FORMULA 1 WORLD CHAMPIONSHIP

Yearbook

VIRGIN

PUBLISHER: *Nick Hervey*

EDITOR: *Bob Constanduros*

ASSOCIATE EDITOR: *Derick Allsop*

FEATURES EDITOR: *Joe Saward of Autosport*

RESULTS AND STATISTICS: *Jane Constanduros*

DESIGNERS: *Nick Downes, Nigel Gray, Nettie Jacobs, Brigitte Willgoss*

PHOTOGRAPHIC CONSULTANTS: *John Dunbar, Steven Tee*

EDITORIAL DIRECTOR: *Paul Forty*

PRODUCTION DIRECTOR: *Mark Pickard*

SECRETARIES: *Sandra Asubonteng, Angela O'Brien*

EXECUTIVE PUBLISHER: *Tim Hailstone*

First published in Great Britain in 1989 by Virgin Books.

A division of W. H. Allen & Co Plc, Sekforde House, 175-9 St John Street, London EC1V 4LL.

Copyright © 1989 W. H. Allen & Co Plc

ISBN 1-85227-096-9

Design Consultants: *Carter Wong Limited, London W11 1QF*

Typeset in Gill and Perpetua by *Fotographics and DLT Nightlines*

Colour origination: *Dot Gradations Limited, Chelmsford, Essex*

Printed and bound in Great Britain by *BPCC Paulton Book Limited, Paulton, Bristol*

Acknowledgements – The publisher and editor would like to thank the following for their assistance in compiling the FIA Yearbook 89: Rod Vickery, Alan Woollard, Martin Whitaker, Karen Brooke, John Dunbar, Steven Tee, Lee Farrant, Keke Rosberg, Derick Allsop, Joe Saward, Jane Constanduros, David Winter, Guy Jackson, John Blakemore, Bob McCaffrey, Zooom Photographic, LAT, Allsport, Darrell Ingham, Philip Wong, Alison Tomlin, Roger Musgrave, Davide Paolini, David Warren, Peter Collins, Nigel Wollheim, Sophie Sicot, Mario Vecchi, Jaime Manca Graziadei, Daniel Hindenoch, Frederic Dhainaut, Walt Stannard, Mike Earle, Joe Chamberlain, Mireille Poirier, Cesare Fiorio, Manny Oettinger, Melanie Brown, Jackie Oliver, John Bisignano, Ryder Houston, Alan Harrison, Herbie Blash, David Stubbs, Bob Tyrrell, Ken Tyrrell, Ann Bradshaw, Sally Shackleton, Stuart Sykes, Frank Williams, Colin Cordy, Alain Prost, Ayrton Senna, Sally Hart, John Connor, Ron Dennis, Creighton Brown, Agnes Carlier, Peter Burns, Ekrem Sami, Eric Silbermann, Bob McMurray, Shaune McMurray, Ian Phillips, Matthew Argenti, Louise Goodman, Nick Underwood, Sue Goffin, Steve Hallam, Noel Stanbury, Rupert Mainwearing, Peter Warr, Tilman Bechem, Kaspar Arnet, Roland Bruynseraede, Jean Jacques Delaruwiere, John Barnard, Jo Ramirez, Ross Brawn, Brian Hart, Gordon Murray, Michael Holt, Barry Griffin, Lee Gaug.

Photographs in the FIA Yearbook '89 have been contributed by: Zooom Photographic, John Dunbar, Lee Farrant, David Winter, Darren Heath, Patrick Gosling, LAT, Steven Tee, Allsport, Keith Sutton, John Blakemore, Peter Nygaard, Lukas Gorys, Colorsport, David Phipps, Ferdi Kraling, Sporting Pictures, Hiroshi Kaneko, Pamela Lausen, Bernard Asset, Stephen Davis, Jon Eisberg, Jeff Bloxham, Ercole Colombo, Agence Vandystadt, Nigel Snowdon, Diana Burnet, Herke de Vries, Dominique Leroy, Dave Kennard, Pascal Rondeau, Alois Rottensteiner, Jean-Francois Galeron of Autopresse, Steve Domenjoz, Kaz Winiemko, Jens Hoffmeister, Jori Potiker, Wolfgang Scholvien, Nick Downes, Phil Wong, Justin de Villeneuve Alain Patrice, J- Marc Loubat

CONTENTS

FORMULA 1 WORLD CHAMPIONSHIP

FOREWORD

Another year in the history of Formula One has passed and again history has been made.

We have seen event attendance increase by an average of 20 per cent. Television viewers have increased. The number of countries broadcasting Formula One races has increased. Now the accepted use of cameras on board the cars has added a new dimension to the interest, with millions of television viewers being able to share some of the sensations of the drivers. Although the championship ended controversially, Formula One is big enough to overcome this, and you know who your champion is. As the FIA

Formula One World Championship is made up of 16 events in 15 countries on 5 continents we should not highlight any one of these, but I must say that I am personally very proud of the 25 drivers who took part in the Australian round of the championship, as they demonstrated what Formula One is really all about — the FIA Formula One World Drivers Championship.

I sincerely hope that you enjoyed the 1989 FIA Formula One World Championship, and hope that 1990 will eclipse even this year.

Bernie Ecclestone

Bernie Ecclestone

1989
FIA FORMULA 1
CONSTRUCTORS
WORLD
CHAMPION

Entrant	Car/Chassis	Engine	Tyres	Fuel/Oil	Plugs	Brakes	Dampers	Brazil	San Marino	Monaco	Mexico	Phoenix	Canada	France	Britain	Germany	Hungary	Belgium	Italy	Portugal	Spain	Japan	Australia	World Championship Points	Grand Prix Started	Total points to date	Grand Prix wins	Pole Positions
McLaren International	McLaren MP4/5	Honda V10	Goodyear	Shell	NGK	Brembo/SEP	Showa	6	15	15	11	9	–	9	9	15	9	15	9	6	13	–	–	141	330	1422·5	80	55
Williams Grand Prix Eng.	Williams FW12C/FW13	Renault V10	Goodyear	Elf	Champion	AP/SEP	Williams/Penske	–	3*	–	6*	7*	15*	4*	–	3*	4*	3*	7*	–	2*	10	13	77	249	880·5	42	30
Scuderia Ferrari	Ferrari 640	Ferrari V12	Goodyear	AGIP	Champion	Brembo/SEP	Penske	9	–	–	–	–	–	6	6	4	9	4	6	9	–	–	–	59	456	1563	97	107
Benetton Formula	Benetton B188/B189	Ford DFR V8	Goodyear	Mobil	Champion	AP/SEP	Koni	4*	4*	–	3*	2*	–	–	4	–	–	2	–	3	–	9	8	39	121	158	2	3
Tyrrell Racing Org.	Tyrrell 017/018	Ford DFR V8	Goodyear	–	Unipart	AP/AP	Koni	–	1	2	4	–	–	3	–	–	–	–	2	1	3	–	–	16	272	556	23	14
Team Lotus	Lotus 101	Judd V8	Goodyear	Elf	NGK	Brembo/SEP	Bilstein	–	–	–	–	–	3	–	3	2	1	–	–	–	–	3	3	15	411	1319	79	107
Arrows Grand Prix Int.	Arrows A11	Ford DFR V8	Goodyear	Mobil	Champion	AP/SEP	Arrows	2	2	–	–	4	–	–	–	1	2	1	–	–	1	–	–	13	183	111	0	1
Scuderia Italia	BMS Dallara 189	Ford DFR V8	Pirelli	AGIP	Champion	Brembo/SEP	Koni	–	–	3	–	–	5	–	–	–	–	–	1	–	2	–	–	8	30	8	0	0
Motor Racing Devs.	Brabham BT58	Judd V8	Pirelli	Elf	Champion	AP/SEP	Koni/Penske	–	–	5	–	–	–	2	–	–	–	–	–	4	–	–	–	6	359	831	35	39
Onyx Grand Prix	Onyx ORE 1	Ford DFR V8	Goodyear	–	Champion	AP/SEP	Onyx	–	–	–	–	–	–	2	–	–	–	–	4	–	–	–	–	6	12	6	0	0
Minardi Team	Minardi M188/M189	Ford DFR V8	Pirelli	AGIP	Champion	Brembo/SEP	Koni	–	–	–	–	–	–	3	–	–	–	2	–	–	1	–	–	6	76	7	0	0
Leyton House Racing	March 881/CG891	Judd V8	Goodyear	BP	Champion	AP/SEP	Koni	4*	–	–	–	–	–	–	–	–	–	–	–	–	–	–	–	4	184	167·5	3	5
Rial Racing	Rial ARC 2	Ford DFR V8	Goodyear	–	Champion	Brembo/SEP	Koni	–	–	–	–	3	–	–	–	–	–	–	–	–	–	–	–	3	20	6	0	0
Ligier Sport	Ligier JS33	Ford DFR V8	Goodyear	Elf	Champion	AP/SEP	Koni	–	–	–	–	–	2	1	–	–	–	–	–	–	–	–	–	3	213	307	8	9
AGS	AGS JH23/JH24	Ford DFR V8	Goodyear	–	Champion	Brembo/SEP	Koni	–	–	–	1*	–	–	–	–	–	–	–	–	–	–	–	–	1	47	6	0	1
Ecurie Larrousse	Lola LC88B/LC89	Lamborghini V12	Goodyear	BP	Champion	Brembo/SEP	Bilstein	–	–	–	–	–	–	–	–	–	–	–	–	–	1	–	–	0	123	7	0	0
Osella Squadra Corse	Osella FA1M	Ford DFR V8	Pirelli	AGIP	Champion	Brembo/SEP	Koni	–	–	–	–	–	–	–	–	–	–	–	–	–	–	–	–	0	54	2	0	0
Zakspeed Formula	Zakspeed 891	Yamaha V8	Pirelli	–	NGK	Brembo/SEP	Koni	–	–	–	–	–	–	–	–	–	–	–	–	–	–	–	–	0	13	0	0	0
Coloni Racing	Coloni C188/C3	Ford DFR V8	Pirelli	–	Champion	Brembo/SEP	Koni	–	–	–	–	–	–	–	–	–	–	–	–	–	–	–	–	0	13	0	0	0
Eurobrun Racing	Eurobrun ER 189	Judd V8	Pirelli	–	Champion	Brembo/SEP	Bilstein	–	–	–	–	–	–	–	–	–	–	–	–	–	–	–	–	0	12	0	0	0

* = Points scored with earlier chassis

1989 FIA FORMULA 1 DRIVERS WORLD CHAMPION

No.	Driver	Nationality	Team	Brazil	San Marino	Monaco	Mexico	Phoenix	Canada	France	Britain	Germany	Hungary	Belgium	Italy	Portugal	Spain	Japan	Australia	World Championship Points	Grand Prix Started	Total Points to date	Grand Prix wins	Pole Positions
2	Alain Prost	F	McLaren	2	2	2	5	1	R	1	1	2	4	2	1	2	3	R	R	76	153	587·5	39	20
1	Ayrton Senna	BR	McLaren	11	1	1	1	R	7	R	R	1	2	1	R	R	1	D	R	60	94	317	20	42
6	Riccardo Patrese	I	Williams	R	R	15	2	2	2	3	R	4	R	R	4	R	5	2	3	40	192	129	2	3
27	Nigel Mansell	GB	Ferrari	1	R	R	R	R	D	2	2	3	1	3	R	R		R	R	38	133	252	15	12
5	Thierry Boutsen	B	Williams	R	4	10	R	6	1	R	10	R	3	4	3	R	R	3	1	37	105	100	2	0
19	Alessandro Nannini	I	Benetton	6	3	8	4	R	D	R	3	R	R	5	R	4	R	1	2	32	63	47	1	0
28	Gerhard Berger	A	Ferrari	R	R			R	R	R	R	R	R	2	1	2	R	R		21	83	119	5	4
11	Nelson Piquet	BR	Lotus	R	R	R	11	R	4	8	4	5	6	DNQ	R	R	8	4	R	12	172	413	20	24
4	Jean Alesi	F	Tyrrell							4	R	10	9		5		4	R	R	8	8	8	0	0
9	Derek Warwick	GB	Arrows	5	5	R	R	R	R		9	6	10	6	R	R	9	6	R	7	115	62	0	0
10	Eddie Cheever	USA	Arrows	R	9	7	7	3	R	7	DNQ	R	5	R	DNQ	R	R	8	R	6	132	69	0	0
4 / 29	Michele Alboreto	I	Tyrrell / Larrousse	10	DNQ	5	3	R	R			R	R	R	R	11	DNPQ	DNQ	DNPQ	6	131	179.5	5	2
36	Stefan Johansson	S	Onyx	DNPQ	DNPQ	DNPQ	R	R	D	5	DNPQ	R	R	8	DNPQ	3	DNPQ	DNPQ	DNPQ	6	75	88	0	0
20 / 4	Johnny Herbert	GB	Benetton / Tyrrell	4	11	14	15	5	DNQ			R		DNQ						5	6	5	0	0
23	Pierluigi Martini	I	Minardi	R	R	R	R	R	R	R	5	9	R	9	7	5	R		6	5	39	6	0	0
22	Andrea de Cesaris	I	BMS Dallara	13	10	13	R	R	3	DNQ	R	7	R	11	R	7	10		R	4	135	38	0	1
21	Alex Caffi	I	BMS Dallara	DNPQ	7	4	13	R	6	R	DNPQ	R	7	R	R	R	9	R		4	43	4	0	0
7	Martin Brundle	GB	Brabham	R	R	6	9	R	DNPQ	DNPQ	R	8	12	R	6	R	5	R		4	62	14	0	0
15	Mauricio Gugelmin	BR	Leyton House	3	R	R	DNQ	R	R	14	R	R	R	7	R	10	R	7	R	4	31	9	0	0
8	Stefano Modena	I	Brabham	R	R	3	10	R	R	R	R	R	11	R	D	14	R	R	R	4	27	4	0	0
12	Satoru Nakajima	J	Lotus	8	R	DNQ	R	R	DNQ	R	8	R	R	DNQ	10	7	R	R	4	3	43	11	0	0
38	Christian Danner	D	Rial	14	DNQ	DNQ	12	4	8	DNQ	DNQ	DNQ	DNQ	DNQ	DNQ	DNQ				3		4	0	0
3	Jonathan Palmer	GB	Tyrrell	7	6	9	R	R	R	10	R	R	13	14	R	6	10	R	DNQ	2	4	14	0	0
25	Rene Arnoux	F	Ligier	DNQ	DNQ	12	14	DNQ	5	R	DNQ	11	R	9	13	DNQ	DNQ	R		2	149	181	7	18
20	Emanuelle Pirro	I	Benetton							9	11	R	8	10	R	R	R	R	5	2	10	2	0	0
26	Olivier Grouillard	F	Ligier	9	D	R	8	DNQ	DNQ	6	7	R	DNQ	13	R	DNQ	R	R	R	1	11	11	0	0
24	Luis Perez-Sala	E	Minardi	R	R	R	DNQ	R	R	DNQ	6	DNQ	R	15	8	12	R	R	DNQ	1	26	1	0	0
30	Phillipe Alliot	F	Larrousse	12	R	R	R	R	R	R	R	DNPQ	16	R	9	6	R	R		1	79	5	0	0
40	Gabriele Tarquini	I	AGS	W	8	R	6	R	R	R	DNQ	DNPQ	DNPQ	DNPQ	DNPQ	DNPQ	DNPQ	DNPQ	DNPQ	1	16	1	0	0
16	Ivan Capelli	I	Leyton House	R	R	11	R	R	R	R	R	R	12	R	R	R	R	R	R	0	50	19	0	0
34	Bernd Schneider	D	Zakspeed	R	DNPQ	DNPQ	DNPQ	DNPQ	DNPQ	DNPQ	DNPQ	DNPQ	DNPQ	DNPQ	DNPQ	DNPQ	R	DNPQ		0	8	0	0	0
17	Nicola Larini	I	Osella	R	R	DNPQ	DNPQ	DNPQ	DNPQ	DNPQ	DNPQ	DNPQ	DNPQ	DNPQ	DNPQ	DNPQ	R	R		0	19	0	0	0
29	Yannick Dalmas	F	Larrousse / AGS	DNQ	R	DNQ	DNQ	DNQ	DNQ	DNPQ	DNPQ	DNPQ	DNPQ	DNPQ	DNPQ	DNPQ	DNPQ	DNPQ		0	17	2	0	0
33	Gregor Foitek	CH	Eurobrun / Rial	DNQ	DNQ	DNQ	DNQ	DNQ	DNQ	DNQ	DNQ	DNQ	DNQ	DNQ		DNQ				0	0	0	0	0
31	Roberto Moreno	BR	Coloni	DNQ	DNQ	R	DNQ	DNQ	R	DNQ	R	DNQ	DNPQ	DNPQ	DNPQ	R	DNPQ	DNPQ	DNPQ	0	6	1	0	0
18	Piercarlo Ghinzani	I	Osella	DNPQ	DNPQ	DNPQ	DNPQ	DNPQ	DNPQ	DNPQ	DNPQ	DNPQ	R	DNPQ	DNPQ	DNPQ	R	DNPQ	R	0	76	2	0	0
39	Volker Weidler	D	Rial	DNPQ	DNPQ	DNPQ	DNPQ	DNPQ	DNPQ	DNPQ	DNPQ	DNPQ	DNQ							0	0	0	0	0
32	Pierre-Henri Raphanel	F	Coloni / Rial	DNPQ	DNPQ	R	DNPQ	DNPQ	DNPQ	DNPQ	DNPQ	DNPQ	DNPQ	DNQ	DNQ	DNQ	DNQ	DNQ	DNQ	0	1	0	0	0
41	Joachim Winkelhock	D	AGS	DNPQ	DNPQ	DNPQ	DNPQ	DNPQ	DNPQ	DNPQ										0	0	0	0	0
35	Aguri Suzuki	J	Zakspeed	DNPQ	DNPQ	DNPQ	DNPQ	DNPQ	DNPQ	DNPQ	DNPQ	DNPQ	DNPQ	DNPQ	DNPQ	DNPQ	DNPQ	DNPQ		0	1	0	0	0
37	Bertrand Gachot	B	Onyx / Rial	DNPQ	DNPQ	DNPQ	DNPQ	DNPQ	DNPQ	13	12	DNQ	R	R	R			DNQ	DNQ	0	5	0	0	0
9	Martin Donnelly	GB	Arrows							12							0	1	0	0	1			
29	Eric Bernard	F	Larrousse							11	R						0	2	0	0	2			
32	Enrico Bertaggia	I	Coloni										DNPQ	DNPQ	DNPQ	DNPQ	DNPQ	DNPQ	0	0	0	0	0		
33	Oscar Larrauri	ARG	Eurobrun										DNPQ	DNPQ	DNPQ	DNPQ	DNPQ	0	8	0	0	0			
37	J. J. Lehto	SF	Onyx											DNPQ	R	DNPQ	R	0	2	0	0	0			
23	Paolo Barilla	I	Minardi													R		0	1	0	0	0			

W – Entry withdrawn
D – Disqualified
DNQ – Did not qualify
DNPQ – Did not pre-qualify

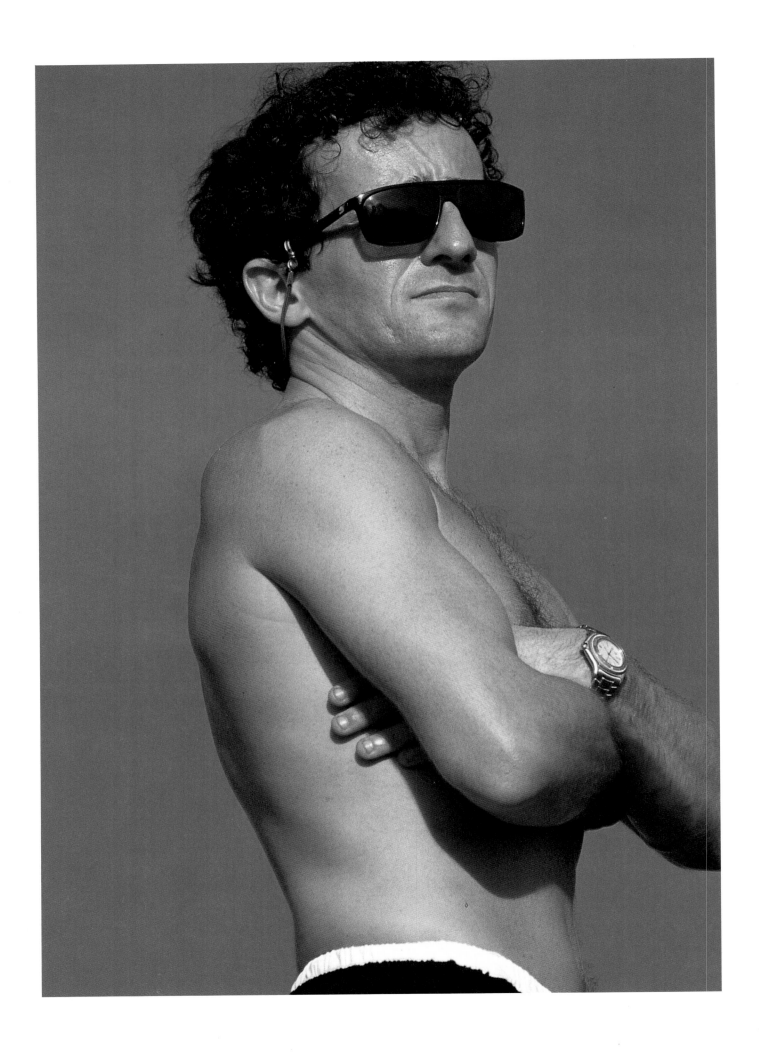

1989 DRIVERS' CHAMPIONSHIP

Suddenly there was a kind of peace, perhaps no more than a lull in the crossfire of accusations and vitriol, but Alain Prost was grateful for the moment. Whatever any further appeals or legal proceedings might produce, he was content to consider himself champion. FIA had said so. Finally and emphatically. That was good enough for Prost. The rest, alas, was not. Reflecting on the course of the season, he was overcome by a sense of sadness rather than bitterness.

'Formula One has always been a business, but don't forget it is also a sport and we are sportsmen,' he said. 'Everyone is talking about business, money, fines or politics, but at the end of the day we are all sportsmen. When you arrive on the podium after winning the race in front of 100,000 people, all applauding you, you don't think about anything else. Nobody exists beside you. You just take the pleasure because that's part of the sport.'

The day Prost savoured triumph at Monza was the day all pretence of harmony in the Marlboro McLaren-Honda camp collapsed. The Frenchman, bound for Ferrari in 1990, lowered his trophy into the throng of Italian fans.

Ron Dennis was furious and Prost followed up by delivering his most scathing condemnation of his treatment by the team. He had won only because of Ayrton Senna's late retirement and felt that it was time to go on the record. As for giving away a piece of silverware, Prost maintains that was merely a reciprocal gesture to an enthusiastic crowd welcoming him to the fold.

'I enjoyed the reception I got,' he says. 'But that was because I had just signed for Ferrari and my reaction followed that. It was not because it was not permitted, not because it was against anyone in the team or the team itself.'

Prost was simply playing the role of sportsman, the role he loves, the role he carries off with style and grace. Throughout his years at McLaren he has demonstrated that success can be gained – and failure endured – with dignity.

After the Italian Grand Prix the bottled-up fears and frustrations finally exploded. Many were aghast, even disenchanted. This wasn't the normal Alain Prost, the Alain Prost everyone respected. But in Prost's eyes this was not a normal season.

By the end of it Senna, having resorted to desperate tactics in Japan, had been discredited by officialdom. As a consequence, Prost regained not only the World Championship but also his public esteem. Nothing, however, could heal the wounds of the season. He had his third title, he had extended his record total of Grand Prix victories, and yet he was left with a hollow feeling.

It has to be said that over the course of the championship he was outpaced and outraced by Senna. Comprehensively so. The Brazilian's displays in qualifying were astonishing, his wins achieved with massive conviction.

Senna was ultimately thwarted by a combination of misfortune and his own impetuosity. His talent, commitment and courage are undeniable. But there remains a chink in the armour, a chink that still separates him from true greatness. It is not in Senna's nature to accept second best, whereas Prost, five years his senior, has learnt to adopt a more pragmatic approach. The lesson has served him well. For Prost, however, that still isn't enough. All the acrimony and rancour, all the claims and counter-claims had turned the victory champagne sour.

'After this season,' he said, 'I could not be satisfied whether I won or lost. Of course, it's better to win, but this is not satisfying for me the way my other two championship wins were. The first championship is obviously very special, to me, to any driver. My second, though, was especially satisfying. In '85 the car was still the best, but in '86 the Williams had come through. Lotus, too, were close. We were close right to the end. We really had to work for it in '86 – as a team. That was our strength. We were a team, all working together, trying to keep the championship for McLaren.

'Now look at the team situation in '89 ... It makes it frustrating because I expect something different. It's not very good to fight in this manner. I am just happy it is finished and I can think about next year. It's very sad after so many good years here. It's very bad that I was waiting for the end of the championship and that I'm happy to leave. But I was stretched just a bit too much.

'Very often I was asked about the pressures in '89 but I didn't have pressures. I just had problems, which is different. Last year we had pressure. For sure, the relationship was not fantastic, but it was never bad. We were very close in racing terms and the Grands Prix were very difficult. This year, only problems.

'Pressure means extra stress when you compete. When you don't feel easy, you don't compete. You don't enjoy it. This season I was just coming in in the morning and "clocking-on". Like working at Peugeot or Renault on the production line. Even in qualifying, when I pushed a bit harder, I didn't feel any pleasure. I can have no joy, no pleasure, fighting someone in the same car – theoretically – and in the same team but not in a fair way. I don't feel any motivation. The motivation will come back next year.'

The Prost-Senna alliance gave McLaren the driving ability their standards demanded. Dennis's declared intention was to pursue excellence. Backed by Marlboro's millions, he established a phenomenal team. John Barnard's car dominated the mid-eighties and subsequent generations have led the field in the late eighties.

Honda power has been a vital factor over the past two years. Dennis anticipated as much and did something about it. When he signed Senna he proudly paraded 'the two best drivers in the world'. For Dennis it had to be the best of everything. The factory, naturally, is sensational. But best of all, perhaps, was the team he built, the organisation he developed. Professional, slick, consistent. Team personnel even looked the part.

Prost was very much a part of that team. He progressed and matured with his colleagues and they admired and respected him as a man as well as a driver. So did Niki Lauda. The Austrian couldn't get over how 'nice' his new team-mate was. He also had to acknowledge Prost was a 'fast son of a bitch'.

Prost put a brave smile on second place behind Lauda in 1984 and had his reward in '85. Victory over the formidable Williams-Hondas the following year was, as the man says, more satisfying still. Ultimately he required a little luck, but that is always part of the package. He stayed in the hunt through skill, judgement and cunning.

In '87 even Prost could do nothing to contain the Williams pair, Nigel Mansell and the eventual champion, Nelson Piquet. Still, he managed to eclipse Jackie Stewart's all-time record of 27 wins, so it wasn't such a bad season. Besides, he had plenty to look forward to in '88. He was confident McLaren would be back on top.

The opposition was blitzed, the championship rendered a no-contest. The first half of the season went well for Prost. Certainly Senna was quick, but the older head seemed in control. For Prost the roles were now reversed. Just as he had been the young charger snapping at Niki's heels, so here was this upstart from Sao Paulo having a go at his. Again, though, experience appeared to be vital.

Until Silverstone. When Prost pulled out of the wet British Grand Prix there was a mixed reaction. He was criticised for being chicken and applauded for being brave. The car was not good, so perhaps he is entitled to the benefit of the doubt. But perhaps it was the first sign that Senna was tipping the scales. Perhaps, in the psychological warfare, he had struck a crucial blow. Possibly, deep down, Prost was beginning to realise that he had met his match.

Back-to-back victories in France and Britain (previous page) firmly established Prost's claim to the championship.

Prost defiantly fought on, particularly at Estoril, where Senna almost squeezed him up against the pit wall. An irate Prost had words with his partner after the race. The alliance was crumbling. Senna clinched his first championship title in Japan and Prost must have had no illusions about '89.

Imola was the final straw. It was there, also, that they had their final conversation. They had a 'no overtaking' pact for the first corner. Prost led from the line but Senna was ahead when they emerged from the turn. Prost was livid, claiming their agreement had been broken. Senna, 'for the good of the team', apologised, yet later insisted he had overtaken Prost 'well before the first corner'.

Senna said: 'It is finished between me and Prost. Maybe in ten years' time we'll exchange banalities, but I doubt it.' The champion contemptuously dismissed his teammate on another occasion, saying: 'He goes only for second places. I race only to win. Always.'

At that stage McLaren were still attempting to put on a united front. Prost had announced his decision to leave at the end of the season, but maybe he would take a sabbatical and return, refreshed, in 1991. The contract was there, ready and waiting.

Instead he went to the major opposition. The mechanics felt betrayed. They expressed their disgust by putting a plate of pasta and a bottle of Italian red wine in his car at Monza. Prost wasn't amused. He wasn't meant to be. Now all the bitterness came pouring out.

In the championship Prost held a huge advantage and although Senna won in Spain he still needed nothing less than victory in both Japan and Australia to keep his crown. Prost went to Suzuka in determined mood. He talked about Senna thinking of himself as 'immortal' and taking risks because he thought he was guided by God. But it was not defeatist talk. He warned Senna that he was going to be positive and that he wouldn't be leaving the door open to him.

He was as good as his word. This was more like the old Prost (or, to be more precise, the young Prost). He made a superb start, pulled away and stayed there. In the second half of the race Senna chipped away at

the deficit but with six laps remaining he still couldn't find a way through. Prost was driving impeccably, always coming out of the corners with the power to fend off his partner.

Senna had to try something and reckoned the chicane presented him with his only chance. He dived inside but Prost, as he'd said, refused to leave the door open. They slid off in an inevitable tangle. Yet as Prost climbed from his cockpit, Senna demanded a push. He returned to the track from the back of the chicane, went into the pits for repairs and took the chequered flag.

Senna's disqualification was upheld by an appeal court (he was also fined $100,000 and given a suspended six-month ban) which confirmed Prost as champion. He would take with him to Ferrari the No. 1.

Dennis is adamant the number means nothing to him. Prost believes otherwise. 'I never thought about winning the championship to take the number with me,' he said. 'I just think it's sad that it could create a problem because it does mean something to some people. It's about ego. It's sad. I think I stayed one or two years too long at McLaren, but six years and three championships with one team is something you cannot forget. Now is the right moment to leave and Ferrari is the right team to join. Next year I think it is very possible they will win the championship.'

Prost's contribution will be scrutinised with interest. His new team-mate is Nigel Mansell, and although they are friends Prost is aware of the Englishman's ambition as well as his speed. Whatever the grounds for his complaints at McLaren, it is just possible the frustration of not being able to keep pace with Senna got the better of him. Next season will provide another stern test.

'I am a little less quick now', he admits, 'and much less persistent, less willing to take risks. I often feel mad because in private testing, on my own, I am very much quicker. But when I am racing I have many more problems motivating myself.

'Next year, though, will be different. I will have no problem. My biggest motivation is for Ferrari to win the championship. It's a new challenge. I prefer to win it myself, but if Nigel wins it will still be a victory for me. To be part of the team, that's what I like.

'I think Nigel is driving the Ferrari better than anything he has driven. He is motivated and I think we can work well together. We have the same sort of feeling about motor racing.

'I wanted to work with John Barnard and I think his going to Benetton is a loss. But maybe there were some problems I don't know about, so we have to try to win without him. I will be involved in technical discussions there.

'My only plan now is to concentrate on the job at Ferrari next year. I'm not going to concentrate on any other business, on building a team, retiring or anything else. I just want to do the job, go racing and enjoy it. As a sport.'

McLaren

1989 CONSTRUCTORS' CHAMPIONSHIP

McLaren's 1988 act was a hard one for any team in motor racing to follow. Fifteen victories from sixteen races was a record envied by everyone throughout the sport, even though the word 'domination' was one which many had overused and which most people were heartily sick of by the end of the year.

Yet before the turn of the turbo era there were indications that all the old cliches might have to be dredged out of the word processors' memories again for 1989. Initial testing of McLaren-Honda's 1989 challenger, complete with new, normally aspirated V10 engine, suggested that turbo times would take a battering. This was not in the scheme of things. The return to normally aspirated engines was made because of the spiralling increase in turbo cars' speed. Normally aspirated engines were meant to be slower.

But the suggestion of quicker cars came about because McLaren and Honda were running a test programme long before anyone else had apparently begun. Frank Williams would admit that he had the mock-up of Honda's V10 in his factory in May 1987. Sure, lots changed on the engine since then but at least Honda and McLaren knew what they were going to do and how they were going to do it at a very early stage.

But their supporting cast was of the highest quality. They had proven drivers in Ayrton Senna (current World Champion) and Alain Prost, proven engine development and design in Honda, and a galaxy of proven high-profile race designers and engineers in (count them) Gordon Murray, Steve Nichols, Neil Oatley and Tim Wright.

Perhaps the surprising thing is that they lost as many races as they did, but then that proves just how competitive Formula One is, and the races that did go to the opposition in the first three-quarters of the season were, in some cases, out of the ordinary.

From a Honda point of view, the 1989 Constructors' Championship gave them more satisfaction than the 1988 win with the V6 turbo

engine. 'The turbo engine's basic design started with the engine that originally ran in Formula Two in the early eighties,' points out Osamu Goto, Honda's Formula One Project leader. 'The V10 engine was completely new to racing in 1989 – and we haven't really finished development of it yet.'

But quite obviously, both Honda and McLaren actually tackled the season earlier and better than their rivals, even though there were weak points in the campaign. The race cars, for instance, were very late in being completed, and there was no doubt that, partly because of testing delays, they were not really ready for the first race in Brazil.

But it was typical of McLaren and Honda that they then went to Imola for their massive eight-day test to sort out not only chassis but engines – and virtually everything else. In spite of their apparent readiness for the start of the season, the engine specification taken to Brazil was slightly down on power in comparison to later models, intended purely for reliability, suggesting that this was a stop-gap measure.

'Our basic engine, developed during the Imola test, had more power and good driveability,' points out Goto. 'We then introduced the specification five engine in Belgium which again has good power and improved driveability. And then there was specification four at Monza with improved top-end power for faster circuits.' There was also a weight-saving programme which saw a saving of three kilos prior to the Monaco Grand Prix.

Along the way, however, there had been a number of problems. Senna's car suffered an electrical fault in Phoenix and then came the problem of pumping out oil, first experienced at the Canadian Grand Prix which resulted in an oil tank re-design which in itself caused problems at the British Grand Prix due to a manufacturing fault. However, loss of oil also caused Senna's Italian Grand Prix blow-up.

Goto's team also worked on the combustion side of the engine which had given rise to Alain Prost's voluble comments. Goto explains that Prost often only uses part of the throttle, and when the throttle is only partly open, combustion is poor, although the post-Italian Grand Prix test at the Hungaroring helped to cure it.

Goto went on to explain that 'combustion can be good in the morning, perfect, no problem, and then it can suddenly start to change in the afternoon, even though the engine hasn't been touched. The atmospheric conditions might have changed, and that in turn can change the ease of combustion.'

Prost's comments after the Italian Grand Prix did not endear him to Honda, and his own team weren't pleased either. But then McLaren's image of a Family at War had unfortunately been growing for some time.

While this side of things was over-stated, there's no doubt that everyone would have preferred an easier working relationship. But as Ron Dennis would explain, within a team where the two drivers are so competitive, it is difficult to maintain that relationship. 'It's just not possible, in the environment of our team, to get an edge. When you have two people who are as competitive as they are, pushing very hard, it's quite logical that there can only be one winner.

'The problem in a team such as ours is not handling the performance of the person who is winning, but handling the performance of the person who is not winning. You have to support them, you continuously have to demonstrate that you are supporting them, and that you are supportive of their problems. That's what we try desperately to do.'

Above left: Gordon Murray, Technical Director, now turning his attention to the McLaren road-car project. Above: Senna — the will to win. Left: the face shows the pressure.

The relationship between the two drivers was a little shaky, of course, in 1988 but it had virtually been patched up again at the end of the season. The problems began again in 1989 at Imola where an agreement not to overtake at the first corner was breached by Senna. Prost was furious, and after a confrontation the pair settled down to a fairly individualistic approach to the rest of the year. However, the team's actual position was not affected: the pair not surprisingly talked to their engineers who in turned worked together, and all things technical were discussed quite openly. It was not felt that the team's position was compromised.

Prost's accusations that he and his teammate were receiving different equipment were not well received. Dennis had constantly reassured Prost ever since the French Grand Prix when he first stated his intention to leave the team that he would receive exactly the same equipment. Indeed, at the start of the Italian Grand Prix weekend, Dennis had gathered together his workforce to underline to them the importance of thorough preparation and to put more care into developing and operating the cars equally. Prost's comment, post-race at Monza, that taking the number one away from McLaren would be too much for the egos of some people was pre-empted by Dennis who, before the race, stated that 'much more important than winning the World Championship is the fundamental integrity of the company and the team. We value highly our reputation for providing and the ability to provide equal equipment for both drivers.

'In Neil Oatley, Alain's engineer, you have a man who has the highest integrity of any engineer in the pit lane. That's a well-known fact and there is absolutely no way that Alain isn't getting the same as everyone else, and that's going to continue.' This, however, was the down side of McLaren's year. They frequently demonstrated that they were better prepared to take on a championship season than almost anyone else, although with a budget said to be approaching £30m and no engine or tyre bills they were perhaps better funded to do so.

The eight-day Imola test was a case in point, meeting the problems and the task in hand head-on and not letting go until they had been solved. The oil tank re-design showed an organisation at work which some teams would find hard to rival, at the same time launching a brand new transverse gearbox.

This had already been delayed so that its first race would not take place too far from home – in case things went wrong. Anyone who saw the rows of rear-end assemblies outside McLaren's truck during the British Grand Prix couldn't have helped but be impressed. Senna ostensibly retired from that race with a spin caused by being unable to select third gear, but when the gearbox was stripped, nothing was found amiss.

McLaren were no less susceptible to gearbox problems during the year than anyone else. At many races their drivers complained of gear selection problems, but there had been a false sense of security during the previous years when fuel consumption had been so important. Gearboxes had not been roughly treated. Come 1989 and people were racing again – and everyone's self-built gear had its toughest test. McLaren had their fair share of troubles.

There were two more instances in the season when McLaren showed what they were made of. In Germany, Senna ran over a kerb and a stone punctured his monocoque. McLaren intercepted a test truck waiting at Dijon for just such an occurrence and it promptly diverted to Germany. There a test chassis became the spare car, replacing the spare which had become Senna's race car. Dennis blamed the subsequent all-nighter for mistakes in the pit stops the next day.

After their problems of traction and handling at the subsequent Hungarian Grand Prix, McLaren recognised the potential problem, noting that they could have difficulties in both Portugal and Spain, similar circuits to the Hungaroring. Their reaction was, once again, to tackle the problem head-on: test at Hungaroring until it was sorted out. New suspension geometry resulted, and although the subsequent handling wasn't ideal, improvements had been made.

Many would say that McLaren couldn't fail to win the series: they had the best drivers, the best engineers and the best engines. But they also made the best use of them too, and when things didn't go right – which they certainly didn't all the time – under Dennis's leadership, the team went for the problem and sought to solve it. The approach was as important as the assets, and if teams wish to break the McLaren stranglehold on the series, then they have to take a leaf out of their book.

A NEW ERA AT MARANELLO

Ferrari is like a beautiful woman: irresistible to any Italian male; capable of stopping the show; forgiven the occasional tantrum, even the odd outrage. In 1989 the scarlet creature was at her most alluring and controversial.

A season approached with, at best, cautious optimism, exploded from the blocks in triumph at Rio, almost turned to disaster at Imola, rose again in glory at Budapest and then served up a bitter-sweet cocktail at Estoril. It could only have happened to Ferrari.

Formula One is ever-changing, constantly on the move. Drivers and key personnel shuttle around at a frantic pace befitting this restless sport. Designs are revised, sometimes revolutionised. Not all moves are in an obviously forward direction, but the philosophy seems to be that any movement is better than none.

Ferrari, true to type, have made some of the more drastic changes. Their new driver for 1989, Nigel Mansell, observed with some bewilderment that all the people he had negotiated with had disappeared from the Maranello scene by the time he joined the team.

Still there at the start of the season, though not by the end, was John Barnard. 'There', in Barnard's case, being rustic Surrey, where he made his base. The GTO concept was always a bone of contention as, in the

early part of the season, was the semi-automatic, seven-speed gearbox. But with time came reliability, and with reliability came results.

With results, ultimately, came Alain Prost. Disenchanted with life at McLaren but not yet ready to take a sabbatical, set up his own team, or join Williams, he decided it would be Ferrari for him in 1990.

At the helm through this first full season after Enzo Ferrari's death was Cesare Fiorio, a man who had honed his competitive instincts in rallying. He was not afraid to steer a bold course and take, if necessary, a few bumps along the way.

The early season struggle for reliability destroyed any prospect of a Championship challenge, but by late summer Fiorio's team had emerged as the most serious and consistent threat to McLaren's domination. They were distinct No. 2, their advance one of the successes of the year. If any team is going to topple McLaren in 1990, Ferrari appears to be the most likely candidate.

That, no doubt, will be another story. The story of Ferrari's 1989 had a fairy-tale beginning. Two days of practice for the Brazilian Grand Prix had done little to raise expectations and after the Sunday morning warm-up Mansell was in a state of despair. Battle-hardened members of the Italian Press corps predicted Ferrari would last no more than ten laps. 'There they go,' said Mansell drily, 'exaggerating again. We'll not last five.'

Gerhard Berger's Ferrari got no further than the first corner, victim of a collision of egos with Ayrton Senna and his McLaren. The champion's car was patched up and continued, but his home Grand Prix was out of reach.

Five laps into the race Mansell was still running. Ten laps . . . still

running. Not only that, the Ferrari was running well. This new Prancing Horse had the measure of its opponents and the man holding the reins responded. He took the lead with a daring charge outside Riccardo Patrese's Williams as they hurtled down the long straight, then settled for more orthodox manoeuvres to see off Prost's McLaren.

As the Ferrari voraciously ate up the laps, it occurred to the Englishman he might not only stay the course but even win. On his debut. He tried to resist the thought but couldn't. Surely something would go wrong, he feared. He was in torment. So were his crew, anxiously watching and listening for him coming round the back of the paddock, through the right-hander that seems to go forever, and on to the straight. His wife Rosanne, too, was standing, waiting, nervously managing a smile.

Amazingly, almost impossibly, the Ferrari made it. Mansell had won his first race for the team. All Italy celebrated and acclaimed a new hero. Not for the first time, Ferrari had defied all logic.

Despite the euphoria that welcomed Ferrari to their own backyard, reason prevailed in the San Marino Grand Prix. The acceleration of the McLaren Hondas was simply too much. In the event, that mattered little. For Ferrari the day was always going to bring failure. It very nearly brought tragedy.

Berger's car went straight on instead of swinging left into the Tamburello curve, smashed into a concrete wall at 180 mph, went into a series of pirouettes and came to a standstill only to burst into flames. Marshals and doctors were on the scene in 15 seconds. The fire was quickly extinguished, Berger carefully released and that night he was in hospital in Austria. Astonishingly, he missed only one race, the Monaco Grand Prix, and returned in Mexico.

While the world outside was amazed at Berger's survival, closer to home there were inquiries about what 'broke'. There were further concerns when Mansell had a 'nasty moment' at Monte Carlo. A hasty 'stiffening' job was ordered.

The trip across the Atlantic – to take in Mexico City, Phoenix and Montreal – fuelled scepticism about the gearbox. Mansell was charging, but his equipment was letting him down.

Barnard was determined to go with the system because he felt this was one area which offered scope for improvement and the opportunity to gain an advantage. Ferrari were down on power compared with Honda but a good chassis and a perfected gearbox might redress the balance.

Whatever Ferrari's private apprehensions were, Fiorio publicly supported the project, maintaining that they accepted patience was required. 'We had so little chance to test in the winter,' he said. 'The testing we should have done is now having to be done as we race.'

Fiorio was also occupied with the task of trying to secure the services of Mansell for the following year. He faced strong competition. Williams were keen to have him back and Benetton, then under the guidance of Fiorio's old chum Peter Collins, had joined the bidding.

Mansell plumped for the team that had made him feel wanted and offered what he believed was the best prospect of challenging for the World Championship in 1990. Between the United States and Canadian Grands Prix, he signed a new contract that would give him outright No. 1 status.

The smiles were wiped off Ferrari faces before the Montreal race had begun. A drying track convinced Mansell he should dive into the pits at the end of the parade lap and change to slicks. Alessandro Nannini, in the Benetton, followed him. Both blasted back on to the track, unaware that the race hadn't started. They were black-flagged but protested there had been no marshal or red light to stop them. All, alas, to no avail. Their race was run.

Ferrari returned to Europe for the French Grand Prix, the seventh on the calendar, with only one finish – Mansell's win in Brazil – to show for their endeavours. Ricard was to prove a turning point, though not for Berger.

The Austrian's frustrations would continue for some time yet, but Mansell's luck changed when he survived aerial bombardment from Mauricio Gugelmin's March at the first corner. For the restart he had to take Berger's discarded race car. It was hurriedly adjusted, lined up in the pit lane and proceeded to race through to second place.

Mansell had another second at Silverstone and a third at Hockenheim. One half of the Ferrari camp, at least, was in business. Reliability was being achieved. Coming up next was the Hungaroring. Narrow, meandering, ideally suited to the Ferrari chassis.

Watching Mansell's car halfway through the weekend, however, you wouldn't have thought so. After the Saturday morning practice session he made a bold decision. He would spend the final qualifying hour preparing for the race. 'I know I'm going to lose places on the grid and that can make life difficult here,' he said. 'But I've got to get it right for tomorrow.'

He did precisely that. From twelfth place on the grid he immediately surged up to eighth, then patiently sat in the queue before mounting his second assault. Prost graciously accepted his fate but Senna wouldn't be so accommodating. It would take stealth, opportunism and courage to pick off the Brazilian. The Englishman was equal to the task.

Mansell savoured 'one of my best and most satisfying wins' while Fiorio applauded 'one of the greatest drivers Ferrari have ever had'.

For Berger, however, it was yet another early cut. By now his disappointment was turning to despair. 'How come I have all the bad luck?' he demanded of no one in particular.

It had, perhaps, not all been bad luck for Berger and he soon found himself off the wet road at Spa. Mansell stayed around to put on another show but couldn't quite prise second place from Prost.

Just before Monza, Prost signed a Ferrari contract for 1990, Mansell having agreed to re-negotiate a deal making them joint No. 1. Berger, already signed by McLaren, finally broke his duck, finishing second. Mansell's car, always struggling to compete, eventually pulled out of the race.

It had been an eventful season for Italy's beloved marque but nothing could have prepared us for the drama about to unfold on the Iberian peninsula. Berger led the early part of the race and soon Mansell was on the prowl, taking Senna, taking his partner.

Then, at the pit stop, it all started to go horribly wrong for the No. 27. Mansell overshot his crew and in his anxiety engaged reverse. An offence. Mansell stormed back on to the track and was hounding Senna again when the black flag was displayed. They raced by the flag three times before colliding and spinning out.

Mansell was fined $50,000 and banned for one race. FISA insisted he must miss the following race, in Spain, despite the fact that his appeal would not be heard until four days later. Mansell was adamant he did not see the flag and threatened to quit Formula One unless he was satisfied with the outcome of the case.

Italian critics suggested that had Fiorio adopted a diplomatic, rather than aggressive posture, Mansell might have been spared the ban. But then Fiorio is what he is. Just as Mansell is what he is. Diplomats are not necessarily winners. 'He reminds of Colin Chapman,' says Mansell of Fiorio. 'He's a strong, determined leader.'

Amid all the furore, Berger actually won the race in Portugal and followed up with second place in Spain. Ferrari confirmed the departure of Barnard, who then confirmed he was joining Benetton on a five-year contract.

Barnard told me early in the season that, if nothing else, he would have the satisfaction of being able to say 'I designed a Ferrari.' By the end of the season he was entitled to be proud that he had created a fine Ferrari.

Life at Ferrari had tested Barnard's resolve. He said: 'I was warned that it would destroy me and it nearly did.' But he had the courage of his convictions and emerged in one piece to pursue new challenges and more 'silly targets' elsewhere.

FIA's Appeal Court, meanwhile, decided they could not reach a verdict on Mansell's case until the Portuguese National Court had deliberated, though FISA president Jean-Marie Balestre maintained the original decision would be confirmed. The legal jousting wasn't confined to the Portuguese controversy. Mansell and Ferrari were also contesting the disqualification in Canada. Then, suddenly, Ferrari withdrew the appeals 'to remove any disturbing element from Formula One racing'. Mansell was 'glad to go racing again'.

Triumph and near tragedy, trials and tribulations. All the ingredients of the corniest soap opera. In reality, of course, it's just an everyday story of Ferrari folk.

BOTTOMING OUT

The 1989 season was not exactly what one might call an easy year for Camel Team Lotus. It will not be remembered fondly by anyone associated with the team, or indeed by the many fans who have followed Lotus since the days when Colin Chapman ran the show, when Lotus was THE team.

Was this really the same team which had collected 107 pole positions and 79 Grand Prix victories; the team with seven Constructors' and six Drivers' World Championships behind it?

How was it then that at Spa-Francorchamps – the scene of five Lotus World Championship race wins – that the team failed to qualify both its cars?

That had never happened before in the 31-year history of the team and it was hard to comprehend that such a thing could ever happen to Lotus. But as the season unfolded the unthinkable gradually began to cross the minds of even the most ardent Lotus fans.

Similar disasters have befallen other top teams. All good teams go through their ups and downs, but somehow Lotus always seemed to be different. Like Ferrari it has acquired a certain mystique over the years – an aura of achievement, backed up by statistics and heroic tales.

It was depressing to discover that Lotus was still merely a racing team, rather than a phenomenon.

During the bad patches, the best teams restructure, get the correct combination for success and then fight back. That has always been the way, yet Lotus has not won the World Championship since way back in the glory days of Mario Andretti and Ronnie Peterson in 1978.

There has not been a race win since Ayrton Senna was with the team early in 1987 – and even more damning, there has not even seemed the likelihood of such a thing occurring.

Things have not been going at all well: Senna departed at the end of that year, taking his startling talents to McLaren, for which he won the 1988 World Championship. In his time with the team, Ayrton had become the hub around which the Lotus wheel rotated. When he left, the team slowly collapsed from the inside. Honda pulled out at the end

of 1988; Technical Director Gerard Ducarouge departed for the Larrousse team; even the Camel sponsorship seemed to be in danger.

Nelson Piquet, one sensed, was not driving with quite the same vigour that had given him three World Championship victories. Satoru Nakajima was something of a leftover from the days of Honda, yet he could run quicker than Piquet on occasion – which, to the critics, did not reflect well on Satoru, merely badly on Nelson.

Team morale had gone through rock-bottom.

And then, within a matter of days, Lotus Chairman Fred Bushell was arrested on charges related to the Delorean scandal, and Peter Warr, the Team Director, decided that there were other ways to make a living and, after a lengthy career based around Lotus, left the team for a second time.

Yet the ultimate humiliation was still to come when Piquet and Nakajima failed to qualify for the Belgian GP on a dreadful soggy day in the Ardennes. It hurt. It hurt a lot.

'See you tomorrow,' people said to Lotus folk on that miserable Saturday night.

'Yes,' replied the team personnel. 'We will have plenty of time to talk. There isn't much else to do.'

And yet, seemingly at the nadir of the team's fortunes, there was a strange, almost macabre, sense of humour.

The team knew it had already turned the corner.

It was beginning to fight back, rather than rolling with the punches as it had in the early part of the season.

While the Jonahs declared after Spa that the end of the world was in sight for the once-mighty Lotus team, the new management shrugged.

Spa had been 'one of those things'. The double non-qualification had been unlucky – a case of being caught out at the wrong time by circumstances. It happens. McLaren discovered that at Monaco in 1983.

In fact, Lotus watchers had noted a change of atmosphere at the German GP.

In the Hockenheim pits the mechanics had put up a sign to ward off enquiries about the management changes in the week before the race:

'Don't mention the Warr', it said.

There, instead of Warr, was Tony Rudd, an avuncular – almost cuddly figure. The great British eccentric brought in to sort everything out.

'I hope the reshuffle has happened now,' he said merrily at Hockenheim. 'My instructions are to win races. The latent talent is here. It is part of my job to find the good people and encourage them.'

It all sound like good home-spun logic, but the man who looked like shark-bait in the deep waters of F1 was no idle swimmer. He knew the rules of the game and how to play it.

The bubbly atmosphere in the Lotus pit at Hockenheim was evidence that everyone felt that a new chapter was beginning in the history of Lotus and the disaster in Belgium would not dent that belief.

Frank Dernie, the voluble and ambitious Technical Director, had formed what seemed like a strong bond with his assorted boffins. The car began to improve by leaps and bounds. Piquet's interest seemed to rekindle.

The new Lotus management settled itself under Rudd's weathered eye: Rupert Manwaring, the team manager since the start of the season, emerged from the shadow cast by Warr's presence; Noel Stanbury, looking after promotions and sponsor liaison, put on his hard-talking hat and went after the sponsors.

Everything began to tick again.

As happened when Gerard Ducarouge arrived and galvanised the team to action in the summer of 1983 – building the Lotus-Renault 94T in a matter of weeks – a great motivator was at work.

Less than six weeks after he took over – a fortnight after the supposed debacle at Spa – Rudd was able to unveil the future plans of Lotus.

Piquet and Nakajima would leave Lotus at the end of the year. Derek Warwick would finally join the team – after several abortive attempts – and would be backed up by Formula 3000 graduate and Lotus test driver Martin Donnelly.

Camel was staying on. Given the dramas in the weeks and months before the decision was taken, it was almost a surprise that the cigarette company should stay with the team.

Lastly, Lotus would have a multi-cylinder engine for the 1990 season.

Clockwise from left: Nakajima never set the yellow cars alight. Neither did triple World Champion Piquet. Twenty years with Lotus, Tony Rudd has been installed as chairman to change this.

A V12 from Lamborghini!

If the investigative press had not dug up the story in advance it would have been a stunning revelation.

'The driving team is organised,' said Tony Rudd proudly, 'the money is organised. What we intend to do now is to have a movement of effort sideways. We will have more emphasis on research and development – on innovation.'

Rudd's words must have gladdened the hearts of Lotus fans everywhere, for this policy was turning the clock back to the original Lotus principles; back to the most successful approach in motor racing – finding the unfair advantage.

It was this principle which gave the Lotus team such success in its history; which had resulted in such breakthroughs as the invention of the monocoque chassis and the discovery of ground-effect.

It all made a lot of sense. The combination might take some time to overrun the tried and tested McLaren-Honda combination and the mighty – and resurgent Ferrari – but it was a step on the path back to competitiveness.

The driver line-up was a neat mixture of youth and experience; the Lamborghini engine was powerful and gaining reliability – and there were longer-term aims at which the team would only hint.

'This is the ideal opportunity for me to join Lotus,' explained a genuinely delighted Derek Warwick. 'There are two divisions in Formula One at the moment: Ferrari, Honda and Renault are out in front. With this package there is the opportunity to challenge Division One.

The most striking thing about Lotus in the summer of 1989 was not the collapse of the team, nor even the grandiose talk of future plans. What stood out was the change that took place in the space of a few days between the British and German Grands Prix.

Perhaps, also, there is a moral in all this: winning drivers may need to be in total control of a team to achieve the level of support they require to sustain their challenge.

In the end, the drivers always move on.

A body does not function without a heart.

Johnny Herbert takes an interest in the performance of replacement Pirro.

Young Guns

TOMORROW'S STARS TODAY

In the words of the old French proverb: 'There is no such thing as a pretty good omelette.'

Today there is no such thing as a pretty good Formula 1 driver.

They are all good but, contrary to the belief of some in the pitlane, Grand Prix racing does not have a monopoly on the talent and there are always new F1 drivers arriving, banging on the door and demanding a seat among the exalted 26 men who sit on the grid for a Grand Prix . . .

In recent years, very few new boys have been admitted into this exclusive society. The likes of Ayrton Senna and Gerhard Berger had sufficient 'extra' to bludgeon their way to the top, but otherwise the supporting cast remained, with only the occasional change and the annual round of musical chairs.

The survivors did not damage cars and produced the occasional good performance. They might even bring some money to help the team along.

This year that has changed. As the winter months grind on towards a new season, many of the names which have been integral to Formula 1 are finding themselves having to look elsewhere for future employment. A new broom is sweeping through Grand Prix racing.

Why? Is this a particularly good new generation? Is it the effect of the McLaren-Honda domination, forcing team managements to take more risks in their choice of drivers? Has F1 tired of its safe choices? Or is the reason that, in the topsy-turvy world behind the multi-cylinder cars, a greater number of young drivers have had the opportunity to show what they can do? One weekend a man will run in the top ten, the next he will fail to qualify.

Formula 1 is now gaining more and more children of the sixties. Ayrton Senna has been the most precocious. The Brazilian is the first to be born in the sixties to have won a race, the first to have won the World Championship. No other driver from the sixties has yet done either.

But the signs are that in the next year, the old order will become ever more threatened. The turbocharged days, when young careers were sacrificed in favour of the old guard, have gone.

In 1989 that change was more noticeable than ever.

Not all the 'new boys' of 1989 were actually new, but they had never before been able to show off their pace.

We have had Ivan Capelli and Yannick Dalmas showing their potential since 1987, but in 1989 a new wave arrived, and the vanguard of this latest generation made its presence felt in Rio de Janeiro.

Mauricio Gugelmin (born 20 April 1963), finished third in the Brazilian GP, after a solid first season with March in 1988. But it was GP debutant Johnny Herbert (born 25 June 1964) who truly stole the thunder.

The young Englishman could scarcely walk, yet this pale, pained figure outqualified his more experienced Benetton teammate Alessandro Nannini and went on to finish fourth.

On the same day Ligier's Olivier Grouillard put in a solid performance to finish ninth on his F1 debut, completely overshadowing the vastly experienced Rene Arnoux.

At San Marino others began to emerge from the shadows: Scuderia Italia's Alex Caffi (born 18 March 1964) and AGS's Gabriele Tarquini (born 2 March 1963) both marked their cards for future stardom.

At Monaco it was the turn of Stefano Modena (born 12 May 1963), emerging from an awful debut year with the hopeless EuroBrun team to take his Brabham to third place. Caffi was fourth, and Tarquini had run fifth before retiring.

Capelli (born 24 May 1963) was fourth on the grid in Mexico and Tarquini came home sixth. In Phoenix Caffi ran second and Herbert struggled home in fifth. In Montreal Nicola Larini (born 19 March 1964) took an Osella to run third in the wet. Caffi was sixth.

But the new boys were merely warming up: all but Herbert and Grouillard had some previous experience in F1.

By the French GP, Herbert was gone from F1, the victim of his injured legs and the political exploitation of his unfortunate position. But there were others to take up the torch.

On 9 July 1989, F1 crossed a new frontier. It was an important day for it marked the F1 debuts of Jean Alesi (born 11 June 1964), Eric Bernard (24 August 1964), Martin Donnelly (26 March 1964), Bertrand Gachot (22 December 1962) and Emanuele Pirro (12 January 1962).

Alesi ran second and finished fourth, Grouillard scored his first point in sixth. The others all impressed.

The young bloods already in F1 responded. At the British GP Pierluigi Martini (born 23 April 1961) showed flashes of the talent everyone knew he had.

And so it went on. In Germany, Pirro ran in third; in Hungary Caffi qualified third; in Italy Alesi was in the points; in Portugal Martini led the race for half a lap and finished fifth, in Spain Alesi was fourth and J. J. Lehto (born 31 January 1966) showed well for Onyx.

But what did it all mean? Why, suddenly, were the youngsters beginning to figure?

The older men argued that it was a technical point. The new men were drawn to the 3-litre Formula 3000 cars, with their rock-hard suspensions and twitchy characteristics. The older generation had to 're-learn' how to drive without turbocharging. There was probably some truth in that.

Clockwise from top left: Modena — the best? Gachot — fired by Onyx! Caffi — always consistent in the Dallara. Larini has his options. Alesi — a Tyrrell find?

The youngsters were able to show well because, being both hungry for success and desperate to make a good impression, they were willing to take more risks on qualifying tyres – a phenomenon which had been absent from F1 for a couple of years.

Generally, with the new generation arriving all at the same time, there was an edge of desperation among the youngsters that had been lacking in F1 for some time.

There were plenty of theories as to the whys and wherefores, but no real evidence to give a definitive answer.

Perhaps it was purely the march of time. The young men had to arrive at some point. It just all happened in 1989.

The question to which most people wanted an answer was, which of these young heroes was the best?

For some years the Italians have been sitting on a very bright heap of talent. Those who followed the 1986 Italian F3 series knew that there were four young men who would all make it to F1: Larini (the champion), Alex Caffi, Stefano Modena and Marco Apicella (born 7 October 1965).

The first three have already succeeded and the fourth, with a little luck, will eventually join them.

In 1987 Formula 3000 highlighted Modena's considerable talents as he swept to the championship.

But who was the best? Which of the Italians would lead his generation? And how do these drivers compare with the French newcomers? Was Alesi better than Bernard? And what about Gachot? Again there is no clear-cut answer. Bernard, Alesi and Gachot first met in the finals of the Paul Ricard Elf Winfield racing school. That was in November 1983. The three finalists fought it out: Bernard won.

Two seasons later Bernard had won the French Fomule Renault title. Alesi was fifth. Two years on and the rivals fought over the French F3 title – Alesi won. In 1989 it was F3000 and Alesi did it again.

And what about those trained in the rough-and-tumble world of British club racing?

How did Gachot compare to Herbert or Donnelly?

Of course, there are no answers. A driver is only as good as his car. To compare talents is a risky game – but one which everyone in F1 has to play if they are to snap up THE hotshot.

Memories are short and already the new generation has had victims. Careers have been blighted by a poor year here, or a bad decision there.

Dalmas, hailed as a future champion a couple of seasons past, seemed to lose his way in 1989; Capelli, very much the hero of 1988, had little to show for his 1989 season. In F1 you are only as good as your last race.

Herbert's F1 future is by no means certain, although he is under contract to return to Benetton in 1991. Larini is under option to Ferrari until 1993.

Others are not so lucky. Pirro lost his seat at Benetton to Nelson Piquet, Emanuele's vast experience as a McLaren test driver seemingly not being taken into account.

Bernd Schneider (20 July 1964), Volker Weidler (18 March 1962), Joachim Winkelhock (24 October 1960), Gregor Foitek (27 March 1965), Pierre-Henri Raphanel (27 May 1961), Aguri Suzuki (21 March 1960) and Enrico Bertaggia (19 September 1964) all struggled in pre-qualifying.

Yet even for the new young men life in F1 will not get any easier. The arrival of new blood may mean the older F1 men have to look over their shoulders, but the new drivers too have little in the way of security. The volatile skills of the new men mean mistakes are made; there are hirings and firings. And, more than ever, there are more youngsters queuing up for a place in F1: Apicella, Erik Comas (28 September 1963), Mark Blundell (8 April 1966), Allan McNish, David Brabham and Gianni Morbidelli. It will not be long before the men of the sixties become established figures, looking over their shoulders at those born in the seventies . . .

It is hard to explain the phenomenon of the 1989 explosion of youth, but it is certainly an unusual thing.

Luckily, it is also extremely exciting to watch such talents flowering.

And who knows which one is the best? Modena, maybe? Only time will tell. . . .

Changes

KEKE ROSBERG

An astute and knowledgeable observer, Keke Rosberg was also the last World Champion before the dominance of the turbo era. Here he describes the differences he sees between normally aspirated Formula One in 1982 and its return seven years later.

The turbo era that succeeded my World Championship in 1982 was one of constant confusion. First the turbos had power but they blew up. Then they had power and didn't blow up and went too fast. So then they needed fuel restrictions to slow them down. There was no consistency at all.

I guess the public thought that as we were going back to normally aspirated engines we were going back to the Formula One of the seventies. But you can't turn the clock back. We now have a Formula One which benefits from a lot of the technology of the turbocharged era — but I'll come to that in a moment.

Away from the teams themselves, there are two areas which have changed, one for the better, one for the worse. Circuits, their facilities, safety and organisation have improved a lot in all areas. I think Derek

Ongaro was a vital factor in safety improvement because he was keen to do his job well and by staying there for a while there was some stability. Here was a guy who niggled and niggled and improved things bit by bit. You ain't going to change the world in a day, and I think that was an important factor. At the moment, Formula One tracks really present the highest standard with the greatest safety that you can get. A great improvement also was Bernie Ecclestone's demand for 5-year GP contracts.

There will always be places that are out of date. But until you start running on airfields without spectators, you have to accept that motor racing is dangerous. You want to bring spectators as close to the action as you dare, but you have to protect them at the same time.

So the circuit safety and organisational situation is good. What is bad

Left: Keke, Monaco 1982.
Right: Some aspects of safety really make Keke see red.

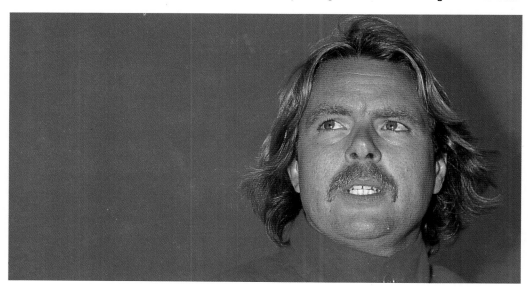

are drivers' track manners. At the end of the seventies there was a certain code of ethics amongst Formula One drivers. It wasn't a gentleman's game but there were certain rules. For instance, you could block somebody on the last two, maybe three laps if you were desperate, but you would never block them on the first or second lap. Nobody ever did that, it wasn't part of the game. If he was quicker he was going to get by you anyway.

These days a guy moves from side to side or tries to run you into the wall. That is very, very sad. But then we're talking about different eras. All this kind of behaviour starts in the lower formulae where drivers used to race as a hobby. Now it's no longer a hobby, so there are huge, fraught battles where manners aren't very good and drivers bring their manners with them.

There should be some kind of a way that when a new driver comes in, an experienced driver gives him a few words of friendly advice as to how the game is played. When I first raced in Formula One in South Africa in 1978, no one even realised I was there. But Mario Andretti walked over to me in the paddock and said, 'Good to see you here. I hope you have a great future and you like this game. But now let me tell you a few points.'

It was all said in a very brotherly way and I appreciated it a lot. I didn't mind at all. If you did that to today's kids they would give you a finger and say, 'I know that already.' There isn't that respect for others any more. Young drivers think it's automatic to get into Formula One and race the same as everyone else.

Yet there are team managers in the paddock who tell new drivers not to worry about their mirrors, about who is trying to overtake them. That's ridiculous. A team manager's responsibility is to educate a new driver. Formula One is a dangerous game with lots of money and interests at stake.

There are some people in Formula One who haven't even realised, after many, many years, that they have two mirrors on their car. Yet that situation has almost been accepted and approved. When you see one of those guys on the track you watch out for him because it's a well-known fact that either he doesn't know you're behind him or he ignores the fact. Those drivers' reputations are so widespread that any driver who arrives in Formula One knows the two worst culprits.

If I can make another small complaint, it is that speeds in the pit lane after tyre changes during the race are way too high. One day somebody is going to lose a car in the pit lane when they are passing other teams and if something like that happens to a car – it only has to lose a wrongly-fitted wheel – it could wipe out 50 people.

There's no excuse for high speeds in the pits during practice. They're not prepared for that. In the race people are trying to be prepared for faster speeds, but the poor mechanics can't move away because their driver might be coming in two seconds later.

World Champion Keke, pre-turbos.

Yet at the same time, a driver from a team closest to the pit lane entrance can be in sixth gear by the time he reaches the last team in the pit lane after his tyre stop. He's on cold tyres which means that the car is unpredictable and it's a piece of road on which he's never driven at such speed. It's very dangerous.

I think Gerard Ducarouge's idea of putting up a speed trap in the pit lane is the best idea in the world. Sixty miles an hours is quick enough for everyone, and it would be quite easy for a driver to work out how many revs in which gear would be sufficiently slow for him. It would eliminate one danger element that currently exists in Formula One.

I mentioned earlier how Formula One has grown up via the turbo era. You can see it in the paddock. There are computer trucks, fuel trucks, engine trucks, not to mention the size of hospitality – but that's another thing.

The engine has become the dominating factor. Engine manufacturers have power. Teams who have contracts with engine manufacturers have power, because without an engine manufacturer today you are an also-ran. But there are many more manufacturers involved in Formula One these days. Ten years ago there was just Ford, Ferrari and Matra. . . .

Now the larger number of manufacturers has meant two things. First of all they have brought in technology from the turbo era, which includes all the electronics which have taken such a dominating role. In the old days you just had someone to check that the engine was running, and providing it was popping and banging you knew that it was fine. But with more people, you have more possibilities.

Having said that leads me on to the second point. An engine manufacturer being involved means you enter into a very heavy test programme. It sets great demands on the team and a lot of the teams which are running Cosworths or other available engines don't realise what they are saying when they say they need an engine manufacturer. Admittedly the gap between the readily available engines and the manufacturers' engines is big and next year it will be bigger. It's not the difference that existed between an old Cosworth DFV and a Ferrari

V12. The Ferrari, everyone said, had more power being a 12 cylinder. But the disadvantage was that it was heavy and used a lot of fuel.

Now electronics have brought fuel consumption down to new levels – and it's the multi-cylinder manufacturers who have the better electronics. Furthermore, they are making their V10s and V12s smaller and smaller. Ten years ago, you could make up that difference between V8 and V12 power with a superior chassis – but you can't do that now.

I do believe that Formula One should be for normally aspirated cars. People claimed that turbo technology and development could benefit mankind, but that's bullshit. They are doing exactly the same things with normally aspirated engines and this development will benefit mankind much more because of the fuel situation. The engine people are really working within smaller parameters and doing more refined work, working with a fuel which is closer to that which is in everyday use.

Secondly, electronics in fuel consumption is still an important factor because fuel is weight. The less fuel you need, the less weight you have. The turbo era and its fuel consumption restraints are still influencing modern Formula One.

The very presence of fuel trucks in the paddock is a legacy of the turbo era. During the old, normally aspirated days, I don't remember fuel companies being involved at all. Nobody ever air-freighted their fuel to Brazil for instance, but now they have to do it for every test and race because of the increased research into fuel and the sort of things that you can do with it within FISA's regulations.

So even though we are in the first year of a new, normally aspirated engines era we are already showing signs of alarmingly quick progress. At Jerez they lapped 3.5s below the pole position winning time of the previous year. Cornering speeds, thanks to normally aspirated engines and improved chassis, have grown again; for me, alarmingly so.

At the same time the emphasis is more on the drivers. The driving has become more physical, and they are having to do more debriefs: discussing chassis, tyres and now the engine too. In the car, we had a rev counter and a switch to switch it on and off and an electrical fuel pump if you were sophisticated which you usually forgot anyway.

Now you're talking about the recirculation of oil, damper controls and, of course, the electronic gearbox. But engine development takes up a lot of the driver's time and it can be completely wasted. You can change something on the engine which in turn changes its behaviour and that might put different demands on the chassis. On one setting the engine can be better low down so that quite suddenly all the chassis improvement that you've made for better traction has just gone out of the window. On the other hand telemetry has taken one responsibility off the driver's shoulders in that you no longer rely on him to suggest that the engine might be better a notch leaner, for instance. You know what is happening out there. You don't guess any more which gives you unlimited possibilities.

All this, of course, increases the role of the potential test driver. When you have got something to try, you use the test driver. As we see now, test drivers are working on active ride suspension which is still unreliable, heavy and complicated but ultimately has advantages. But it's being given to test drivers eager to get into Formula One. To be brutally frank, you ain't going to send your five-million-dollar number one to test an active ride system. He might hurt himself, but the guy you are buying in for $25,000 a year is hired to see if it works.

The teams themselves have changed a lot. You used to have 50 people on a team, but a big team nowadays has 160 to 180 people. Carbon fibre has changed it all, raising costs enormously and increasing manpower. It requires highly qualified and accurate people who perform their jobs exactly and know what they are doing.

The standard of manufacturing race cars is incredibly high when you think of the past. There's tremendous accuracy for starters. When you bolt a car together everything fits perfectly, which it didn't in the past. The cars are incredibly light which makes them safer as well because they stop more quickly when they hit something. The cars are virtually one piece too which provides great protection for the driver.

However, I don't like the way a cockpit sometimes ends right in front of the face of the driver. Seat belts stretch, as they must, but if a driver hits his head on a carbon fibre cockpit, it doesn't bend as fibreglass did, it's as hard as steel.

I don't think that cars are any more comfortable than they used to be. There's still no suspension movement. You lift the car up, the wheels don't go down. But regulations allow designers to make cars that in my opinion are far too small inside. The drivers are wearing knee and elbow pads because they are getting banged about in the cockpit. I can't even imagine what it would be like to be one of the bigger guys.

The one area that perhaps has become easier is the tyre situation. In my day I might run three different compounds in one race, several times on four different corners. That doesn't happen today.

But much of the increase in speed today has come from tyre development. We have completely changed from cross-plies to radials, unheard-of until Michelin arrived. To see these cars running on cross-plies would be fun, because they are running so low to the ground, and you can't control a cross-ply as you can a radial.

Tyres, in fact, have become a dominant factor and have influenced some of the best races that we've seen this year. With the engine becoming so dominant, circuits that equalise all engines, such as the Jerez and Budapests of the season, actually result in good races where ultimately tyre choice makes the difference.

But already, in the three years since I last drove, the development that has taken place in all sorts of areas is incredible. Formula One is even more expensive and fascinating, and I'm sure it will continue to be what it always has been – a great sport.

Moody clouds reflect the feeling of the Zakspeed team.

UNLUCKY 13?

It's early Friday morning. There's a chill in the air and a dusty racing track. At this time of day, a sane soul would be rolling over in bed and re-setting the alarm clock.

But not the 13 Formula 1 pre-qualifiers. They'll be up waiting nervously for 8 a.m. when, for 60 minutes, they will have the chance to produce one of the four best times. If they fail in this task, they will have to pack up their trucks and leave.

This was the story of the 1989 Grand Prix season and, on the face of it, it was not a fair system. A successful pre-qualifier might go on to gain a good grid position, might even finish the weekend in the top six places — or even on the podium.

At Estoril Stefan Johansson was third in the Portuguese GP, yet a week later he failed to pre-qualify the Spanish GP.

The lap times produced in the hectic hour were often faster than those achieved later by successful qualifiers. It mattered not. If you were not one of the top four, your weekend was over.

But how did such a bizarre system develop? Purely and simply, pre-qualifying was a response to Formula 1 being too popular. There were too many teams to fit into the paddock and the pits and on to the tracks.

The decision to hold pre-qualifying was taken to 'weed out' the slower cars. An immediate side-effect of this was to raise the game of the little teams. To be successful in pre-qualifying required a well-sorted, well-built car and some snappy driving.

The pre-qualifying rules developed as they went along. At the start of the year, the unlucky 13 were made up of the left-overs of the 1988 championship and the new teams.

By mid-season this had changed. The top 13 teams in the previous two half-seasons gained automatic inclusion in the official practice. The rest had to pre-qualify.

It all made for spectacular viewing, for many of the smaller teams had hired young drivers, desperate to make their mark on F1. It was a recipe for hotshoes to turn their racing cars into component parts if they tried too hard.

It happened regularly. Gregor Foitek demolished his EuroBrun in Canada, Pierre-Henri Raphanel destroyed his Coloni at Hockenheim.

'It was my fast lap and I had to keep my foot down,' explained Raphanal later. 'It was my only chance.' The result was a very bent Coloni as Raphanel hit a kerb and launched his car into the unforgiving barriers.

Raphanel eventually left Coloni for Rial
— out of the frying pan into the fire.

There was luck involved, of course, for with the one-lap 'gum-ball' qualifying tyres of 1989 the pre-qualifiers often had just one chance to make the grade. A wasted set of qualifiers would mean a wasted weekend.

If there was traffic in the way on that one lap, the unacceptable risk had to be taken.

The 60-minute session called for unusual approaches. The Larrousse team had a fleet of motorcycles stationed around the track in Germany to ensure that if one of the cars broke down, the driver could be returned to the pits in time to take over the spare car.

The system could be beaten, as Brabham proved. In the first eight races Stefano Modena and Martin Brundle were consistently successful in pre-qualifying and as they gained championship points in the races, so the threat of having to continue pre-qualifying in the second half of the season faded. Alex Caffi also escaped after eight races, but the curious system also had its stranger side.

Christian Danner's Rial scored a fortunate three points in Phoenix and, as a result, Volker Weidler (who had never looked likely to make it through pre-qualifying) found himself an automatic entry to official practice after the British GP. Thereafter neither of the Rials ever looked like qualifying, while the Lolas, AGSs and Onyxes had to fight for one of the four places, despite being obviously quicker than the German cars. So luck played its part.

Only one man managed to retain a 100 per cent record, Modena succeeding on all eight occasions when he was called to pre-qualify. Even such experienced drivers as Martin Brundle, Michele Alboreto, Stefan Johansson and Philippe Alliot did not always make the cut.

As the teams became ever more competitive, so the line between success and failure became ever finer. We thought Martin Brundle had cut it as fine as was possible in Monaco when he slipped in by just 0.021s quicker than Piercarlo Ghinzani's Osella, but it could be even closer than that.

In Canada Alex Caffi began his flying lap just five seconds before the chequered flag came out to mark the end of the session. He bumped out Martin Brundle on that very lap.

But it could go closer than that. At the German GP Michele Alboreto edged out Yannick Dalmas's AGS by the smallest possible margin available with the Olivetti/Longines timing system – 0.001s – and that in the closing minutes of the session.

The pressure on pre-qualifiers was not merely restricted to that wild hour, for at the British GP the pre-qualifers were to change over with teams which had gone into the top 13 list at mid-season, moving into the ranks of the automatic qualifiers.

At the French GP Stefan Johansson finished fifth for Onyx. Two points would be enough.

Seven days later Onyx fortunes dived again, as Pierluigi Martini and

Clockwise from left: Eric Zakowski hopes for better things in 1990. Lack of reliability demoted the Larrousse team to pre-qualifying. Wiedler sprints back for another attempt – DNQ. Johansson and Lehto surely shouldn't be in this lottery.

Luis Sala took their Minardis to fifth and sixth in the British GP – scoring three points . . .

The pressures ultimately led to considerable frustrations in the teams which failed to make it, and as the season progressed so the hirings and firings increased in intensity; Joachim Winkelhock lost his AGS seat to Dalmas; Raphanel, desperate for a place among the automatic entries, switched to Rial replacing Weidler; Gregor Foitek fell out with EuroBrun and was replaced by Oscar Larrauri and Bertrand Gachot was replaced by J. J. Lehto.

It was not a fair system. It had many faults and inconsistencies, but it was exciting – and there were races in 1989 when a little excitement was needed in the face of the McLaren-Honda onslaught.

McLaren – champions again. McLaren's strengths and difficulties in challenging for the Constructors' and Drivers' Championships in 1989 are covered in detail elsewhere, so this review concentrates on a race-to-race action replay. Both Honda and McLaren tackled the Brazilian race almost on a one-off basis. There would be a gap of about a month after the first round of the series, giving them plenty of time to sort out any problems with their MP4/5 which, once again, appeared very much at the last minute. And when rain washed out some of the pre-race testing, there were rumours, firmly put down by Ron Dennis, that the car wasn't very good.

Senna started from pole in Brazil, Prost from row three. Senna was soon involved in a first-corner tussle with Berger while Patrese went round the outside of the two of them. Senna never recovered from the first lap stop for a new nose cone and finished eleventh, while Prost could not believe how good his car was, but losing his clutch prevented a second tyre stop and he had to settle for second place.

The team then went off to Imola for eight solid days' testing which established chassis and engine set-ups for the season. And when the Grand Prix circus revisited Imola, McLaren showed their class: front row of the grid, with Mansell third, 1.4 s behind second-placed Prost. Nannini, the first V8-powered runner, was 2.8 s behind poleman Senna.

But the race saw an upset which would slowly spread like a cancer. Senna led Prost at the first start but when Berger crashed and they had to start again, Prost led Senna, only for the Brazilian to dive down inside Prost's wide-open door, breaking an agreement that the two would not battle at the first corner. And that was the way they finished, in spite of Prost spinning because of a blistered tyre. Senna, also on blistering tyres and suffering brake troubles, and Prost were a lap ahead of the rest.

So by Monaco the relationship was seriously soured. Again it was Senna from Prost on the front row and Prost kept up the pressure on the leading Senna in the race. But with help from Rene Arnoux, Senna rapidly pulled away as Prost was held up, and the ridiculous traffic jam instigated by de Cesaris and Piquet at Loew's put Prost further behind. There were gearbox problems for Senna which he tried hard to disguise to prevent Prost from knowing, but once again, the pair were a lap ahead of the rest.

Mexico saw the same grid formation, but this was a tyre race, and while Senna chose a mixture with Goodyear's Bs on the harder used left side, Prost went for the softer Cs all round. Although Alboreto, for instance, made the choice work, Prost, in pursuit of Senna, couldn't. So the Brazilian scored his hat trick, and Prost was only fifth after two tyre stops.

A week later in Phoenix, Prost damaged a McLaren chassis in qualifying for the first time. Once again it was Senna – Prost on the front row. Senna began to pull away from Prost when suddenly his car began to misfire and this would ultimately stop him. Prost, meanwhile, scored his first victory in America, suspecting that his tyre choice would have brought him a win anyway.

Canada was the team's biggest disaster of the year. This time Prost claimed pole position after a rather strange qualifying session. Mixed conditions in the race saw Prost retire early with a broken front suspension mounting, but Senna was leading, in spite of two tyre stops, when his engine expired having pumped out all its oil, a problem that was to dog the team for the next two races. So both McLarens had retired for the first time in many races.

In fact the oil problem didn't seem so serious in France where Prost announced that he was going to leave the team at the end of the year, then put the car on the front row of the grid and, when Senna's transmission broke at the second start, proceeded to dominate the race.

In Britain a week later, a new transverse gearbox meant a new oil tank and that in turn produced problems which were finally solved on raceday. Senna started from pole position only to have difficulty engaging a gear and spun off, handing the race to Prost.

But in Germany two weeks later, it was Senna who ultimately had some good luck. The pair were once more on the front row, and here they fought the first of their duels, Senna leading from Prost. But at the pit stops there were problems, and that gave the lead back to Prost. We were all wondering how it would end when Prost found that he couldn't engage fifth gear. Senna swooped past and was back on the rostrum again for the first time since Mexico.

Hungary provided upsets galore with the track not giving the grip that others were able to find. Senna at least ran second to Patrese, and then led as Prost fought up to third. But Senna lost out to Mansell, and Prost had to make two pit stops, so McLarens finished second and fourth in the end.

In spite of wet conditions, Prost made a battle of it in Belgium, holding off Mansell to finish a fighting second behind Senna, both drivers complaining of the driveability of their engines in spite of a fine one-two.

With Prost now destined for Ferrari, he was the tifosi's blue-eyed boy in Italy but Senna was on pole and Prost fourth with the Ferraris in between. Senna looked as though he would win, until once again his

engine lost its oil. Prost took care of both Ferraris to inherit the win, although he had much to say about the power of his engine afterwards, for which he would later apologise.

With the championship moving into its final, crucial stage, Portugal was all-important for Senna and once again he started from pole with Prost back in fourth. In fact the Ferraris seemed to have the McLarens beaten when Mansell had trouble at his stop, then came charging back to challenge second-placed Senna, only for the two to collide. Prost survived to finish second to Berger.

Now Senna had to win everything to stay in contention, and he fulfilled that contract in Spain with Prost happy in third place. Then came Japan and the ultimate showdown. It was a championship that had everything, more than was necessary for some. The McLarens were rarely perfect: there always seemed to be a little something that wasn't quite right, and gearboxes in general came in for more stick than usual now that there were no fuel restrictions. But whenever McLaren drivers described their problems, the reaction of most other drivers was, 'those are problems that I could live with if I had a McLaren and a Honda engine'.

Ferrari – the challenger when reliable. Ferrari were without doubt McLaren's main challengers throughout the season, and on occasions much more than that. Look at the Portuguese Grand Prix where they were quite obviously superior to McLaren, and Hungary where Mansell came through from 12th on the grid to beat both red-and-white cars in a straight fight.

But this success was hard-earned by a team that chiselled away at the job in hand and came up with suitable modifications which were particularly successful on circuits where McLaren were scrabbling for grip. There were many who said that Ferrari had the better chassis by the end of the season.

The changeover from turbos saw a number of changes within the team. Gone was sporting director Marco Piccinnini, replaced by Lancia's successful rally team manager Cesare Fiorio. The Italian press couldn't believe it when Mansell won first time out for the team in Brazil. 'Everything Fiorio touches turns to gold,' they said.

But if the truth were told, new driver Mansell, replacing Michele

Alboreto, couldn't believe it either. The fact that a Ferrari didn't see a chequered flag for another seven races tells the reason why. Indeed, the departing Berger wouldn't finish a race until the 12th of the year.

Ferrari tackled the season with what they called the 640, developed from the 639 which was their normally aspirated, turbo-chassis test car. Moreno had started testing this car the previous year, together with John Barnard's electronically operated hydraulic gearbox system, controlled by levers behind the steering wheel.

It was this gearbox and its various valves and electronic systems that caused Mansell's incredulity after the first race, for he'd had a succession of bothers with the box, many of them quite alarming. Virtually nothing else on the car caused problems throughout the year; this superb system, for which the drivers virtually sacrificed the season, was the cause of most of Ferrari's problems when the drivers didn't make their own mistakes. There were moments when one thought that they had the problem licked – only for another problem to rear its head. A failure of some sort never seemed to be far away.

In the meantime, Ferrari modified the suspension with a new anti-roll bar system for the French Grand Prix and there the engine was also lighter and more powerful. A further increase in power, with a smoother power curve, was the team's final modification for the year.

Although neither driver regularly slagged off the team, there were murmurs of discontent occasionally. Berger, not surprisingly, became frustrated with his non-finishes and was vociferous when a gearbox problem in one warm-up wasn't rectified for the race and caused retirement. Mansell also had reason to be upset: twice he ran out of petrol in qualifying and he was not happy when he found the spare wasn't prepared for him after the first corner accident in France.

Mansell was involved in two incidents which would cause him grief. In Canada he exited the pit lane before the race had started and was subsequently disqualified. Ferrari later dropped both this appeal and the one against his disqualification for ignoring the black flag in Portugal.

That was three-tiered hassle. A missed pit entry meant reversing in the pit lane which earned the black flag. Mansell didn't see it and then collided with Senna, putting them both out of the race. It was another incident in a contentious season, and not an easy debut for Fiorio in Grand Prix motor racing.

Adding to his complications was the accident which befell Berger at Imola. The Austrian had a miraculous escape, but it did take some time for any idea of what had happened to emerge. Later Berger's nose section came flying off in the German Grand Prix, and the so-called sages nodded wisely, suggesting that this had been the original problem at Imola.

Comparison between the two drivers is difficult. It took a while for Berger to get over his accident, longer than he would admit, and the lack of reliability dented his confidence too. A pattern emerges in the two drivers' qualifying performances, with Berger quickest up to the accident, and then only out-qualifying Mansell again from Hungary onwards. His victory in Portugal was sadly overshadowed by other events but he was in control for most of the race, even before the elimination of his two greatest threats.

Mansell, meanwhile, drove hard throughout and was frequently the driver who enlivened an otherwise dull race. His race to victory in Hungary was nothing short of exceptional and was probably the drive of the year. Ferrari gave him the background, support and confidence that he needs, and he in turn rewarded the team with his commitment. He would admit that he had never been so relaxed during a Grand Prix season. It was a partnership that was ideal – not everyone would have imagined that it would go so well at the start of the year.

For Ferrari, then, it was the year of the special gearbox, dominated by the perfection of a superb development. But its inventor was gone by the end of the year and so too was Berger, to be replaced by Prost. It would be he and Mansell who would consolidate the development work on one of the team's greatest assets.

Williams-Renault return. After one year in the doldrums, Williams bounced back into division one partially thanks to their membership of the exclusive 'multi-cylinder' club via Renault with their V10. This was probably the newest of the non-V8s and therefore had the steepest development curve, but by the end of the year Renault were delighted with their progress, and Williams had begun their 1990 programme with the late launch of the FW13.

After a difficult year running the Judd V8 and active suspension in 1988, there were quite a few defections from the Williams team over the winter, in spite of the obvious promise that could be expected from the liaison with Renault, returning to Formula One after their turbo programme ended three years previously. Among those leaving were team manager Dave Stubbs (to Brabham), Frank Dernie (to Lotus), race engineer James Robinson (to Arrows) and of course Nigel Mansell (to Ferrari). All of which left Patrick Head at the head of the engineering team with Dave Brown handling the second car. Renault's willingness to test, particularly at their comprehensive facility at Circuit Paul Ricard, meant that the engineering team had quite a busy time.

The team, in fact, spent most of the year working with the FW12C, the design which originally handled power from John Judd's V8 and which was then adapted to V10 Renault power. This worked better on downforce circuits, while the team's long-awaited 1989/1990 design, the FW13, appeared only for Portugal after a very brief test session. An imbalance between new front and old rear suspension and the incorrect operation of the front suspension necessitated a lengthy test after Spain, but the drivers would still admit that the car was tricky in fast corners, although the traction was excellent.

Of the three principal multi-cylinder producers, Renault were the last to produce their engine, and therefore were the furthest behind in development. But there were constant improvements, highlighted by a revised engine at Silverstone and electrical improvements in Hungary while there was a quiet commitment which proved that the Frenchmen were tackling this year in a somewhat more reserved way in terms of publicity compared to their previous efforts, but with just as much behind-the-scenes work by Bernard Dudot and his team.

Progress was remarkably swift. Patrese started from the front row in Brazil with Boutsen behind him, and after the first lap kerfuffle the pair found themselves first and second. Boutsen was soon out, however, but Patrese held off Mansell for 15 laps, eventually to retire just after half-distance with engine problems like Boutsen.

They were a little less competitive in the McLaren-dominated San Marino Grand Prix, but Patrese was once again battling with Mansell, this time for third place, when his timing belt broke on lap 19. Boutsen started from the pits following a puncture caused by debris from Berger's accident but then fought through to fourth place only to have it taken away from him by the officials. It wasn't for several months that Williams were able to claim their first points of 1989.

Much could be expected with Boutsen third on the grid ahead of the two Ferraris at Monaco. But Patrese's car would not start on the dummy grid, and after running third for the first 18 laps, Boutsen had to pit for a new rear wing after both he and Patrese suffered failures. From here, however, they both drove their hearts out to the chequered flag, but to little effect in terms of points. Here, however was the reliability they were looking for.

This was consolidated by the pair in Mexico where the McLarens, Ferraris and Williamses ran two by two until Boutsen retired when his engine cut. When both Ferraris quit, Patrese found himself on the rostrum for the first time in 1989, already providing Renault with surprises.

Patrese was there again a week later in Phoenix after the worst qualifying session of the year where the pair were 14th (Patrese) and 16th (Boutsen). But they fought through the field early on until Boutsen was delayed, while Patrese continued to make progress which, with retirement, resulted in second place. Boutsen was in the points too with a lucky sixth.

Two weeks later, of course, came the new liaison's greatest hour. On the tricky, slippery Circuit Gilles Villeneuve, the pair kept their cars on the road when others didn't, and the material once again proved reliable, although poor Patrese was relegated to second by his own teammate when his undertray came loose with twenty laps to go. But this was their result of the year: first Boutsen, second Patrese.

Patrese was on the rostrum again in France while Boutsen was there in Hungary. This was really Patrese's race for while McLaren and Ferrari searched for grip, Grand Prix racing's most experienced driver ever put his Williams-Renault on pole position in the first session, and it remained unbeaten in the second, bringing an end to a long succession of McLaren poles.

He led all but the last 25 laps too, but a stone had pierced his water radiator (for the second time in three races) and that in turn overheated his engine. But it had been his race and would surely have resulted in another place on the rostrum.

The pair were on the rostrum (subject to appeal) in Japan with the new FW13s, which was encouraging for reliability although both drivers still felt that there was a lot of work to do. Both drivers are very interested in testing, which tends to make their engineers' jobs easier. They are both good-natured (although Boutsen showed his horns when

his gearbox was wrongly assembled in Italy) and they work well together. Patrese was usually the quickest qualifier which is a great testament to his motivation as he nears his 200th Grand Prix.

This was a year of consolidation for Williams, still supported by a loyal band of sponsors. They were usually number three in the multi-cylinder pecking order, but they would be well prepared for the 1990 season, and Renault proved that they had lost no commitment, the new regime actually looking more determined than ever to get the job done.

Benetton – change of regime. This was not an easy year for Benetton. There was a team leadership change mid-season, a driver was replaced, and the team's latest car and engine were late arriving. Yet at the same time, they maintained their position as head of the V8 runners and late in the season an engine modification even suggested that they could get in amongst the multi-cylinders on a regular basis. With the addition of John Barnard on the R&D strength, the new season is eagerly awaited.

The team started off with the B188 and Ford's DFR engine with the latest HB engine on the stocks. This unit, normally known simply as the Ford V8, was a brand–new unit of a compact 75° rather than the 92° of the DFR. Ford were determined not to race their latest-born before it was ready, but the post-Monaco Grand Prix Ricard test revealed that the crankshaft was rather too close to technological limits. It was fine on the test bed, for example, but once affected by a race car's vibrations, it would only last, say, 300 kilometres. Clearly this wasn't enough and so Ford went back to the drawing board to design and build a whole new batch of crankshafts, and this accounted for the two-month delay; relatively little considering the task in hand.

So the first half of the season saw the team use Rory Byrne's old B188. Joining Nannini as Boutsen's replacement was team manager Peter Collins's gamble, Johnny Herbert, still working hard to recover from injuries sustained in the Brands Hatch F3000 race the previous August. Collins, however, believed firmly in Herbert and his faith initially seemed justified. Herbert finished a fine fourth in Brazil where Nannini was sixth with a multitude of small problems.

Things looked good when Nannini finished third at Imola behind the McLarens, but this was more a case of picking up the points left by the multi-cylinders when they failed. In Monaco, however, the pair weren't in the ballpark at all in qualifying, even blown off by fellow DFR users. A lack of development because of the impending arrival of the new car was the quite logical reason, and things were little better in Mexico.

By now the crankshaft problem was public knowledge so questions were being asked. Yet just one race later, with some crafty tyre warming in qualifying, Nannini put the car third on the grid at Phoenix. An eventual place on the rostrum was well within his capabilities, but he crashed the car heavily in the warm-up, injuring his neck, and after a couple of spins he decided to pull out of the race.

But from 25th on the grid, in temperature approaching 100 degrees, Herbert slogged it out for two hours on a slippery track to bring home his car in fifth place. Non-qualification in Canada followed and then came news that Herbert was to be stood down and replaced by Grand Prix debutant Emanuele Pirro. Herbert would later agree that this was the right course of action, but for many, it seemed tough on the Essex driver who had shown so well.

The constant schedule of tests and races meant that he was unable to continue his vital training to quite the extent that he would have wished. Furthermore, he was having trouble pushing the brake pedal on certain circuits. He would remain on the driving strength, said Benetton. They subsequently released him to drive for Tyrrell on a couple of occasions.

Pirro arrived at about the same time as the B189 with its new V8. Nannini got his for the French Grand Prix, qualified fourth and was running a great second when the rear suspension broke. A week later in Britain he qualified ninth but overtook Piquet to claim third.

The pair were seventh (Nannini) and ninth (Pirro) in Germany where Nannini was an early retirement with an ignition problem. But Pirro was in fourth place when he crashed spectacularly through polystyrene blocks. From now on, Nannini's rightful place in qualifying would be behind the multi-cylinders, which occasionally included Alliot's Lola-Lamborghini, and ahead of the rest, unless there was a dirty circuit where Pirelli's runners came on strong.

The B189, however, wasn't as easy to set up as the B188. The new car was more sensitive to track conditions such as bumps, and everything needed to be favourable before it came right. There were points for Nannini in Belgium and Portugal, and then came the great Japanese Grand Prix win – where Alessandro had the good grace to admit that he would prefer to have won by overtaking Senna.

Here Nannini put his Benetton, powered by Ford's latest development engine with smoother power curve, in amongst the multi-cylinders for the first time, but it was Pirro who raced with the development engine after qualifying a lowly 22nd. He was eighth, heading for fourth, when he collided with de Cesaris. Things looked good for the future.

By now, Piquet had been signed for 1990, and so had John Barnard on the R&D side. Team manager Collins, who departed in August, had maintained the strong R&D connection with Dave Price in charge of a test team working on the relatively unfashionable active suspension for which Johnny Dumfries was test driver.

The now more Italian regime, with Gordon Message handling the day-to-day team managing, certainly has its sights set in the right direction, but many would suggest that in spite of all Cosworth's experience, the V8 configuration is not likely to produce the same power as say a V10 or V12 . . .

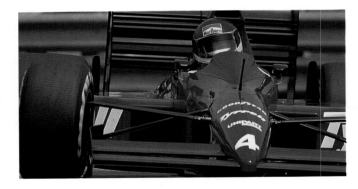

Tyrrell – points on the breadline. Few people in motor racing would suggest that there's any substitute for experience – and that puts Ken Tyrrell number one in the league. Working within the confines of a tight budget – when indeed it existed at all – Ken and his closely knit team used that vital ingredient to maximum effect and it showed in 1989.

Tyrrell had established his newly structured team with Harvey

Postlethwaite at the engineering helm during the 1988 season, no doubt working on the principle that if you have the engineers and the drivers, then the money will follow. He retained the services of Jonathan Palmer, and Michele Alboreto (out of favour at Ferrari) returned to the fold.

There was one thing missing in Brazil for the start of the season: sponsorship. Postlethwaite's new 018 wasn't ready, so 017s were the makeweights for the first couple of races. They were plain black, and when the new cars did come along, they were plain blue! It wasn't for seven races that the name of a sponsor – apart from 'Tyrrell', that is – appeared on the car.

When that sponsor did appear, it was for good reason. The 018 model was competitive right from its very first race. One car made its appearance at Imola, but Alboreto didn't qualify it, so Palmer used it for the race. They were still working out settings on the grid, and when the race was stopped because of Berger's accident, they made further modifications. The result was a delightful and satisfying fifth place which eventually became sixth when Boutsen was reinstated.

Alboreto got his car for Monaco's second qualifying session, qualified in 12th and once again scored points. The team's peak was reached in Mexico, where the car really did come into its own on a tricky circuit. Speed trap times revealed it to be effective in the corners as well as on the straights, in spite of the Brian Hart-tuned V8s sounding as tame as F3 engines in comparison with the wailing multi-cylinders.

Alboreto qualified seventh, Palmer 14th, and with multi-cylinder retirements, the Italian made his C-compound tyres last the entire race to finish third. 'Now,' said Alboreto, 'perhaps we can get some sponsorship so we can afford to go testing the car.'

But within two more races, when both cars retired, Michele was on his way out as the sponsorship began to come in. What happened between Ken and Michele has never been openly explained, so it just remains one of those falling-outs, but his replacement was future F3000 champion Jean Alesi who would soon assume the role of team pace-setter.

Alesi's first race in France saw him tenth in the first qualifying session, dropping to 16th when he failed to improve in the second. Palmer was ninth, but this was almost the last time that the Briton would outqualify the Frenchman. Alesi raced hard to a great fourth place and after a shunt in England, he proceeded to finish races and score points, occasionally on the 'stay out as long as you can on the tyres and you could pick up points' principle practised by Ken.

Palmer came in sixth in Portugal while Alesi qualified ninth and raced through to a tenuous fourth in Spain, even overtaking Senna on the way. The way he picked off other cars during the opening laps of the Japanese Grand Prix was inspirational to the team. This is a driver they want to work with and he figures in Ken's plans for 1989.

Palmer, sadly, had rather waned in the face of his new teammate. He still scores points, and he fits the Tyrrell philosophy ideally. You could only feel immense sympathy with him as he struggled to bring home his drastically misfiring car in Spain.

But this was a year that Tyrrell kept their heads above water, no doubt hoping to attract the big sponsor and engine supplier for the future. They certainly maintained a good profile, their points score being the envy of all but the 'works' teams.

Lotus – towards 1990. By the time the 1990 season starts, there will have been an almost total change in terms of equipment and personnel within the Lotus team over the preceding 18 months.

At the start of the 1989 season, the team had a new technical director in Frank Dernie, and they had lost Honda's engines, becoming virtually a 'customer' of Judd's. By the end of the year, that engine programme, including the Tickford five valve head development, had been shelved and Lamborghinis were already on the horizon. Fred Bushell and Peter Warr had already been replaced by Tony Rudd and Rupert Manwaring, and drivers Piquet and Nakajima had been replaced by Warwick and former Lotus test driver Donnelly.

It was one of Lotus's most difficult years. A combination of facts brought about a major downturn in fortunes. From a technical point of view, Dernie and Judd were two major changes while Dernie's first-born, the 101, was late appearing and designed around a 1988 generation Goodyear tyre that was not being used in 1989.

Piquet qualified ninth and eighth in the first two Grands Prix, but then his performance dropped off badly. There were reliability problems and accidents here and there, but the bright spot was his fourth place in the rain in Canada where Nakajima failed to qualify at all.

This, in fact, was the low spot of the year for the team, in spite of the later non-qualification of both cars in Belgium. Team director Fred Bushell was in trouble and management morale was at a low ebb. Many of those involved were beginning to make alternative plans . . .

It was therefore remarkable that they made such a push at the Silverstone test, with some four cars and three drivers in action, including test driver Martin Donnelly, about to make his Grand Prix debut with Arrows.

But it wasn't until after the British race, where Piquet seemed to have found new fire, that the team really pulled itself together. Bushell stood down in favour of the immensely experienced and respected Tony Rudd. Peter Warr also left the team and the Tickford programme was shelved as it wasn't producing the projected advantage.

Rudd now set about getting reliability into the Judd and welding the team together for the 1990s. Piquet reacted by scoring points in Britain, Germany and Hungary. The Belgian non-qualification was simply the unfortunate result of adverse circumstances. But results, admittedly, were sparse thereafter. In Italy, of course, it was announced that Piquet would be going to Benetton and that the team had two new drivers and Lamborghini power for 1990, but Piquet was in the points again in Japan.

Teammate Nakajima was one of those drivers who should have got into the points at some stage in the year. He failed to qualify in Monaco, Canada and Belgium and usually qualified mid- to late-field. But he was heading for points in Germany and Portugal until retirement intervened.

In many ways this was a year best forgotten by Lotus. That they got as much out of it as they did is a tribute to their experience and long standing, and the leadership of Tony Rudd.

Arrows – promise unfulfilled. The USF&G Arrows team looked as though they would spend this year consolidating their improved position over past years, but early promise with their new Ross Brawn-

designed chassis failed to be fulfilled although there were several notable performances during 1989.

The team once again enjoyed support from USF&G which included the planning and eventual opening of a superb new facility for use in 1990. The principals were pretty much the same as ever, with Jackie Oliver and Alan Rees once again at the helm, Ross Brawn again in charge of engineering, and James Robinson joining late from Williams. Derek Warwick and Eddie Cheever would stay on for another season. But by the end of the year, the situation had changed. Both drivers were moving on, USF&G limited their involvement and the Footwork Corporation of Japan were buying in. Ross Brawn was leaving the team to further his career in sports car racing.

Brawn's A11 lacked testing time when the pit lane opened for Brazilian Grand Prix qualifying, partially due to weather, and also to one or two engineering problems, including engine problems with the Brian Hart-tuned DFRs. In using these engines, Arrows found themselves in the same league, perhaps, as Tyrrell, Minardi and Ligier with DFRs, and Brabham and Lotus with Judds. In Arrows case, all engines were new.

There was every indication of a great season in Brazil, for fifth-placed Derek Warwick was just 18 s behind winner Mansell in spite of two fumbled pit stops. The promise was there, it was now a matter of working on it.

One thing had to be resolved first of all. Cheever simply didn't fit in his car and would have to have the fuel moved around within the car to give him space although he would blame his driving position for his relatively poor qualifying form during the year.

Warwick won the 'customer' Grand Prix with an eventual fifth in Imola and Cheever finished too. He was seventh in Monaco after an early retirement for Warwick, while Eddie was again seventh in Mexico where Warwick again retired.

At home in Phoenix, everything went right for Eddie however. It was, he noted, his first straight race of the year where he could race hard all the way through and that's just what he did, although he eased up on the heels of second-placed Patrese when his brakes disappeared. But Eddie, who had finished third in Italy the year before, maintained his record of a place on the rostrum.

After early retirement in Phoenix, it was Derek's turn for his moment of glory when he led four laps of the Canadian Grand Prix until his engine failed. Eddie had retired when his engine cut.

Warwick missed the French Grand Prix after a karting accident, but stand-in Martin Donnelly brought the spare car home to 12th while Eddie was once again seventh from 25th on the grid.

This would characterise the second half of the season. Derek started 17th and claimed a point in Germany, started ninth in Hungary (his best for many races), started tenth and claimed another point in Belgium.

Eddie meanwhile, came from 16th to finish fifth in Hungary but his qualifying difficulties saw him fail to start at least twice. During the second half of the season he was usually in the twenties rather than the 'teens, which is not his usual form.

What was going wrong? In common with March, the team was governed by fractions of a second which were enough to cost them whole rows. Pirelli's improved form saw some of their drivers come through and regularly pip the Arrows men, while the drivers often found it hard to balance the A11. The car's straightline speed was sometimes suspect too. Rarely, however, were their problems easily solved. They covered a whole variety throughout the scope of a racing car, so there was nothing particularly at fault, and it was a shame that the team should so regularly suffer balance problems which perhaps more comprehensive testing might have solved.

Even so, the team had a points score by the end of the year in keeping with their usual position, and reliability was never particularly suspect – which perhaps made their problems all the more frustrating.

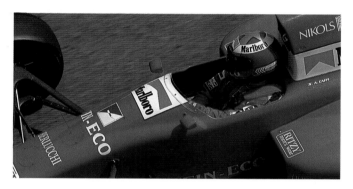

Dallara-Pirelli: the front-runner. The BMS Dallara team became a major force in 1989 with some remarkable qualifying results, and one or two excellent race results. There were low spots, for it would take a little while to adapt the chassis to any new tyres produced by Pirelli but the team was 'quite pleased with its year' and its championship results.

When it came to the non-multi-cylinders, there were those with Judds and those with Cosworths, those with Goodyears and those with Pirellis. Dallara comparison, then, is with Osella, for instance, or Minardi and Coloni. To a lesser extent there were also Brabham and Zakspeed.

But Dallara come out well in these comparisons. They stepped up to being a two-car team in 1989, which is a big step. They worked with Pirelli for the first time, and found one car having to pre-qualify which not only split the team but also put pressure on them.

With the return of 1988 designer Sergio Rhinland to Brabham, the new car was designed by Gianpaolo Dallara, and apart from the Pirelli problem already mentioned, work on a mechanical balance was usually crucial to success. At some circuits, this was a serious handicap.

After Alex Caffi's great 1988, many felt it very unfair that the arrival

of Andrea de Cesaris meant that Caffi had to pre-qualify. He was, the pundits reckoned, one of those who would regularly get through without problems. This wasn't quite the case, for few people appreciated what a knife-edge pre-qualifying was. Consequently, there was no race for Caffi in Brazil or in Britain, but by then he was already confident that he wouldn't have to pre-qualify in the second half of the season.

Once he'd made it through pre-qualifying, however, Caffi knew that he'd get into the race. He never failed to qualify, whereas de Cesaris didn't make it at Silverstone, but then that was one of the team's least successful circuits.

De Cesaris would rarely out-qualify his more determined teammate, and the writing was on the wall as early as Imola that Alex, at least, would score points in 1989. Ninth on the grid, he was then disqualified and then reinstated in seventh place. Just two weeks later he bounced back to qualify on row five with his teammate alongside. He spent much of the race battling with Tarquini for seventh place, while teammate de Cesaris was actually ahead fighting with Modena. He had the crazy collision lapping Piquet at the Loew's hairpin which didn't reflect well on either of them, and when Caffi overtook the slower Tarquini on lap 45 he was in fifth place. Brundle's pit stop elevated him to fourth and that's where he finished. Mexico wasn't one of their circuits – it tended to be a bit like that for Dallara – but Caffi was sixth on the grid and de Cesaris 13th in Phoenix which will probably long remain in Andrea's brain as the ultimate bad dream.

Caffi had run as high as second in this race and was in a fairly solid fifth place when he was taken off by his own teammate, who had collided with Warwick and then had to make a pit stop. Andrea then climbed back up to fifth, only to run out of fuel. The team enlarged the fuel tanks after that.

But he redeemed himself one race later in Canada, where he qualified ninth to Caffi's eighth. The pair were soon running fourth and fifth, only for Alex to go off: Andrea fought up to fourth after a pit stop and then found himself on the rostrum when Senna retired. Pre-qualifying was now a thing of the past.

France, Britain and Germany weren't suited to the car, but Hungary certainly was. The irrepressible Caffi qualified a remarkable third on the grid on this tight circuit. Race tyres, however, weren't so good, and Alex slipped back to finish seventh, but it would be one of his memories of the year. He qualified well in Portugal too but again slipped back in the race and then collided with Piquet. De Cesaris finished seventh from 15th on the grid in Spain, but the team now appeared to have lost a little of its edge.

This was the year Dallara established itself in spite of a number of organisational problems associated with being a two-car team. But under Reno Rananzini, the team acquitted itself well in 1989.

Brabham – promising return. After a year's absence due to lack of suitable power unit, Brabham made a tricky return to Grand Prix racing in 1989 under new ownership and using Judd engines and Pirelli tyres. Even the transfer of ownership to Swiss Joachim Luhti was difficult, however, and there were legal restrictions on the team which were made worse when Luhti was incarcerated later in the year. From the Hungarian Grand Prix onwards the team was unable to speak to its owner.

But at least they were racing and continued to do so in spite of their difficulties, thanks to the continuing faith of sponsors Nippon Shinpan. Herbie Blash remained at the helm, Sergio Rhinland headed the engineering team after his year with Scuderia Italia and Dave Stubbs joined as team manager from Williams. John Baldwin left the team, however, as did Teddy Mayer after a brief, unsuccessful spell as managing director.

All these problems, however, were behind the scenes. Up front, it was Brabham doing a workmanlike job in the difficult business of pre-qualifying, in which at least they were the most experienced team. When they got through pre-qualifying, they always made the race, and thanks to their Monaco performances, pre-qualifying was soon a thing of the past anyway.

Pre-qualifying one and two for the first couple of races, drivers Stefano Modena and Martin Brundle got into both races fairly easily but failed to finish. It was a very different story in Monaco, however, where they both qualified in the top ten and they both finished in the top six with Modena on the rostrum for the first time in his career.

The pair finished in Mexico too, while good qualifying positions and an excellent race were ruined by brake problems in Phoenix. It was here that financiers Nippon Shinpan first appeared on the car, and where Teddy Mayer appeared. But the brake problem was solved by Silverstone with a move to AP, while Mayer was also on his way by then.

Brundle failed to pre-qualify in either Canada or France, while engine problems claimed both cars in Britain. The Judd did tend to use too much oil, but the independent manufacturer solved this problem by the end of the year.

They qualified well again at the dusty Hungaroring, but the promise

was not continued in the race.

Modena qualified a fine eighth in Belgium too, but accidents for both drivers prior to the start wiped out any advantage, while he was disqualified for missing a weigh-in in Italy. Brundle, however, squeezed into the points with sixth place while Portugal's fine qualifying positions were not capitalised upon either. Brundle was just outside the points in Spain when he retired but he finished fifth in Japan where Pirelli came up with new tyres which should see them in good stead in 1990. The car wasn't 100 per cent perfect, and when they did go testing, it was usually to work on tyres rather than the chassis, as rubber gives the greater advantage. But with two very steady drivers, working well together, and an experienced team, Brabham were one of the front-running 'customer' teams in 1989, and it was good to see them back.

Onyx – sizing up the job in hand. That Grand Prix racing's newest team should finish where they did in such a highly competitive year is a tribute to Mike Earle and everyone with him. It wasn't always such a happy situation, however, and anyone who saw Mike during the early stages of the season would never have recognised him as being the same team manager seen regularly in Formula Two and 3000 over the last decade.

'We never appreciated the task we'd taken on,' was a regular admission during the early part of the season. From being a works-assisted team running mass-produced racing cars in the admittedly very competitive division two to designing, building and developing your own car for division one – and the very bottom of division one at that – was a very different kettle of fish.

Earle was lucky, however. He started with a designer whose track record was proven. In Alan Jenkins, he had a man who had worked with McLaren and Penske. He's so particular, they said at Onyx, that he even wants to design the loo doorhandles.

He also had financial support in the shape of Jean-Pierre van Rossem, whose Moneytron sponsorship joined Marlboro's in assuring the team's future, although van Rossem's management skills were sometimes slightly out of place in the high profile world of motor racing. Without him, however, the team would not have enjoyed the same confidence.

But the car was late, so late that it was still being finished in the Rio

paddock, and then a testing accident prior to the San Marino Grand Prix put more strain on the team. Pirelli flattered in Monaco, but when it all went right, then Johansson was able to pre-qualify and qualify thereafter. When Johansson got through pre-qualifying and was sixth in Saturday's untimed session in Mexico there was great excitement.

Of course, once the car was running race distances, teething troubles appeared as the car was developed, but this was only to be expected. A wheel-bearing problem in particular showed up and that nearly cost Gachot his first race effort in France. But he made it through pre-qualifying using the spare and the pair qualified 11th (Gachot) and 13th (Johansson). Both drivers ran in the top six but when Gachot had a battery problem, it was Johansson who came through to claim two points for fifth place.

Pre-qualifying now seemed a thing of the past, but Minardi's Silverstone result put paid to that, and the Onyx men re-set their alarm clocks for early starts on Fridays – but with a little more confidence.

Germany and Hungary didn't favour the cars, however, and it wasn't until Portugal that the team were really able to celebrate, thanks to Johansson's marvellous third place in a race in which he was constantly competitive.

By now, however, he had a new teammate. Gachot, who had been instrumental in bringing Moneytron's Jean-Pierre van Rossem into the team as a major shareholder and sponsor, was sacked and replaced by J. J. Lehto who immediately impressed the team. Such are the vagaries of pre-qualifying that he made it into the Spanish race a week later, when Johansson didn't, and then neither made it in Japan.

But that's all part of the lottery of pre-qualifying. Onyx's management, drivers and team members sweated it out in 1989. They deserve not to have to do so again in 1990.

Minardi – progress made. This was surely Minardi's best year. In spite of starting the season with a mildly modified version of the previous year's car, the team worked well with Pirelli to haul itself up

the grid dramatically, even if Pirelli's race tyres weren't the match of Goodyear's.

At the end of 1988, Minardi's priority was to establish a good engineering team, and to this end they hired Nigel Cowperthwaite, the former Lotus aerodynamicist, who worked on the new car with Aldo Costa. It was late arriving, however, and the team began its year testing Pirelli tyres with the older car, but this certainly stood them in good stead later in the year.

Even the older car seemed competitive during the early stages of the season. Martini qualified eleventh at Imola but was an early retirement; neither he nor Sala finished the first three races, and the situation was no better when the new car appeared in Mexico and immediately proved to have an inherent cooling problem. This cost both drivers their engines in Phoenix and Martini his in France.

But help was on the way. Back in Faenza, the team was working on larger cooling intake and bigger radiators and in the nick of time they worked, for pre-qualifying was by now looming large. The drivers qualified 11th (Martini) and 15th (Sala) at Silverstone, and Martini was soon running eighth. Hearts, no doubt, sank when Martini's engine temperature rocketed to 130 degrees within a couple of laps. But when he pitted, they found paper in the intakes, and once back on the track he drove superbly to pip teammate Sala for fifth place, the Spaniard's sixth place giving them the vital point needed to avoid pre-qualifying.

Now the team could concentrate on sorting out their new car and after hovering around the midfield grid positions, the team made a concerted leap up the grid in Portugal and Spain where Martini qualified fifth and then fourth. Sala was ninth in Portugal, the drivers admitting that all their Pirelli tyre testing in the winter had been a great help.

An excellent set-up on race tyres saw Martini run in fifth place, ahead of the two new Williams-Renault FW13s during the early stages, and a late pit stop saw Minardi leading a Grand Prix for the first time ever! But Martini lost out to Johansson and Nannini during his tyre stop, although he eventually finished fifth with Sala twelfth.

However, Martini had run over a kerb and damaged a rib which was further agravated in Spain a week later. He qualified a remarkable fourth, lost out a place at the start and was then overtaken by Pirro before spinning out after pushing his tyres hard during the early stages.

Martini's rib injury caused him to miss Japan where his good friend Paolo Barilla took his place and qualified well on a track he knows better than many, although the race was less of a success. Here Sala took over the role of team leader admirably, after a season in which he appeared psychologically out-qualified by his teammate.

At the end of 1989, Minardi had improved its status as a team in Grand Prix racing, making an excellent base on which to build with improved organisation and increasing respect from the more established teams. They were looking forward to 1990 with great expectations.

Leyton House March – ambitious year of disappointment. The Leyton House March team had a great year in 1988, impressing onlookers both on and off the circuit with an atmosphere second to none. Sadly, this wasn't followed up by a similar 1989. There were many reasons for this, but the result was that the team faced pre-qualification which was unthinkable the previous year. There were positive signs to 1989, however. After the loss of mentor Cesare Garibaldi in a car crash, the principals remained very much the same in Mr Akagi's team: Ian Phillips took over as managing director with Adrian Newey heading the design staff along with Tim Holloway. The drivers remained too, Ivan Capelli once again joining Mauricio Gugelmin. It may have been a difficult year but no one was fleeing the ship.

So what were the difficulties? A basic problem arose when Leyton House decided to buy out of the March Group, taking certain facilities and leaving others. During this period, virtually nothing could be done. And once the takeover had been completed, the new company had to set up manufacturing facilities to replace those previously enjoyed within the March Group.

The team used its old and very capable 881 design for the first two races in the season, and from 12th on the grid Gugelmin raced to a great third at the finish in what was a very close race. But when Capelli crashed out of seventh place on lap two of the San Marino Grand Prix he placed the team in a tricky position.

The new CG891 was ready, with its new 75° Judd engine which had been designed and built in six months. The team didn't want to race the new car, but Capelli's accident meant they had to take it to Monaco and then away to the Americas for three races. There was virtually no time to test either car or engine.

Yet amazingly Capelli was heading for a point in Monaco when his electrics failed just three laps from home. He found an amazing two seconds in himself in Mexico to put his car fourth on the grid, yet a split brake hose was found when the race stopped after a lap, and he had to climb in Gugelmin's car – the Brazilian hadn't qualified – and all the good of that grid position was lost as he started from the pits. The transmission broke in the end anyway. Neither driver finished in either Phoenix or Canada.

Gugelmin, of course, was the unwilling star of the French Grand Prix, and then set fastest lap of the race after starting from the pit lane. But Capelli charged up to fourth place and was second when the engine failed just after half distance.

They were competitive in Britain but again Gugelmin had to start in the pits because of a water leak. Capelli retired from seventh place with a failed clutch release bearing, while Gugelmin again raced well but retired from fifth place with ten laps to go, the gearbox out of commission.

Gugelmin was in the points when he retired in Germany, both retired in Hungary, but Gugelmin finished a steady seventh in Belgium. Both again retired in Italy, and Capelli was out in Portugal and in Spain. Gugelmin might have scored a point in Japan but was just pipped by Warwick.

By now, however, qualifying had become a tough job. Midfield, fractions of a second could make the difference between whole rows. During the North American races, the team had discovered a basic casting problem with the gearbox and its long lead-in time meant that it wasn't replaced for some races. When it was, weaknesses were discovered with the engine.

This was an ambitious, perhaps over-ambitious year with a car that was sensitive to changes causing a narrow operating band. The team would admit that they needed a greater understanding of it. Judd's engine programme was remarkable given the timescale and it provided more power in some areas, but not all.

The drivers were once again consistently competitive, although Capelli was somewhat patchy mid-season. But this was a year in which Gugelmin really showed class with some fine drives during the year.

The team deserved better, but the trials and tribulations could mean that it will be stronger in the years to come. 'It was meant to be difficult,' said Phillips, 'but perhaps not that difficult. In the long term, however, it has built a stronger team, and I think it will prove that we've made the right moves at the right time.'

Rial – backwards. Thanks to Andrea de Cesaris's performances in the Gustav Brunner-designed Rial in 1988, at least one of the team's cars didn't have to pre-qualify in 1989, and in the second half of the season, neither of them did. However, by this stage the ageing design was beginning to creak under pressure, and Rial was a team in a downward slide in the second half of the season, much to the annoyance of teams trying hard to pre-qualify. By this stage, too, neither of the drivers who started the season were still with the team, although at least they now had a designer.

The cars were little more than modifications of Brunner's original design, with Christian Danner not having to pre-qualify, although teammate Volker Weidler would. The latter seemed out of his depth almost throughout, and it was a tall order to ask him to get through the hurly-burly of pre-qualifying in his first year. Before he left the scene after Hungary, he had been spared pre-qualifying thanks to Danner's performance in Phoenix, but by then neither he nor the car looked remotely like qualifying for a race.

Danner was always on the limit of qualifying – apart from in Brazil where he got in easily in 17th place, although his car was rather less new than most people's. He was classified too, although his gearbox had caused him to stop. He saw the chequered flag in Mexico as well, the next race for which he qualified, and he just scraped on to the grid in Phoenix. But here the German driver stuck to the job in hand and drove admirably to pick up three valuable points in finishing fourth, ahead of Herbert's Benetton and Boutsen's Williams. Some people may have regarded the result as a fluke, but they couldn't take it away from him: he'd earned it. Indeed, two weeks later, he finished eighth in Canada.

But that was the last time a Rial even saw a chequered flag. Danner's result spared them pre-qualifying, but he was happy to leave the team after Portugal, for by now things were breaking on the car, as a wing did a week later when Foitek took over from the German in Spain.

That was enough as far as he was concerned too, and the determined Gachot took over for the last two races. By this stage Raphanel was in the other car, having brought Christian van der Pleyn with him, but all the French engineer was able to do was highlight the shortcomings of the car and start work on some improvement.

So the year ran out for Rial, with Danner providing the no doubt hard-working team with its only reward.

Ligier – heavy. France's national team – which included 14 Britons and a Brazilian designer – did not have a happy year, although marginally better than the previous one. Having abandoned Judd engines, and with newcomer Olivier Grouillard replacing Stefan Johansson, the team also had a new designer in Richard Divila who had already designed a Grand Prix car for FIRST of which no more was seen.

Joining in late November, Divila found a part-designed and somewhat large car, which he and Michel Beaujon set about slimming down. Various bits were salvaged from the JS31 which would be used on the new car and March's 1988 gearbox was destined for the rear end. When it arrived, it was found to upset the weight distribution, while Divila had to mount a rescue operation to sort out Specialised Mouldings' construction of the monocoque, which resulted in spiralling weight. But over the year, the team would discover that the car was quite sensitive to adjustment, that the suspensions were average and that it was quite easy to find downforce.

The car was only just ready for the first race, while at race two in Imola, the team was pleasantly surprised to find new boy Grouillard tenth on the grid. He would qualify eleventh in Mexico and finish eighth, and it began to be him rather than his teammate who established the set-up. Preferring a harder set-up, this caused a string of non-qualifications for Arnoux who preferred a softer one.

In the meantime, testing was not going so well. Altogether four chassis were written off during the year, which simply added weight to the existing cars so that by the end the cars were up to nearly 550 kilos.

But Arnoux scored a fifth place in Canada, and Grouillard scored a point in his home Grand Prix two weeks later. By now, however, the Frenchman was out of favour with the team, having been rather too vociferous in Phoenix when expressing his views on what he felt was wrong with it. When he blew the clutch at the start of the German Grand Prix, that was virtually the last straw. Indeed, the team had 'retired' Rene Arnoux from the end of the year, and the Frenchman's track manners had finally attracted the wrath of FISA when he held up Prost at Monaco: few teams would want a driver with such a reputation.

As the season wore on, the car became heavier and the drivers less motivated, and the team rapidly came to the conclusion that it would be pre-qualifying in 1990. Ligier himself was unwilling to invest in further development, preferring to work on the team's 1990 design.

He would be seen less and less frequently around the circuits, and by mid-season the team was virtually rudderless as he was the only one with any authority. It would be up to him to begin rebuilding the team for the horrors of pre-qualifying in 1990.

AGS – disappointment in difficult circumstances. AGS are a part of motor racing folklore in many ways: one of the smallest teams to run in the premier formula, they always seemed to salvage things with at least one good result per year. Small was beautiful.

But then the team began to grow, and running two cars under new ownership proved a tough task for the little team from Gonfaron. By the end of the year, they had managed to score a single point, and no doubt they would often have got into the race, but from mid-season both cars had been sentenced to pre-qualifying, and they never got any further.

The team suffered a tragedy even before the season had begun. Philippe Streiff suffered a dreadful accident during the Brazil test which left him partially paralysed. The driver who for so long had been associated with AGS, and whom they were looking forward to running again, would not be a part of the team.

This was not only a logistical blow but a particularly grave psychological upset. The team had expanded to run Camel driver Joachim Winkelhock and Streiff. The German would have to pre-qualify while Streiff wouldn't. Indeed, the German never got any closer than ninth quickest in pre-qualifying, and never looked like making the grade, ultimately quitting after the French Grand Prix with bad sciatica.

The question was, who would replace Streiff? By sheer coincidence, the FIRST effort, for whom Gabriele Tarquini was scheduled to drive, simply never happened, leaving him free. Holder of a super-licence, and with a respectable record for racing, he was called in to replace Streiff from Imola onwards in the team's JH23 design.

It was only towards mid-season that his qualifying performances began to flag. At Imola he was 18th, and finished a very promising seventh. In Monaco he qualified 13th and had a long battle with Caffi (eventually placed fourth) before electrical problems intervened.

He qualified 17th in Mexico, challenged Warwick for many laps and, although overtaken by Prost, earned a World Championship point with sixth place. A week later in Phoenix, he might have made a second point but for a misfire from the start and then swapping sixth place with Boutsen on the very last lap, relegating him to seventh. Arnoux, placed fifth, took him off in Canada two weeks after that. This was a real 'if only' story.

The smooth surfaces and fast configurations of the upcoming tracks have never been AGS's strong point, and an engine failure in France and non-qualification at Silverstone meant that the unfortunate Tarquini was now a pre-qualifier along with his new teammate, Lola refugee Yannick Dalmas.

Claude Galopin's new JH24 design, which appeared about this time, failed to offer salvation, although the team worked hard at their local track, Le Luc. But Tarquini never got closer to pre-qualifying than fifth in Spain, while Dalmas was similarly placed in Germany. The big disappointment for the French driver was Portugal where he pre-qualified, only to be disqualified for using tyres that had been used to wheel the car up from the paddock and were not marked for that race.

AGS scored a point and looked like scoring more, but it never happened. Firmly and disappointingly down amongst the pre-qualifiers, regrouping is now imperative to ensure that they start 1990 on a competitive note.

Larrousse – Lamborghini development. Lamborghini was almost certainly the most exciting arrival of the year but they threw in their lot with a team that from the start of the season was troubled. Gerard Larrousse's partner, Didier Calmels, was incarcerated before the season had even begun, and this, certainly, had a most destabilising effect on the team for much of the year.

The team, however, had use of the Lola chassis for which various designers claim credit. It was even suggested that Lola's first design was ditched when Gerard Ducarouge joined the team, but he and Chris Murphy were certainly joint collaborators on the final chassis.

Unfortunately, that was late, and the team was ill-prepared for the first two Grands Prix of the year. Of course, they were also working with an engine that was making its Grand Prix debut, and however talented Mauro Forghieri may have been, there would inevitably be production problems with his young engine.

The team began the year with Yannick Dalmas, now recovered – but how completely? – from Legionnaire's disease, and Philippe Alliot. Doubts were cast on the former's health and he only qualified once, in the first Grand Prix with the new car in San Marino, when the engine wouldn't start. Indeed, the teething troubles with the glorious V12 were not a little to blame for his string of non-qualifications.

Alliot, meanwhile, finished the team's first race in Brazil but was struggling with reliability for much of the first half of the season. His own mistakes also prevented him from taking the chequered flag on occasions. But in qualifying he made great strides: from qualifying 26th in Brazil, he went on to qualifying 20th, 17th, 16th, 12th and 10th in the next five races, and the progression didn't stop there. He ran strongly in Canada, too, but only actually finished the Brazilian race. What was sorely lacking was reliability. And that turning step came in France. Firstly, there was some doubt as to whether either driver would be retained after Canada, and there were stories of shortage of money.

But Alliot was retained, while Eric Bernard replaced Dalmas. There were reliability problems, but Alliot qualified seventh and Bernard was 15th. Alliot was in the top six until his engine failed, but Bernard was seventh when his engine failed three laps from home.

The pair were 12th and 13th in qualifying for Silverstone, but when both retired in the race, pre-qualifying for the second half of the year became a reality. At least, however, there was some reliability and they could now go testing and develop the chassis as well as the engine. Furthermore, Michele Alboreto joined from Tyrrell.

In fact the Italian didn't really impress, although he undoubtedly suffered bad luck. He qualified last in Germany, last in Hungary and was at best midfield in Belgium, Italy and Portugal. He failed to get into the last three races at all.

Alliot, meanwhile, had his problems, although he was rarely out of the top half of the field. But a real measure of the season can be taken from the fact that he finally qualified seventh in Italy, first of the non-Honda, Ferrari and Renault runners. This was where he'd expected to be long before.

That he then slid off and disappeared within a couple of laps was rather too typical but two races later he qualified fifth and came home to claim the team's first point of the year with sixth place. It was unlikely to be enough to stave off pre-qualifying, however.

But the promise was still there, and despite Alliot's days with the team being numbered, he was still putting in determined performances – even if they were punctuated by spins.

By the end of the year, Larrousse had taken a new step, securing

Japanese finance and a new pair of drivers. Their progression stood them in good stead, but now they needed stability throughout.

Osella – surprise. It may seem unjust, but for most people it was a surprise to find an Osella tenth on the grid in Japan or eleventh in Spain and Australia. A pleasant surprise, though, for these were performances that were unrivalled in the history of Enzo Osella's team, and after so many disheartening years when the team has been at the bottom of the pile, it was only right that they should get a little glory.

Both Nicola Larini and Piercarlo Ghinzani were sentenced to pre-qualifying, such was the team's previous form. But they had a new model Osella to work with, powered by Cosworth engines and running on Pirelli tyres.

Larini proved to be the team's saviour, for not only did he get through pre-qualifying in 50 per cent of the races, but when he did so, he also got into the race. Apart from Portugal, where he was disqualified, he never pre-qualified lower than seventh, and four times he missed the cut by one place. But there was every reason to believe that Pirelli's advance in qualifying tyres had more than a little to do with this.

Once through pre-qualifying, he rarely even looked as though he might not make the race. In Brazil he was 19th on the grid, but missed his grid slot at the start and was black-flagged. At Imola he was 14th and was running seventh towards the end of the race when the rear suspension collapsed, pitching him into the wall.

After a string of non-pre-qualifications, he started 15th on the grid in Canada, and was lying an amazing fourth at half distance when the electrics failed. Failing to start in France, he ducked out of the British Grand Prix with handling problems. Now came another gap – while teammate Ghinzani qualified for the first time in Hungary – before a lowly grid position in Italy was followed by the promising performances at the end of the year.

But apart from being classified tenth in Imola, he never, for one reason or other, finished a race. By the last part of the season, teammate Ghinzani, one of the most vociferous critics of the pre-qualifying system, was also getting into races. But he had trouble finishing too, and by the end of the year had already announced that this was his last Grand Prix season.

But still it was good that two Osellas started in Spain and Australia. In the latter case, the mechanics were so glad that Ghinzani had pre-qualified that they doused him in champagne.

Whatever Pirelli's products had to do with it, Osella's eventual taste of glory was still very pleasing.

Zakspeed – little reward. Erich Zakowski doesn't look like a gambler, but on occasions that's what he appears to be. After running his own engines in Formula One for several years, he then took on Yamaha's V8 engine to run in 1989 on their Grand Prix racing debut, and a tough year it proved to be. But rather like Ken Tyrrell, Zakowski puts a brave face on hardship and there never seemed to be a time when he was depressed, in spite of a singular lack of success.

He'd hired Gustav Brunner from Rial before the end of the previous year and Brunner was able to design his car around the neat little Yamaha V8 engine. This was originally designed for F3000, and included in the package was Aguri Suzuki who had made his debut with Lola the previous year.

However, this was no Honda deal, low-key being a more appropriate description. With cynicism worthy of a journalist, Brunner began to time how long the engines lasted. One self-destructed within six seconds . . .

If the truth be known, however, progress was made during the year and the team tested and sorted out the car slowly but surely. They used Pirelli tyres, but a combination of the engine problems and chassis problems meant that it was difficult to make any rapid progress, and as others did, so Zakspeed fell behind.

The season started deceptively well. Due to Philippe Streiff's severe accident, AGS ran just one car in Brazil which meant that there were only 25 which didn't have to pre-qualify. Wrongly, as it turned out, FISA allowed in an extra pre-qualifier into qualifying itself to make up the 30

– and number five was Bernd Schneider.

Having got that far, he also made it on to the grid too, albeit in 25th spot but ahead of Alliot, Arnoux and Dalmas, and also fellow pre-qualifiers Foitek and Moreno. He lasted some 36 laps towards the back of the field before the front suspension broke, pitching him into Cheever and out of the race.

From then on he and Suzuki never looked like pre-qualifying. There were hopes that improvements in Belgium might make them a little more competitive, but these were not realised. Only when they reached Japan did Schneider get through pre-qualifying and then on to the grid in 21st spot, but a gearbox failure prevented him from doing more than a lap.

By this stage sponsors West and designer Brunner had left. The latter's chassis did come in for some criticism although the team would say that they had troubles 'from A to Y', an obvious reference to the engine suppliers.

But in true Formula One spirit, everyone had signed up for more of the same in 1990, so even if 1989 was depressing, some improvement was obviously expected.

Coloni – an inherent problem. Life at the sharp end might mean McLaren & Co for some, but it could just as easily embrace teams at the other end of the field, succinctly illustrated by the Coloni story.

A well-staffed, well-equipped and financially sound team at the beginning of the year ended the season as two drivers, six mechanics and a team manager in Australia. There were great hopes at the start of the year but these were progressively shattered in spite of the amazing determination to survive, characteristic of all Grand Prix teams, in circumstances where other businesses would collapse.

Coloni's problems perhaps began with the lateness of their 1989 challenger. What should have been ready prior to Brazil didn't appear for another three months by which time it was difficult to begin development. Only in the later stages of the year did the now diminished team get itself together again.

They began the year with the 1988 car which wasn't really competitive, illustrated by Pierre-Henri Raphanel failing to pre-qualify, and Roberto Moreno failing to qualify for the first two races. Raphanel, who had brought sponsorship to the team, used his muscle to secure the more modified car for pre-qualifying in Monaco, and with different engine, brakes and wings, got the car into qualifying. The pair both qualified for the race which was an accomplishment in itself, even though they both retired with gearbox trouble.

Now every effort was being put into the new car, and after running only a skeleton team in Mexico and Phoenix, it finally appeared in Canada, once again for Raphanel. He failed to pre-qualify it, but Moreno managed to get it into the race, only to lose a wheel and then suffer more gearbox trouble with the brand-new car.

Raphanel got his new car for France but there was virtually no time to test and develop it. Nonetheless Moreno qualified for the British Grand Prix, but gearbox trouble struck again.

Now both drivers had to pre-qualify, and the situation worsened when designer Christian van der Pleyn left after Germany and Michel Costa followed two weeks later. The draughtsmen also left; and the cupboard looked even more bare when Raphanel took himself and his money off to Rial after Hungary.

Enrico Bertaggia joined Moreno in the team, the Brazilian now calling on the services of Gary Anderson, the freelance engineer who the previous year had helped him win the European F3000 championship. A couple of tests with Anderson improved the car, and a day in the wind tunnel gave birth to a Brabham-type nose section which improved the aerodynamic balance.

Moreno managed to get through pre-qualifying easily in Portugal, but then the vital nose was destroyed in an accident with Cheever after the driver had qualified an excellent 15th. On-going electrical problems with the loom saw the Brazilian retire from the race, and of course there was no new nose for Spain.

There *was* one for Japan, but lack of straightline speed cost the team dearly there, and so the year ran out, with Enzo Coloni trying desperately to build up his team for the 1990 Grand Prix season. The moral is that life at both ends can be very tough . . .

EuroBrun – non-event. Poor EuroBrun have the dubious honour of being the only team not to qualify for a single event, although newcomer Gregor Foitek did get further than Enrico Bertaggia, his own

replacement Oscar Larrauri, Aguri Suzuki and Joachim Winkelhock by at least qualifying for one event.

The team began the year with last year's car coupled to a Judd engine rather than the Cosworths they were running in 1988. This gave them the advantage over several unprepared teams in Brazil, and Foitek made it through pre-qualifying in third place, admittedly 1.5s slower than Modena ahead of him, but just ahead of Larini. But his engine blew in the second qualifying session, and his 24th quickest time from the first session was only good enough for 29th in the combined times.

He was often in the first half of the pre-qualifying 13 thereafter, but the closest he got to actually getting through pre-qualifying was sixth at Imola and in Mexico. But being a brave driver, he often over-extended himself and by mid-season the team was beginning to run a little short of machinery.

However, Brun had regrouped. Euroracing's involvement was due to come to an end anyway, and a splinter group under George Righton was set up in Britain to begin work on the 1990 contender with a number of other well-qualified backroom boys.

The latest challenger, the ER189, appeared in Germany but a lack of testing never really gave it a chance. Foitek stepped down in Italy and his place was taken by Brun's long-term driver Oscar Larrauri. However, the Argentinian had no more luck than his predecessor.

The term 'rudderless' has been used elsewhere in this review, but it is certainly applicable to EuroBrun as well. Euroracing's form had been proven the previous year, but Brun was too interested and involved in his sports car projects to try to lend any credence or morale to his Italian partners.

This season was no better than 1988, and it served little purpose, whether or not the team is allowed to remain in Grand Prix racing.

GRANDE PRÊMIO DO BRASIL · 26 MARÇO

The sun always shines over Rio and on the day it shone over Ferrari.

There was a decidedly euphoric mood in the paddock after the Brazilian Grand Prix. Quite simply, it was because everyone had just witnessed a great race, with great performances from several different drivers. And they not only included established stars, but also one or two whose star was no longer in the ascendant, and one or two newcomers.

Following the previous year's domination by McLaren-Honda, there was a distinct feeling that, after the closest top-six finish in Grand Prix history, real racing had returned to Formula One with the reappearance of normally aspirated engines. The ban on turbos was just what was needed; FISA has perhaps got it right this time.

Prost and Mansell: camaraderie that's refreshing in Formula 1.

The sound was fantastic, the emphasis was back on the drivers' ability, with cornering speeds higher than ever but lower straightline speeds. The drivers were right, it was going to be much closer with normally aspirated engines. And we had the proof: 18.2s covered the points winners, the smallest margin ever.

Furthermore, we had seen three different leaders and six leadership changes in Rio. On three occasions Nigel Mansell had taken the lead by overtaking another car. (That may sound banal, but think back to 1988!) There had been several other potential winners, but it was a dream debut for Nigel Mansell at Ferrari and now only Ferrari could score a full house of wins in 1989.

Down that long back straight, we no longer saw one turbo car pull out effortlessly and swoop by another. Even McLaren-Hondas would pull out, have a look around the slower car, and then, more often than not, pull back in respectfully. Yes, it was much closer. The only fear that one had was for the V8 runners. The consensus of opinion was that V10s and 12s were more powerful than V8s. The multi-cylinders, as they became known, filled the first six places on the grid. Yet Derek Warwick's performance in the Ford V8-powered Arrows, which lost more time in the pits than separated Derek from the winner, suggested that a V8 was still good enough.

But for a pit-stop hiccup, Warwick would have been on the podium.

A permanent object of attention throughout the three days was Johnny Herbert, from the moment he set 11th fastest time in the first session. Eighth that afternoon, he was fifth the next morning and ended up in the top ten. A fortuitous early tyre stop in the race saw him running third just before half distance, but again he made an early stop and was right up with Prost and Gugelmin at the end in spite of suffering fatigue. Everyone felt admiration for the English driver who spent most of the weekend on a bicycle to save his legs, still recovering from a serious accident in F3000 the previous August.

In spite of concentrating on their new car, March could also be pleased with their drivers' performances. Capelli started seventh on the grid, and Gugelmin might have been higher but for a handling problem. But he was fifth in the warm-up and both drivers were in the top eight and looking promising at one-third distance. Capelli, however, soon went out with a broken bolt in the rear suspension, but a delighted Gugelmin scored his best result to date with third, in spite of rising engine temperatures and low tyre pressures.

Olivier Grouillard was a promising ninth in the race for Ligier's 200th Grand Prix. He had qualified 22nd where team mate Arnoux had failed, been 12th fastest in the warm-up but then tangled with Sala at the second corner due to a sticking throttle. Thereafter, the car never handled ideally, but Grouillard brought it home a lap down in spite of a late oil leak.

RACE DEBRIEF

The first Grand Prix of the year gave everyone hope of a full, open season, the like of which we hadn't known for a year or two. Nigel Mansell surprised himself and many others with a great debut win, but even he was surprised that Ferrari's new electronically operated gearbox had lasted the distance. Renault, Honda and Ferrari had all vied for honours, with Renault taking early retirement after Riccardo Patrese led the first 15 laps. In spite of an unusually early tyre stop, Alain Prost could not stop again as he lost his clutch and was twice overtaken

Local Heroes — Piquet, distracted, by the condition of his countryman's car, leaves his braking very late.

by the charging Mansell, as he made the almost obligatory two tyre stops. Prost then followed Mansell home, but Gugelmin, Herbert, Warwick and Nannini were only 18.2s behind the winner. It had never been closer.

Most of the Grand Prix teams had been in Rio for at least a week before the race, indulging in a long test which simply ran into the Grand Prix. Some teams had managed to accomplish a lot, in spite of rain, whereas others didn't have such good luck. Philippe Streiff and Thierry Boutsen both had big accidents, the former being badly injured and sadly taking no further part in the season. Boutsen later admitted that his accident upset him for the first few races.

The new pre-qualifying system did not provide the expected excitement at the first race, although the two Brabhams' performances were not surprising. Caffi's and Johansson's non-pre-qualification were disappointing.

Qualifying itself was dominated by the powerful V10s and V12s – even though this circuit was not the power circuit that Imola would be. While Senna put his McLaren on pole, confounding the stories that the new McLaren-Honda wasn't a success, Riccardo Patrese was only 0.8s behind him with a time set in the first session, but reliability would be the key to Renault's race.

Gerhard Berger chipped in with third quickest time, but the Ferrari's electronically operated gearchange was in doubt after several failures, and Boutsen made Williams look strong–with fourth quickest time although the Belgian was not on top form after his accident.

Prost, upset by traffic, was still sorting out his McLaren, while Mansell fell victim to the Ferrari gearbox problem; yet he was still sixth and only 1.4s from pole.

Best of the V8s was Capelli's 1988 March which still looked remarkably good in newer company. Warwick was still improving the Arrows after unproductive testing, so eighth on the grid was very encouraging. Piquet's ninth place at home in the new Lotus was encouraging, particularly as he was still recovering from ribs broken in a fall on his boat.

Johnny Herbert was another man recovering from injury, although his limp tended to make things seem worse than he claimed they were. Like so many, he didn't really get to grips with the qualifiers that were now de rigeur in Formula One, following the reappearance of Pirelli. In fact it was his first session time that counted after traffic ruined his second session.

But he out-qualified Nannini who preferred to concentrate on a race set-up for the older Benetton. Gugelmin, 12th, was another who relied on his first session time, so might have gone quicker; but he preceded the two Brabhams, Brundle and Modena filling row seven, best of the Pirelli-shod runners although less competitive as the thermometer nudged the 40-degree mark.

Behind them came de Cesaris, Martini in the older Minardi, the unsponsored Tyrrells and Danner's Rial ahead of heavy hitters such as Nakajima and Cheever. Arnoux, however, joined non-qualifiers Dalmas, Foitek and Moreno.

The warm-up suggested a McLaren walkover: Prost was half a second quicker than Senna and a second quicker than Patrese, third. Brundle was fourth, ahead of Gugelmin. Piquet didn't set a time at all, due to engine failure and all three Ferraris stopped with gearbox trouble.

'Three into one doesn't go,' explained Senna philosophically when it came to describing the first corner at Rio. Berger went down the inside, Patrese made a good start round the outside, and Senna was trapped in the middle. 'The only way was upwards,' and that's just where his nose section went. Berger, tight into the grass, noted that he wasn't going to give way anyway, otherwise Senna would also expect him to give way . . . but it cost them both their race. Berger's engine ingested something and failed later the same lap, and Senna went two laps down with a pit stop. Patrese came out of it unharmed and had Boutsen in second place with Mansell up to third ahead of Prost. Capelli led the V8s from Warwick, Herbert, Nannini, Gugelmin, Brundle, Piquet and de Cesaris.

Herbert soon gave best to Nannini but Mansell was showing determination. 'The car was very good overtaking,' he would say later, and went on to prove it by getting past Boutsen, who promptly stopped with engine failure. Next in Mansell's sights was Patrese, and by lap eight, he was right behind the second Williams.

But his former teammate proved difficult to overtake and only after another eight laps did Mansell get past. By now, the pit stops for new tyres had already begun: the Pirelli runners first, then Herbert, Prost, Capelli and Nannini together, then a slow one for Warwick, followed by Mansell.

Capelli went out soon after with a broken rear suspension bolt while Patrese was the last to stop for new tyres, after he'd been overtaken by both Prost and Mansell. The Frenchman's early stop had stood him in good stead, and he was leading, only for Mansell to loom in his mirrors and swoop by again on lap 28.

Nannini took his second set just three laps later and would have to stop again nine laps later, just after Warwick (another slow stop), Herbert and Gugelmin pitted.

When Mansell came in for tyres, he was already 25 seconds ahead of Prost who in turn was losing time to Patrese, now seven seconds away. Both Mansell and Patrese pitted for new tyres, the Ferrari driver finding himself three seconds behind Prost when he emerged. And there was nothing that Prost could do. 'I lost the clutch which made it impossible for me to stop a second time for tyres. It was just too risky, so it was impossible for me to go quickly,' explained the Frenchman.

Within a few laps, Mansell had swooped past Prost again and was gone, all the way to the chequered flag. But Prost began to come under

Above: Nannini on the horizon. Left: Rio's Carnival reputation is always in evidence, even at the Autodromo.

pressure during the closing stages. Gugelmin had made two well-judged pit stops and found himself third when Mansell took the lead. He came under pressure from Patrese after the Williams driver pitted, but then a camshaft pulley broke in the Renault, and the Brazilian was able to concentrate on the McLaren ahead of him. Pushed by Herbert who came up behind him, he would challenge the McLaren, but admitted that his Judd just didn't have the power of the Honda.

Herbert, however, was having trouble with his neck, and was perfectly happy to take fourth in his first-ever Grand Prix. Warwick, knowing that he should have been on the rostrum but for his pit stop troubles, was a frustrated fifth, just holding off Nannini's Benetton which stopped so often.

Best of the rest was Palmer in a typically tigering drive, while the Pirelli challenge faded, both Brabhams retiring and de Cesaris stopping out of fuel, a familiar complaint. Cheever collapsed after tangling with Schneider's stricken Zakspeed, proving just what a tight fit it was for him in the Arrows, although it was subsequently modified.

A great start, then, for Mansell, Ferrari and Grand Prix racing. Would it last, though?

MILESTONES

First Grand Prix for Herbert, Grouillard, Lamborghini and Yamaha

Ligier's 200th Grand Prix

Smallest ever margin covering top six

First points for Herbert

First podium appearance for Gugelmin

Gugelmin's distinctive coloured Leyton House on its way to third and his first podium bottle of Moet.

FORMULA 1 WORLD CHAMPIONSHIP

GRANDE PRÊMIO DO BRASIL

ENTRIES · PRACTICE · RESULTS

Pos	Driver/Nationality		No.	Car/Engine	P.Q. (sunny, warm)	Practice I (sunny, hot)	Practice 2 (sunny, hot)	Warm-up (pos) (sunny, hot)	Laps	Time/Retirement (sunny, very hot)
I	N. Mansell	GB	27	Ferrari 640 Ferrari V12	–	1:27.249	**1:26.772**	2:10.117 (24)	61	1hr38m 58.744
2	A. Prost	F	2	McLaren MP4/5 Honda V10	–	1:27.095	**1:26.620**	1:32.274 (1)	61	1hr39m06.553
3	M. Gugelmin	BR	15	March 881 Judd V8	–	**1:27.956**	1:28.581	1:33.346 (5)	61	1hr39m08.114
4	J. Herbert	GB	20	Benetton B188 Ford DFR V8	–	**1:27.626**	1:27.754	1:33.657 (8)	61	1hr39m09.237
5	D. Warwick	GB	9	Arrows A11 Ford V8	–	**1:27.937**	1:27.408	1:34.551 (11)	61	1hr39m16.610
6	A. Nannini	I	19	Benetton B188 Ford DFR V8	–	1:28.394	**1:27.865**	1:33.576 (7)	61	1hr39m16.985
7	J. Palmer	GB	3	Tyrrell 017 Ford DFR V8	–	1:30.443	**1:29.573**	1:40.283 (23)	60	1hr39m58.271
8	S. Nakajima	J	12	Lotus 101 Judd V8	–	1:30.942	**1:30.375**	1:36.542 (18)	60	1hr40m17.613
9	O. Grouillard	F	26	Ligier JS33 Ford DFR V8	–	1:30.410	**1:30.666**	1:35.411 (12)	60	1hr40m38.703
10	M. Alboreto	I	4	Tyrrell 017 Ford DFR V8	–	1:32.260	**1:30.255**	1:36.888 (20)	59	1hr39m53.587
II	A. Senna	BR	1	McLaren MP4/5 Honda V10	–	1:26.205	**1:25.302**	1:32.797 (2)	59	1hr40m22.265
12	P. Alliot	F	30	Lola LC88B Lamborghini V12	–	1:31.872	**1:31.009**	1:37.793 (22)	58	1hr39m57.938
13	A. de Cesaris	I	22	Dallara BMS 189 Ford DFR V8	–	1:29.005	**1:29.206**	1:35.834 (16)	57	out of fuel
14	C. Danner	D	38	Rial ARC02 Ford DFR V8	–	1:30.460	**1:29.455**	1:37.557 (21)	56	gearbox
15	R. Patrese	I	6	Williams FW12C Renault V10	–	**1:26.172**	7:12.732	1:33.296 (3)	51	camshaft pulley
16	E. Cheever	USA	10	Arrows A11 Ford DFR V8	–	**1:30.657**	1:31.068	1:35.517 (13)	37	collision/Schneider
17	B. Schneider	D	34	Zakspeed ZK189 Yamaha V8	1:30.417	**1:32.346**	1:30.861	1:36.266 (17)	36	susp., collision/Cheever
18	M. Brundle	GB	7	Brabham BT58 Judd V8	1:27.764	1:29.138	**1:28.274**	1:33.297 (4)	27	electrical loom
19	I. Capelli	I	16	March 881 Judd V8	–	1:27.525	**1:27.035**	1:33.756 (9)	22	broken rear susp. bolt
20	N. Piquet	BR	11	Lotus 101 Judd V8	–	1:28.423	**1:27.437**	No time	10	fuel pump
21	M. Larini	I	17	Osella FAIM Ford DFR V8	1:29.679	1:31.341	**1:30.146**	1:35.552 (14)	10	black flag
22	S. Modena	I	8	Brabham BT58 Judd V8	1:28.147	1:28.621	**1:28.942**	5:40.506 (25)	9	constant velocity joint
23	T. Boutsen	B	5	Williams FW12c Renault V10	–	1:27.367	**1:26.459**	1:33.512 (6)	3	engine
24	P. Martini	I	23	Minardi M188B Ford DFR V8	–	Time D/A	**1:29.435**	1:35.683 (15)	2	engine mounting
25	G. Berger	A	28	Ferrari 640 Ferrari V12	–	1:26.271	**1:26.394**	1:33.760 (10)	0	accident damage/engine
26	L. Sala	E	24	Minardi M188B Ford DFR V8	–	1:30.702	**1:30.643**	1:36.796 (19)	0	collision/Grouillard
27	Y. Dalmas	F	29	Lola LC88B Lamborghini V12	–	1:32.411	**1:31.260**	DNQ		
28	R. Arnoux	F	25	Ligier JS33 Ford DFR V8	–	Time D/A	**1:31.376**	DNQ		
29	G. Foitek	CH	33	Eurobrun ER188B Judd V8	1:29.604	**1:31.791**	1:53.570	DNQ		
30	R. Moreno	BR	31	Coloni C188B Ford DFR V8	–	**1:32.561**	1:34.894	DNQ		
–	A. Caffi	I	21	Dallara BMS 189 Ford DFR V8	1:30.747	DNPQ	DNPQ			
–	P. Ghinzani	I	18	Osella FAIM Ford DFR V8	1:31.150	DNPQ	DNPQ			
–	V. Weidler	D	39	Rial ARC02 Ford DFR V8	1:31.964	DNPQ	DNPQ			
–	P-H. Raphanel	F	32	Coloni C188B Ford DFR V8	1:32.019	DNPQ	DNPQ			
–	J. Winkelhock	D	41	AGS JH23 DFR V8	1:32.982	DNPQ	DNPQ			
–	A. Suzuki	J	35	Zakspeed ZK189 Yamaha V8	1:33.079	DNPQ	DNPQ			
–	S. Johansson	S	36	Onyx ORE1 Ford DFR V8	1:35.232	DNPQ	DNPQ			
–	B. Gachot	F	37	Onyx ORE1 Ford DFR V8	1:37.932	DNPQ	DNPQ			

Circuit Data: Autodromo Nelson Piquet, length 3.126 miles/5.031 km, race distance 61 laps = 190.7 miles/306.9 km, race weather sunny and very hot.
Notes: Only one AGS for Joachim Winkelhock, Gabriele Tarquini did not race the other car, nor did Philippe Streiff, the scheduled driver. Because of this, five cars go through from pre-qualifying (they shouldn't have, but they did).

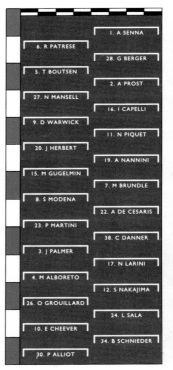

1. A SENNA
6. R PATRESE
28. G BERGER
5. T BOUTSEN
2. A PROST
27. N MANSELL
16. I CAPELLI
9. D WARWICK
11. N PIQUET
20. J HERBERT
19. A NANNINI
15. M GUGELMIN
7. M BRUNDLE
8. S MODENA
22. A DE CESARIS
23. P MARTINI
38. C DANNER
3. J PALMER
17. N LARINI
4. M ALBORETO
12. S NAKAJIMA
26. O GROUILLARD
24. L SALA
10. E CHEEVER
34. B SCHNIEDER
30. P ALLIOT

LAP CHART

Grid Order	Lap positions (laps 1–61)
1 A. Senna	6 6 6 6 6 6 6 6 6 6 6 6 6 6 6 27 27 27 27 27 6 6 2 2 2 2 2 2 27 27 27 27 27 27 27 27 27 27 27 27 27 27 27 27 27 27 27 2 2 27 27 27 27 27 27 27 27 27 27 27 27
6 R. Patrese	5 5 27 27 27 27 27 27 27 27 27 27 27 27 27 6 6 6 6 6 2 2 6 27 27 27 2 2 2 2 2 2 2 2 2 2 2 2 2 2 2 2 2 2 2 2 2 27 27 2 2 2 2 2 2 2 2 2 2 2 2
28 G. Berger	27 27 5 2 2 2 2 2 2 2 2 2 2 2 16 9 9 9 2 2 27 27 27 6 20 20 20 9 9 9 9 9 9 9 9 15 6 6 6 6 6 6 15 15 15 15 15 15 15 15 15 15 15 15 15 15 15 15 15 15 15
5 T. Boutsen	2 2 2 16 16 16 16 16 16 16 16 16 16 9 16 15 15 15 20 20 20 20 9 9 20 20 20 20 20 20 15 15 9 15 19 15 15 15 15 15 15 20 6 6 6 20 20 20 20 20 20 20 20 20 20
2 A. Prost	16 16 16 9 9 9 9 9 9 9 9 9 9 19 15 2 2 20 16 19 19 19 9 19 15 15 15 15 15 15 15 20 6 6 6 19 15 19 20 20 20 20 20 6 20 20 20 20 20 6 9 9 9 9 9 9 9 9 9 9 9
27 N. Mansell	9 9 19 19 19 19 19 19 19 19 19 19 19 19 20 16 19 9 9 9 19 15 19 19 19 6 6 6 6 6 20 20 20 20 20 20 9 9 9 9 9 9 9 9 9 9 9 19 19 19 19 19 19 19 19 19 19 19 19 19 19
16 I. Capelli	19 19 19 20 20 20 20 20 20 20 15 15 15 2 16 16 9 9 9 19 15 19 19 19 6 6 6 6 6 20 20 20 20 20 9 9 9 9 9 9 9 9 9 9 9 9 19 19 19 19 19 19 19 19 22 22 22 22 22 3 3 3
9 D. Warwick	20 20 20 15 15 15 15 15 15 15 20 22 22 20 19 9 15 16 7 7 22 22 22 22 22 22 22 22 22 22 22 22 22 22 22 22 22 22 22 22 22 22 22 22 22 22 3 3 3 3 3 12 12 12
11 N. Piquet	15 15 15 7 7 7 7 7 22 22 22 20 20 20 10 10 10 10 10 7 22 22 7 10 10 10 10 10 10 10 10 10 10 10 10 38 38 38 38 12 12 12 12 12 12 12 3 3 3 12 12 12 12 12 12 26 26
20 J. Herbert	7 7 7 11 22 22 22 22 22 22 7 10 10 10 10 10 38 38 4 4 7 7 24 4 4 4 12 12 10 10 10 12 12 12 12 12 3 3 3 3 3 3 3 12 12 26 26 26 26 26 26 26 4 4
19 A. Nannini	11 11 11 11 22 11 8 8 10 38 38 38 38 4 4 7 7 24 4 4 12 4 12 10 38 38 38 38 38 38 38 38 38 38 38 12 26 3 3 3 38 38 38 26 26 26 26 26 26 26 4 4 4 4 4 1 1
15 M. Gugelmin	22 22 22 8 8 11 11 11 11 11 38 12 12 4 4 4 7 7 22 22 22 4 12 10 10 12 4 7 3 3 3 3 3 38 38 38 26 26 26 26 26 26 26 4 4 4 4 4 1 1 1 1 1 30
7 M. Brundle	8 8 8 10 10 10 10 10 10 12 4 12 12 22 22 38 26 26 10 38 38 38 7 3 26 26 26 26 26 26 26 26 4 3 26 26 26 26 4 30 30 30 1 1 1 30 30 30 30 30 30 30 30
8 S. Modena	10 10 10 38 38 38 38 38 4 3 3 3 3 12 26 26 26 12 38 3 3 3 26 34 34 34 34 34 4 4 4 4 3 26 26 26 26 4 30 30 30 1 1 1 30 30 30 30 38 38 38 38
22 A. de Cesaris	23 38 38 12 12 12 12 12 4 3 3 26 26 26 7 7 3 12 38 38 26 26 26 26 34 4 4 4 4 4 34 34 34 34 30 1 1 1 1 1 1 1 38 38 38 38 38 38
23 P. Martini	38 12 12 4 4 4 4 4 11 34 34 7 26 26 26 34 3 3 3 16 34 34 34 4 7 30 30 30 30 30 30 30 30 30 1
38 C. Danner	12 17 4 3 3 3 3 3 26 7 34 34 34 30 30 34 34 30 30 30 34 30 30 30 30 30 30 1
3 J. Palmer	17 4 17 17 17 17 17 17 4 34 30 30 30 30 30 3 34 30 30 30 30 1 1 1 1 1
17 N. Larini	4 3 3 26 26 26 26 26 26 17 1 1 1 1 1 1 1 1 1 1 1
4 M. Alboreto	3 26 26 34 34 34 34 34 34 30
12 S. Nakajima	34 34 34 30 30 30 30 30 30 1
26 O. Grouillard	26 23 30 1 1 1 1 1
24 L. Sala	30 30 1
10 E. Cheever	1 1
34 B. Schneider	
30 P. Alliot	

FASTEST LAPS

Pos.	Car No.	Driver/Team	Time
1	6	R. Patrese/Williams	(N.R.) 1:32.507
2	19	A. Nannini/Benetton	1:33.361
3	1	A. Senna/McLaren	1:33.685
4	9	D. Warwick/Arrows	1:33.699
5	15	M. Gugelmin/March	1:33.774
6	27	N. Mansell/Ferrari	1:33.948
7	20	J. Herbert/Benetton	1:34.167
8	16	I. Capelli/March	1:34.479
9	7	M. Brundle/Brabham	1:35.284
10	3	J. Palmer/Tyrrell	1:35.327
11	2	A. Prost/McLaren	1:35.341
12	22	A. de Cesaris/BMS Dallara	1:35.402
13	5	T. Boutsen/Williams	1:35.696
14	26	O. Grouillard/Ligier	1:35.807
15	38	C. Danner/Rial	1:36.199
16	10	E. Cheever/Arrows	1:36.394
17	4	M. Alboreto/Tyrrell	1:36.747
18	12	S. Nakajima/Lotus	1:36.932
19	8	S. Modena/Brabham	1:37.470
20	11	N. Piquet/Lotus	1:37.665
21	34	B. Schneider/Zakspeed	1:37.789
22	17	N. Larini/Osella	1:38.682
23	30	P. Alliot/Larrousse	1:38.740
24	23	P. Martini/Minardi	1:46.060

N.R. = New lap record

CHAMPIONSHIP POINTS

Drivers		Constructors	
1 Mansell	9 pts	1 Ferrari	9 pts
2 Prost	6 pts	2 McLaren	6 pts
3 Gugelmin	4 pts	3 March	4 pts
4 Herbert	3 pts	4 Benetton	4 pts
5 Warwick	2 pts	5 Arrows	2 pts
6 Nannini	1 pt		

Left: the newcomers to Formula 1 arrived in Rio but neither driver got in.

Existing qualifying lap record (before 1989 edition): Ayrton Senna, Lotus-Renault 98T, 1m 25.501s, 211.829 kph/131.624 mph in 1986

Existing race lap record (before 1989 edition): Gerhard Berger, Ferrari F1/88, 1m 32.943s, 194.868 kph/121.085 mph in 1988

Existing distance record: Alain Prost, McLaren-Honda MP4/4, 60 laps in 1hr 36m 06.857s, 188.438 kph/117.090 mph in 1988

PAST WINNERS

Year	Driver	Nat.	Car	Circuit
1979	Jacques Laffite	F	3.0 Ligier JS11 Ford	Interlagos
1980	René Arnoux	F	1.5 Renault RS t/c	Interlagos
1981	Carlos Reutemann	RA	3.0 Williams FW07C Ford	Rio de Janeiro
1982	Alain Prost	F	1.5 Renault RS t/c	Rio de Janeiro
1983	Nelson Piquet	BR	1.5 Brabham BT52 BMW t/c	Rio de Janeiro
1984	Alain Prost	F	1.5 McLaren MP4/2 TAG t/c	Rio de Janeiro
1985	Alain Prost	F	1.5 McLaren MP4/2B TAG t/c	Rio de Janeiro
1986	Nelson Piquet	BR	1.5 Williams FW11 Honda t/c	Rio de Janeiro
1987	Alain Prost	F	1.5 McLaren MP4/3 TAG t/c	Rio de Janeiro
1988	Alain Prost	F	1.5 McLaren MP4/4 Honda t/c	Rio de Janeiro

Imola

GRAN PREMIO KRONENBOURG DI SAN MARINO · 23 APRILE

There were three outstanding impressions from the San Marino Grand Prix. The first was that McLaren and Honda's eight-day test had really put them back where they had left off in 1988, a fact proven by their dominating one-two. The second was that

Ferrari homeground and recent success brought the tifosi out in their thousands, all jostling for the best view.

despite their remarkable form, there was a chink in the armour again: the Senna/Prost disagreement regarding overtaking manoeuvres at the first corner had been breached; relationships were not good. And thirdly there was the happy fact that Gerhard Berger had survived his spectacular accident without serious injury, and that the Imola marshals had done a superb job in rescuing him.

San Marino had something of Rio about it: many Formula One teams seemed to have been there for days before the race weekend got under way, and that was because it had been a month between the races, culminating in a test prior to the race itself.

But McLaren had been there long before the test. By their own admission, they had once again left it late in finalising their latest car – the MP4/5 – prior to Brazil, and Ron Dennis had not been happy with suggestions that his drivers weren't happy with the car in Brazil. Sure, the pair had been on the front row and fastest in warm-up; but while everyone else might have thought that Brazil was a great race, for Ron, as he mused on the plane home, it had been one of the worst.

His reaction was to book into Imola for eight days before the San Marino Grand Prix. Honda could work on their engines, McLaren could work on the chassis. The racing car, after all, is a double-edged sword. Take two basic factors, get them both working to their optimum, and you have a powerful weapon. McLaren, then, did exactly that.

No sooner were the drivers setting times at least a second faster than the rest (1.5 seconds quicker in the warm-up) than they fell out again. The pair had once again made their sensible pact, that whoever led up to the first corner would not be overtaken by his teammate. At the first corner of the second start, Alain was clearly leading and left the door wide open into Tosa, when who should come up on the inside and take the lead but his teammate, breaching the agreement.

Senna won, a livid Prost refused to go to the post-race press conference (for which he was later fined), and promptly registered his annoyance with Dennis. Later Senna broke down, admitting that he had breached the agreement. While relations would remain cool, the pair would continue to work together, but there would be no agreements.

There had been two starts because Gerhard Berger had crashed at the start of lap four. The fifth-placed Ferrari inexplicably went straight on at the Tamburello, slamming into the wall at around 180 mph and then spinning to a halt, whereupon it burst into flames, the driver unconscious inside.

It was an appalling sight, and one wondered how long it would endure.

Of course, it seemed like an age, but in truth it was only 14 seconds before the first help arrived, and a further 11 before the fire was put out. Thought to have been caused by a faulty nose wing, the accident proved the remarkable strength of modern Formula One cars and the sheer efficiency of the Italian marshals. Gerhard suffered burns to back and hands, but within 30 minutes of the crash he was already thinking of his next race! Indeed within five weeks he was back in the driving seat.

Imola's fire marshals can feel pleased with a job well done.

running out of brakes at Rivazza and sliding off just as Capelli had already and Larini would later.

The Osella driver had scraped through pre-qualifying and almost immediately fallen foul of engine and electrical problems in a car that had been crashed in testing. But in Friday's wet qualifying he was a fine 12th and in spite of leaving the car parked in the barriers, he ended up 14th in the next day's dry qualifying.

He made excellent progress in the race, overtaking Caffi to take eighth place on lap four. Cheever later came by, as did Boutsen. As the fuel load lightened, a vibration set in. He succumbed to Herbert, then Palmer and later both Tarquini and Caffi. Even so he overtook the stricken Cheever and then a hub broke, pitching him into the barriers at Rivazza when lying ninth.

The honour of best of the rest in qualifying went to Nannini. From the word go he'd been in seventh spot and in spite of a spin in the wet, he was again seventh the next morning and stayed there in the next day's qualifying session, even though he reckoned he'd lost a tenth or two due to traffic. Interestingly, he just pipped Piquet with whom he'd had such a titanic struggle the year before.

He could provide no resistance to Mansell during the early stages and dropped to fifth place, but that became fourth and then third when the battling Patrese and Mansell both retired. From then on life became lonely, but a place on the rostrum in such company was not to be sneezed at. Nannini found that the Williams and Ferrari were not much quicker, and a rapid pace proved quite comfortable.

Mansell had a difficult decision to make after Berger crashed. Could the same thing happen to his car? There were pressures in both directions, but he got into the car and drove a hard race, battling with former teammate Patrese until gearbox-induced retirement after 20 laps.

'The car's like a breath of fresh air,' said Jonathan Palmer after the race. 'It's the first time that I've enjoyed a motor race for a long while.' Tyrrell's brand new sponsorless 018 had been handled by Alboreto for the first half of the weekend, this being Italy. The usual teething troubles had seen the understeering Alboreto struggle to 27th and therefore out of the race.

Despite a brave effort, Johansson's Onyx — carbon fibre discs glowing red-hot — fails to make it through pre-qualifying.

Capelli spins off in spectacular style at Rivazza. Below right: Larini's Osella qualified well and was impressive in the wet, but on race day joined Capelli in the sand trap at Rivazza.

BRIGHT SPARKS

McLaren's performance, of course, was one of the high points of this San Marino Grand Prix. The two drivers were a lap ahead of the rest of the opposition at the end, but then this was to be expected in some ways, if the V12s and other V10s were unable to challenge them.

The best of the V8s, then, was a coveted title, and one which was liable to earn points. Stefano Modena might have been one of those to challenge the multi-cylinders on this circuit. In Friday's pre-qualifying session, he set a 1m 27.350s which would have been good enough for third spot on the grid ahead of Mansell. But several mechanical problems intervened leaving him 17th. He never really recovered from that,

MORTE A RICOTTI

Right: The Brabhams are on the limit as they fight to hold a charging Dr. Palmer in the new Tyrrell. Right middle: Piquet contemplates another qualifying lap. Right bottom: Gugelmin adds to Leyton House's misery.

The Scuderia Italia/Dallaras, also on home ground, cannot command the praise of the tifosi quite like the other red cars.

Enter teammate J. Palmer, having qualified 25th in the older 017. He takes over the new car, eighth in the warm-up on half tanks, and well embroiled with the likes of Caffi, Gugelmin, Tarquini, Nakajima and both Brabhams, finds himself tenth at half distance. He overtakes Tarquini and Cheever and ends up a delighted fifth. Harvey Postlethwaite's heat-of-the-moment words with regard to former job satisfaction are best left unquoted!

A quick word about Tarquini: his first Formula One race with AGS, qualifies 18th in spite of traffic. Delayed behind de Cesaris, overtakes Caffi who passes him again when he loses the clutch in the final stages. Finishes eighth but promoted to sixth and thus his first championship points, following disqualifications of Caffi and Boutsen.

RACE DEBRIEF

'A power circuit,' said Frank Williams several months before the start of the season. Power, we knew by now, came from cars with multi-cylinder engines. V12s and V10s had the edge on V8s, particularly at Imola where it was all chicanes and straights. Take Friday's untimed session: Prost, Senna, Berger, Patrese, Boutsen and Mansell. Find a V8 amongst that lot.

It didn't vary much although Friday's wet session was interesting in that Cheever slotted into fourth behind Berger, Senna and Prost, while Nannini was next ahead of Brundle, Nakajima, and Sala and Martini in

some surprises.

Thank heavens the race was stopped. Senna made the best start first time round from Prost, Mansell and Patrese, and at the end of lap one, Senna led Prost by two seconds and he led Mansell by 2.2s from Patrese, Berger and Boutsen.

These gaps did not get smaller. Senna pulled away from Prost who pulled away from Mansell. In turn, he pulled away from Patrese battling with Berger and Boutsen, a sort of Berger burger. Capelli had already flown out of seventh place when he hit oil at Rivazza.

But then Berger's Ferrari just went straight on at Tamburello. Piquet had crashed there two years before, but hit the wall side on. Berger went in straight. 'The front wing came off,' said the following Boutsen. Berger seemed not to turn. The impact looked huge, although experts would say it was relatively little. The car disintegrated as it spun down the wall: wheels, bodywork, side pods, wings. Finally coming to rest, it burst into flames.

There was no reaction within the cockpit. The worst was feared. The marshals were on the move within seconds, however. A fire crew and a running marshal had extinguished the flames in a few more seconds, and Berger was lifted clear. The news was good: he was conscious, relatively unhurt and lucid. That evening he was back in Austria. He had burns to hands and back, fractured ribs and collar-bones, but was otherwise unhurt. He was hailed 'the miracle of Imola'.

Once the mess was cleaned up, the race was restarted, three laps having been run and 55 to go. This time Prost made the better start, but believing that he and teammate Senna still had a non-overtaking pact concerning the first corner, he left the door wide open at Tosa only to find Senna taking the lead.

The Brazilian quickly pulled away, opening up a gap of 4.8 seconds within three laps but the gap to Patrese leading first Nanni and then Mansell was even bigger and growing. This was McLaren's, no contest.

When Prost recaught Senna after 12 laps, the pair were more than 20 seconds ahead of Patrese who was still battling with Mansell. Nannini was next, now having a lonely race having shaken off Piquet who was coping with Warwick, whose Arrows' gearbox had already shown signs of weakness by smoking on lap four. Larini was next having been caught by Cheever, after both had been bottled up behind de Cesaris. Boutsen,

The Benetton Formula team always put on a colourful show.

Prost again put in his usual faultless performance despite his anger with Senna.

With Berger out Mansell was the
tifosi's only representative.

The mid-field runners, bunched together in the early laps.

however, had started from the pit lane with Caffi while Grouillard had started on the grid, all three requiring attention after Boutsen ran over debris from Berger's accident and the other two collided when the black flag came out. Clearly a case that would run and run.

Senna versus Prost continued from lap 12 to 20, and then the Brazilian began to pull away. 'My car wasn't too good under heavy braking,' he declared later, 'but I was under a lot of pressure for the first few laps and Prost was a little quicker. But I didn't want to force hard because my car was not good on full tanks.'

As they began to lap backmarkers, however, the gap began to open up. Soon they had no worries at all from behind. Patrese pulled out of third place when the engine's timing belt broke, and two laps later it was Mansell's turn to pull off with gearbox failure. The locals went home in their droves.

It seemed now that the race was over. Senna pulled away from Prost early on, then there was a huge gap to Nannini, Piquet pulling away from Warwick, Boutsen up to sixth place, Cheever already in trouble with a broken exhaust, Larini next and then Herbert. Palmer and Tarquini were lapped.

The gap between first and second hovered around the five, then six second mark, before returning to five seconds. In the meantime, Piquet had retired from fourth place with an engine failure when under pressure from Warwick. Herbert had a time-consuming spin and aftermath at Tosa while Caffi dropped back to Palmer's advantage, making short work of Larini and then Cheever, both Arrows now suffering broken exhausts, although Cheever was the worse off with two broken primaries.

When Prost spun because of a blistered tyre on lap 43, the race seemed set. Although Senna had problems with second gear, and had to cool his brakes as well, he cruised home to a 40-second win. Both he and the furious Prost were a lap ahead of the rest.

Nannini came into third place in spite of a small vibration during the last ten laps, managing to resist pressure from Boutsen. Warwick came next with his broken exhaust, gear selection trouble and virtually no oil in the engine for the last three laps. Palmer was ecstatic at being sixth on the road ahead of Caffi, who had battled hard with Tarquini during the closing stages, the AGS driver having no clutch from the 20th lap. Larini had come off at Rivazza a few laps from home.

After the celebrations, mystery endured: why were Boutsen and Caffi disqualified? Was it for receiving outside assistance prior to the second start? FISA later changed the rules to ensure that it didn't happen again, but for the present, the arguments raged on.

MILESTONES

- Tyrrell's 018 races for first time
- Lola debut new LC89

*Mansell, courageous even to start after
Berger's accident, ran as high as third
until the gearbox gave up.*

GRAN PREMIO KRONENBOURG DI SAN MARINO

ENTRIES · PRACTICE · RESULTS

Pos	Driver/Nationality		No.	Car/Engine	P.Q. (sunny)	Practice I (sunny, hot)	Practice 2 (warm, cloudy)	Warm-up (pos) (cool, sunny)	Laps (hot, sunny)	Time/Retirement
1	A. Senna	BR	1	McLaren MP4/5 Honda V10	–	1:42.939	1:26.010	1:28.571 (2)	58	1hr26m51.245
2	A. Prost	F	2	McLaren MP4/5 Honda V10	–	1:44.558	1:26.235	1:28.566 (1)	58	1hr27m31.471
3	A. Nannini	I	19	Benetton B188 Ford DFR V8	–	1:45.536	1:28.854	1:32.537 (19)	57	1hr27m06.457
4	T. Boutsen	B	5	Williams FW12C Renault V10	–	1:49.451	1:28.308	1:30.722 (6)	57	1hr27m18.100
5	D. Warwick	GB	9	Arrows A11 Ford DFR V8	–	1:47.859	1:29.281	1:31.798 (12)	57	1hr27m56.364
6	J. Palmer	GB	3	Tyrrell 017 (p) 018 (R) Ford DFR V8	–	1:51.229	1:30.928	1:31.508 (8)	57	1hr28m15.929
7	A. Caffi	I	21	Dallara BMS 189 Ford DFR V8	1:29.346	1:48.868	1:29.069	1:32.292 (16)	57	1hr28m19.526
8	G. Tarquini	I	40	AGS JH23 Ford DFR V8	–	1:48.795	1:29.913	1:32.489 (17)	57	1hr28m22.598
9	E. Cheever	USA	10	Arrows A11 Ford DFR V8	–	1:45.375	1:30.233	1:32.068 (13)	56	1hr27m40.576
10	A. de Cesaris	I	22	Dallara BMS 189 Ford DFR V8	–	1:53.681	1:29.669	1:34.017 (24)	56	1hr27m49.033
11	J. Herbert	GB	20	Benetton B188 Ford DFR V8	–	2:05.126	1:30.347	1:32.874 (22)	56	1hr28m40.601
12	N. Larini	I	17	Osella FA1M Ford DFR V8	1:29.787	1:47.577	1:29.488	1:32.749 (21)	52	accident
13	M. Brundle	GB	7	Brabham BT58 Judd V8	1:28.197	1:46.279	1:30.271	1:32.246 (15)	51	fuel pressure
14	S. Nakajima	J	12	Lotus 101 Judd V8	–	1:46.483	1:30.697	1:31.693 (10)	46	electrics
15	L. Sala	E	24	Minardi M188B Ford DFR V8	–	1:46.800	1:29.503	1:33.630 (23)	43	accident
16	M. Gugelmin	BR	15	March 881 Judd V8	–	1:52.119	1:30.163	1:32.553 (20)	39	clutch and gearbox
17	N. Piquet	BR	11	Lotus 101 Judd V8	–	1:48.124	1:29.057	1:31.272 (7)	29	engine
18	N. Mansell	GB	27	Ferrari 640 Ferrari V12	–	1:49.665	1:27.652	1:30.147 (3)	23	gearbox
19	R. Patrese	I	6	Williams FW12C Renault V10	–	1:47.486	1:27.920	1:30.531 (4)	21	timing belt
20	S. Modena	I	8	Brabham BT48 Judd V8	1:27.350	1:48.415	1:29.761	1:31.637 (9)	19	brakes/accident
21	P. Martini	I	23	Minardi M188B Ford DFR V8	–	1:47.321	1:29.152	1:32.224 (14)	6	fourth gear
22	O. Grouillard	F	26	Ligier JS33 Ford DFR V8	–	1:47.371	1:29.104	1:31.778 (11)	4	black flag
23	G. Berger	A	28	Ferrari 640 Ferrari V12	–	1:42.781	1:28.089	1:30.596 (5)	3	accident
24	I. Capelli	I	16	March 881 Judd V8	–	1:48.178	1:29.385	1:32.504 (18)	1	accident
25	P. Alliot	F	30	Lola LC89 Lamborghini V12	–	2:00.293	1:30.168	1:35.649 (26)	0	plugs
26	Y. Dalmas	F	29	Lola LC89 Lamborghini V12	–	1:58.083	1:31.137	1:34.607 (25)	0	would not start
27	M. Alboreto	I	4	Tyrrell 018 Ford DFR V8	–	1:31.206	1:31.206	DNQ		
28	R. Arnoux	F	25	Ligier JS33 Ford DFR V8	–	1:48.091	1:31.268	DNQ		
29	C. Danner	D	38	Rial ARC02 Ford DFR V8	–	1:47.967	1:31.342	DNQ		
30	R. Moreno	BR	31	Coloni C188B Ford DFR V8	–	1:50.947	1:31.775	DNQ		
–	B. Gachot	B	37	Onyx ORE1 Ford DFR V8	1:30.384	DNPQ	DNPQ			
–	G. Foitek	CH	33	Eurobrun ER188B Judd V8	1:30.620	DNPQ	DNPQ			
–	P. Ghinzani	I	18	Osella FA1M Ford DFR V8	1:30.631	DNPQ	DNPQ			
–	S. Johansson	S	36	Onyx ORE1 Ford DFR V8	1:30.647	DNPQ	DNPQ			
–	J. Winkelhock	D	41	AGS JH23 Ford DFR V8	1:32.071	DNPQ	DNPQ			
–	P-H. Raphanel	F	32	Coloni C188B Ford DFR V8	1:32.267	DNPQ	DNPQ			
–	A. Suzuki	J	35	Zakspeed ZK189 Yamaha V8	1:32.287	DNPQ	DNPQ			
–	B. Schneider	D	34	Zakspeed ZK189 Yamaha V8	1:32.855	DNPQ	DNPQ			
–	V. Weidler	D	39	Rial ARC02 Ford DFR V8	1:36.480	DNPQ	DNPQ			

Circuit Data: Autodromo Enzo e Dino Ferrari, length 3.132 miles/5.040 km, race distance 58 laps = 181.6 miles/292.3 km, race weather sunny and warm.
Notes: Gabriele Tarquini (I) joins the fray in the AGS JH23 with Ford V8 engine. Tyrrell debut 018; note!! Alboreto drives 018 in practice but doesn't qualify; Jonathan Palmer drives 017 in practice, then drives 018 in warm-up and race. Lola debuts LC89 for both drivers. Both Boutsen and Caffi were originally disqualified.

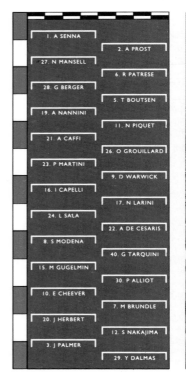

1. A SENNA
2. A PROST
27. N MANSELL
6. R PATRESE
28. G BERGER
5. T BOUTSEN
19. A NANNINI
11. N PIQUET
21. A CAFFI
26. O GROUILLARD
23. P MARTINI
9. D WARWICK
16. I CAPELLI
17. N LARINI
24. L SALA
22. A DE CESARIS
8. S MODENA
40. G TARQUINI
15. M GUGELMIN
30. P ALLIOT
10. E CHEEVER
7. M BRUNDLE
20. J HERBERT
12. S NAKAJIMA
3. J PALMER
29. Y DALMAS

LAP CHART

Grid Order	1 2 3 4 5 6 7 8 9 10 11 12 13 14 15 16 17 18 19 20 21 22 23 24 25 26 27 28 29 30 31 32 33 34 35 36 37 38 39 40 41 42 43 44 45 46 47 48 49 50 51 52 53 54 55 56 57 58
1 A. Senna	1 1 1 1 1 1 1 1 1 1 1 1 1 1 1 1 1 1 1 1 1 1 1 1 1 1 1 1 1 1 1 1 1 1 1 1 1 1 1 1 1 1 1 1 1 1 1 1 1 1 1 1 1 1 1 1 1 1
2 A. Prost	2 2 2 2 2 2 2 2 2 2 2 2 2 2 2 2 2 2 2 2 2 2 2 2 2 2 2 2 2 2 2 2 2 2 2 2 2 2 2 2 2 2 2 2 2 2 2 2 2 2 2 2 2 2 2 2 2 2
27 A. Mansell	27 27 27 27 27 27 27 27 27 27 27 27 27 27 27 27 27 27 27 27 27 27 27 27 27 27 27 27 19 19 19 19 19 19 19 19 19 19 19 19 19 19 19 19 19 19 19 19 19 19 19 19 19 19 19 19 19 19
6 R. Patrese	6 6 6 6 6 6 6 6 6 6 6 6 6 6 6 6 6 6 6 6 6 6 6 19 19 11 11 11 11 11 11 11 11 11 5 5 5 5 5 5 5 5 5 5 5 5 5 5 5 5 5 5 5 5 5 5 5 5
28 G. Berger	28 28 28 19 19 19 19 19 19 19 19 19 19 19 19 19 19 19 19 19 19 11 11 9 9 9 9 5 5 9 9 9 9 9 9 9 9 9 9 9 9 9 9 9 9 9 9 9 9 9 9 9 9 9 9 9 9 9
5 T. Boutsen	5 5 5 11 11 11 11 11 11 11 11 11 11 11 11 11 11 11 11 11 11 11 11 11 11 9 9 5 5 5 5 5 9 9 10 10 10 10 10 10 10 10 10 17 17 17 17 21 21 21 21 3 3 3 3 3 3 3 3 3
19 A. Nannini	16 19 19 9 9 9 9 9 9 9 9 9 9 9 9 9 9 9 9 9 9 9 9 5 5 10 10 10 10 10 10 10 17 17 17 17 17 17 17 17 17 10 10 21 21 40 3 3 3 21 21 21 21 21 21 21 21 21
11 N. Piquet	19 11 11 5 5 5 5 5 5 5 5 5 5 5 5 5 5 5 5 17 10 17 17 17 17 17 17 20 21 21 21 21 21 21 21 21 21 10 10 3 40 40 40 40 40 40 40 40 40 40 40 40 40 40 40 40 40 40
21 A. Caffi	11 1 9 9 17 17 17 17 17 17 17 17 17 17 17 17 17 10 10 10 17 20 20 20 20 20 40 40 40 40 40 40 40 40 40 40 40 17 17 17 17 17 17 17 10 10 10 10
26 O. Grouillard	9 26 26 22 22 22 22 22 10 10 10 10 10 10 10 10 10 17 17 20 20 40 40 40 40 40 21 3 3 3 3 3 3 3 3 3 3 10 10 10 10 10 10 10 10 22 22 22 22
23 P. Martini	26 21 21 23 23 10 10 10 10 22 22 22 20 20 20 20 20 20 20 40 40 21 21 21 21 21 3 22 22 22 22 22 22 24 24 22 22 22 22 22 22 22 22 22 20 20 20
9 D. Warwick	21 17 17 10 10 40 40 40 40 20 20 20 22 22 22 22 22 22 15 15 40 21 21 22 22 22 22 22 3 22 24 24 24 24 24 24 24 22 22 22 24 24 24 7 7 7 7 7 7 7 7 7 20
16 I. Capelli	17 22 22 40 40 8 20 20 20 40 21 21 21 21 21 21 15 15 22 40 15 22 22 3 3 3 3 3 22 24 7 7 7 7 7 7 7 7 7 7 7 20 20 20 20 20 20 20
17 N. Larini	22 40 23 8 20 8 21 21 21 40 40 40 40 40 40 40 21 21 22 22 7 7 24 24 24 24 24 24 7 20 20 20 20 20 20 20 20 20 20 20 20 12 12 12
24 L. Sala	40 23 40 21 20 21 21 8 8 8 8 8 8 8 15 15 40 40 21 21 3 3 7 7 7 7 7 15 15 15 15 15 15 15 15 15 15 12 12 12 12
22 A. de Cesaris	23 8 8 20 21 15 15 15 15 15 15 15 15 8 8 8 8 7 7 24 24 15 15 15 15 15 15 15 12 12 12 12 12 12 12 12 12 12 12 12 12
8 S. Modena	8 10 10 15 15 12 12 12 12 12 12 12 12 12 12 7 7 3 3 15 12 12 12 12 12 12 12
40 G. Tarquini	10 20 20 12 12 7 7 7 7 7 7 7 7 7 7 3 3 24 24 12 12
15 M. Gugelmin	20 15 15 7 7 24 24 24 24 3 3 3 3 3 3 3 3 3 24 24 12 12
30 P. Alliot	24 24 24 24 24 3 3 3 3 24 24 24 24 24 24 24 24 12 12
10 E. Cheever	15 12 7 26 3 23
7 M. Brundle	12 7 24 3
20 J. Herbert	7 3 3
12 S. Nakajima	3
3 J. Palmer	
29 Y. Dalmas	

FASTEST LAPS

Pos.	Car No./Driver/Team	Time
1	2 A. Prost/McLaren	(N.R.) 1:26.795
2	1 A. Senna/McLaren	1:27.273
3	5 T. Boutsen/Williams	1:29.571
4	27 N. Mansell/Ferrari	1:29.849
5	19 A. Nannini/Benetton	1:29.868
6	6 R. Patrese/Williams	1:29.959
7	22 A. de Cesaris/BMS Dallara	1:29.959
8	3 J. Palmer/Tyrrell	1:30.164
9	40 G. Tarquini/AGS	1:30.364
10	21 A. Caffi/BMS Dallara	1:30.371
11	10 E. Cheever/Arrows	1:30.728
12	9 D. Warwick/Arrows	1:30.749
13	11 N. Piquet/Lotus	1:30.771
14	20 J. Herbert/Benetton	1:31.020
15	17 N. Larini/Osella	1:31.791
16	24 L. Sala/Minardi	1:31.948
17	12 S. Nakajima/Lotus	1:31.970
18	15 M. Gugelmin/March	1:32.038
19	7 M. Brundle/Brabham	1:32.189
20	8 S. Modena/Brabham	1:32.618
21	28 G. Berger/Ferrari	1:33.319
22	26 O. Grouillard/Ligier	1:34.472
23	23 P. Martini/Minardi	1:34.525
24	16 I. Capelli/March	1:42.912

Existing qualifying lap record: *Ayrton Senna, Lotus-Renault 98T, 1m 25.050s, 213.333 kph/132.559 mph in 1986*

Existing race lap record: *Nelson Piquet, Williams-Honda FW11, 1m 28.667s, 204.631 kph/127.152 mph in 1986*

Existing distance record: *Alain Prost, McLaren-TAG/Porsche MP4/2C, 60 laps in 1 hr 32m 28.408s at 196.208 kph/121.918 mph in 1986*

CHAMPIONSHIP POINTS

Drivers			Constructors	
1	Prost	12 pts	1 McLaren	21 pts
2	Senna	9 pts	2 Ferrari	9 pts
	Mansell	9 pts	3 Benetton	8 pts
4	Nannini	5 pts	4 March	4 pts
5	Gugelmin	4 pts	5 Arrows	4 pts
	Warwick	4 pts	6 Williams	3 pts
7	Boutsen	3 pts	7 Tyrrell	1 pt
	Herbert	3 pts		
9	Palmer	1 pt		

Left: a predominance of Ferrari red in the Imola grandstands.

PAST WINNERS

Year	Driver	Nat.	Car	Circuit
1981	Nelson Piquet	BR	3.0 Brabham BT 49C Ford	Imola
1982	Didier Pironi	F	1.5 Ferrari 126C2 t/c V6	Imola
1983	Patrick Tambay	F	1.5 Ferrari 126C2/B/ t/c V6	Imola
1984	Alain Prost	F	1.5 McLaren MP4/2/ TAG t/c	Imola
1985	Elio de Angelis	I	1.5 Lotus 97T Renault t/c V6	Imola
1986	Alain Prost	F	1.5 McLaren MP4/2C TAG t/c V6	Imola
1987	Nigel Mansell	GB	1.5 Williams FW11B Honda t/c V6	Imola
1988	Ayrton Senna	BR	1.5 McLaren MP4/4 Honda t/v V6	Imola

Monte Carlo

GRAND PRIX DE MONACO · 7 MAI

How did he do it? Ayrton Senna had led the race from the word go. When he and a pursuing Prost had got into traffic, he'd put the

Benetton Formula and Monte Carlo, the two most colourful aspects of Grand Prix racing.

hammer down, taken the risks where Alain wouldn't, and the gap had risen from 2.8 seconds to 15 seconds in four laps, thanks in great part to one R. Arnoux who did his usual hatchet job on his old pal Alain. This time, however, he got his knuckles rapped for it.

But from half distance onwards, Ayrton was in trouble with first gear and then second disappeared. 'I had to keep Alain from knowing I was in trouble,' he explained. How do you get around Monaco without one gear, and disguise the fact from your teammate?

It goes like this. 'I'd had the problem with first gear jumping out on the Thursday morning, so I had had a bit of practice in coping with it. You use it three times around here. I started using second gear for the hairpins which wasn't too bad – but a few laps later, second gear broke too. I had a big problem now. I had to keep Alain from knowing that I was in trouble so that he wouldn't try to come back at me. I lost three seconds a lap while I worked on how I could keep him from knowing. What I had to do was go very close to the barriers in the slow corners, keeping up the revs, sliding a bit. It wasn't easy lapping the slower cars either, because I had no acceleration to overtake them.'

Ayrton succeeded, and this time, there were no mistakes. With problems like that, there were no lapses of concentration, the mind was fully occupied. And the ruse worked.

Alain was no doubt stunned by the way that Ayrton had weaved his way through the traffic early, completely wiping out any challenge that the brilliant Frenchman might have mounted. Ayrton made room where perhaps there wasn't any. Alain admitted that he wasn't aggressive enough in similar circumstances. Gugelmin and later Arnoux cost him time where the yellow helmet seemed to scythe through.

And he had no idea that Ayrton was in trouble. 'I had no real problems with my car. It was in good shape. If I'd known that Ayrton was in trouble, perhaps I could have caught him. I could have lapped at two or three seconds a lap quicker.' The McLarens had been all-conquering, but whatever the slightly bemused Prost had to say about being happy to come first or second at Monaco, there was the feeling that he was a little frustrated to have had the wool pulled over his eyes and not been able to react to Aryton's problems.

Senna and Prost ran nose to tail until a Ligier intervened.

The Lola Lamborghini winds
through Monaco's tight streets.

A flat battery spoilt Brundle's
excellent drive.

If there was another impression, then it was that Pirelli were firmly back in business. Both the Pirelli-shod Brabhams and the Dallaras were in the top ten with Martini 11th. The non-qualifiers were all Goodyear runners. Brundle ran very strongly in the race, so did Modena and de Cesaris (until his ridiculous tangle with Piquet) and Caffi was there too: three Pirelli runners in the top six.

But Goodyear knew what the situation was. 'Our tyres aren't soft enough,' explained Goodyear's Lee Gaug. 'Everyone is taking off wing to try and run with the McLarens, and we're not getting the heat into the tyres. We'll be bringing softer compounds from now on.'

BRIGHT SPARKS

There were many staggering performances at Monaco, although Ayrton Senna's was probably the most obvious. Elsewhere, however, there were other performances of note around this difficult circuit, some of which were rewarded, and some which weren't.

There was no doubt, for instance, that Pirelli's tyres were just as competitive – if not more so – than Goodyear's, the Americans admitting that their tyres were too hard. But Brabham and Dallara in particular went well on the Italian tyres, and reaped just reward.

The Brabhams were there from the start, with Stefano Modena setting best time in pre-qualifying followed up by eighth on the grid. Only in Thursday's qualifying did he dip outside the top ten when he had gear selection problems.

Teammate Brundle admitted that he'd almost left his pre-qualifying run too late and ended up in fourth place on the grid, four places ahead of his teammate. Brundle spent much of the early part of the race battling with Mansell, moving up to third place just before the Ferrari retired. Modena, meanwhile, was pushing fourth-placed de Cesaris when the Dallara tangled with Piquet's Lotus, so that at half distance the Brabhams were third and fourth behind the McLarens. Brundle was chipping away at the gap between himself and Prost when his battery went flat and he had to pit for a new one, but Modena inherited his place and went on to finish third, with the recovered Brundle taking sixth two laps from home.

Alex Caffi had been the second pre-qualifier and took ninth spot on the grid, just ahead of teammate de Cesaris. But de Cesaris made the better start, and for many laps, Caffi found himself following Gabriele Tarquini's eighth-placed AGS.

Tarquini, in fact, probably hoped to be even higher up the order having qualified fifth on the Thursday. His DFZ-based engine had more low-down power which was suited to the circuit, but he dropped to 13th on the Saturday, 'reaching my limits and the car's'.

He was able to hold Caffi in spite of a misfire, but when it reappeared, he had to let the Dallaras through. Tarquini's race ended when his electrics melted when he was in sixth place.

Caffi, however, was then left in a fine fourth place when Brundle pitted, delighting both his team and his friends within the sport.

The unhappiest man at Monaco was probably Ivan Capelli. It isn't the easiest circuit in the world to sort out a new car, but March had brought CG891 to make its debut in the Principality as well as their older 881s. Twenty-eighth on Thursday morning became 25th that afternoon, 29th on Saturday morning and thankfully 22nd in qualifying. After a morning warm-up spin in Casino Square, Ivan was soon up to 14th, overtook Cheever when the Arrows driver spun, got by Nannini and found himself in sixth spot towards the end. 'Arnoux and I touched at the hairpin on lap one, and that broke a plate that protects the electrics,' explained

Top right: Mansell leads Brundle – having passed Arnoux – into Loews hairpin. Right: Moreno surrounded by the colour of Monaco.

Capelli in action.

the Italian. 'The car felt good, a little understeer and losing traction, but then the electrics caught fire three laps from home and the engine stopped.' Still no points, then, for Ivan . . .

RACE DEBRIEF

The Monaco Grand Prix was all about the McLaren drivers. Rumours abounded about the breach of the Imola agreement. Of course the pair were constantly at the head of the time sheets, Prost and Senna sharing fastest times in the sessions, although Senna was always the quicker in the important qualifying sessions.

Even so, Senna admitted a slight mistake on his best lap. 'I went over the bump in Casino Square a little too quickly, and had to lift off which cost me a couple of tenths. Otherwise it was a good lap without traffic. The engine is very good and a great improvement.' Prost also acknowledged that Ayrton's time – 1.6 seconds under his pole-winning time in 1988 – was quick.

Alain tried very hard to maintain a challenge to his teammate throughout the race. Although he and Senna were a couple of seconds apart after two laps, Prost soon cut the gap to sit on his teammate's tail.

But then there were a couple of gatecrashers in the party. Third-placed Thierry Boutsen was pushed up to join Prost by Mansell, who had Brundle pushing him. Within 10 laps, this duo had become a quintet.

Boutsen experiences a Formula 1 traffic jam. Main shot: the cause — Piquet and de Cesaris.

But then came the backmarkers, and Senna set the fastest lap of the race so far. Down went the hammer, and the gap grew. Senna was 2.1 seconds ahead when he and Prost first hit backmarkers. A lap later, that was up to 3.0 seconds, then 3.8 seconds. Prost struggled to bring the gap down again; then – happily for him – Boutsen drifted out and then disappeared altogether on lap 18 to collect a new rear wing, the original having begun to break up. Prost found himself safely in second place by 12.7 seconds.

He tried hard to cut the gap to Senna, but then came up behind his old adversary, Rene Arnoux. Arnoux recognised the yellow helmet in the red and white car as being one that tends to push through, takes its chances. The blue and white helmet is, perhaps by its own admission, more wary. It didn't push, and Rene wasn't about to let his old teammate past. The gap of 4.2 seconds became 6.6 seconds on lap 21, 11 seconds on lap 22 and 15 seconds on lap 23. Mansell and Brundle were only 7.9 seconds behind.

Prost pushed hard, and pulled away from Mansell who promptly disappeared. He had controlled Brundle's Brabham, but then the electronic gearbox played up, and that was the end of the lone Ferrari challenge. There was no Berger here, of course, at least not in a car.

Brundle slotted into third place, around 25 seconds behind Prost, and then came de Cesaris, struggling, as at the start of the race, to stay ahead of Modena.

Prost had actually cut the lead down to 12.9 seconds on lap 33, and we could but hope that he was closing on Senna. But then de Cesaris came up to lap an off-form Piquet. As de Cesaris went down the inside of the Lotus into the Loews hairpin, Piquet came back across on the exit. The two interlocked wheels and squealed to a halt.

De Cesaris then did his imitation of a Roman taxi driver, getting out, waving his arms and shouting. Throughout this performance Piquet sat impassively. Marshals struggled to separate the cars, while a queue built up behind – including Alain Prost. 'It was laughable,' said Prost, 'I don't think I have ever, in my whole racing life, put the lever into neutral and waited during a race.'

Gugelmin's Leyton House negotiates Loews.

Below left: Herbert follows Arnoux's wide Ligier with the Port. Below: Modena impressive in the Brabham heads for third.

Wait he did, however, and when he finally got going again, the lead gap had risen to 36.8 seconds. That, it seemed, was that. But just a few laps later came a little rise in Senna's lap times which might have given Prost the hint he needed. 'I had a problem with first gear which we use three times around here. I lost nearly three seconds a lap, then I broke second gear too, and I had no acceleration to overtake slower cars. But I tried hard not to give any indication to Alain that I was in trouble.'

Senna succeeded. 'I didn't know that Ayrton had problems at the end. Perhaps I might have caught him because I had no real problems with my car, but Monaco is very difficult, so it's good to come first or second. I don't mind.'

Alain showed that he could have gone a lot quicker. Senna's lap times hovered around 1m 27s to 1m 30s during the second half of the race, with a couple of visits to 1m 26s. Prost, however, twice dipped into 1m 25s before lap 60, with a fastest lap of 1m 25.5s.

Another McLaren one-two, then, but after Mansell's retirement, and the delay to both Williamses (Patrese had started at the back anyway due to low fuel pressure) it was the Brabhams who came into the picture, holding third and fourth at half distance. But then Brundle pitted for a new battery, putting Modena up into third, a fine result for a pre-qualifier. Then Caffi, another pre-qualifier, came next after tussling with Tarquini who quit after an early misfire.

One of the best and longest battles was that headed by Alboreto in his brand new Tyrrell. He had decided against driving the cramped and older 017 on the Thursday, preferring to wait for the roomier new 018 being hurried to him in Monaco. When it did arrive, Michele put it into 12th on the grid, and after a gearbox panic in the warm-up, grappled with Nannini until Alliot, Cheever and Capelli joined in.

Alboreto fighting with the new Tyrrell.

Centre: De Cesaris crosses the lines. Top: Patrese on the limit. Above: another close battle in the streets of Monaco.

This got a little too crowded, but Michele was able to pull away again. And although he upset lapped teammate Palmer for not letting him past during the later stages, Michele confirmed the ability of both himself and the new 018 with a fine fifth place.

Sixth was in question until the very end. Nannini slipped back with overheating brakes and clipped the barrier once, and in spite of braking later and later, he was overtaken by Ivan Capelli who looked to be heading for sixth place in the brand-new March in which he had started 22nd. Unfortunately a contact with Arnoux on lap one had broken a part protecting the electrics. These caught fire right at the end, and the engine stopped; a desperately disappointing and frustrating way to finish the car's first race.

And who should be right there to take that final point but Brundle

after his disjointed drive. He had known that the battery was flat, and after hopping from his Brabham for the replacement to be fitted, had hopped back in again and resumed in tenth place on lap 49.

He soon overtook Palmer and then Nannini, while Cheever, the Arrows driver was caught with handling troubles, seven laps from the end. Capelli's demise on the penultimate lap gave Brundle his well-deserved sixth place, with Cheever seventh, ahead of Nannini, Palmer and Boutsen, the three covered by less than a second.

The Monaco Grand Prix was full of intrigue, more behind the scenes than on track, although Messrs Arnoux, Piquet and de Cesaris tried to put that right. Pirelli had three runners in the top six, and Goodyear would later react. For the moment, however, Prost and Senna were equal first in the World Championship . . .

Above: spectators cram the balconies of Monaco, watching Warwick lead out of Loews. Left: Raphanel thunders through the tunnel in his first Grand Prix.

FIA
FORMULA 1
WORLD
CHAMPIONSHIP

GRAND PRIX DE MONACO

ENTRIES · PRACTICE · RESULTS

Pos	Driver/Nationality		No.	Car/Engine	P/Q	Practice 1 (cloudy)	Practice 2 (sunny)	Warm-up (pos) (cloudy)	Laps (sunny)	Time/Retirement (sunny)
1	A. Senna	BR	1	McLaren MP4/5 Honda V10	–	1:24.126	**1:22.308**	1:26.214 (1)	77	1hr53m33.251
2	A. Prost	F	2	McLaren MP4/5 Honda V10	–	1:24.671	**1:23.456**	1:26.590 (2)	77	1hr54m25.780
3	S. Modena	I	8	Brabham BT58 Judd V8	1:26.957	1:27.598	**1:25.086**	1:28.435 (5)	76	1hr53m48.938
4	A. Caffi	I	21	Dallara BMS 189 Ford DFR V8	1:27.098	27.894	**1:25.481**	1:33.292 (26)	75	1hr53m33.659
5	M. Alboreto	I	4	Tyrrell 018 Ford DFR V8	–	no time	**1:26.388**	1:32.026 (24)	75	1hr53m59.595
6	M. Brundle	GB	7	Brabham BT58 Judd V8	1:27.774	1:26.970	**1:24.580**	1:28.867 (7)	75	1hr53m12.305
7	E. Cheever	USA	10	Arrows A11 Ford DFR V8	–	1:28.461	**1:27.117**	1:30.545 (14)	75	1hr54m23.537
8	A. Nannini	I	19	Benetton B188 Ford DFR V8	–	1:28.608	**1:26.599**	1:29.641 (11)	74	1hr53m41.508
9	J. Palmer	GB	3	Tyrrell 018 Ford DFR V8	–	1:29.151	**1:27.452**	1:29.849 (12)	74	1hr53m42.353
10	T. Boutsen	B	5	Williams FW12C Renault V10	–	1:25.540	**1:24.332**	1:29.336 (9)	74	1hr53m42.43866
11	I. Capelli	I	16	March CG891 Judd V8	–	1:39.800	**1:27.302**	1:30.653 (16)	73	accident/electrics
12	R. Arnoux	F	25	Ligier JS33 Ford DFR V8	–	1:30.003	**1:27.182**	1:32.065 (25)	73	1hr53m40.319
13	A. de Cesaris	I	22	Dallara BMS 189 Ford DFR V8	–	1:26.617	**1:25.515**	1:29.049 (8)	73	1hr54m03.717
14	J. Herbert	GB	20	Benetton B188 Ford DFR V8	–	1:29.661	**1:27.706**	1:31.018 (18)	73	1hr54m20.335
15	R. Patrese	I	6	Williams FW12C Renault V10	–	1:27.138	**1:25.021**	1:28.427 (4)	73	1hr54m29.947
16	L. Sala	E	24	Minardi M 188B Ford DFR V8	–	1:28.886	**1:27.786**	1:31.169 (19)	48	engine
17	G. Tarquini	I	40	AGS JH23 Ford DFR V8	–	1:26.603	**1:26.422**	1:31.209 (40)	46	electrics
18	R. Moreno	BR	31	Coloni C188B Ford DFR V8	–	1:30.209	**1:27.721**	1:31.899 (22)	44	hearbox
19	P. Alliot	F	30	Lola LC89 Lamborghini	–	1:26.975	**1:26.857**	1:29.379 (30)	38	engine
20	M. Gugelmin	BR	15	March CG891 (p) 881 (r) Judd V8	–	1:28.917	**1:26.522**	1:30.294 (13)	36	oil pump
21	N. Piquet	BR	11	Lotus 101 Judd V8	–	1:29.047	**1:27.046**	1:30.887 (17)	32	collision/de Cesaris
22	N. Mansell	GB	27	Ferrari 640 Ferrari V12	–	1:25.363	**1:24.735**	1:26.861 (3)	30	electrics
23	P-H. Raphanel	F	32	Coloni C188B Ford DFR V8	1:27.590	1:30.264	**1:27.011**	1:31.982 (23)	19	gearbox
24	O. Grouillard	F	26	Ligier JS53 Ford DFR V8	–	1:27.040	**1:26.792**	1:31.644 (21)	4	gearbox
25	P. Martini	I	23	Minardi M188B Ford DFR V8	–	1:28.469	**1:26.288**	1:30.599 (15)	3	gear linkage
26	D. Warwick	GB	9	Arrows A11 Ford DFR V8	–	1:26.606	**1:24.791**	1:28.726 (6)	2	electrics
27	C. Danner	D	38	Rial ARC02 Ford DFR V8	–	1:28.737	**1:27.910**	DNQ		
28	Y. Dalmas	F	29	Lola LC89 Lamborghini V12	–	1:29.794	**1:27.946**	DNQ		
29	S. Nakajima	J	12	Lotus 101 Judd V8	–	1:28.568	**1:28.419**	DNQ		
–	P. Ghinzani	I	18	Osella FA1M Ford DFR V8	1:27.795	DNPQ	DNPQ			
–	S. Johansson	S	36	Onyx ORE1 Ford DFR V8	1:27.821	DNPQ	DNPQ			
–	N. Larini	I	17	Osella FA1M Ford DFR V8	1:28.555	DNPQ	DNPQ			
–	B. Schneider	D	34	Zakspeed ZK189 Yamaha V8	1:28.610	DNPQ	DNPQ			
–	B. Gachot	B	37	Onyx ORE1 Ford DFR V8	1:28.897	DNPQ	DNPQ			
–	G. Foitek	S	33	Eurobrun ER188 Judd V8	1:29.423	DNPQ	DNPQ			
–	V. Weidler	D	39	Rial ARC02 Ford DFR V8	1:29.498	DNPQ	DNPQ			
–	A. Suzuki	J	35	Zakspeed ZK189 Yamaha V8	1:30.528	DNPQ	DNPQ			
–	J. Winkelhock	D	41	AGS JH23 Ford DFR V8	1:32.274	DNPQ	DNPQ			

Circuit Data: Circuit de Monaco, length 2.069 miles/3.328 km, race distance 77 laps = 159.2 miles/256.3 km, race weather sunny.
Notes: Both Tyrrell drivers have 018s, Alboreto didn't practice on Thursday because he was waiting for his new car. Both March drivers have new CG891s, but Gugelmin races 881.
Berger does not race, 29 cars in qualifying, four only go through from pre-qualifying.

1. A SENNA
2. A PROST
5. T BOUTSEN
7. M BRUNDLE
27. N MANSELL
9. D WARWICK
6. R PATRESE
8. S MODENA
21. A CAFFI
22. A DE CESARIS
23. P MARTINI
4. A ALBORETO
40. G TARQUINI
15. M GUGELMIN
19. A NANNINI
26. O GROUILLARD
30. P ALLIOT
32. P RAPHANEL
11. N PIQUET
10. E CHEEVER
25. R ARNOUX
16. I CAPELLI
3. J PALMER
20. J HERBERT
31. R MORENO
24. L SALA

LAP CHART

Grid Order	1 2 3 4 5 6 7 8 9 10 11 12 13 14 15 16 17 18 19 20 21 22 23 24 25 26 27 28 29 30 31 32 33 34 35 36 37 38 39 40 41 42 43 44 45 46 47 48 49 50 51 52 53 54 55 56 57 58 59 60 61 62 63 64 65 66 67 68 69 70 71 72 73 74 75 76 77
1 A. Senna	1 1 1 1 1 1 1 1 1 1 1 1 1 1 1 1 1 1 1 1 1 1 1 1 1 1 1 1 1 1 1 1 1 1 1 1 1 1 1 1 1 1 1 1 1 1 1 1 1 1 1 1 1 1 1 1 1 1 1 1 1 1 1 1 1 1 1 1 1 1 1 1 1 1 1 1 1
2 A. Prost	2 2 2 2 2 2 2 2 2 2 2 2 2 2 2 2 2 2 2 2 2 2 2 2 2 2 2 2 2 2 2 2 2 2 2 2 2 2 2 2 2 2 2 2 2 2 2 2 2 2 2 2 2 2 2 2 2 2 2 2 2 2 2 2 2 2 2 2 2 2 2 2 2 2 2 2 2
5 R. Patrese	5 5 5 5 5 5 5 5 5 5 5 5 5 5 5 5 5 5 5 5 5 5 5 5 5 27 27 27 27 27 27 27 27 27 27 7 7 7 7 7 7 7 7 7 7 7 7 7 7 7 7 7 7 7 7 7 7 7 7 7 7 7 7 8 8 8 8 8 8 8 8 8 8 8 8 8 8
7 M. Brundle	27 27 27 27 27 27 27 27 27 27 27 27 27 27 27 27 27 27 27 7 7 7 7 7 7 7 7 27 27 22 22 22 8 8 8 8 8 8 8 8 8 8 8 8 8 8 8 8 8 8 8 8 8 21 21 21 21 21 21 21 21 21 21 21 21 21 21 21 21 21 21 21 21 21 21 21 21
27 N. Mansell	7 7 7 7 7 7 7 7 7 7 7 7 7 7 7 7 7 22 22 22 22 22 22 22 22 22 22 27 8 8 40 40 40 40 40 40 40 40 40 40 21 21 21 21 4 4 4 4 4 4 4 4 4 4 4 4 4 4 4 4 4 4 4 4 4 4 4 4 4 4 4 4 4 4 4 4 4
9 D. Warwick	9 9 22 22 22 22 22 22 22 22 22 22 22 22 22 22 8 8 8 8 8 8 8 8 8 8 8 8 40 40 40 21 21 21 21 21 21 21 21 4 40 40 4 19 19 19 16 16 16 16 16 16 16 16 16 16 16 16 16 16 16 16 16 16 16 16 16 16 16 16 16 16 7 7
6 T. Boutsen	22 22 8 8 8 8 8 8 8 8 8 8 8 8 8 40 40 40 40 40 40 40 40 40 40 40 21 21 21 4 4 4 4 4 4 4 4 4 4 19 19 16 16 16 16 16 19 19 19 19 19 19 19 19 10 10 10 10 10 10 10 10 10 10 10 10 10 10 10 10 10 10 10 10 10
8 S. Modena	8 8 23 40 40 40 40 40 40 40 40 40 40 40 21 21 21 21 21 21 21 21 21 21 21 4 4 4 19 19 19 19 19 19 19 19 19 19 19 16 10 10 10 10 10 10 10 10 10 10 10 10 10 10 19 19 19 19 19 19 7 7 7 7 7 7 7 10 10 10 10 19
21 A. Caffi	23 23 40 21 21 21 21 21 21 21 21 21 21 21 4 4 4 4 4 4 4 4 4 4 4 19 19 19 30 30 30 30 16 16 16 16 16 16 16 10 10 3 3 7 7 7 7 7 7 7 7 7 7 7 19 19 19 19 19 19 19 19 19 19 19 19 19 3
22 A. de Cesaris	40 40 21 4 4 4 4 4 4 4 4 4 4 4 19 19 19 19 19 19 19 19 19 19 19 30 30 30 10 10 10 10 10 10 10 10 10 10 10 3 3 7 3 3 3 3 3 3 3 3 3 3 3 3 3 3 3 3 3 3 3 3 3 3 3 3 3 5
23 P. Martini	21 21 4 19 19 19 19 19 19 19 19 19 19 19 30 30 30 30 30 30 30 30 30 30 30 10 10 10 16 16 16 16 25 25 25 25 25 25 3 24 24 25 25 25 25 25 5 5 5 5 5 5 5 5 5 5 5 5 5 5 5 5 5 5 5 5 5
4 M. Alboreto	4 19 30 30 30 30 30 30 30 30 30 30 10 10 10 10 10 10 10 10 10 10 10 10 10 16 16 16 25 25 25 25 3 3 3 3 3 3 24 25 25 5 5 5 5 25 25 25 25 25 25 25 25 25 25 25 25 25 25 25 25 25 25 25 25 25 25
40 G. Tarquini	19 19 10 10 10 10 10 10 10 10 10 10 16 16 16 16 16 16 16 16 16 16 11 11 20 20 20 3 24 24 24 24 24 24 25 5 20 20 20 20 20 20 20 20 20 20 20 20 20 20 20 20 22 22
15 M. Gugelmin	26 26 16 16 16 16 16 16 16 16 16 16 25 25 25 25 25 25 25 11 11 11 11 11 25 25 20 3 3 24 24 31 5 5 5 5 5 5 20 20 22 22 22 22 22 22 22 22 22 22 22 22 22 20 20
19 A. Nannini	30 30 10 25 25 25 6 6 6 6 25 25 25 25 32 11 11 11 11 11 11 11 11 25 25 25 25 20 20 3 24 24 24 31 5 31 31 31 20 20 22 22 6 6 6 6 6 6 6 6 6 6 6 6 6 6 6 6 6 6 6 6 6 6
26 O. Grouillard	10 10 16 32 6 6 6 25 25 25 25 32 32 32 32 32 11 20 20 20 20 20 20 20 20 20 3 3 24 31 31 5 5 20 20 20 20 20 22 22 6 6
30 P. Alliot	32 16 32 26 32 32 32 32 32 32 32 11 11 11 11 11 11 20 32 3 3 3 3 3 3 3 3 24 31 15 15 5 20 20 22 22 22 22 22 22 6 6
32 P.H. Raphanel	16 32 25 6 11 11 11 11 11 11 11 20 20 20 20 20 3 24 24 24 24 24 24 24 24 31 15 15 5 5 15 22 22 6 6 6 6 6 6
11 N. Piquet	25 25 6 11 20 20 20 20 20 20 3 3 3 3 24 24 31 31 31 31 31 31 31 31 31 15 15 5 22 22 22 22 6 6
10 E. Cheever	11 6 11 20 3 3 3 3 3 3 24 24 24 24 24 31 15 15 15 15 15 15 15 15 15 15 15 5 5 6 6 6 6
25 R. Arnoux	6 11 20 3 31 31 24 24 24 24 24 31 31 31 31 15 5 5 5 5 5 5 5 5 5 5 6
16 I. Cappelli	20 20 3 31 24 24 31 31 31 31 15 15 15 15 15 5 5 6 6 6 6 6 6 6 6 6 6
3 J. Palmer	3 3 31 24 15 15 15 15 15 15 15 6 6 6 6 6 6
20 J. Herbert	31 31 24 15
31 R. Moreno	24 24 15
24 L. Sala	15 15

FASTEST LAPS

Pos.	Car No./Driver/Team	Time
1	2 A. Prost/McLaren	(N.R.) 1:25.501
2	7 M. Brundle/Brabham	1:25.882
3	1 A. Senna/McLaren	1:26.017
4	27 N. Mansell/Ferrari	1:26.946
5	6 R. Patrese/Williams	1:26.369
6	22 A. de Cesaris/BMS Dallara	1:27.240
7	5 T. Boutsen/Williams	1:27.290
8	3 J. Palmer/Tyrrell	1:27.745
9	8 S. Modena/Brabham	1:28.188
10	16 I. Capelli/March	1:28.204
11	11 E. Cheever/Arrows	1:28.506
12	21 A. Caffi/BMS Dallara	1:28.680
13	4 M. Alboreto/Tyrrell	1:29.063
14	40 G. Tarquini/AGS	1:29.203
15	19 A. Nannini/Benetton	1:29.251
16	30 P. Alliot/Larrousse	1:29.446
17	20 J. Herbert/Benetton	1:29.685
18	11 N. Piquet/Lotus	1:29.808
19	24 L. Sala/Minardi	1:30.890
20	31 R. Moreno/Coloni	1:31.114
21	32 P. Raphanel/Coloni	1:31.253
22	25 R. Arnoux/Ligier	1:31.358
23	9 D. Warwick/Arrows	1:32.050
24	23 P. Martini/Minardi	1:32.270
25	15 M. Gugelmin/March	1:32.334
26	26 O. Grouillard/Ligier	1:34.265

N.R. = New lap record

Existing qualifying lap record: Alain Prost, McLaren-TAG/Porsche MP4/2C, 1m 22.627s, 144.999 kph/90.098 mph in 1986

Existing race lap record: Ayrton Senna, McLaren-Honda MP4/4, 1m 26.321s, 138.794 kph/86.243 mph in 1988

Existing distance record: Alain Prost, McLaren-TAG/Porsche MP4/2C, 78 laps in 1 hr 55m 41.060s at 134.634 kph/83.658 mph in 1986

CHAMPIONSHIP POINTS

	Drivers			Constructors	
1	Senna	18 pts	1	McLaren	36 pts
2	Prost	18 pts	2	Ferrari	9 pts
3	Mansell	9 pts	3	Benetton	8 pts
4	Nannini	5 pts	4	Brabham	5 pts
5	Gugelmin	4 pts	5	March	4 pts
	Modena	4 pts	6	Arrows	4 pts
7	Warwick	4 pts	7	Williams	3 pts
8	Boutsen	3 pts		Dallara	3 pts
	Herbert	3 pts	9	Tyrrell	3 pts
	Caffi	3 pts			
11	Alboreto	2 pts			
12	Palmer	1 pt			
	Brundle	1 pt			

Left: a clean-up operation for the Monaco marshals at Loews.

PAST WINNERS

Year	Driver	Nat.	Car	Circuit
1979	Jody Scheckter	ZA	3.0 Ferrari 312T-4	Monte Carlo
1980	Carlos Reutemann	RA	3.0 Williams-Ford FW07B	Monte Carlo
1981	Gilles Villeneuve	CDN	1.5 Ferrari 126CK	Monte Carlo
1982	Riccardo Patrese	I	3.0 Brabham-Ford BT49D	Monte Carlo
1983	Keke Rosberg	SF	3.0 Williams-Ford FW08C	Monte Carlo
1984	Alain Prost	F	1.5 McLaren-TAG MP4/2 t/c	Monte Carlo
1985	Alain Prost	F	1.5 McLaren-TAG MP4/2B t/c	Monte Carlo
1986	Alain Prost	F	1.5 McLaren-TAG MP4/2C t/c	Monte Carlo
1987	Ayrton Senna	BR	1.5 Lotus-Honda 99T t/c	Monte Carlo
1988	Alain Prost	F	1.5 McLaren-Honda MP4/4 t/c	Monte Carlo

Mexico City

GRAN PREMIO DE MEXICO · 28 MAYO

available. Their users dominated the top six, while Pirelli's top runners, Brabhams, were only ninth and tenth. But what was the

Pressure too great for Caffi causing a Mexican two-step.

This was a tyre race. We hadn't had one of those, it seemed, for many years, although admittedly this was a one-sided tyre race. After Pirelli were flattered, as Goodyear put it, in Monaco, the American tyre company reacted in Mexico, making a variety of rubber

right choice for Goodyear runners?

'We've got to bring out some softer tyres,' said Goodyear's Lee Gaug in Monaco. 'People are using so little wing to try and catch the McLaren-Hondas that they're not getting our tyres up to temperature.'

nd for that reason, Goodyear brought Bs and Cs to Mexico, the Bs being the harder of the two compounds. Crucial to any driver's tyre choice for the race was the thought of the left-hand front having to work hard through that long fast final corner 69 times. That's where the wear would come.

Consequently, Senna chose a mix: the harder Bs on the left, the softer Cs on the right. No-one copied him, and no-one headed him. But he would later say: 'The tyre choice was fundamental to my success. It was a gamble and I'm normally not too successful when I gamble. But I was worried about the choice, and I thought it would be safer with the hard left.'

In the early stages, Senna's chief rival was Prost, wearing the softer Cs. If anyone could make them last, said the pundits, Prost could. But after 20 laps he was in the pits for a change of tyres. 'I thought I could make it, and I was quicker than Senna for a while,' said the Frenchman, 'but I took a lot out of the tyres trying to stay with him and they blistered, and then so did the second set.'

Two tyre stops for Prost, then, and still not able to make them last. Mansell stuck fairly close to Senna too, until retirement, yet he was on Cs and making them last, but the man who inherited second place from the Ferrari, Riccardo Patrese, was on the harder Bs.

'We chose the harder compound because we didn't think we could manage the softer one,' explained the Italian. 'The grip wasn't fantastic

but it was consistent.' And behind him was a delighted Michele Alboreto on Goodyear's Cs again and making them last quite happily.

If there was another overriding impression, it was seeing these two Italians on the rostrum. Both were in teams that hadn't had a happy time so far in 1989: at this stage, Williams-Renault didn't have a championship point (although Boutsen's fourth place in Imola was in dispute) and Ken Tyrrell's obviously competitive 018s were still plain blue.

And in the championship, the McLaren-Hondas were certainly easing away, with Senna having taken his third race victory in succession and

Clockwise from left: third in a row for Senna. Ken Tyrrell waited all day for sponsors to ring after Alboreto's great third. Renault were thrilled with Patrese's second place.

pulling out a seven-point lead over teammate Prost after a quarter of the season. Mansell, from his single win in Brazil, was in third place with a remarkable 15 scorers in the championship out of a potential 24. In some ways it looked dominated, in others it looked open.

BRIGHT SPARKS

We had become accustomed to seeing pre-qualifiers get all the way through to the race, and even winning points, but the pattern had perhaps become over-established. The two Brabhams

always made it, Caffi usually did. It was just down to who would fill place number four. Larini, Foitek, Schneider and Raphanel had all made it in their time, but when, oh when, was an Onyx going to get a race?

The answer finally came in Mexico, for there was Johansson fourth and Gachot knocking on the door in fifth. Now Onyx were into a whole new ball game: setting up the car with plenty of time instead of pre-qualifying's do-or-die 60-minute dash.

At Saturday lunchtime, they were able to phone team sponsor Jean-Pierre van Rossem in Belgium that they were sixth in the unofficial session. There was an explosion of glee from the other end. Stefan's time that morning would have put him 10th on the eventual grid, but sadly he was 0.8 seconds slower, having not got the best from his qualifiers – and in this super-competitive world of Grand Prix racing, that resulted in 21st on the grid.

Ninth in the warm-up, Stefan was up to 17th on the first lap, and then fought past Modena, Herbert, Brundle and Grouillard. But just as he was joining the Warwick/Tarquini battle for eighth, the clutch broke and he was out.

Tarquini, in fact, was rather confounding the suggestion that the AGS is only good on slow circuits. Having found a slot in 17th spot for most of practice and qualifying, he leaped up four places on the first lap and picked off Modena, then de Cesaris and Grouillard, only to get stuck behind Warwick who was too quick in a straight line, although the Arrows driver lost third gear very early on. When Warwick's engine cut out, Tarquini briefly found himself in fifth place, but was knocked back to sixth as Prost came back after another pit stop for tyres. But the Italian claimed what he called his 'first real championship point' – for the moment, potential salvation from pre-qualifying.

For Williams-Renault and Patrese, this was a vital result. No-one was looking at the 40-second gap between Senna and Patrese on lap 53, preferring the 15-second gap at the end of the race. But after retirement in the first two Grands Prix and a wing problem in Monaco, it was great to score points with second place in Mexico, even though teammate Boutsen went out with failed electrics when he was just behind Patrese.

As for Tyrrell, this was sheer confirmation that Harvey Postle-thwaite's 018 worked exceptionally well. Very quick on the straight, and across the start/finish line; grip in the final corner as well as speed at the end of the straight. Palmer was already fifth in Friday's first session and Alboreto seventh but the next morning the doctor went off after bottoming because of stiffer springs. After its rebuild the car didn't handle so well, and left Jonathan 14th on the grid, although Michele was a more competitive seventh.

Fourth in the warm-up, he stuck rigidly to the back end of Patrese's Williams-Renault throughout, and only in the final stages did the gap creep up as Michele consolidated his third place. You win some, you lose some: Palmer took early retirement with broken throttle linkage.

If there was another performance to mention, it was Ivan Capelli's great fourth place on the grid in what was still a very new March —

Clockwise from left: it took two starts to get the Mexican Grand Prix under way, after incidents first time round. Gerhard Berger made a welcome return after his Imola accident. A split brake pipe cost Ivan Capelli his fourth on the grid.

although Gugelmin didn't qualify when the session was cut short by late session rain. But then Capelli had to take Gugelmin's car and start from the pits after a rear brake pipe split at the first start. The CV joint broke after just one lap.

RACE DEBRIEF

The outcome of the Mexico Grand Prix revolved around tyre choice. But until that moment, it had been one of those races where McLaren were up against the rest of the field, with Ferrari and Mansell knocking on the door, Williams-Renault right up with them, and then various other challengers also seeking a look-in. The Tyrrells, Capelli's March, the Brabhams and Warwick's Arrows were all among the top ten.

And the grid might even have taken on a new look but for a short sharp heavy shower which abbreviated a potentially very exciting last few minutes of qualifying. In the end Ayrton Senna was on pole, his record-equalling 33rd and his record-breaking seventh in a row. Furthermore, his time was just 0.4 seconds off his turbo time for pole last year.

For all this, however, he didn't have nice things to say about the circuit, particularly the long, slightly banked flat in fifth final corner. 'Every time I go through that corner, I'm not sure that I'm going to come out of it in the right direction. The responsible people must understand that they have to change it.'

Brundle went off there, so did de Cesaris, Palmer and Danner, who called it 'the number one corner in the world'. None did so with the severity that Philippe Alliot had the previous year: it had, however, earned him celebrity status in Mexico.

McLarens on the front row, then: Senna to Prost, 0.9 seconds; Prost to Mansell, 0.4 seconds; Mansell to Capelli, 0.2 seconds; the rest were all close behind, but the McLarens did look good out front. Prost was quickest in the warm-up from Mansell and then Senna with Alboreto right up there with them in 1m 21s. At least the warm-up looked closer than qualifying.

At Indianapolis that same day, Emerson Fittipaldi's red and white Penske was the class of the field, in spite of the late race incident. Few people would bet that red and white wouldn't be the colours to watch at the front of the Mexican Grand Prix.

Indeed Senna made a great getaway, while the Ferraris were exceptionally fleet, with Mansell heading Berger into the first corner, the Austrian soon to be overtaken by Prost. De Cesaris and Nakajima had an incident on that first lap, while Modena went off going into the final corner and Danner, Grouillard and Caffi were also slightly involved. The race was stopped, and everyone lined up for a new start.

Everyone, that is, except for Modena from the pit lane, joined there by the unfortunate Capelli who had to take Gugelmin's car after his own split a brake pipe.

Prost made a better start this time, trailing Senna around the first lap and sticking with him every inch of the way for the first ten laps or so. Admittedly, he was then into the lappery, but Senna pulled away as Prost's tyres began to suffer. For four laps the gap widened by a second a lap, and Prost felt the pinch from third-placed Nigel Mansell.

Prost realised very quickly that the tyre choice was wrong. But when he did decide to come in he got another set of Cs, and the stop wasn't the quickest at 14 seconds. He dropped to sixth, behind Senna, now 6.7 seconds ahead of Mansell, in turn some 15 seconds ahead of Patrese, who was 3.2 seconds ahead of Alboreto. Then came Nannini, and then Prost.

Already gone was Berger, who had led Mansell for the first seven laps and then retired ten laps later with a gear-shift problem. Boutsen had been right up with teammate Patrese, protecting him from the Alboreto threat until his electrics cut out on lap 16, while Johansson had climbed up to tenth and was embroiled in the eighth-place battle with Warwick and Tarquini when his clutch went.

Mansell now hung on bravely, the gap of 6.7 seconds that he inherited dipping into the fives (with fastest lap), then creeping back into the sixes, sevens (fastest lap to Senna), eights, then nines (held up by Nakajima). Senna's lead crept through the ten-second barrier and into the elevens, Mansell setting a fastest lap twice to bring it down into the tens again, only to pull off with an oil line failure to the gearbox, on lap 44.

Patrese was the man to inherit second place, but even then he was 41 seconds behind and only 4.4 seconds ahead of Alboreto. Nannini was in fourth place, his Benetton understeering in the medium-speed corners

McLaren and Ferrari on lap one.
Senna's nearest challenger was 17
seconds behind at the end.

Ex-Ferrari, ex-McLaren,
Johansson qualifies his Onyx for
its first race of '89.

which feature so notably at the Autodromo Hermanos Rodriguez.

Prost had made a second stop within 14 laps of getting his second set of Cs, dropping from fifth – ahead of Nannini at the time – to eighth and last of the unlapped. He was even behind the on-going Warwick/Tarquini tussle. Warwick had lost third gear early on, and was struggling with second gear. Then a coil lead came off, and his race was run.

Prost was overtaken by his own teammate on lap 36, but trailed Senna to pick up one place when he overtook Tarquini on lap 42, and he unlapped himself on lap 57. But although he wasn't far behind Nannini (13 seconds on lap 59), he never made much impression on the Benetton, finishing 11 seconds behind him, although the Italian admitted that his tyres were finished by the end.

Senna's lead was as much as 40 seconds on lap 52, all the way through to lap 57, but then it began to drop: 31 seconds on lap 63, 28 seconds on lap 66 and only 15 seconds at the end. But he wasn't worried: far from it, he was delighted by the result.

If he didn't show it, his rostrum-sharers did. Patrese clearly saw this as an important result for team, engine supplier and himself. Alboreto's joy almost matched that of Ken Tyrrell, who looked as though he had won the World Championship, and back in sixth place the little AGS team had soldiered through to score their point. Grouillard had been up there all the time, even heading Tarquini at the start. But then he lost his clutch and in turn lost out to Cheever who had started on the penultimate row and, on Bs, raced hard to finish seventh (again) after having a long wait behind Brundle, ultimately best of the Pirelli runners.

Piquet, Caffi and Arnoux all finished, but there was little glory in that: no points, and final finishers in a field where there were only 11 retirements, relatively few.

The pit lane was not for Ligier: Grouillard, Arnoux both finished, the newcomer ahead.

MILESTONES

- Johansson pre-qualifies and qualifies 21st: first Grand Prix for Onyx
- First World Championship point for Gabriele Tarquini
- Senna's record-breaking seventh successive pole position

GRAN PREMIO DE MEXICO

ENTRIES · PRACTICE · RESULTS

Pos	Driver/Nationality		No.	Car/Engine	P.Q. (sunny)	Practice I (sunny, hot)	Practice 2 (warm, cloudy)	Warm-up (pos) (cool, sunny)	Laps (hot, sunny)	Time/Retirement
I	A. Senna	BR	I	McLaren MP4/5 Honda V10	–	1:19.112	1:17.876	1:21.461 (3)	69	1hr35m21.431
2	R. Patrese	I	6	Williams FW12C Renault V10	–	1:21.763	1:19.656	1:22.782 (6)	69	1hr35m36.991
3	M. Alboreto	I	4	Tyrrell 018 Ford DFR V4	–	1:22.150	1:20.066	1:21.749 (4)	69	1hr35m52.685
4	A. Nannini	I	19	Benetton B188 Frd DFR V8	–	1:21.791	1:20.888	1:23.617 (15)	69	1hr36m06.926
5	A. Prost	F	2	McLaren MP4/5 Honda V10	–	1:20.401	1:18.773	1:21.017 (1)	69	1hr35m17.544
6	G. Tarquini	I	40	AGS JH23 Ford DFR V8	–	1:23.004	1:21.031	1:23.987 (19)	68	1hr35m25.008
7	E. Cheever	USA	10	Arrows A11 Ford DFR V8	–	1:23.427	1:21.716	1:23.681 (16)	68	1hr35m33.821
8	O. Grouillard	F	26	Ligier JS33 Ford DFR V8	–	1:23.053	1:20.859	1:23.142 (10)	68	1hr35m39.759
9	M. Brundle	GB	7	Brabham BT58 Judd V8	1:21.770	1:23.375	1:21.217	1:24.557 (21)	68	1hr35m42.666
10	S. Modena	I	8	Brabham BR58 Judd V8	1:22.211	1:22.640	1:20.505	1:24.361 (20)	68	1hr35m49.134
11	N. Piquet	BR	11	Lotus 101 Judd V8	–	1:23.090	1:21.831	1:23.170 (12)	68	1hr36m18.967
12	C. Danner	G	38	Rial ARC02 Ford DFR V8	–	1:22.931	1:21.696	1:25.484 (25)	67	1hr35m32.801
13	A. Caffi	I	21	Dallara BMS 189 Ford DFR V8	1:22.876	1:22.705	1:21.139	1:25.197 (23)	67	1hr36m41.990
14	R. Arnoux	F	25	Ligier JS33 Ford DFR V8	–	1:24.890	1:21.830	1:25.231 (24)	66	1hr35m28.345
15	J. Herbert	GB	20	Benetton B188 Ford DFR V8	–	1:22.553	1:21.105	1:23.778 (18)	66	1hr35m51.120
16	P. Martini	I	23	Minardi M189 Ford DFR V8	–	1:24.181	1:21.471	1:24.903 (22)	53	engine
17	N. Mansell	GB	27	Ferrari 640 Ferrari V12	–	1:21.170	1:19.137	1:21.423 (2)	43	gearbox oil line
18	D. Warwick	GB	9	Arrows A11 Ford DFR V8	–	1:23.245	1:20.601	1:23.327 (14)	35	coil lead
19	S. Nakajima	J	12	Lotus 101 Judd V8	–	1:22.438	1:20.943	1:23.713 (17)	35	spin
20	P. Alliot	F	30	Lola LC89 Lamborghini V12	–	1:22.014	1:21.031	1:22.556 (5)	28	running not classified
21	A. de Cesaris	I	22	Dallara BMS 189 Ford DFR V8	–	1:23.066	1:20.873	1:27.051 (26)	20	accident damage
22	G. Berger	A	28	Ferrari 640 Ferrari V12	–	1:21.564	1:19.835	1:22.976 (8)	16	gearbox electrics
23	S. Johansson	S	36	Onyx ORE1 Ford DFR V8	1:23.288	1:23.746	1:21.358	1:22.994 (9)	16	clutch
24	T. Boutsen	B	5	Williams FW12C Renault V10	–	1:21.456	1:20.234	1:23.188 (13)	15	electrics
25	J. Palmer	GB	3	Tyrrell 018 Ford FR V8	–	1:21.561	1:20.888	1:22.819 (7)	9	throttle linkage
26	I. Capelli	I	16	March CG891 Judd V8	–	1:24.720	1:19.337	1:23.160 (11)	I	constants velocity joint
27	L. Sala	S	24	Minardi M189 Ford DFR V8	–	1:26.567	1:21.935	DNQ		
28	M. Gugelmin	BR	15	March CG891 Judd V8	–	1:22.712	1:22.081	DNQ		
29	Y. Dalmas	F	29	Lola LC89 Lamborghini V8	–	1:25.651	9:27.789	DNQ		
30	R. Moreno	BR	31	Coloni C188B Ford DFR V8	–	no time	3:32.095	DNQ		
–	B. Gachot	B	37	Onyx ORE1 Ford DFR V8	1:23.752	DNPQ	DNPQ			
–	G. Foitek	CH	33	Eurobrun ER188B Judd V8	1:24.351	DNPQ	DNPQ			
–	N. Larini	I	17	Osella FA1M Ford DFR V8	1:24.392	DNPQ	DNPQ			
–	V. Weidler	D	39	Rial ARC02 Ford DFR V8	1:24.966	DNPQ	DNPQ			
–	B. Schneider	D	34	Zakspeed ZK189 Yamaha V8	1:25.418	DNPQ	DNPQ			
–	A. Suzuki	J	35	Zakspeed ZK189 Yamaha V8	1:25.658	DNPQ	DNPQ			
–	P. Ghinzani	I	18	Osella FA1M Ford DFR V8	TDA	DNPQ	DNPQ			
–	J. Winkelhock	D	41	AGS JH 23 Ford DFR V8	1:26.754	DNPQ	DNPQ			
–	P-H. Raphanel	F	32	Coloni C188B Ford DFR V8	1:34.357	DNPQ	DNPQ			

Circuit Data: Autodromo Hermanos Rodriguez, length 2.747 miles/4.421 km, race distance 69 laps = 189.5 miles/305 km, race weather hot and sunny.
Notes: Minardi debut new M189 for both drivers.

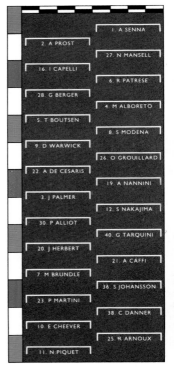

	1. A SENNA
2. A PROST	
	27. N MANSELL
16. I CAPELLI	
	6. R PATRESE
28. G BERGER	
	4. M ALBORETO
5. T BOUTSEN	
	8. S MODENA
9. D WARWICK	
	26. O GROUILLARD
22. A DE CESARIS	
	19. A NANNINI
3. J PALMER	
	12. S NAKAJIMA
30. P ALLIOT	
	40. G TARQUINI
20. J HERBERT	
	21. A CAFFI
7. M BRUNDLE	
	36. S JOHANSSON
23. P MARTINI	
	38. C DANNER
10. E CHEEVER	
	25. R ARNOUX
11. N PIQUET	

LAP CHART

Grid Order	Lap progression (laps 1–69)
1 A. Senna	1 1 1 1 1 1 1 1 1 1 1 1 1 1 1 1 1 1 1 1 1 1 1 1 1 1 1 1 1 1 1 1 1 1 1 1 1 1 1 1 1 1 1 1 1 1 1 1 1 1 1 1 1 1 1 1 1 1 1 1 1 1 1 1 1 1 1 1 1
2 A. Prost	2 2 2 2 2 2 2 2 2 2 2 2 2 2 2 2 2 2 2 2 2 2 2 2 27 27 27 27 27 27 27 27 27 27 27 27 27 27 27 27 27 27 27 27 27 27 27 27 27 27 27 27 27 6 6 6 6 6 6 6 6 6 6 6 6 6 6 6
27 N. Mansell	28 28 28 28 28 28 28 28 27 27 27 27 27 27 27 27 27 27 27 6 6 6 6 6 6 6 6 6 6 6 6 6 6 6 6 6 6 6 6 6 6 6 6 6 6 4 4 4 4 4 4 4 4 4 4 4 4 4 4 4 4 4 4 4 4 4 4 4 4
16 I. Capelli	27 27 27 27 27 27 28 28 28 28 28 28 28 28 6 6 6 4 4 4 4 4 4 4 4 4 4 4 4 4 4 4 4 4 4 4 4 4 4 4 4 4 19 19 19 19 19 19 19 19 19 19 19 19 19 19 19 19 19 19 19 19 19 19 19 19 19 19 19
6 R. Patrese	6 6 6 6 6 6 6 6 6 6 6 6 6 6 4 4 4 2 19 19 19 19 19 2 2 2 2 2 2 2 19 19 19 19 19 19 19 19 19 19 2 2 2 2 2 2 2 2 2 2 2 2 2 2 2 2 2 2 2 2 2 2 2 2 2 2 2 2 2
28 G. Berger	5 5 5 5 5 5 5 5 5 5 5 5 5 5 4 19 19 19 19 2 2 2 2 2 19 19 19 19 19 19 19 9 9 40 40 40 40 40 40 40 2 2 40 40 40 40 40 40 40 40 40 40 40 40 40 40 40 40 40 40 40 40 40 40 40 40 40 40 40
4 M. Alboreto	4 4 4 4 4 4 4 4 4 4 4 4 4 4 19 9 9 9 9 9 9 9 9 9 9 9 9 9 9 9 9 40 40 2 2 2 2 2 40 10 10 10 10 10 10 10 10 10 10 10 10 10 10 10 10 10 10 10 10 10 10 10 10 10 10 10 10 10 10
5 T. Boutsen	9 9 19 19 19 19 19 19 19 19 19 19 19 9 40 40 40 40 40 40 40 40 40 40 40 40 40 40 40 40 40 2 2 10 10 10 10 10 10 10 10 10 10 10 10 10 10 10 10 10 10 10 10 10 10 10 10 10 10 10 10 10 10 10 10 10 10 10 10
8 S. Modena	19 19 9 9 9 9 9 9 9 9 9 9 9 40 26 26 26 26 26 26 26 26 26 26 26 26 10 10 10 10 10 26 26 26 26 26 26 26 26 7 7 7 7 7 7 7 7 7 7 7 7 7 7 7 7 7 7 7 7 7 7 7 7 7 7 7 7 7 7
9 D. Warwick	22 22 26 26 26 40 40 40 40 40 40 40 40 36 7 7 10 10 10 10 10 10 10 10 10 10 26 26 26 7 7 7 7 7 7 8 8 8 8 8 8 8 8 8 8 8 8 8 8 8 8 8 8 8 8 8 8 8 8 8 8 8 8 8 8 8 8 8 8
26 O. Grouillard	26 26 22 40 40 40 26 26 26 26 36 36 26 10 10 7 7 7 7 7 7 7 7 7 7 7 8 8 8 8 8 8 8 8 11 11 11 11 11 11 11 11 11 11 11 11 11 11 11 11 11 11 11 11 11 11 11 11 11 11 11 11 11 11 11 11 11 11 11
22 A. de Cesaris	8 40 40 22 22 3 3 3 3 36 36 26 26 7 12 12 12 12 12 12 12 12 12 12 12 12 7 7 7 11 11 11 11 11 11 20 20 38 38 38 38 38 38 38 38 38 38 38 38 38 38 38 38 38 38 38 38 38 38 38 38 38 38 38 38 38 38 38
19 A. Nannini	40 8 8 8 3 22 22 36 36 7 7 7 7 7 10 8 8 8 8 8 8 8 8 8 8 8 8 8 8 8 20 20 20 20 20 20 38 21 21 21 21 21 21 21 21 21 21 21 21 21 21 21 21 21 21 21 21 21 21 21 21 21 21 21 21 21 21 21 21
3 J. Palmer	21 7 7 3 8 7 7 7 20 10 10 10 10 10 12 21 21 21 21 21 21 21 21 11 11 11 11 11 11 11 11 11 11 11 21 38 38 38 38 38 25 25 25 25 25 25 25 25 25 25 25 25 25 25 25 25 25 25 25 25 25 25 25 25 25 25 25 25 25
12 S. Nakajima	7 3 20 7 20 36 20 20 10 12 12 12 12 8 11 11 11 11 11 11 11 11 11 21 21 21 21 21 21 21 21 21 21 20 38 21 21 21 21 21 25 25 25 25 25 25 20 20 20 20 20 20 20 20 20 20 20 20 20 20 20 20 20 20 20 20 20 20 20
30 P. Alliot	3 20 3 20 36 20 10 10 12 8 8 8 8 8 21 25 25 25 25 25 25 25 25 25 25 25 25 20 20 20 20 21 25 25 25 21 21 23 23 23 23 23 23 25 25 20 20 20 20 20 20 20 20 20 20 20 20 20 20 20 20 20 20 20 20 20 20 20 20
40 G. Tarquini	36 36 36 12 36 8 10 12 12 8 21 21 21 21 11 38 38 38 38 38 38 38 38 38 38 20 25 25 25 23 38 23 23 23 23 23 23 23 23
20 J. Herbert	20 12 12 36 12 10 8 8 8 21 11 11 11 11 11 25 20 20 20 20 20 20 20 20 20 38 38 38 38 38 25
21 A. Caffi	12 10 10 10 10 12 12 21 11 11 25 25 25 25 38 23 23 23 23 23 23 23 23 23 23 23 23 23 23 23 23
7 M. Brundle	23 23 23 23 23 21 21 11 11 11 25 38 38 38 38 38 23 22 22 22 22 22 30 30 30 30 30 30 30 30
36 S. Johansson	10 21 21 21 21 23 11 25 25 38 30 30 30 30 23 20 30 30 30 30 30
23 P. Martini	25 25 25 25 25 25 23 38 38 30 23 23 23 23 20 22
38 C. Danner	38 38 38 38 11 11 11 25 23 23 20 20 20 20 22 30
10 E. Cheever	11 11 11 11 11 11 38 38 38 30 30 22 22 22 22 22 30
25 R. Arnoux	30 30 30 30 30 30 30 22 22
11 N. Piquet	16

FASTEST LAPS

Pos.	Car No./Driver/Team	Time
1	27 N. Mansell/Ferrari	1:20.420
2	2 A. Prost/McLaren	1:20.506
3	1 A. Senna/McLaren	1:20.585
4	4 M. Alboreto/Tyrrell	1:21.230
5	6 R. Patrese/Williams	1:21.383
6	26 O. Grouillard/Ligier	1:22.093
7	19 A. Nannini/Benetton	1:22.110
8	10 E. Cheever/Arrows	1:22.111
9	8 S. Modena/Brabham	1:22.233
10	40 G. Tarquini/AGS	1:22.318
11	7 M. Brundle/Brabham	1:22.344
12	11 N. Piquet/Lotus	1:22.560
13	30 P. Alliot/Larrousse	1:22.593
14	9 D. Warwick/Arrows	1:22.777
15	12 S. Nakajima/Lotus	1:22.907
16	28 G. Berger/Ferrari	1:22.981
17	5 T. Boutsen/Williams	1:22.991
18	20 J. Herbert/Benetton	1:23.095
19	36 S. Johansson/Onyx	1:23.416
20	38 C. Danner/Rial	1:23.524
21	23 P. Martini/Minardi	1:23.539
22	25 R. Arnoux/Ligier	1:23.867
23	21 A. Caffi/BMS Dallara	1:24.527
24	3 J. Palmer/Tyrrell	1:24.660
25	22 A de Cesaris/BMS Dallara	1:25.424
26	16 I. Capelli/March	1:46.744

CHAMPIONSHIP POINTS

	Drivers			Constructors	
1	Senna	27 pts	1	McLaren	47 pts
2	Prost	20 pts	2	Benetton	11 pts
3	Mansell	9 pts	3	Ferrari	9 pts
4	Nannini	8 pts	4	Williams	9 pts
5	Patrese	6 pts	5	Tyrrell	7 pts
6	Alboreto	6 pts	6	Brabham	5 pts
7	Gugelmin	4 pts	7	March	4 pts
	Modena	4 pts	8	Arrows	4 pts
9	Warwick	4 pts	9	Dallara	3 pts
10	Boutsen	3 pts	10	AGS	1 pt
	Herbert	3 pts			
	Caffi	3 pts			
13	Palmer	1 pt			
	Brundle	1 pt			
	Tarquini	1 pt			

Left: It's better than egg on your face.

Existing qualifying lap record: *Ayrton Senna, Lotus-Renault 98T, 1m 16.990s, 206.723 kph/128.452 mph in 1986*

Existing race lap record: *Alain Prost, McLaren-Honda MP4/4, 1m 18.608s, 202.468 kph/125.808 mph in 1988*

Existing distance record: *Alain Prost, McLaren-Honda MP4/4, 1hr 30m 15.737s at 196.898 kph/122.347 mph in 1988*

PAST WINNERS

Year	Driver	Nat.	Car	Circuit
1966	John Surtees	GB	3.0 Cooper T81 Maserati	Mexico City
1967	Jim Clark	GB	3.0 Lotus 49 Ford	Mexico City
1968	Graham Hill	GB	3.0 Lotus 49B Ford	Mexico City
1969	Denny Hulme	NZ	3.0 McLaren M7A Ford	Mexico City
1970	Jacky Ickx	B	3.0 Ferrari 312B	Mexico City
1986	Gerhard Berger	A	1.5 Benetton B186 BMW t/c	Mexico City
1987	Nigel Mansell	GB	1.5 Williams FW11B Honda t/c	Mexico City
1988	Alain Prost	F	1.5 McLaren MP4/4 Honda t/c	Mexico City

Phoenix

ICEBERG USA GRAND PRIX · 4 JUNE

A new US Grand Prix venue is always eagerly welcomed. The Grand Prix fraternity like the country, the people, know the importance of Grand Prix racing in the USA, yet there's always a little curiosity as to what the venue will be like. Long Beach's

Grand Prix racing headed one way from Mexico, but the Arizona truck stop brought no change to Ferrari fortunes.

track, down the street from the porn cinema, complete with built-in high jump, was one novelty. Then came Las Vegas and the 'Car

Park Grand Prix'. Detroit gradually got its act together, but just when everyone became used to it the venue was changed, then it was dropped altogether amid a 'good riddance' chorus from the natives who all preferred good ol' home-baked CART racing: chassis from Bicester, Huntingdon and Poole, engines from Northampton, and drivers from the world over!

F ISA's vice-president for promotions sought suitable replacement
venues, and from Phoenix, Laguna Seca and Road Atlanta,
eventually preferred the former.

Only Eddie Cheever knew Phoenix, Arizona; he was born there. All
he would say in Mexico was that it would be hot. Sure it was, but it was
a dry heat, less than 10 per cent humidity. There were few complaints
about that.

But then the track location was a concrete jungle, chucking that heat
up off the pavement. You longed for a little grass or something to walk
on. Staying downtown within yards of the circuit was fine, but more
expensive, and you never saw much more than concrete and tarmac.

Phoenix, in fact, impressed many people, but it wasn't the race track
area that pleased them. There were resort hotels, some of them
glorious white elephants charging 40 bucks a night and never likely to
make a profit, but offering luxury which would cost five times as much
in Monaco.

The Grand Prix venue itself wasn't too newsworthy. The good news
was that it was well organised. Here and there were small problems, no
doubt sorted out by Grand Prix 2, but overall it ran like clockwork.
Everyone could remember the delays associated with new Grand Prix
venues the world over, but at Phoenix there was none of those.

Unlike Detroit, there were permanent garages for the teams to work
in, and a permanent control tower. ESPN handled the TV coverage
(their biggest-ever outside broadcast), and the locals tried to make
Grand Prix racing as welcome as they could.

The race itself was a case of 'chuck the cards in the air, and see where they fall'. Nothing wrong with that, once in a while. Gives everyone a chance of glory. Cope with a slippery circuit, ridden with 90-degree corners, the heat, dust, some oil and you could be like Brundle and Caffi, fifth and sixth on the grid ahead of Berger; or like Alboreto, Warwick and Modena, ahead of eventual winner Prost in the warm-up.

Or finally, you could have been a delighted Prost, winning for the first time in the United States; Patrese, happy with his second place in eight days. Or Eddie Cheever, a dream result in your home Grand Prix, with a special bonus for American sponsors USF&G. What about Christian Danner charging home fourth with a broken exhaust, Johnny Herbert fifth without fourth gear, and Thierry Boutsen swopping sixth place with Gabriele Tarquini on the last lap as fuel ran low? Everyone had a tale to tell from Phoenix. Maybe not the nicest configuration or location, not even well-attended, but a race not to be discounted.

BRIGHT SPARKS

Clockwise from below: Alboreto contemplates two hours in 100 degrees. European technology, American architecture. Local boys made good: third for Cheever at home.

This was one of the longest Grands Prix in the season, the chequered flag coming out at the two-hour mark. Two hours of heat in the nineties shouldn't have been too much fun, yet there weren't too many complaints after the race. Maybe everyone who finished was glad to survive; there were so many who didn't.

As ever on such a circuit, there were many contacts with the concrete walls, resulting in various degrees of damage. Aguri Suzuki set the

Senna's run of wins came to an end in Phoenix but the man beat Jim Clark's record for pole positions.

standard early on when pre-qualifying got under way bang on time. Within the hour, he'd hit the wall four times.

Of his fellow, more successful pre-qualifiers, only one would start below seventh! Brundle was fifth on the grid, Caffi sixth and Modena seventh. Only Johansson was 20th, having got through the morning mad dash without second gear — and virtually every 90-degree corner in Phoenix was second gear. Stefan was even third on Saturday morning and heading for a point the next afternoon when the front suspension collapsed, worn away after Stefan had suffered a puncture.

But then Phoenix was full of hard-luck tales. Take Nannini. We'd heard nothing but sob stories the previous weekend when it was announced that the new car and engine wouldn't be ready for weeks; how the old Benetton was no longer being developed, how it was really suffering, uncompetitive, etc. Nannini was fifth in the first session, seventh in the second, sixth the next day and third on the grid.

But it all went wrong in the warm-up. He spun into the wall backwards, badly damaging his race car and hurting his neck and back. After a few laps of the race, he pulled out.

Teammate Herbert, however, never looked competitive in qualifying, even though he was high up the order in the free practice sessions. He didn't seem to be able to get the car to handle; yet when it came to the race, he stuck in there with best of them, finishing a lap down on the leaders, even without fourth gear and with a front brake that was grabbing.

You couldn't help but be happy for Eddie Cheever. Born in Phoenix, he had family and friends all around him throughout the weekend, although both he and teammate Derek Warwick tested the more solid part of the circuit to the detriment of their Arrows. Eddie qualified 17th, and simply stuck in there, usually to the back of Patrese's Williams. Only when the brake pedal went to the floor with five laps to go did Eddie finally ease up, deciding that discretion was the better part of valour. But third not only delighted his fellow Phoenicians, but also sponsors USF&G. It was a dream come true for all of them.

There was good and bad for McLaren. Senna claimed his 34th and record-breaking pole position but retired from the race. Prost, alongside his teammate, took up the reins and no-one ever came close. 'It's my first win in the USA so I'm very happy,' said Prost, 'and although Ayrton led the first part, I think the second part would have been very different even if he hadn't retired, because we were on different tyres and mine were just coming good.' Nine points to Alain, then, and the championship lead by two points. As well as Cheever opening his account, there was Danner too, soldiering around from 26th on the grid to pick up three points. As Prost said, 'The heat didn't really affect me, but it was difficult to concentrate.' Those who saw the chequered flag had concentrated for 75 laps, on one of the most difficult race tracks they were likely to encounter. They deserved their points but there were quite a few who deserved points which just eluded them.

RACE DEBRIEF

We first heard the misfire on lap 25 – incredulously. Was this really one of those perfect McLaren-Hondas showing a sign of failure? We'd already had one incredulous moment this weekend. Prost had damaged a McLaren against one of Phoenix's unforgiving walls. 'It's the first time that I've done that at McLaren,' said Alain of his damaged monocoque, as the locals from Hercules and ICI tried to repair it.

Apart from that, however, practice, qualifying and the first 27 laps of the race had gone pretty much according to the usual script. Senna was on pole again, although the occasional spin and the exclusion of some times as an added oil cooler exceeded dimensions upset the flow a little.

A new record of pole positions for Ayrton, then, and teammate Prost alongside in spite of his indiscretion, and the odd problem. These also included a sticking throttle which saw Prost back in seventh spot to Senna's fastest time in the warm-up.

And so to the race. Prost on Goodyear's harder B compound this weekend to Senna's Mexico mix, Cs on the left, Bs on the harder-worked right. The Cs, said Goodyear, would give more grip but would pick up more. The Bs would feel more stable and cool quicker on the straight, but wouldn't give as much grip. Hmm.

When Phoenix's lights turned green for the first time, Prost made a great start on the long, wide drag down to 90-degree right, turn one. But just as it looked as though he'd got the lead, Senna passed him in a flash. There was good reason. 'I was on the right of the track where there's a bad bump. I went to change up just as I went over it, got wheelspin and hit the rev limiter. The engine stopped and Senna went round me on the left.'

Status quo restored, as it were. In those opening laps, Senna eased out a lead over Prost, who in turn was little troubled by those behind. By lap six, Senna had a 3.3 second lead and 10 laps later it was only 0.9

seconds more. Then suddenly it jumped to eight seconds. Was Prost in trouble? 'I dropped back because of high oil and water temperatures. I was worried about them when I was running behind Ayrton, so I dropped back on purpose.'

Alain was optimistic that his tyre choice was right at this stage. And he soon brought down that gap from eight seconds back into the fives, even though they were now lapping backmarkers. Then, suddenly, there was a cackle instead of the Honda V10 bark. What was that? It was gone again on the next lap. Must have been mistaken, or they've ironed it out from the pits. The gap between the two McLarens actually went up.

Three laps later and there it was again: this time the gap had tumbled a second and a half. It came down again on the next two laps, and then Senna set fastest lap of the race so far. So . . . yet there it was again. Prost sets fastest lap, and the gap is down to 1.2 seconds – and Senna's in the pits.

The mechanics changed the black box and battery, he lost a lap and it seemed as though they'd sorted out the problem. But six laps later, he was back in again, this time for a change of plugs. When that didn't sort

Clockwise from right: new sponsor for Brabham but no finish. Still no more points for Mansell, none at all for Piquet. Herbert's resilience brought two points in Phoenix in the familiar, concrete and wire environment of American street racing.

it, Senna quit, the first time in 21 races with McLaren-Honda that he'd had a mechanical problem.

When Senna pitted on lap 34, Prost was left with a 41-second lead over – remarkably enough – none other than Alex Caffi. Nannini had withdrawn from second place early on and then into the frame came Nigel Mansell. Fourth on the grid, both he and teammate Berger had suffered a kind of motion sickness around the streets of Phoenix and he had also touched a wall in final qualifying.

Caffi had given him a hard time for the first few laps, but then he'd left the Italian to cope with compatriot Modena, while the second Brabham of Brundle was holding off Berger in the next two places further back.

But on lap seven, when Mansell was already 7.6 seconds behind Prost, Modena took third-placed Caffi and began to move up on the Ferrari. Only seven laps later did Mansell begin to shake off the Brabham, but he was making little impression on the McLarens ahead. Behind Modena, Caffi and Brundle, Berger was struggling now to contain the advances of Patrese, Capelli, Cheever and Johansson.

The March driver soon disappeared with a broken driveshaft, and the Onyx began to drop back with a puncture. But as Senna's misfire began to take hold, so third-placed Mansell was being caught by Caffi, Brundle had caught teammate Modena, and the Patrese/Cheever duo were beginning to close in on fifth-placed Berger.

But no sooner did that threaten than Mansell was in the pits for a new battery. But this failed to cure his alternator problem, and on lap 32 he pulled off to retire. Caffi was up to third. Brundle was fourth, now unchallenged by teammate Modena who had had a brake problem which caused a spin, and had wisely pitted.

Berger managed to pull away from the Patrese/Cheever duo and was able to pass Brundle who was suffering brake trouble like teammate Modena. When Senna quit on lap 34, Brundle lost two places to Patrese and Cheever, and looming in his mirrors was Palmer, after Johansson had pitted to replace his punctured tyre.

So on lap 37, half distance, the order was Prost, some 46 seconds ahead of Caffi, who in turn was 6.3 seconds and losing to Berger, closely pursued by Patrese and Cheever. Sixth-placed Brundle was falling into the grip of Palmer, while Piquet, Herbert, Danner, Tarquini, Johansson, de Cesaris, Senna (for the moment) and Boutsen were all lapped, the Belgian having earlier pitted with a puncture.

Berger was soon up to second place ahead of Caffi, who promptly pitted for fresh tyres and moved back to fifth, just ahead of the Brundle/Palmer battle. This soon went the way of the Tyrrell driver, the Brabham immediately retiring.

First and second were really no contest for a while. Cheever was too close to Patrese for the Williams driver to do anything about Berger's second-placed Ferrari just ahead, but then that began to suffer alternator problems which in turn were affecting the car's electronic gearchange mechanism. Steadily the duo closed, and on lap 51 the Austrian plummeted from second to fourth. He was even being caught by the recovered Caffi, once the Italian had shaken off Jonathan Palmer's challenge; but then Caffi was taken out by his own teammate, de Cesaris, who had already had a brush with an optimistic Derek Warwick earlier in the race. The sight of the two teammates colliding was something to behold, although one or two team managers must have thought 'There but for the grace of God go I.'

At two-thirds distance, even Cheever seemed to have briefly tired of his study of Patrese's Williams suspension and had allowed himself some breathing space. Prost was way out in front, Patrese second from Cheever, then Berger losing ground and Palmer. Danner, at one time overtaken by the recovered Johansson, was first of the unlapped, from

Herbert, de Cesaris and Tarquini, while two laps down was Boutsen.

The track was fairly quiet, and to become quieter on lap 62 when Berger quit just as Mansell had before him. It allowed the Patrese/Cheever battle to join again, though only for seven laps, because then Cheever's brake pedal went to the floor, and he settled for third place. At the same time Palmer disappeared, out of fuel, ironic because Ken Tyrrell didn't want the race shortened. De Cesaris also disappeared from what was then fifth place, while right at the back there was a twist as Boutsen caught and passed Tarquini's sixth-placed AGS, only for the Williams-Renault to lose fifth gear at the end, and Tarquini to get his place back on the last lap. But it wasn't over yet. The AGS ran out of fuel, and Boutsen, his car failing, took the final point. It was that kind of a race.

MILESTONES

- Senna claims 34th pole, beats Jim Clark's record
- Prost's 36th win, first in USA, damages McLaren monocoque for the first time too!
- The US's eighth Grand Prix location, no other country had had so many Grand Prix circuits
- Lotus's 400th Grand Prix
- Caffi's best-ever grid position: 6th

Left: perseverance brings rewards: Danner, last early on, scooped fourth, while Boutsen grabbed sixth on the last lap.
Below: Senna's stuttering Honda came as a shock.

Above: the Arizona sun encouraged Minardi's overheating.

FORMULA 1 WORLD CHAMPIONSHIP

ICEBERG USA GRAND PRIX

ENTRIES · PRACTICE · RESULTS

Pos	Driver/Nationality		No.	Car/Engine	P.Q. (sunny, hot)	Practice 1 (sunny, v. hot)	Practice 2 (sunny, v. hot)	Warm-up (pos) (sunny, hot)	Laps	Time/Retirement (sunny, v. hot)
1	A. Prost	F	2	McLaren MP4/5 Honda V10	–	1:31.620	**1:31.517**	1:35.696 (7)	75	2hr01m33.133
2	R. Patrese	I	6	Williams FW12C Renault V10	–	1:34.523	**1:32.795**	1:37.263 (21)	75	2hr02m12.829
3	E. Cheever	USA	10	Arrows A11 Judd V8	–	**1:33.214**	1:33.361	1:36.090 (12)	75	2hr02m16.343
4	C. Danner	D	38	Rial ARC02 Ford DFR V8	–	1:35.453	**1:33.848**	1:37.961 (23)	74	2hr02m13.863
5	J. Herbert	GB	20	Benetton B188 Ford DFR V8	–	1:35.377	**1:33.806**	1:37.053 (19)	74	2hr02m49.649
6	T. Boutsen	B	5	Williams FW12C Renault V10	–	1:36.227	**1:33.044**	1:36.984 (18)	74	2hr03m15.567
7	G. Tarquini	I	40	AGS JH23 Ford DFR V8	–	1:34.455	**1:33.790**	1:36.417 (14)	73	out of fuel
8	A. de Cesaris	I	22	Dallara BMS 189 Ford DFR V8	–	1:33.061	**1:32.649**	1:37.817 (22)	70	out of fuel
9	J. Palmer	GB	3	Tyrrell 018 Ford DFR V8	–	1:34.748	**1:33.741**	1:35.893 (10)	69	out of fuel
10	G. Berger	A	28	Ferrari 640 Ferrari V12	–	1:33.697	**1:32.364**	1:34.707 (3)	61	alternator
11	A. Caffi	I	21	Dallara BMS 189 Ford DFR V8	1:32.992	1:32.819	**1:32.160**	1:39.313 (26)	52	collision/de Cesaris
12	N. Piquet	BR	11	Lotus 101 Judd V8	–	**1:33.745**	1:33.804	1:36.713 (16)	52	accident damage
13	S. Johansson	S	36	Onyx ORE1 Ford DFR V8	1:33.768	1:34.637	**1:33.370**	1:36.005 (11)	50	front suspension
14	L. Sala	E	24	Minardi M189 Ford DFR V8	–	1:34.636	**1:33.724**	1:38.527 (24)	46	overheating
15	A. Senna	BR	1	McLaren MP4/5 Honda V10	–	**1:30.108**	1:30.710	1:33.949 (1)	44	misfire
16	M. Brundle	GB	7	Brabham BT58 Judd V8	1:32.293	1:32.750	**1:31.960**	1:35.736 (8)	43	brakes overheating
17	S. Modena	I	8	Brabham BT58 Judd V8	1:33.924	1:34.267	**1:32.286**	1:35.367 (6)	37	brakes overheating
18	N. Mansell	GB	27	Ferrari 640 Ferrari V12	–	**1:31.927**	1:33.383	1:34.590 (2)	31	alternator
19	P. Martini	I	23	Minardi M189 Ford DFR V8	–	1:34.794	**1:33.031**	1:36.650 (15)	26	overheating
20	S. Nakajima	J	12	Lotus 101 Judd V8	–	1:35.188	**1:33.782**	1:37.222 (20)	24	throttle cable bracket
21	I. Capelli	I	16	Leyton House CG891 Judd V8	–	1:36.135	**1:32.493**	1:38.560 (25)	22	driveshaft
22	M. Gugelmin	BR	15	Leyton House CG891 Judd V8	–	1:35.236	**1:33.324**	1:36.235 (13)	20	black flag
23	M. Alboreto	I	4	Tyrrell 018 Ford DFR V8	–	1:33.377	**1:32.491**	1:35.109 (4)	17	gearbox
24	A. Nannini	I	19	Benetton B188 Ford DFR V8	–	1:32.924	**1:31.799**	1:36.919 (17)	10	withdrew
25	D. Warwick	GB	9	Arrows A11 Judd V8	–	1:32.640	**1:32.492**	1:35.223 (5)	7	collision/de Cesaris
26	P. Alliot	F	30	Lola LC89 Lamborghini V12	–	1:34.721	**1:32.562**	1:35.762 (9)	3	spun/stalled
27	O. Grouillard	I	26	Ligier JS33 Ford DFR V8	–	1:35.124	**1:34.153**	DNQ		
28	R. Moreno	BR	31	Coloni C188B Ford DFR V8	–	2:10.795	**1:34.352**	DNQ		
29	R. Arnoux	F	25	Ligier JS33 Ford DFR V8	–	1:35.823	**1:34.798**	DNQ		
30	Y. Dalmas	F	29	Lola LC89 Lamborghini V12	–	1:35.771	**1:35.496**	DNQ		
–	P. Ghinzani	I	18	Osella FA1M Ford DFR V8	1:34.281	DNPQ	DNPQ			
–	P. Raphanel	F	32	Coloni C188B Ford DFR V8	1:35.1102	DNPQ	DNPQ			
–	G. Foitek	S	33	EuroBrun ER188B Judd V8	1:35.805	DNPQ	DNPQ			
–	N. Larini	I	17	Osella FA1M Ford DFR V8	1:36.470	DNPQ	DNPQ			
–	J. Winkelhock	D	41	AGS JH 23 Ford DFR V8	1:36.498	DNPQ	DNPQ			
–	V. Weidler	D	39	Rial ARC02 Ford DFR V8	1:36.583	DNPQ	DNPQ			
–	B. Schneider	D	34	Zakspeed ZK189 Yamaha V8	1:36.610	DNPQ	DNPQ			
–	A. Suzuki	J	35	Zakspeed ZK189 Yamaha V8	1:37.776	DNPQ	DNPQ			
–	B. Gachot	B	37	Onyx ORE1 Ford DFR V8	1:45.530	DNPQ	DNPQ			

Circuit Data: Circuit of Phoenix, length 2.36 miles/3.798 km, race distance 75 laps = 177 miles/284.8 km, race weather sunny and very hot.
Notes: New Grand Prix circuit no existing lap records. Leyton House President Akira Akagi buys March Formula 1 team out of March Group – now known as Leyton House Racing.

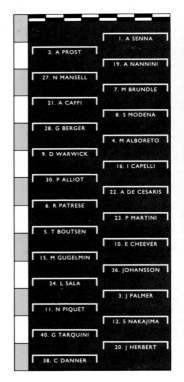

	1. A SENNA
2. A PROST	
	19. A NANNINI
27. N MANSELL	
	7. M BRUNDLE
21. A CAFFI	
	8. S MODENA
28. G BERGER	
	4. M ALBORETO
9. D WARWICK	
	16. I CAPELLI
30. P ALLIOT	
	22. A DE CESARIS
6. R PATRESE	
	23. P MARTINI
5. T BOUTSEN	
	10. E CHEEVER
15. M GUGELMIN	
	36. JOHANSSON
24. L SALA	
	3. J PALMER
11. N PIQUET	
	12. S NAKAJIMA
40. G TARQUINI	
	20. J HERBERT
38. C DANNER	

LAP CHART

Grid Order		Laps 1–75
1	A. Senna	1 1 1 1 1 1 1 1 1 1 1 1 1 1 1 1 1 1 1 1 1 1 1 1 1 1 1 1 1 1 1 1 1 1 2 2 2 2 2 2 2 2 2 2 2 2 2 2 2 2 2 2 2 2 2 2 2 2 2 2 2 2 2 2 2 2 2 2 2 2 2 2 2 2 2
2	A. Prost	2 2 2 2 2 2 2 2 2 2 2 2 2 2 2 2 2 2 2 2 2 2 2 2 2 2 2 2 2 2 2 2 2 2 2 21 21 21 21 21 28 28 28 28 28 28 28 28 6 6 6 6 6 6 6 6 6 6 6 6 6 6 6 6 6 6 6 6 6 6 6 6 6 6 6
19	A. Nannini	19 19 19 27 27 27 27 27 27 27 27 27 27 27 27 27 27 27 27 27 27 27 27 27 27 27 27 27 27 21 21 21 21 21 28 28 28 28 28 21 6 6 6 6 6 6 6 6 6 10 10 10 10 10 10 10 10 10 10 10 10 10 10 10 10 10 10 10 10 10 10 10 10 10 10
27	N. Mansell	27 27 27 21 21 21 8 8 8 8 8 8 8 8 8 8 8 8 8 8 8 21 21 21 7 7 7 7 7 7 6 6 6 6 6 6 10 10 10 10 10 10 10 10 10 10 10 10 28 28 28 28 28 28 28 28 28 3 3 3 3 3 3 38 38 38 38
7	M. Brundle	21 21 21 8 8 8 21 21 21 21 21 21 21 21 21 21 21 21 21 21 21 8 8 8 28 28 28 6 10 10 10 10 10 10 10 10 21 21 21 21 21 21 21 21 3 3 3 3 3 3 3 38 38 38 38 38 38 38 22 20 20 20 20
21	A. Caffi	8 8 8 7 7 7 7 7 7 7 7 7 7 7 7 7 7 7 7 7 7 7 7 28 6 6 6 10 7 7 7 7 7 7 3 3 3 3 3 3 3 3 38 38 38 38 38 38 38 38 38 38 20 20 20 22 22 22 22 22 22 40 5 5 5
8	S. Modena	7 7 7 28 28 28 28 28 28 28 28 28 28 28 28 28 28 28 28 28 28 28 6 10 10 10 10 36 3 3 3 3 3 3 7 1 1 1 38 38 38 38 38 38 20 20 20 20 20 22 22 22 20 20 20 20 40 5 40 40
28	G. Berger	28 28 28 19 19 19 19 19 19 19 4 4 4 4 4 4 6 6 16 16 16 6 6 6 6 10 36 36 36 3 1 1 1 1 1 1 1 1 1 1 1 20 20 20 36 36 38 20 20 22 22 22 22 22 22 22 40 40 40 40 40 40 40 5
4	M. Alboreto	22 22 22 22 22 22 4 4 4 4 6 6 6 6 6 16 6 6 6 10 10 10 10 10 10 36 3 3 3 11 20 20 20 20 20 20 20 38 38 36 20 20 20 20 11 11 40 40 40 40 40 40 40 40 5 5 5 5 5 5 5
9	D. Warwick	4 4 4 4 4 4 22 6 6 16 16 16 16 16 6 10 10 10 10 36 36 36 36 3 11 11 11 11 20 40 38 38 38 38 38 38 36 36 22 22 22 22 22 22 22 5 5 5 5 5 5 5 5 5 5
16	A. Capelli	9 9 9 9 9 9 16 16 10 10 10 10 10 10 36 36 36 36 23 23 23 23 11 3 11 20 20 20 40 38 40 40 40 40 36 36 22 22 11 11 11 11 11 11 11 40 40
30	P. Alliot	6 6 6 6 6 6 10 10 10 36 36 36 36 36 36 5 5 5 5 5 11 11 11 3 11 40 40 40 40 38 36 36 36 36 36 22 22 22 40 40 40 40 40 40 5 5
22	A. de Cesaris	16 16 16 16 16 16 36 36 36 5 5 5 5 5 23 23 23 23 23 11 11 2 3 40 40 20 38 38 38 22 22 22 22 22 22 40 40 40 5 5 5 5 5 5
6	R. Patrese	10 10 10 10 10 10 10 5 5 23 23 23 23 23 11 11 11 11 11 11 12 3 40 40 20 38 22 22 22 22 5 5 1 1 1 5 5 5 24 24 24
23	P. Martini	30 30 30 5 5 5 23 23 23 11 11 11 11 11 11 11 11 40 40 12 12 12 3 40 20 20 38 38 22 5 5 5 5 1 1 5 5 5 24 24 24 24 1
5	T. Boutsen	5 5 5 36 36 36 11 11 11 40 40 40 40 40 40 12 12 40 3 40 20 38 38 22 22 5 24 24 24 24 24 24 24 24 24 1 1 1 1
10	E. Cheever	23 23 36 23 23 23 40 40 40 12 12 12 12 12 12 3 3 3 40 40 20 38 22 22 5 5 24 8 8 8 8 8 8 8
15	M. Gugelmin	36 36 23 11 11 11 11 11 15 12 12 20 20 20 20 20 3 20 20 20 20 38 22 5 5 24 24 27 27 27
36	S. Johansson	11 11 11 11 11 15 40 40 40 12 20 20 3 3 3 3 20 20 38 38 38 38 38 22 5 24 24
24	L. Sala	15 15 15 40 15 15 15 20 3 3 38 38 38 38 38 38 24 24 24 24 22 24 24
3	J. Palmer	12 12 12 12 12 12 12 3 38 38 24 24 24 24 24 24 22 22 22 22 24
11	N. Piquet	40 40 40 20 20 20 20 38 24 24 22 22 22 22 22 22 15 15 15
12	S. Nakajima	20 20 20 3 3 3 24 22 22 15 15 15 15 15 15 15
40	G. Tarquini	3 3 3 38 38 38 22 15 15
20	J. Herbert	38 38 38 24 24 24 24
38	C. Danner	24 24 24

FASTEST LAPS

Pos.	Car No./Driver/Team		Time
1	1	A. Senna/McLaren	(N.R.) 1:33.969
2	2	A. Prost/McLaren	1:34.957
3	22	A. de Cesaris/BMS Dallara	1:35.155
4	27	N. Mansell/Ferrari	1:35.168
5	21	A. Caffi/BMS Dallara	1:35.291
6	3	J. Palmer/Tyrrell	1:35.349
7	36	S. Johansson/Onyx	1:35.435
8	5	T. Boutsen/Williams	1:35.526
9	10	E. Cheever/Arrows	1:35.650
10	11	N. Piquet/Lotus	1:35.837
11	28	G. Berger/Ferrari	1:35.930
12	6	R. Patrese/Williams	1:35.973
13	4	M. Alboreto/Tyrrell	1:36.140
14	8	S. Modena/Brabham	1:36.213
15	7	M. Brundle/Brabham	1:36.391
16	16	I. Capelli/Leyton House	1:36.722
17	38	C. Danner/Rial	1:36.901
18	19	A. Nannini/Benetton	1:37.134
19	40	G. Tarquini/AGS	1:37.216
20	20	J. Herbert/Benetton	1:37.287
21	12	S. Nakajima/Lotus	1:37.415
22	23	P. Martini/Minardi	1:38.135
23	9	D. Warwick/Arrows	1:38.223
24	30	P. Alliot/Larrousse	1:38.690
25	15	M. Gugelmin/Leyton House	1:38.762
26	24	L. Sala/Minardi	1:39.506

N.R. = New lap record

Left: Piquet extols the virtue of water-cooling hats to Berger.

CHAMPIONSHIP POINTS

Drivers		Constructors	
1 Prost	29 pts	1 McLaren	56 pts
2 Senna	27 pts	2 Williams	16 pts
3 Patrese	12 pts	3 Benetton	13 pts
4 Mansell	9 pts	4 Ferrari	9 pts
5 Nannini	8 pts	5 Arrows	8 pts
6 Alboreto	6 pts	6 Tyrrell	7 pts
7 Herbert	5 pts	7 Brabham	5 pts
8 Gugelmin	4 pts	8 Leyton House	4 pts
Modena	4 pts	9 Dallara	3 pts
Cheever	4 pts	Rial	3 pts
11 Boutsen	4 pts	11 AGS	1 pt
12 Warwick	4 pts		
13 Danner	3 pts		
Caffi	3 pts		
15 Tarquini	1 pt		
Brundle	1 pt		
Palmer	1 pt		

Left: another venue for Formula 1 in the USA.

PAST WINNERS

Year	Driver	Nat.	Car	Circuit
1982	John Watson	GB	3.0 McLaren MP4B Ford	Detroit
1983	Michele Alboreto	I	3.0 Tyrrell 011 Ford	Detroit
1984	Nelson Piquet	BR	1.5 Brabham BT53 BMW t/c	Detroit
1985	Keke Rosberg	SF	1.5 Williams FW10 Honda t/c	Detroit
1986	Ayrton Senna	BR	1.5 Lotus 98T Renault t/c	Detroit
1987	Ayrton Senna	BR	1.5 Lotus 99T Honda t/c	Detroit
1988	Ayrton Senna	BR	1.5 McLaren MP4/4 Honda t/c	Detroit

Montréal

There's a well-known motor racing saying that 'If my aunt had balls, she'd be my uncle.' It's motor racing's somewhat crude way of saying that there are no ifs in the sport.

That Ayrton Senna would have won the Canadian Grand Prix is in no doubt. That he didn't, pulling off just a few laps from home, brings home the above epigram in all its glory. That may not be good news to the undoubted realists at McLaren-Honda, but it should be underlined for the sake of those from Williams and Renault.

No doubt Renault and Williams cheered loudly when Senna pulled off the track. They had everything

Water, water everywhere – but it couldn't dampen Canada's bright sparks.

to gain. There were cheers elsewhere too, but with less moral reason, except for relief from the on-going run of McLaren wins.

Sadly, however, there were a number of people who had begun to lose sight of just what a good job McLaren were doing, and that the reason for their endless victories was perhaps not that they were doing so well, but that others were unable to touch them, from whatever causes.

Everyone, though, was delighted for the first victory of the Williams-Renault combination with the placid Thierry Boutsen. It is refreshing when another driver joins that select band of Grand Prix winners. Thierry became the ninth Grand Prix winner in the field. Of these, only six can be considered even potential winners these days, including the McLaren pair.

Honda congratulated Renault on their win, perhaps cognisant of the effort required to get so far. And perhaps they were also looking warily at the learning curve which Renault had climbed. Second and fourth on the grid, the two Williams-Renaults had run first and second in Brazil before early retirement. On the Imola power circuit, Patrese had been battling over third with Mansell when he retired; Boutsen started from the pits to claim fourth, but was disqualified. Only after his win, two and half months later, did he get his points back.

The Williams pair found engine reliability in Monaco, but you might not have known it. After running third, Boutsen had to pit on lap 18 when his rear wing began to break up; Patrese, starting late, suffered the same fate. But they finished, tenth and 15th respectively.

Then came Mexico: second for Patrese, 15s behind Senna. He was second again a week later in Phoenix after continued handling problems in practice which persisted in Boutsen's car, leaving him sixth.

And then came Montreal. It was a mixture of Mexico and Phoenix: a race of attrition aggravated by a wet track and a difficult tyre choice early in the race. McLaren-Honda eventually suffered their two rare retirements, one because of a chassis problem, one because of an engine; no shame there, happens to most teams. But then McLaren's record and standards are higher than most.

In the conditions, in the circumstances, Montreal was a true test of driving skills and reliability. Williams-Renault and the drivers were eagerly awaiting the coming European races, when they might consolidate the advantages of their successful American campaign.

BRIGHT SPARKS

There were a number of drivers who found themselves up, when they expected to be otherwise, and vice versa. The Canadian Grand Prix, so soon after the Phoenician lottery in the slippery streets of the Arizona desert town, was a similar race, except that it started even earlier.

Ron Dennis perhaps gave a mild slap on the wrist to one of his drivers in saying 'This [the changing track conditions] emphasises the importance of not always taking for granted that the circuit will always

improve and get faster.'

Ayrton Senna lost the opportunity to increase his record of consecutive poles on Saturday, when the increasing headwind and dirt blowing onto the track made it doubly slower. Only down in 23rd spot did you find the first Saturday improvement. Prost had pipped his own teammate to fastest time on the Friday, and he would become Montreal's 'off-line' poleman on Sunday.

But that was later. First pleasant surprise was Nicola Larini setting second quickest time in pre-qualifying; rumour had it that he'd asked Pirelli for better treatment. When given it, he obliged. The Osella was 15th in the first official session, and that's just where it stayed for the start.

By lap ten, Larini had grabbed all opportunities to hold sixth place, and after a dust-up with the Dallaras, held third place at half distance. But soon after Senna swept past, the electrics cut, and Larini was out.

Preceding Larini in pre-qualifying had been Stefano Modena, succeed-

ing where teammate Martin Brundle had failed for a succession of niggling reasons. Ninth in the morning free practice session, Modena qualified seventh that afternoon, and was fifth in both the next day's sessions. Seventh in the warm-up also looked promising, but a first-lap tangle with Martini (another one) put paid to any further hopes.

The Minardi driver had qualified in eleventh place. The point he won at Detroit on his return to the team in 1988 had served them well to avoid pre-qualification etc, but now mid-season was looming large. Thirteenth in the warm-up, there was plenty of time for heroics late in the race, but on the slippery surface of lap one, it all went wrong, and with Sala later crashing heavily, pre-qualifying was closing in on Minardi.

It looked as though it might have been for others too. Alliot was tenth in both the first two sessions, eighth on Saturday morning and in the warm-up. How quickly it can go wrong; two spins and an accident in the barrier during the pre-race warm-up laps were followed by a good race performance in the spare, until a spin on lap 17 was followed by a grassy

A succession of mechanical problems resulted in a DNQ for Dalmas, the writing was on the wall at Lola . . .

moment on lap 18 in which he overtook three cars, and then a terminal spin on lap 26. That was enough for one day, it seemed.

But points there were out there, if you waited for them. The Dallaras were eighth and ninth on the grid with de Cesaris consistently the better placed of the two drivers. He battled with teammate Caffi without the Phoenix consequences, but the less experienced driver had the greater number of incidents, and Andrea scored four World Championship and many plus points with his third place, while Caffi was a fine sixth.

Both Piquet and Arnoux opened their own and their team's World Championship accounts with points-winning results. Lotus, in particular, were delighted with their result, although one sage reminded them that Colin Chapman would have been horrified at

celebrations for a fourth gained by a three-times World Champion . . . Ligier, however, had probably avoided pre-qualifying with Arnoux's fifth place.

RACE DEBRIEF

Two weeks after the form book was all but torn up in Phoenix, the same thing happened again in Canada. Admittedly this was with the help of an afternoon of showers on the Ile de Notre Dame, and some uncharacteristic unreliability on the parts of both McLaren and Honda.

But perhaps we should have guessed. Williams, after all, won the first wet race of the weekend, the now traditional raft race across the former Olympic rowing basin. Arrows capsized early on, March, motor-

powered, didn't win and nor did McLaren-Honda in their Anglo-Japanese raft. Even Lotus improved on last year's performance.

Practice was strange too. Brundle didn't pre-qualify, thanks to a succession of problems. The track didn't get quicker on day two, as it normally does. The headwind blowing dust onto the circuit meant that Prost's time from Friday earned pole – although Senna was alongside. The so-called multi-cylinders followed: Patrese, Berger ahead of Mansell, and Boutsen. Then came pre-qualifiers Modena and Caffi ahead of teammate (remember Phoenix) de Cesaris, with Alliot and Martini both doing well. Warwick, Nannini and Palmer weren't so happy. Larini was in 15th while Gugelmin had the first March in 17th just ahead of Johansson. Piquet was 19th from Alboreto and Capelli. First driver to

Clockwise from top: Moreno suffered an unscheduled wheel stop. Martini collided with Modena on lap one. Kerb-crawling Berger. Warwick led four laps.

Clockwise from below: Piquet 3pts, Alboreto 0. Larini fourth! — for a while. Victory for Boutsen, confusion for Mansell. First points for Arnoux. Prost made best use of Montreal's unfashionable pole.

But it wasn't to last. Senna was charging through the field, overtaking the Englishman after just four laps in the lead, and pulling away. But Warwick would only last another two laps, his engine sidelining him on lap 41.

Now Senna led from Patrese from Boutsen and de Cesaris, the margins being equidistant at around 24s. But on lap 46, Patrese's lead over teammate Boutsen begain to disappear. From 23 seconds it had dropped to 10 seconds in ten laps, and just four laps later, the Williamses were nose to tail. Second place wasn't easy for Boutsen, but it was his on lap 63 and he was pulling away.

He was incredulous when he saw the leading McLaren pull off at the start of lap 67. 'When Senna stopped, I didn't know which position I was in,' said the Belgian. 'And then I was very very careful. I was petrified in case I didn't finish the race.'

Senna's McLaren had pumped out all its oil, the engine was broken. Williams scored a popular one-two, Patrese privately frustrated with his third second place in as many races. De Cesaris had erased all memories of two weeks previously, while Piquet and Arnoux enhanced their flagging reputations with points. Caffi scored the final one, after an incident-packed race, while Danner was the only other driver still running, once again with a broken exhaust. It was, however, another interesting and incident-packed race, and no one grudged Williams-Renault nor Boutsen their victory.

MILESTONES

- Thierry Boutsen and Williams-Renault's first Grand Prix victory
- Neither Prost or Senna in points, first time for McLaren-Honda in nine races

GRAND PRIX MOLSON DU CANADA

ENTRIES · PRACTICE · RESULTS

Pos	Driver/Nationality		No.	Car/Engine	P.Q. (overcast, cool)	Practice 1 (damp)	Practice 2 (warm, windy)	Warm-up (pos) (rain)	Laps (showery)	Time/Retirement
1	T. Boutsen	B	5	Williams FW12C Renault V10	–	1:22.311	1:24.004	1:45.457 (2)	69	2hr01m24.073
2	R. Patrese	I	6	Williams FW12C Renault V10	–	1:21.783	1:23.738	1:48.349 (11)	69	2hr01m54.080
3	A. de Cesaris	I	22	Dallara BMS 189 Ford DFR V8	–	1:23.050	1:24.444	1:48.732 (12)	69	2hr03m00.722
4	N. Piquet	BR	11	Lotus 101 Judd V8	–	1:24.029	1:25.825	1:47.940 (6)	69	2hr03m05.557
5	R. Arnoux	F	25	Ligier JS33 Ford DFR V8	–	1:24.558	1:25.394	1:50.228 (16)	68	2hr03m00.337
6	A. Caffi	I	21	Dallara BMS 189 Ford DFR V8	1:24.778	1:22.901	1:24.957	1:51.682 (20)	67	2hr01m46.163
7	A. Senna	BR	1	McLaren MP4/5 Honda V10	–	1:21.049	1:21.269	1:47.149 (4)	66	1hr55m51.463
8	C. Danner	D	38	Rial ARC02 Ford DFR V8	–	1:25.298	1:24.727	1:56.090 (23)	66	2hr02m07.535
9	R. Moreno	BR	31	Coloni C188B Ford DFR V8	–	1:24.470	1:25.037	1:47.869 (5)	57	gearbox
10	D. Warwick	GB	9	Arrows A11 Ford DFR V8	–	1:23.348	1:23.833	1:50.070 (15)	40	engine
11	J. Palmer	GB	3	Tyrrell 018 Ford DFR V8	–	1:23.665	1:23.876	1:48.112 (10)	35	accident
12	N. Larini	I	17	Osella FA1M Ford DFR V8	1:24.550	1:23.799	1:25.289	1:49.739 (14)	33	water in electrics
13	I. Capelli	I	16	Leyton House CG891 Judd V8	–	1:24.406	1:25.094	2:38.818 (26)	28	accident
14	P. Alliot	F	30	Lola LC89 Lamborghini V12	–	1:23.059	no time	1:47.988 (8)	26	spin
15	S. Johansson	S	36	Onyx ORE1 Ford DFR V8	1:24.764	1:23.979	1:24.918	1:51.835 (21)	13	black flag
16	L. Sala	E	24	Minardi M189 Ford DFR V8	–	1:24.786	1:25.570	1:52.409 (22)	11	accident
17	M. Gugelmin	BR	15	Leyton House CG891 Judd V8	–	1:23.863	1:24.734	1:50.656 (17)	11	electrics
18	G. Berger	A	28	Ferrari 640 Ferrari V12	–	1:21.946	1:22.305	2:07.088 (25)	6	gearbox management syst.
19	G. Tarquini	I	40	AGS JH23 Ford DFR V8	–	1:24.793	1:25.246	1:50.755 (18)	6	collision/Arnoux
20	E. Cheever	USA	10	Arrows A11 Ford DFR V8	–	1:23.828	1:24.693	1:51.562 (19)	3	electrics
21	A. Prost	F	1	McLaren MP4/5 Honda V10	–	1:20.973	1:22.269	1:47.052 (3)	2	suspension mounting
22	A. Nannini	I	19	Benetton B189 Ford DFR V8	–	1:23.542	1:24.279	1:48.004 (9)	–	disqualified
23	N. Mansell	GB	27	Ferrari 640 Ferrari V12	–	1:22.165	1:22.751	1:45.416 (1)	–	disqualified
24	M. Alboreto	I	4	Tyrrell 018 Ford DFR V8	–	1:24.296	1:25.412	2:03.208 (24)	–	alternator
25	S. Modena	I	8	Brabham BT58 Judd V8	1:23.398	1:22.612	1:23.599	1:47.975 (7)	–	collision/Martini
26	P. Martini	I	23	Minardi M189 Ford DFR V8	–	1:23.252	1:25.195	1:48.985 (13)	–	collision/Modena
27	S. Nakajima	J	12	Lotus 101 Judd V8	–	1:25.051	1:26.358	DNQ		
28	Y. Dalmas	F	29	Lola LC89 Lamborghini V12	–	1:25.317	1:25.161	DNQ		
29	J. Herbert	GB	20	Benetton B188 Ford DFR V8	–	1:25.335	1:25.282	DNQ		
30	O. Grouillard	I	26	Ligier JS33 Ford DFR V8	–	1:25.382	1:25.289	DNQ		
–	M. Brundle	GB	7	Brabham BT58 Judd V8	1:25.275	DNPQ	DNPQ			
–	B. Gachot	B	37	Onyx ORE1 Ford DFR V8	1:25.952	DNPQ	DNPQ			
–	G. Foitek	S	33	EuroBrun ER188B Judd V8	1:26.365	DNPQ	DNPQ			
–	P. Ghinzani	I	18	Osella FA1M Ford DFR V8	1:26.807	DNPQ	DNPQ			
–	B. Schneider	D	34	Zakspeed ZK189 Yamaha V8	1:27.073	DNPQ	DNPQ			
–	J. Winkelhock	D	41	AGS JH23 Ford DFR V8	1:28.545	DNPQ	DNPQ			
–	V. Weidler	D	39	Rial ARAC02 Ford DFR V8	1:31.455	DNPQ	DNPQ			
–	A. Suzuki	J	35	Zakspeed ZK189 Yamaha V8	1:53.327	DNPQ	DNPQ			
–	P. Raphanel	F	32	Coloni C188B Ford DFR V8	1:59.693	DNPQ	DNPQ			

Circuit Data: Circuit Giles Villeneuve, length 2.728 miles/4.390 km, race distance 69 laps = 188.232 miles/302.910 km, race weather wet and showery.
Note: Coloni now running Coloni C3 for both drivers.

Starting grid:
1. A SENNA / 2. A PROST
28. G BERGER / 6. R PATRESE
5. T BOUTSEN / 27. N MANSELL
21. A CAFFI / 8. S MODENA
30. P ALLIOT / 22. A DE CESARIS
9. D WARWICK / 23. P MARTINI
3. J PALMER / 19. A NANNINI
10. E CHEEVER / 17. N LARINI
36. S JOHANSSON / 15. M GUGELMIN
4. M ALBORETO / 11. N PIQUET
25. R ARNOUX / 16. I CAPELLI
24. L SALA / 38. C DANNER
31. R MORENO / 40. G TARQUINI

LAP CHART

Grid Order	1	2	3	4	5	6	7	8	9	10	11	12	13	14	15	16	17	18	19	20	21	22	23	24	25	26	27	28	29	30	31	32	33	34	35	36	37	38	39	40	41	42	43	44	45	46	47	48	49	50	51	52	53	54	55	56	57	58	59	60	61	62	63	64	65	66	67	68	69
2 A.Prost	2	1	1	6	6	6	6	6	6	6	6	6	6	6	6	6	6	6	6	6	6	6	6	6	6	6	6	6	6	6	6	6	6	6	6	6	6	6	6	9	9	9	1	1	1	1	1	1	1	1	1	1	1	1	1	1	1	1	1	1	1	1	1	1	1	1	5	5	5
1 A.Senna	1	6	6	5	28	28	5	5	5	5	1	1	1	1	1	1	1	1	1	1	9	9	9	9	9	9	9	9	9	9	9	9	9	9	9	9	1	1	1	1	9	9	6	6	6	6	6	6	6	6	6	6	6	6	6	6	6	6	6	6	6	6	6	6	6	5	5	5	
6 R.Patrese	6	5	5	28	5	5	1	1	1	30	30	30	9	9	9	9	9	9	9	22	17	17	17	17	17	17	17	17	1	1	1	1	6	6	6	6	6	6	5	5	5	5	5	5	5	5	5	5	5	5	5	5	5	5	5	6	6	6	22	22	22								
28 G.Berger	28	28	28	30	30	1	30	30	30	30	9	9	9	30	17	21	21	22	22	17	22	21	1	1	1	1	1	1	17	17	5	5	5	5	5	5	22	22	22	22	22	22	22	22	22	22	22	22	22	22	22	22	22	22	22	22	22	22	22	22	22	22	11	11	11				
27 N.Mansell	5	30	30	1	1	30	9	9	9	17	17	17	17	30	22	22	21	17	21	1	25	25	25	25	25	5	5	5	5	22	22	22	22	22	22	22	11	11	11	11	11	11	11	11	11	11	11	11	11	11	11	11	11	11	11	11	11	11	11	11	11	11	11	11	25	25			
5 T.Boutsen	22	17	3	17	9	9	17	17	17	25	25	25	25	21	21	17	17	21	1	1	25	30	30	30	38	5	25	25	25	25	25	25	25	25	25	25	25	25	25	25	25	25	25	25	25	25	25	25	25	25	25	25	25	25	25	25	25	25	25	25	25	21							
8 S.Modena	30	9	17	9	17	25	25	25	38	38	38	21	22	22	5	5	25	25	25	25	38	38	38	38	5	38	22	22	22	22	22	3	3	11	11	11	11	11	38	38	38	38	38	21	21	21	21	21	21	21	21	21	21	21	21	21	21	21	21	21	21								
21 A.Caffi	17	3	10	15	25	40	38	38	38	24	21	21	21	25	5	30	25	38	38	38	38	30	5	5	5	22	38	38	3	3	3	11	11	38	38	38	38	21	21	21	21	21	21	21	21	21	38	38	38	38	38	38	38	38	38	38	38	38	38	38	38								
22 A.de Cesaris	3	10	9	16	40	25	16	16	16	21	22	22	38	5	25	25	38	11	11	30	30	22	22	22	22	3	3	3	38	38	38	38	38	21	21	21	21	31	31	31	31	31	31	31	31	31	31	31	31	31	31	31	31	31															
30 P.Alliot	10	16	15	25	38	38	24	24	24	24	22	5	5	5	38	38	38	11	3	30	11	5	5	21	3	31	11	11	11	11	11	11	11	11	21	21	31	31	31	31	31																												
23 P.Martini	9	15	16	11	24	24	21	21	21	21	5	3	3	3	3	3	11	3	30	5	11	11	3	11	11	21	21	21	21	21	21	21	21	31	31																																		
9 D.Warwick	36	25	25	40	16	16	22	22	22	22	3	11	11	11	11	11	11	11	3	30	5	5	3	3	3	11	21	21	16	16	31	31	31	31	31																																	
19 A.Nannini	16	11	11	38	21	21	3	3	3	3	11	16	16	16	16	16	16	16	16	16	16	16	16	16	16	16	31	31																																							
3 J.Palmer	15	40	40	24	3	22	11	11	11	11	11	16	31	31	31	31	31	31	31	31	31	31	31	31																																											
17 N.Larini	25	31	38	31	22	3	15	15	15	15	15	36	36																																																					
10 E.Cheever	11	38	31	21	11	11	11	31	31	31	36	31																																																					
15 M.Gugelmin	40	24	24	3	15	15	36	36	36	31	36																																																					
36 S.Johansson	31	2	21	22	23	31	31																																																									
11 N.Piquet	38	21	22	36	36	36																																																								
4 M.Alboreto	24	22	36																																																										
16 I.Capelli	21	36																																																										
25 R.Arnoux																																																												
38 C.Danner																																																												
24 L.Sala																																																												
40 G.Tarquini																																																												
31 R.Moreno																																																												

FASTEST LAPS

Pos.	Car No./Driver/Team		Time
1	3	J.Palmer/Tyrrell	1:31.925
2	1	A.Senna/McLaren	1:32.143
3	11	N.Piquet/Lotus	1:32.422
4	22	A.de Cesaris/BMS Dallara	1:32.481
5	16	I.Capelli/Leyton House	1:32.742
6	21	A.Caffi/BMS Dallara	1:33.167
7	5	T.Boutsen/Williams	1:33.790
8	15	M.Gugelmin/Leyton House	1:34.231
9	24	L.Sala/Minardi	1:34.509
10	6	R.Patrese/Williams	1:35.251
11	36	S.Johansson/Onyx	1:35.333
12	31	R.Moreno/Coloni	1:35.369
13	17	N.Larini/Osella	1:35.726
14	38	C.Danner/Rial	1:35.970
15	9	D.Warwick/Arrows	1:36.443
16	30	P.Alliot/Larrousse	1:36.687
17	25	R.Arnoux/Ligier	1:37.131
18	28	G.Berger/Ferrari	1:37.916
19	40	G.Tarquini/AGS	1:38.284
20	10	E.Cheever/Arrows	1:38.631
21	2	A.Prost/McLaren	1:41.751

CHAMPIONSHIP POINTS

Drivers			Drivers/Constructors		
1	A.Prost	29pts	18	R.Arnoux	2pts
2	A.Senna	27pts		J.Palmer	2pts
3	R.Patrese	18pts	20	M.Brundle	1pt
4	T.Boutsen	10pts			
5	N.Mansell	9pts	1	McLaren	56pts
6	A.Nannini	8pts	2	Williams	28pts
7	M.Alboreto	6pts	3	Benetton	13pts
8	J.Herbert	5pts	4	Ferrari	9pts
	D.Warwick	5pts		Arrows	9pts
10	A.de Cesaris	4pts	6	BMS Dallara	8pts
	M.Gugelmin	4pts		Tyrrell	8pts
	E.Cheever	4pts	8	Brabham	5pts
	S.Modena	4pts	9	Leyton House	4pts
14	A.Caffi	4pts	10	Rial	3pts
15	C.Danner	3pts		Lotus	3pts
	N.Piquet	3pts	12	AGS	2pts
17	G.Tarquini	2pts		Ligier	2pts

Existing qualifying lap record: Ayrton Senna, McLaren-Honda MP4/4, 1m 21.681s, at 193.484 kph/120.225 mph in 1988

Existing race lap record: Ayrton Senna, McLaren-Honda MP4/4, 1m 24.973s, 185.988 kph/115.568 mph in 1988

Existing distance record: Ayrton Senna, McLaren-Honda MP4/4, 69 laps in 1 hr 39m 46.618s at 182.152 kph/113.184 mph in 1988

PAST WINNERS

Year	Driver	Nat.	Car	Circuit
1979	Alan Jones	AUS	3.0 Williams FW07 Ford	Ile Notre-Dame
1980	Alan Jones	AUS	3.0 Williams FW07B Ford	Ile Notre-Dame
1981	Jacques Lafitte	F	3.0 Ligier JS17 Matra	Ile Notre-Dame
1982	Nelson Piquet	BR	1.5 Brabham BT50 BMW t/c	Ile Notre-Dame
1983	René Arnoux	F	1.5 Ferrari 126C2/B t/c	Ile Notre-Dame
1984	Nelson Piquet	BR	1.5 Brabham BT53 BMW t/c	Ile Notre-Dame
1985	Michele Alboreto	I	1.5 Ferrari 156/85 t/c	Ile Notre-Dame
1986	Nigel Mansell	GB	1.5 Williams FW11 Honda t/c	Ile Notre-Dame
1988	Ayrton Senna	BR	1.5 McLaren MP4/4 Honda t/c	Ile Notre-Dame

Paul Ricard

RHÔNE-POULENC GRAND PRIX DE FRANCE · 9 JUILLET

Ron Dennis said it: 'Too many people are getting too close. We will have to try harder at Silverstone.' No doubt after the race, he had reason to re-evaluate. Prost had won, extending his championship lead to 11 points. Senna had become McLaren-Honda's fourth retirement from the last six starts. Ferrari had come close, the new Benetton-Ford shone on its debut and Williams-Renault scored again, although not without problems.

Paul Ricard, famous for his spirits also lends his name to this colourful circuit.

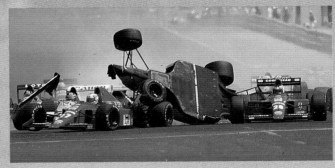

There were signs that the McLaren domination was being threatened, even if Alain Prost did delight in not only taking pole but winning at home, on the weekend that he announced that he would be leaving the McLaren team at the end of the year.

'I am happy for the team,' he stated, 'because it proves to them that I am still highly motivated, even though I am leaving at the end of the season.'

But while Renault ran its Evolution 2 engine, Benetton ran its new Ford second-generation V8 engine, and Ferrari showed reliability and revitalised handling, McLaren also had a card up its sleeve.

The team's transverse gearbox had been tested the week before, and although it had given satisfaction at Silverstone where Prost had set fastest time, McLaren had decided that they would run it a week later, where they were close to base in case anything went wrong. The team's MP4/5s had been designed in this configuration . . .

Elsewhere, a wind of change was blowing through the paddock. Murmurs of dissatisfaction had been heard for several weeks.

At Silverstone, for instance, Lola had tested four new drivers, completely ignoring both their existing duo during the test.

The key to the situation seemed to be Emanuele Pirro, a key member

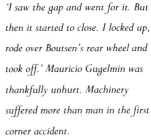

'I saw the gap and went for it. But then it started to close. I locked up, rode over Boutsen's rear wheel and took off.' Mauricio Gugelmin was thankfully unhurt. Machinery suffered more than man in the first corner accident.

of the McLaren team due to his endless testing in Japan. Now he was being offered seats elsewhere. He tested and was offered the Lola, and then took the Benetton seat vacated by Johnny Herbert at the last minute. McLaren had lost their test driver. The Englishman was standing down to recover fully from his injuries sustained nearly a year before.

Larrousse had sought to replace the unlucky Dalmas, and second choice was Eric Bernard, already committed to DAMS in F3000 but able to do this race. Camel support for the increasingly sponsored Tyrrells saw Marlboro-supported Michele Alboreto withdraw, his seat in France being taken by F3000 championship leader Jean Alesi. The Frenchman's

F3000 teammate, Martin Donnelly, was also busy after Derek Warwick had crashed a kart in Jersey and severely bruised himself.

These changes, together with Lotus trying their Tickford-headed Judd engine for the first time, made for a new-look Formula One grid. The remarkable thing was that they all seemed so competitive. It may have been Ricard's notorious surface, but many previously unfancied combinations had their moment of glory in France.

Yet the championship positions speak for themselves. Onyx scored their first points thanks to Johansson, Alesi instantly shone with fourth place, and Grouillard opened his account with sixth place. Fourteen teams and 23 drivers had scored World Championship points even before half distance. This was a record season, indeed, and McLaren weren't winning all the points.

BRIGHT SPARKS

There seemed to be an underlying trend running through the French Grand Prix of drivers either using the same car or using someone else's in which to perform.

The former was the case in Onyx's remarkable one-two in pre-qualifying. Johansson had spun out on the circuit, and then Gachot had an overheating wheel bearing, so they both took their turns in the spare car. While Johansson set his time, good enough for second, Gachot was pacing up and down, spiritually beating his teammate's time. Sure enough, both Onyxes got through pre-qualifying, and they qualified admirably in 11th (Gachot) and 13th (Johansson) places too.

Within a few laps they were running tenth and eleventh, closing on the Tyrrells and briefly battling with the delayed Ferraris. Relatively early tyre stops dropped them down the order, and then Gachot had to have a battery replaced soon after he'd overtaken a superbly on-form Bernard for sixth. But Johansson followed him through and overtook Grouillard to claim a great fifth place and Onyx's first-ever World Championship points.

The Tyrrell pair also shared a car in first qualifying after Palmer's had caught fire out on the track in the morning. Alesi was a remarkable tenth in that session, his uncomfortable teammate two places further back.

When the track was quicker next day, however, it was Palmer who improved to start ninth, while Alesi never found a hole in the traffic and dropped to 16th. Sixth in the warm-up, Palmer led his teammate early on. But damage to his undertray in the first-lap accident resulted in poor handling and two extra tyre stops, slowing him until Alesi took the initiative after 19 laps. From then on Alesi never looked back. 'I wasn't all that keen to pit for new tyres,' he said, getting out of the car in remarkably good shape after 80 laps in 90-degree heat.

Clockwise from left: Frenchmen have eyes for none but Prost at home. Palmer finished tenth, Gachot eleventh, but Alesi's Grand Prix debut reaped a superb fourth. Johansson's fifth suggested pre-qualifying relief for Onyx – but only for a week.

Lola Lamborghini debutant Eric Bernard.

Warwick in Arrows

- Jean Alesi scores World Championship points in debut Grand Prix, replacing Alboreto at Tyrrell
- Eric Bernard makes Grand Prix debut replacing Yannick Dalmas in Lola-Lamborghini
- Emanuele Pirro's Grand Prix debut replacing Herbert at Benetton.
- Bertrand Gachot makes Grand Prix debut
- Grouillard scores first World Championship points
- Onyx scores first World Championship points, 14th team to score points in 1989

FIA FORMULA 1 WORLD CHAMPIONSHIP

RHÔNE-POULENC GRAND PRIX DE FRANCE

ENTRIES · PRACTICE · RESULTS

Pos	Driver/Nationality		No.	Car/Engine	P.Q. (overcast, cool)	Practice I (warm, sunny)	Practice 2 (hot, sunny)	Warm-up (pos) (sunny)	Laps (hot, sunny)	Time/Retirement
I	A. Prost	F	2	McLaren MP4/5 Honda V10	–	1:08.285	**1:07.203**	1:10.400 (1)	80	1hr38m39.411
2	N. Mansell	GB	27	Ferrari 640 Ferrari V12	–	1:09.030	**1:07.455**	1:10.894 (2)	80	1hr39m13.428
3	R. Patrese	I	6	Williams FW12C Renault V10	–	1:09.326	**1:08.993**	6:32.292 (26)	80	1hr39m36.332
4	J. Alesi	F	4	Tyrrell 018 Ford DFR V8	–	1:09.668	**1:09.909**	1:12.862 (17)	80	1hr39m42.643
5	S. Johansson	S	36	Onyx ORE1 Ford DFR V8	1:09.668	1:10.600	**1:09.299**	1:12.297 (12)	79	1hr38m44.650
6	O. Grouillard	F	26	Ligier JS33 Ford DFR V8	–	1:10.410	**1:09.717**	1:12.830 (16)	79	1hr39m04.027
7	E. Cheever	USA	10	Arrows A11 Ford DFR V8	–	**1:10.372**	time d/a	1:12.670 (15)	79	1hr39m41.525
8	N. Piquet	BR	11	Lotus 010 Judd V8	–	1:10.473	**1:10.135**	1:12.262 (11)	78	1hr38m36.963
9	E. Pirro	I	20	Benetton B188 Ford DFR V8	–	1:11.566	**1:10.292**	1:13.117 (21)	78	1hr38m37.905
10	J. Palmer	GB	3	Tyrrell 018 Ford DFR V8	–	1:10.2328	**1:09.026**	1:11.857 (6)	78	1hr39m20.983
11	E. Bernard	F	29	Lola LC89 Lamborghini V12	–	1:25.401	**1:09.596**	1:121.556 (14)	77	classified – engine
12	M. Donnelly	IRL	9	Arrows A11 Ford DFR V8	–	1:11.223	**1:09.524**	1:13.330 (22)	77	1hr39m16.217
13	B. Gachot	B	37	Onyx ORE1 Ford DFR V8	1:09.617	1:10.564	**1:09.122**	1:11.921 (8)	76	1hr39m32.114
14	M. Gugelmin	BR	15	Leyton House CG891 Judd V8	–	1:10.122	**1:09.036**	1:12.175 (10)	71	1hr39m31.717 (N/C)
15	S. Modena	I	8	Brabham BT58 Judd V8	1:09.917	1:10.910	**1:10.254**	1:14.131 (25)	67	engine
16	T. Boutsen	B	5	Williams FW12C Honda V10	–	1:08.299	**1:08.211**	1:11.883 (7)	50	gearbox
17	S. Nakajima	J	12	Lotus 101 Judd V8	–	1:12.125	**1:10.119**	1:13.090 (20)	49	engine
18	I. Capelli	I	16	Leyton House CG891 Judd V8	–	1:09.569	**1:09.283**	1:11.747 (5)	43	engine
19	A. Nannini	I	19	Benetton B1888 Ford DFR V8	–	1:09.615	**1:08.137**	1:11.966 (9)	40	rear suspension
20	P. Martini	I	23	Minardi M189 Ford DFR V8	–	1:10.640	**1:10.267**	1:12.895 (19)	31	overheating
21	P. Alliot	F	30	Lola LC89 Lamborghini V12	–	1:09.478	**1:08.561**	1:12.405 (13)	30	engine
22	G. Tarquini	I	40	AGS JH23 Ford DFR V8	–	1:11.136	**1:10.216**	1:13.701 (23)	30	water leak/engine
23	G. Berger	A	28	Ferrari 640 Ferrari V12	–	1:09.011	**1:08.233**	1:11.350 (4)	29	gearbox management
24	A. Caffi	I	21	Dallara BMS 189 Ford DFR V8	1:09.726	1:11.409	**1:10.468**	1:13.986 (24)	27	chassis/clutch
25	R. Arnoux	F	25	Ligier JS33 Ford DFR V8	–	1:10.725	**1:10.077**	1:12.866 (18)	14	gearbox
26	A. Senna	BR	1	McLaren MP4/5 Honda V10	–	1:07.920	**1:07.228**	1:10.951 (3)	–	differential
27	A. de Cesaris	I	22	Dallara BMS 189 Ford DFR V8	–	1:12.078	**1:10.591**	DNQ		
28	L. Sala	E	24	Minardi M189 Ford DFR V8	–	1:11.539	**1:11.079**	DNQ		
29	C. Danner	D	38	Rial ARC02 Ford DFR V8	–	1:12.569	**1:11.178**	DNQ		
30	R. Moreno	BR	31	Coloni C3 Ford DFR V8	–	1:14.746	**1:11.372**	DNQ		
–	N. Larini	I	17	Osella FA1M Ford DFR V8	1:09.989	DNPQ	DNPQ			
–	M. Brundle	GB	7	Brabham BT58 Judd V8	1:10.181	DNPQ	DNPQ			
–	V. Weidler	D	39	Rial ARC02 Ford DFR V8	1:11.059	DNPQ	DNPQ			
–	B. Schneider	D	34	Zakspeed ZK189 Yamaha V8	1:11.098	DNPQ	DNPQ			
–	P. Ghinzani	I	18	Osella FA1M Ford DFR V8	1:11.528	DNPQ	DNPQ			
–	P. Raphanel	F	32	Coloni C3 Ford DFR V8	1:11.953	DNPQ	DNPQ			
–	A. Suzuki	J	35	Zakspeed ZK189 Yamaha V8	1:12.031	DNPQ	DNPQ			
–	G. Foitek	S	33	EuroBrun ER188B Judd V8	1:12.179	DNPQ	DNPQ			
–	J. Winkelhock	D	41	AGS JH23 Ford DFR V8	1:13.173	DNPQ	DNPQ			

Circuit Data: Circuit Paul Ricard, length 2.369 miles/3.813 km, race distance 80 laps = 189.51 miles/305 km, race weather dry, hot and sunny.
Notes: Martin Donnelly (GB) replaced Derek Warwick in the Arrows-Ford A11 No. 9 for this race only. Jean Alesi, replaced Michele Alboreto in Tyrrell No. 4. Eric Bernard (F) replaces Yannick Dalmas in Lola No. 29. Emanuele Pirro (I) replaces Johnny Herbert in Benetton No. 20, Nannini now driving Benetton B189 with Ford V8 HB engine rather than B188 with Ford V8 DFR engine.

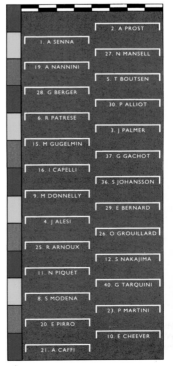

Starting grid:
1. A SENNA / 2. A PROST
19. A NANNINI / 27. N MANSELL
28. G BERGER / 5. T BOUTSEN
6. R PATRESE / 30. P ALLIOT
15. M GUGELMIN / 3. J PALMER
16. I CAPELLI / 37. G GACHOT
9. M DONNELLY / 36. S JOHANSSON
4. J ALESI / 29. E BERNARD
25. R ARNOUX / 26. O GROUILLARD
11. N PIQUET / 12. S NAKAJIMA
8. S MODENA / 40. G TARQUINI
20. E PIRRO / 23. P MARTINI
21. A CAFFI / 10. E CHEEVER

LAP CHART

Grid Order	Laps 1–80
2 A. Prost	2 2 2 2 2 2 2 2 2 2 2 2 2 2 2 2 2 2 2 2 2 2 2 2 2 2 2 2 2 2 2 2 2 2 2 2 2 2 2 2 2 2 2 2 2 2 2 2 2 2 2 2 2 2 2 2 2 2 2 2 2 2 2 2 2 2 2 2 2 2 2 2 2 2 2 2 2 2 2 2
1 A. Senna	28 28 28 28 28 28 28 28 28 28 19 19 19 19 19 19 19 19 19 19 5 5 5 5 5 5 5 5 19 19 19 19 19 19 19 16 16 4 4 4 6 6 6 6 6 6 6 6 27 27 27 27 27 27 27 27 27 27 27 27 27 27 27 27 27 27 27 27 27 27 27 27 27 27 27 27 27 27 27 27
27 N. Mansell	19 19 19 19 19 19 19 19 19 19 5 5 5 5 5 5 5 5 5 5 16 16 16 16 16 9 19 16 16 16 16 16 16 16 16 4 4 6 6 6 6 4 27 27 27 27 27 27 27 27 27 27 27 27 6 6 6 6 6 6 6 6 6 6 6 6 6 6 6 6 6 6 6 6 6 6 6 6 6 6
19 A. Nannini	5 5 5 5 5 5 5 5 5 5 28 28 28 16 16 16 16 16 16 16 19 6 19 19 19 6 16 16 4 4 4 4 4 4 4 6 6 27 27 27 27 27 27 4 4 4 4 4 4 4 4 4 4 4 4 4 4 4 4 4 4 4 4 4 4 4 4 4 4 4 4 4 4 4 4 4 4 4 4 4
5 T. Boutsen	30 30 30 30 16 16 16 16 16 16 16 16 16 28 6 6 6 6 6 6 6 19 6 6 6 16 4 4 5 5 5 5 5 5 5 5 52 27 5 5 5 5 5 29 26 36 36 36 36 36 36 36 36 36 36 36 36 36 36 36 36 36 36 36 36 36 36 36 36 36 36 36 36 36 36 36 36 36 36 36
28 G. Berger	6 6 6 16 30 30 30 30 30 30 30 30 30 30 30 30 30 30 30 30 28 28 4 30 3 3 3 3 3 6 6 6 6 27 5 5 37 37 29 29 29 26 36 26 26 26 26 26 26 26 26 26 26 26 26 26 26 26 26 26 26 26 26 26 26 26 26 26 26 26 26 26 26 26 26 26 26 26 26 26
30 P. Alliot	16 16 16 6 6 6 6 6 6 6 6 6 6 3 3 4 4 4 4 4 4 28 30 4 30 3 6 6 6 6 27 27 27 27 27 29 37 37 29 29 26 26 36 36 29 29 29 29 29 29 29 29 29 29 29 29 29 29 29 29 29 29 29 29 29 29 29 29 29 29 29 29 29 10 10
6 R. Patrese	3 3 3 3 3 3 3 3 3 3 3 3 3 4 4 3 3 28 28 28 28 4 4 30 3 36 27 27 27 27 3 29 29 29 37 29 26 26 26 36 36 36 5 1 1 11 11 11 11 11 11 11 11 11 11 10 10 10 10 10 10 10 10 10 10 10 10 10 10 10 10 10 10 10 10 10 11
3 J. Palmer	37 4 4 4 4 4 4 4 4 4 4 4 4 37 37 27 27 27 28 3 3 3 3 3 28 6 36 29 29 29 29 29 37 37 37 26 26 36 36 36 37 12 11 10 10 10 10 10 10 10 10 10 10 10 11 20 20 20 20 20 20 20 20 20 20 20 20 20 20 20 20 20 20 20 20
15 M. Gugelmin	4 37 37 37 37 37 37 37 37 37 37 37 27 27 27 28 28 37 37 37 37 37 37 27 29 12 12 12 37 37 26 26 26 26 36 36 12 12 12 12 11 11 11 11 11 10 20 20 20 20 20 20 20 20 11 11 11 11 11 11 11 11 11 11 11 11 11 11 11 11 11 11 11 11 11 3
37 B. Gachot	36 36 36 36 36 36 36 36 36 36 36 27 36 28 37 37 37 26 36 36 36 36 36 26 12 37 37 26 26 36 36 36 12 12 12 11 11 11 11 11 10 10 20 8 8 8 8 8 8 8 8 8 8 3 3 3 3 3 3 3 3 3 3 3 3 3 3 3 3 3 3 3 3 3
16 I. Capelli	26 26 26 26 26 26 26 26 26 26 27 36 28 36 36 36 36 36 26 26 26 26 27 27 29 26 26 26 36 12 12 12 12 11 11 11 11 10 10 10 20 20 8 3 3 3 3 3 3 3 3 3 8 8 8 8 8 8 8 8 9 9 9 9 9 9 9 9 9
36 S. Johansson	25 25 25 25 25 25 25 27 27 27 26 26 26 26 26 26 26 29 29 29 27 26 26 12 37 36 36 36 12 12 3 3 10 11 10 10 10 20 20 20 20 8 8 3 9 9 9 9 9 9 9 9 9 9 9 9 9 9 9 9 9 9 37 37 37 37 37 37 37 37
9 D. Warwick	8 8 8 8 29 29 29 27 25 25 25 29 29 29 29 29 29 29 12 12 12 12 29 29 29 37 8 10 10 10 10 10 10 11 10 8 20 20 8 8 8 3 3 9 37 37 37 37 37 37 37 37 37 37 37 37 37 37 15 15 15 15
29 E. Bernard	29 29 29 29 9 8 27 29 29 29 25 12 12 12 12 12 12 12 27 27 27 27 12 12 12 8 10 9 9 9 9 11 11 8 8 20 8 9 9 9 3 3 9 37 15 15 15 15 15 15 15 15 15 15 15 15 15 15 15 15 15 15
4 J. Alesi	12 12 12 12 27 8 8 12 12 12 12 8 8 8 8 8 8 8 8 8 8 8 10 9 8 20 20 20 11 8 8 3 20 9 9 9 3 3 3 9 37 37 15
26 O. Grouillard	40 40 40 40 27 12 12 8 8 8 8 40 40 40 40 40 40 40 40 40 40 9 20 20 11 11 11 8 9 20 20 3 3 3 15 15 15 15 15
25 R. Arnoux	10 10 10 27 40 40 40 40 40 40 40 40 10 10 10 10 10 10 10 10 10 10 10 20 11 11 8 8 20 9 9 15 15
12 S. Nakajima	11 11 27 10 10 10 10 10 10 10 10 10 11 11 11 11 11 11 11 11 11 11 11 11 9 40 23 15 15 15 15 15 15 15 15 15
11 N. Piquet	23 27 11 11 11 11 11 11 11 11 11 11 23 23 23 23 23 23 23 23 23 23 9 9 11 11 15
40 G. Tarquini	27 23 23 23 23 23 23 23 23 23 23 9 9 9 9 9 9 9 9 9 9 20 20 20 23
8 S. Modena	20 20 20 20 20 20 20 9 9 9 20 20 20 20 20 20 20 20 20 20 23 23 15
23 P. Martini	21 21 21 21 9 9 9 9 20 20 20 20 25 21 21 21 21 21 21 21 21 21 15 15
20 E. Pirro	15 9 9 9 21 21 21 21 21 21 21 21 15 15 15 15 15 15 15 15 15 15
10 E. Cheever	9 15 15 15 15 15 15 15 15 15 15 15
21 A. Caffi	

FASTEST LAPS

Pos.	Car No./Driver/Team		Time
1	15	M. Gugelmin/Leyton House	1:12.090
2	19	A. Nannini/Benetton	1:12.406
3	2	A. Prost/McLaren	1:12.500
4	27	N. Mansell/Ferrari	1:12.542
5	11	N. Piquet/Lotus	1:12.723
6	16	I. Capelli/Leyton House	1:12.737
7	5	T. Boutsen/Williams	1:12.755
8	28	G. Berger/Ferrari	1:12.937
9	4	J. Alesi/Tyrrell	1:12.964
10	6	R. Patrese/Williams	1:12.977
11	29	E. Bernard/Larrousse	1:12.144
12	10	E. Cheever/Arrows	1:13.171
13	36	S. Johansson/Onyx	1:13.175
14	3	J. Palmer/Tyrrell	1:13.262
15	37	B. Gachot/Onyx	1:13.358
16	26	O. Grouillard/Ligier	1:13.399
17	12	S. Nakajima/Lotus	1:13.657
18	20	E. Pirro/Benetton	1:13.712
19	30	P. Alliott/Larrousse	1:13.719
20	8	S. Modena/Brabham	1:14.137
21	9	M. Donnelly/Arrows	1:14.538
22	23	P. Martini/Minardi	1:14.631
23	21	A. Caffi/BMS Dallara	1:14.789
24	25	R. Arnoux/Ligier	1:14.956
25	40	G. Tarquini	1:15.437

CHAMPIONSHIP POINTS

	Drivers				Drivers/Constructors	
1	A. Prost	38 pts	20	G. Tarquini		1 pt
2	A. Senna	37 pts		O. Grouillard		1 pt
3	R. Patrese	22 pts		J. Palmer		1 pt
4	N. Mansell	15 pts				
5	T. Boutsen	13 pts	1	McLaren		65 pts
6	A. Nannini	8 pts	2	Williams		35 pts
7	M. Alboreto	6 pts	3	Ferrari		15 pts
8	J. Herbert	5 pts	4	Benetton		13 pts
9	A. de Cesaris	4 pts	5	Tyrrell		10 pts
	M. Gugelmin	4 pts	6	BMS Dallara		8 pts
	E. Cheever	4 pts		Arrows		8 pts
	S. Modena	4 pts	8	Brabham		5 pts
13	A. Caffi	4 pts	9	Leyton House		4 pts
14	D. Warwick	4 pts	10	Rial		3 pts
15	C. Danner	3 pts		Ligier		3 pts
	N. Piquet	3 pts		Lotus		3 pts
	J. Alesi	3 pts	13	Onyx		2 pts
18	R. Arnoux	2 pts	14	AGS		1 pt
19	S. Johansson	2 pts				

Left: a home win for Prost.

Existing qualifying lap record: Nigel Mansell, Williams-Honda FW11B, 1m 06.454s at 206.561 kph/128.351 in 1987

Existing race lap record: Nelson Piquet, Williams-Honda FW11B, 1m 09.548s, 197.372 kph/122.641 mph in 1987

Existing distance record: Nigel Mansell, Williams-Honda FW11B, 80 laps in 1 hr 37m 03.839s at 188.560 kph/177.166 mph in 1987

PAST WINNERS

Year	Driver	Nat.	Car	Circuit
1979	Jean-Pierre Jabouille	F	1.5 Renault RS t/c	Dijon-Prenois
1980	Alan Jones	AUS	3.0 Williams FW07B Ford	Paul Ricard
1981	Alain Prost	F	1.5 Renault RE t/c	Dijon-Prenois
1982	René Arnoux	F	1.5 Renault RE t/c	Paul Ricard
1983	Alain Prost	F	1.5 Renault RE t/c	Paul Ricard
1984	Niki Lauda	A	1.5 McLaren MP4/2 TAG t/c	Dijon-Prenois
1985	Nelson Piquet	BR	1.5 Brabham BT54 BMW t/c	Paul Ricard
1986	Nigel Mansell	GB	1.5 Williams FW11 Honda t/c	Paul Ricard
1987	Nigel Mansell	GB	1.5 Williams FW11B Honda t/c	Paul Ricard
1988	Alain Prost	F	1.5 McLaren MP4/4 Honda t/c	Paul Ricard

Silverstone

SHELL BRITISH GRAND PRIX · 16 JULY

transverse gearbox was waiting in the wings. It had been tested frequently in the run-up to the British Grand Prix but an earlier debut had been delayed so that the new gearbox could be run at home – just in case there were any problems. Perhaps they remembered the new aerodynamics that they had introduced a year before, which then had to be ditched during the weekend.

McLaren really did seem to have problems. Ron Dennis had said that the opposition were getting too close; something would have to be done. The car with the

Silverstone reflects on a Ferrari/McLaren battle, while boasting more aerial manoevres than Heathrow on raceday.

Yet it wasn't the gearbox that cost them time and laps on the Friday and Saturday of the British Grand Prix. Since the Canadian Grand Prix disaster, when Ayrton Senna retired after his engine blew out all its oil, the team had been striving with various different oil systems to correct the problem.

The engine's oil tank is an integral part of the gearbox, and the modified version of what had been run in France was not working. Thin blue smoke followed the McLarens around for much of Friday. Further modifications resulted for Saturday. Still there were problems. On Saturday evening the company helicopter returned to Woking where certain sections of the factory were in full swing, working out what had gone wrong. There was, it seemed, a fault in the manufacture of the subsequent models. By Sunday, the status quo had been restored.

In the meantime, however, Senna was suffering the after-effects of a cold and a sore throat. He and Prost both had transmission problems, and one or two difficulties with the new gearbox.

On Friday, then, while Senna was quickest, Prost was down in fifth spot. Next morning, Prost was quickest and Senna had parked his car out on the track. Problems persisted, and what's more, the track seemed slower.

Yet that afternoon both drivers improved their times to claim the front row of the grid, and the 16th consecutive pole for McLaren. Later, as Prost sat in the sun and waited for the return of the helicopter, screaming Hondas could be heard in the garage, and that persisted next morning as the team fought to find out if they were still blowing out oil.

Although witnesses said that there was still a blue trail following the cars, the team was happy with them next day. And in the afternoon, with their brand new rear ends, the pair led the British Grand Prix.

Senna, of course, would not see the chequered flag. He hadn't been

Clockwise from left: British advertising standards require no Marlboro logos for televised events – so strobe stripes it is as Senna sweeps past Capelli entering the pit lane. The same applies to de Cesaris and Gachot. For Moreno the writing is on the tyre wall!

worried about Prost's World Championship lead of 11 points prior to the race – it had been more the previous year. But his gearbox proved recalcitrant on lap 12 of the 64 laps, and he spun off, leaving Prost to drive to his 38th win and a 20-point lead in the series.

Prost was the first to pay tribute to McLaren's feats over the weekend. 'It's one of the best victories for both me and the team, because it shows that I am still motivated and the team can still react quickly and effectively in the face of problems,' he said, going on to point out that 'I have never had such a big lead in the World Championship...'

BRIGHT SPARKS

McLaren's performance was obviously one of the high points of the British Grand Prix, but then there were several other noteworthy performances. Gachot again got through pre-qualifying, but this time teammate Johansson didn't make it. The Belgian would have to defend his team's chances of final non-pre-qualifiers on his own. Larini was second quickest: Brundle brought his run of two DNPQs to a halt.

The March drivers always looked forward to the British Grand Prix. The previous year they'd qualified fifth and sixth behind the Ferraris and McLarens. Third and fourth on Friday morning looked very hopeful, sixth and eighth that afternoon less so but there they would remain on the grid, once again behind the McLarens and Ferrari (in revised order) and sharing their rows with the Williams-Renaults.

Gugelmin had an engine problem in the warm-up but worse was to come. When a water leak was discovered on the grid, the Brazilian was forced to take the spare and start from the pits for the second race running. Capelli was quickly running in the second bunch, holding eighth place, but had picked up a place when his transmission failed on lap 16.

Yet even at that stage, teammate Gugelmin was more than willing to take up the cudgels on the team's behalf. He was only 24th on lap one, but his teammate's retirement gave him tenth place. At half distance, lap 32, he was last unlapped runner in fifth place. And there he remained until gearbox-induced retirement on lap 54.

A fair amount of flak had been sent Nelson Piquet's way and although Nelson's view was that much of it came from people who didn't know what they were talking about, some took his tenth place on the grid as being as a result of their criticism.

The man himself was a survivor of the second bunch battling over fourth, and then he overtook the gear-troubled Boutsen for third. Just ahead of him an understeering Nannini had stopped for tyres on lap 20, but although the Benetton's exhaust then broke, the Italian came charging back, surprising Piquet with his speed, to pip the Lotus driver on lap 56. Even so, Piquet found the car fantastic, although he had been worried by his engine temperatures for many laps, and didn't think that it would last.

There was a dramatic battle going on for who would and wouldn't have to pre-qualify in the second half of 1989. Onyx had scored two points in France to become team number 13 (and therefore free of pre-qualifying) while Gabriele Tarquini's single point in the AGS was not good enough. Neither Lola nor Minardi had points and looked as though they might have to pre-qualify.

But after qualifying had ended at Silverstone, Martini (Minardi) and Alliot (Lola) both looked good on row six and their respective teammates weren't far behind. Gachot, in the Onyx, was a frustrated 21st but Tarquini's chances had ended with non-qualification.

Martini leaped into eighth at the start but within five laps was in the pits, a piece of paper having caused Minardi's perennial complaint, overheating. Rejoining 23rd, his place was taken by Alliot, who had just been lapped at half distance when sixth, and who went on to fight a stirring battle with Alesi.

Two places behind, however, was Martini's teammate Sala – and Martini himself. With Bernard having retired earlier, Lola's chances disappeared with Alliot's retirement on lap 39, made that much worse by Martini willingly accepting sixth, and when Gugelmin retired, that became fifth. Sala fought off Grouillard during the closing stages to score a third vital point, thus escaping pre-qualifying and sentencing Onyx to that fate; Gachot had never been happy with his handling. Minardi, however, came right at just the most vital moment.

Clockwise from below: Palmer rides the heat haze, a pleasant surprise for Silverstone. Gugelmin, happier with the March, checks times. Running in close company – Grouillard and Nakajima. Pirro on a quick lap, Prost slowing down.

RACE DEBRIEF

Apart from the glorious weather conditions which were partially responsible for making the track slower on Saturday, there were few surprises in the British Grand Prix, apart, of course, from the McLaren team's obvious problems.

But as the track filled on Sunday, there was encouraging news for the patriotic local crowd: Mansell quickest in the warm-up ahead of Prost and Senna, with Berger fourth and then Nannini, Martini chasing hard and Nelson Piquet. The Williamses were just in the top ten, while Sala had an oil-pump failure and was last.

There were two cars in the pits at the start: Gugelmin's March had had a water leak, and Larini had lost a mirror. But it was Prost who got the car off the line the best when the lights turned green, although Senna squeezed by into Copse. 'If we had been any closer, it would have been an accident,' said the Frenchman. The Ferraris followed while the Williamses were in fifth and sixth ahead of Nannini, Martini and Piquet with a small gap already opening up to the rest, although Capelli soon crossed that gap.

When Berger ducked out of fourth place to have his metering unit replaced, that made the break for Senna, Prost and Mansell, leaving Boutsen, Patrese, Nannini, Piquet, Martini and Capelli battling at least four seconds behind the Ferrari. Martini soon pitted from eighth to have paper removed from an inlet duct, while Bernard, three places further back, emitted ominous puffs of smoke.

The first three were very much in line astern: Senna, Prost and Mansell, with no let-up in the pressure. But then suddenly, on lap 12, Senna's McLaren swung around at Becketts, and spun off into the gravel trap. And there it stuck. 'I had difficulty selecting third gear on the downchange from the start, and I almost went off earlier,' explained the Brazilian. 'Then I couldn't get the gear at all, and I couldn't take the corner in neutral . . .'

Senna out, then, for the fourth race running but still Mansell hung on to Prost like a leech. Even so, he was suffering understeer behind the McLarens, not surprisingly given the lack of downforce. But while he stayed as close to the McLaren ahead as he could, at least he didn't have to worry about those behind. Boutsen, Patrese, Nannini, Piquet and Capelli were at least ten seconds down. Alliot, Modena and Alesi were further back again, followed by Nakajima, Gugelmin (from the pits), Sala, Bernard etc. As Prost began to open up the tiniest of gaps to Mansell, so the battling quintet began to fall apart. First to go was Capelli with failed transmission. Patrese took teammate Boutsen after the Belgian had lost his clutch and was now having problems with gear selection.

But then suddenly Patrese was gone too. 'I turned into Club corner and the car just went off. It spun around very quickly and I went into the tyre wall backwards. It was a big one,' said Patrese who received a bang

Clockwise from above: A lonely, but very encouraging run for the Lotuses. Tarquini in the AGS: non-qualification means more pre-qualifying. Forza Mansell!

on the back of the helmet. Subsequent examination of the car revealed a punctured radiator which had then sprayed water onto the rear tyres. As Patrese had gone off, he'd been launched across the gravel trap by the kerbs and slammed hard into the tyre barrier which thankfully had done its job.

So on lap 20, Boutsen, Nannini and Piquet battled over third place, but then Nannini pitted, chronic understeer having destroyed his previous set of Goodyears. Now just Boutsen and Piquet disputed third position, Nannini having joined the Alliot-Alesi-Gugelmin-Modena battle for fifth place. Nakajima and Sala were further back, the last unlapped runners on lap 22.

Boutsen, devoid of a clutch, finally succumbed to the Piquet pressure on lap 24, then headed for the pits three laps later with a puncture. This proved a lengthy operation and effectively put him out of the race, losing 12 places.

At the front, the lead gap had opened out a little, going out to as much as 4.8s amongst the backmarkers, but then closing back up to 3.3s before going out to 8.8s within four laps. Piquet was well out of touch in third place, Nannini some 20s back in fourth followed by Gugelmin and Alliot. The rest, led by Alesi and Modena, were lapped. Almost immediately, however, the turbulence behind the Lola-Lamborghini caused Alesi to spin into the bank and out of the race.

Modena disappeared on lap 32 with engine failure so that Alliot, progressively losing power, found Nakajima, Sala and Martini closing on him. And when Alliot retired rather than blow his engine, it was Martini who suddenly slotted into sixth place, overtaking both Sala and Nakajima. But his place was taken by a determined Grouillard who disposed of the Japanese driver, worried by rising temperatures, and began to pressure Sala.

Mansell had managed to maintain Prost's lead at around seven or eight seconds, but suddenly there were groans around the circuit. The Ferrari had settled down onto its suspension round the back of the circuit, sparks flew from under it and Nigel had to nurse his car back to the pits with a punctured right front tyre.

By the time he was back out on the track again, he was some 53s behind Prost. But when the Frenchman decided to change tyres some four laps later, it was a slow stop at nearly 25 seconds and Prost emerged with a lead of just 12.8s. Once again Mansell was able to keep the gap constant, but not close it.

Further back, however, the gap between third-placed Piquet and Nannini on new tyres was closing, even though the Benetton was obviously suffering a broken exhaust. Gugelmin had been a threat behind Nannini for a while, but a tyre-pressure problem had caused him to slow, and as Nannini closed on Piquet, so the March driver quit with a failed gearbox.

Nannini surprised Piquet with his speed, taking the Lotus on lap 56.

The first four places were settled, then, with Prost coming home to his second Grand Prix victory in just eight days, and opening up as big a championship lead as he's ever had. Mansell was second for the second time in eight days, while Nannini was delighted with third place in the new Benetton, even suggesting that it was especially good to finish third in Britain because it earned him better money . . .

Piquet had to settle for fourth place, enthusing about his car even if

Above: Bernard's Lola leads Capelli and Nannini. Left: A happy day . . . for the Minardi team, three points in the 'bag', both cars in the top six and no pre-qualifying. Below: Patrese's race was a short one.

the temperature warning lights had come on. Martini did a great job to come through to fifth ahead of teammate Sala, who managed to keep Grouillard at bay right to the end.

Minardi's three points would spare them pre-qualification in the second half of 1989 while half-term also saw a twenty-point lead for Prost over Senna, who in turn was only five ahead of Patrese, now just one point ahead of Mansell.

MILESTONES

- McLaren's 16th successive pole position
- Berger records ninth successive retirement, announces he will join McLaren in 1990
- Dalmas replaces Winkelhock at AGS
- Minardi becomes 15th team to score World Championship points in 1988; previous season's record was 14 teams in 1978

SHELL BRITISH GRAND PRIX

ENTRIES · PRACTICE · RESULTS

Pos	Driver/Nationality		No.	Car/Engine	P.Q. (cool, cloudy)	Practice 1 (overcast)	Practice 2 (warm, sunny)	Warm-up (pos) (cloudy)	Laps	Time/Retirement (warm, cloudy)
1	A. Prost	F	2	McLaren MP4/5 Honda V10	–	1:10.156	**1:09.266**	1:12.515 (2)	64	1hr19m22.131
2	N. Mansell	GB	27	Ferrari 640 Ferrari V12	–	**1:09.156**	1:10.279	1:12.130 (1)	64	1hr19m41.500
3	A. Nannini	I	18	Benetton B189 Ford DFR V8	–	1:22.034	**1:10.798**	1:13.371 (5)	64	1hr20m10.150
4	N. Piquet	BR	11	Lotus 101 Judd V8	–	1:11.589	**1:10.925**	1:13.876 (7)	64	1hr20m28.866
5	P. Martini	I	23	Minardi M189 Ford DFR V8	–	**11.368**	1:11.582	1:13.796 (6)	63	1hr19m56.084
6	L. Sala	E	24	Minardi M189 Ford DFR V8	–	**1:11.955**	1:11.826	1:21.185 (26)	63	1hr20m02.435
7	O. Grouillard	F	26	Ligier JS33 Ford DFR V8	–	1:12.853	**1:12.605**	1:15.020 (18)	63	1hr20m03.281
8	S. Nakajima	J	12	Lotus 101 Judd V8	–	1:12.326	**1:11.960**	1:14.424 (12)	63	1hr20m29.578
9	D. Warwick	GB	9	Arrows A11 Ford DFR V8	–	**1:12.295**	1:12.208	1:16.476 (24)	62	1hr19m24.321
10	T. Boutsen	B	5	Williams FW12C Renault V10	–	**1:10.276**	1:10.771	1:14.074 (8)	62	1hr19m28.575
11	E. Pirro	I	20	Benetton B188 Ford HB V8	–	1:13.233	**1:13.148**	1:14.868 (15)	62	1hr19m44.594
12	B. Gachot	B	37	Onyx ORE1 Ford DFR V8	1:11.506	**1:12.329**	1:12.928	1:16.851 (25)	62	1hr20m01.374
13	M. Gugelmin	BR	15	Leyton House CG891 Judd V8	–	**1:10.336**	1:12.655	1:15.489 (20)	54	gearbox
14	M. Brundle	GB	7	Brabham BT58 Judd V8	1:12.021	12.616	**1:12.327**	1:15.974 (23)	49	engine
15	G. Berger	A	28	Ferrari 640 Ferrari V12	–	**1:09.855**	1:10.130	1:12.687 (4)	49	gearbox management
16	E. Bernard	F	29	Lola LC89 Lamborghini V12	–	1:12.193	**1:11.687**	1:14.916 (16)	46	engine
17	P. Alliot	F	30	Lola LC89 Lamborghini V12	–	**1:11.541**	1:12.408	1:15.018 (17)	39	engine
18	J. Palmer	GB	3	Tyrrell 018 Ford DFR V8	–	**1:12.070**	1:12.157	1:14.221 (9)	32	accident
19	S. Modena	I	8	Brabham BT58 Judd V8	1:11.809	1:12.262	**1:11.755**	1:15.340 (19)	31	engine
20	J. Alesi	F	4	Tyrrell 018 Ford DFR V8	–	1:12.994	**1:12.341**	1:14.768 (13)	28	spun/stalled
21	N. Larini	I	17	Osella FA1M Ford DFR V8	1:11.766	**1:12.061**	1:12.395	1:14.792 (14)	23	handling
22	R. Patrese	I	6	Williams FW12C Renault V10	–	**1:09.865**	1:09.963	1:14.225 (10)	19	holed radiator
23	I. Capelli	I	16	Leyton House CG891 Judd V8	–	**1:10.650**	1:11.544	1:14.252 (11)	15	clutch release bearing
24	A. de Cesaris	I	22	Dallara BMS 189 Ford DFR V8	–	1:13.335	**1:13.148**	1:15.898 (22)	14	engine
25	A. Senna	BR	1	McLaren MP4/5 Honda V10	–	1:09.124	**1:09.099**	1:12.530 (3)	11	gearbox/spin
26	R. Moreno	BR	31	Coloni C3 Ford DFR V8	–	1:12.680	**1:12.412**	1:15.774 (21)	2	gearbox
27	R. Arnoux	F	25	Ligier JS33 Ford DFR V8	–	1:13.240	1:13.550	DNQ		
28	E. Cheever	USA	2	Arrows A11 Ford DFR V8	–	1:13.655	**1:13.386**	DNQ		
29	G. Tarquini	I	40	AGS JH23 Ford DFR V8	–	1:13.496	1:13.997	DNQ		
30	C. Danner	D	38	Rial ARC02 Ford DFR V8	–	1:15.387	1:15.394	DNQ		
–	S. Johansson	S	36	Onyx ORE1 Ford DFR V8	1:12.248	DNPQ	DNPQ			
–	A. Caffi	I	21	Dallara BMS 189 Ford DFR V8	1:12.501	DNPQ	DNPQ			
–	G. Foitek	S	33	EuroBrun ER 189 Judd V8	1:13.128	DNPQ	DNPQ			
–	P. Ghinzani	I	18	Osella FA1M Ford DFR V8	1:13.429	DNPQ	DNPQ			
–	Y. Dalmas	F	41	AGS JH23 Ford DFR V8	1:13.720	DNPQ	DNPQ			
–	B. Schneider	D	34	Zakspeed ZK189 Ford DFR V8	1:14.124	DNPQ	DNPQ			
–	P. Raphanel	F	32	Coloni C3 Ford DFR V8	1:14.206	DNPQ	DNPQ			
–	A. Suzuki	J	35	Zakspeed ZK189 Ford DFR V8	1:14.266	DNPQ	DNPQ			
–	V. Weidler	D	39	Rial ARC02 Ford DFR V8	1:15.096	DNPQ	DNPQ			

Circuit Data: Silverstone Grand Prix Circuit, length 2.969 miles/4.778 km, race distance 64 laps = 190 miles/305.8 km, race weather warm and cloudy.
Notes: Warwick drives Arrows No. 9 again. Yannick Dalmas (F) takes over AGS No. 41 from Joachim Winkelhock. Bernard drives Lola No. 29 again.

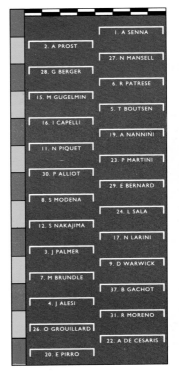

Starting grid:

1. A SENNA
2. A PROST
27. N MANSELL
28. G BERGER
6. R PATRESE
15. M GUGELMIN
5. T BOUTSEN
16. I CAPELLI
19. A NANNINI
11. N PIQUET
23. P MARTINI
30. P ALLIOT
29. E BERNARD
8. S MODENA
24. L SALA
12. S NAKAJIMA
17. N LARINI
3. J PALMER
9. D WARWICK
7. M BRUNDLE
37. B GACHOT
4. J ALESI
31. R MORENO
26. O GROUILLARD
22. A DE CESARIS
20. E PIRRO

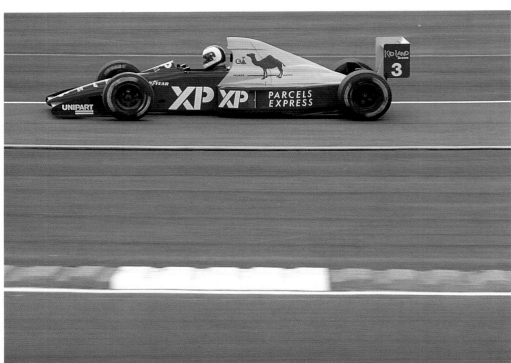

LAP CHART

Grid Order	1 2 3 4 5 6 7 8 9 10 11 12 13 14 15 16 17 18 19 20 21 22 23 24 25 26 27 28 29 30 31 32 33 34 35 36 37 38 39 40 41 42 43 44 45 46 47 48 49 50 51 52 53 54 55 56 57 58 59 60 61 62 63 64
1 A. Senna	1 1 1 1 1 1 1 1 1 1 1 1 1 2 2 2 2 2 2 2 2 2 2 2 2 2 2 2 2 2 2 2 2 2 2 2 2 2 2 2 2 2 2 2 2 2 2 2 2 2 2 2 2 2 2 2 2 2 2 2 2 2 2 2
2 A. Prost	2 2 2 2 2 2 2 2 2 2 27 27 27 27 27 27 27 27 27 27 27 27 27 27 27 27 27 27 27 27 27 27 27 27 27 27 27 27 27 27 27 27 27 27 27 27 27 27 27 27 27 27 27 27 27 27 27 27 27 27 27 27 27 27
27 N. Mansell	27 27 27 27 27 27 27 27 27 27 27 5 5 5 5 6 6 6 6 5 5 5 5 11 11 11 11 11 11 11 11 11 11 11 11 11 11 11 11 11 11 11 11 11 11 11 11 11 11 11 11 11 11 11 11 11 11 11 11 19 19 19 19 19 19 19 19
28 G. Berger	28 28 28 5 5 5 5 5 5 5 6 6 6 6 6 5 5 5 19 11 11 11 11 5 5 5 19 19 19 19 19 19 19 19 19 19 19 19 19 19 19 19 19 19 19 19 19 19 19 19 19 19 19 19 19 11 11 11 11 11 11 11 11 11
6 R. Patrese	5 5 5 6 6 6 6 6 6 6 6 19 19 19 19 19 19 19 11 11 19 30 30 19 19 19 5 15 15 15 15 15 15 15 15 15 15 15 15 15 15 15 15 15 15 15 15 15 15 15 15 15 15 15 23 23 23 23 23 23 23 23 23
15 M. Gugelmin	6 6 6 19 19 19 19 19 19 19 11 11 11 11 11 11 11 11 11 11 11 11 30 30 4 19 15 15 15 15 30 30 30 30 30 30 30 30 23 23 23 23 23 23 23 23 23 23 23 23 23 24 24 24 24 24 24 24 24
5 T. Boutsen	19 19 19 11 11 11 11 11 11 11 11 11 11 16 16 16 16 30 30 30 30 4 4 19 15 30 30 30 30 4 8 8 12 12 12 12 12 12 23 24 24 24 24 24 24 24 24 24 24 24 24 24 24 26 26 26 26 26 26 26 26 26
16 I. Capelli	7 23 23 23 16 16 16 16 16 16 30 30 30 30 4 4 4 4 15 15 15 4 4 4 4 8 12 12 12 24 24 24 24 24 24 12 12 12 26 26 26 26 26 26 26 26 26 26 26 12 12 12 12 12 12 12 12 12
19 A. Nannini	23 11 11 16 30 30 30 30 30 30 30 8 8 8 8 8 8 15 8 8 8 8 8 8 8 12 24 24 24 23 23 23 23 23 24 26 12 12 12 12 12 12 12 12 12 12 12 12 9 9 9 9 9 9 9 9 9
11 N. Piquet	11 16 16 30 8 8 8 8 8 8 4 4 4 4 15 15 15 8 12 12 12 12 12 12 12 12 24 23 23 26 26 26 26 26 26 26 9 9 9 9 9 9 9 9 9 9 9 9 9 9 5 5 5 5 5 5 5 5 5
23 P. Martini	16 30 30 8 29 29 29 4 4 4 4 29 12 12 12 12 12 12 24 24 24 24 24 24 24 23 26 26 26 9 9 9 9 9 9 9 37 37 37 37 5 5 5 5 5 5 5 5 5 5 20 20 20 20 20 20 20 20 20
30 P. Alliot	30 8 8 29 4 4 4 29 29 29 29 24 12 15 15 24 24 24 24 9 9 9 9 9 9 9 26 9 9 9 3 3 37 37 37 37 37 30 5 5 5 20 20 20 20 20 20 20 20 20 20 20 23 37 37 37 37 37 37
29 E. Bernard	8 29 29 4 24 24 24 24 24 24 12 24 24 24 9 9 9 9 26 26 23 23 23 23 23 9 3 3 3 37 5 5 5 5 5 5 5 20 20 20 20 20 37 37 37 37 37 37 37 37 37 37 37 37
8 S. Modena	29 24 4 24 7 7 7 7 7 7 12 15 15 29 9 26 26 26 26 23 23 23 26 26 26 26 3 37 37 37 5 20 20 20 20 20 20 20 7 7 7 7 7 7 7 7 7 7
24 L. Sala	24 4 24 7 12 12 12 12 12 7 9 9 9 26 20 20 20 23 20 20 20 20 20 3 3 37 5 5 5 20 7 7 7 7 7 7 29 29 29 29 29 29 29 28 28 28
12 S. Nakajima	4 7 7 12 9 9 9 9 9 9 26 26 26 20 3 23 20 3 3 3 3 20 37 5 20 20 20 7 29 29 29 29 29 29 29 28 28 28 28 28 28 28
17 N. Larini	12 12 12 9 3 3 3 26 26 15 15 3 3 3 23 23 3 3 37 37 37 37 37 37 20 20 29 29 29 29 28 28 28 28 28 28 28 28
3 J. Palmer	9 9 9 3 26 26 26 15 15 26 20 20 20 23 37 37 37 37 29 29 29 29 29 29 29 29 29 7 7 7 28
9 D. Warwick	3 3 3 26 20 15 15 3 3 3 3 7 23 23 29 29 29 29 29 7 7 7 7 7 7 7 7 7 7 28 28 28
7 M. Brundle	26 26 26 20 15 20 20 20 20 20 23 23 37 37 37 7 7 7 17 17 17 17 17 28 28 28 28 28
37 B. Gachot	20 20 20 15 22 22 37 37 37 23 23 37 37 22 17 17 17 17 17 17 28 28 28 28
4 J. Alesi	37 22 22 22 37 37 22 22 23 23 37 37 22 17 7 7 28 28 28 28
31 R. Moreno	22 37 15 37 23 23 23 22 22 22 22 17 7 22 28
26 O. Grouillard	26 31 15 37 28 17 17 17 17 17 17 17 17 28 28 28
22 A. de Cesaris	15 31 17 17 82 28 28 28 28 28 28 28
20 E. Pirro	17 17

FASTEST LAPS

Pos.	Car No./Driver/Team		Time
1	27	N. Mansell/Ferrari	1:12.017
2	2	A. Prost/McLaren	1:12.193
3	19	A. Nannini/Benetton	1:12.397
4	28	G. Berger/Ferrari	1:13.477
5	11	N. Piquet/Lotus	1:13.565
6	15	M. Gugelmin/Leyton House	1:13.735
7	1	A. Senna/McLaren	1:13.737
8	16	I. Capelli/Leyton House	1:14.224
9	5	T. Boutsen/Williams	1:14.248
10	23	P. Martini/Minardi	1:14.388
11	26	O. Grouillard/Ligier	1:14.446
12	37	B. Gachot/Onyx	1:14.484
13	24	L. Sala/Minardi	1:14.492
14	6	R. Patrese/Williams	1:14.586
15	11	S. Nakajima/Lotus	1:14.720
16	20	E. Pirro/Benetton	1:15.293
17	7	M. Brundle/Brabham	1:15.363
18	30	P. Alliot/Larrousse	1:15.405
19	9	D. Warwick/Arrows	1:15.443
20	8	S. Modena/Brabham	1:15.489
21	4	J. Alesi/Tyrrell	1:15.519
22	3	J. Palmer/Tyrrell	1:15.931
23	29	E. Bernard/Larrousse	1:16.264
24	17	N. Larini/Osella	1:16.901
25	22	A. de Cesaris/BMS Dallara	1:18.076
26	31	R. Moreno/Coloni	1:20.498

Existing qualifying lap record: Nelson Piquet, Williams-Honda FW11B, 1m 07.110s, 256.308 kph/159.262 mph in 1987

Existing race lap record: Nigel Mansell, Williams-Honda FW11B, 1m 09.832s, 246.317 kph/153.054 mph in 1987

Existing distance record: Nigel Mansell, Williams-Honda FW11B, 65 laps in 1hr 19m 11.780s at 235.291 kph/146.203 mph in 1987

CHAMPIONSHIP POINTS

	Drivers		Drivers/Constructors	
1	A. Prost	47 pts	21 O. Grouillard	1 pt
2	A. Senna	27 pts	L. Sala	1 pt
3	R. Patrese	22 pts	M. Brundle	1 pt
4	N. Mansell	21 pts	J. Palmer	1 pt
5	T. Boutsen	13 pts		
6	A. Nannini	12 pts	1 McLaren	74 pts
7	M. Alboreto	6 pts	2 Williams	35 pts
8	N. Piquet	6 pts	3 Ferrari	21 pts
9	J. Herbert	5 pts	4 Benetton	17 pts
10	A. de Cesaris	4 pts	5 Tyrrell	10 pts
	M. Gugelmin	4 pts	6 BMS Dallara	8 pts
	E. Cheever	4 pts	Arrows	8 pts
	S. Modena	4 pts	8 Lotus	6 pts
14	A. Caffi	4 pts	9 Brabham	5 pts
15	D. Warwick	4 pts	10 Leyton House	4 pts
16	C. Danner	3 pts	11 Rial	3 pts
	J. Alesi	3 pts	Ligier	3 pts
18	S. Johansson	2 pts	Minardi	3 pts
	R. Arnoux	2 pts	14 Onyx	2 pts
	P. Martini	2 pts	15 AGS	1 pt
21	G. Tarquini	1 pt		

PAST WINNERS

Year	Driver	Nat.	Car	Circuit
1979	Clay Regazzoni	CH	3.0 Williams FW07 Ford	Silverstone
1980	Alan Jones	AUS	3.0 Williams FW07B Ford	Brands Hatch
1981	John Watson	GB	3.0 McLaren MP4 Ford	Silverstone
1982	Niki Lauda	A	3.0 McLaren MP4B Ford	Brands Hatch
1983	Alain Prost	F	1.5 Renault RE40 t/c	Silverstone
1984	Niki Lauda	A	1.5 McLaren MP4/2 TAG t/c	Brands Hatch
1985	Alain Prost	F	1.5 McLaren MP4/2B TAG t/c	Silverstone
1986	Nigel Mansell	GB	1.5 Williams FW11 Honda t/c	Brands Hatch
1987	Nigel Mansell	GB	1.5 Williams FW11B Honda t/c	Silverstone
1988	Ayrton Senna	BR	1.5 McLaren MP4/4 Honda t/c	Silverstone

Hockenheim

The Hockenheimring weaves through emerald green forests, only diving into the stadium complex for the spectators.

We'd been waiting a long time for this confrontation between Alain Prost and teammate Ayrton Senna. Since their personal relationship (or lack of it) had come out in the open and Prost had stated his reasons for leaving the McLaren team, Senna had retired almost immediately in France, and lasted only eleven laps in Britain.

The German Grand Prix duel (some called it a war) was the battle we'd all waited to see and at the end of it, we felt just a little bit cheated of the final denouement. Only on the last two laps were the pair further apart than their 4.8s on lap 27. Most of the time, indeed, they were three seconds or less apart.

It was a battle of nerves, of talent, of disappointments, of frustrations, a battle where tactics were vital – a waiting game, some might call it, yet one where both attacked throughout. Twenty-eight times the lap record was broken as it was whittled down to 1m 45.884s, a whisker off Mansell's four bar record of 1m 45.718s in 1987. No one else broke 1m 48s!

For the first seventeen laps Prost was rarely more than a second behind Senna, once they'd both overtaken Berger's Ferrari by the second chicane on the first lap. All the leading runners, McLaren of course included, were scheduled to stop for tyres, however. And Prost was the first to pit on lap 17. But it was a relatively long stop at around 15s.

'I had a clutch problem,' said Alain, 'and the rear wheels were spinning. I actually had to take it out of gear so that the mechanics could tighten the rear wheels.'

Advantage Senna, then, but only for two more laps. When he came into the pits, it had seemed a good stop when suddenly he was held again. A mechanic wasn't sure that the right rear wheel was properly seated, and had to take it off again to check. It took 19 seconds all told. 'As I drove down the pit lane, I saw Alain go past through the Armco, so I knew what I had to do,' said Senna.

Ayrton rejoined some 3.2s behind Prost, 'and this time the traffic seemed to go against me', said Ayrton. The gap actually opened up to 4.1s in the next three laps, dipped to 3.5s, then opened up to 4.8s again.

But then Ayrton set to work. He had 15 laps in which to cut that gap.

'I was concentrating on getting close, just easing towards him in case something happened. I needed to get close enough to profit if he should make a mistake. I didn't really have any strategy for overtaking.'

Ayrton knew that his rival wasn't having an easy time, however. 'I knew what it was like following, after being behind during the first part. However, I was having a problem changing gear because of the clutch, and I was being very careful under braking.'

There were three laps to go and the pair were just 1.1s apart when Prost suddenly slowed on his way to the stadium. 'I put it into sixth gear, but there was no drive,' said Alain; it was later diagnosed as a broken part in the selector mechanism.

Senna was past in a flash; that wasn't the ending that we expected, not the final confrontation that we hoped for. The drivers, however, were philosophical, particularly Prost. 'I've won 38 Grand Prix in my career, some when I should have, some when perhaps I've been lucky. Today I've been unlucky.'

For Senna, it was another surprise. 'I was surprised when Gerhard made such a good start, surprised at the pit stop, surprised when Alain slowed, and surprised when I won.'

On the down side, we were surprised when Berger's nose section flew off so suddenly when he went off at the chicane, and surprised when marshals rather carelessly hauled the unfortunate Pirro out of his car. But generally speaking, the usually unexciting Hockenheim will be remembered for the Senna versus Prost tussle. What a shame it didn't last full distance.

Clockwise from left:
Patrese leads Boutsen. Nakajima and
Lotus – happier to be on the fast circuits.
Alliot safely through pre-qualifying
with the help of a scooter. Sala's
Minardi is charged up in the pit lane.

BRIGHT SPARKS

There was a distinct hierarchy at Hockenheim. It went like this: V10 McLaren-Hondas, V12 Ferraris, V10 Williams-Renaults, V8 Benettons, and the rest. Anyone who intruded into that hierarchy was a pleasant relief. Mansell was one of the few to do so, just as his fast- starting teammate would do so in the race.

A relaxed Nigel, however, was perfectly conscious that this wasn't a race for Ferrari, it was a race for McLaren. The chicanes and straights were made for them, he said. Even so, he was looking forward to the race, and was pleased to complete it with reliability and four points. It was a most philosophical view.

One of the most pleasant sights was the two V8 Ford-powered Benettons mixing it with the Williamses. The Renault-powered cars weren't at their best at Hockenheim; the latest Evolution engines weren't forthcoming, and the new chassis was eagerly awaited.

But at Benetton, new boy Pirro had his B189 with the HB engine for the first time, and it had the added benefit of helping Nannini with development. Seventh on the grid, Nannini was past Patrese on lap one and past Boutsen on lap three. On lap four, he set fastest lap of the race so far but pitted two laps later with a misfire.

It was left to teammate Pirro to carry the honours. He'd got by Patrese too at the start, but overtaking Boutsen's Williams had resulted in the Belgian hitting the wall, neither driver particularly blaming the other.

But the banging of wheels had resulted in some damage to the Benetton as well, particularly the balance under braking. After the pit stops, the gap between Pirro and Mansell's third-placed Ferrari ahead was actually coming down when the Benetton put a wheel up on the kerb under braking for the corner into the stadium: the car snapped sideways, and then thumped three of the huge polystyrene bales placed there to direct the racing cars.

Ducarouge watches the times – intent on Alboreto and Alliot pre-qualifying.
Below: They went two by two.
Left: Nannini passes his sponsor's product in the number one Benetton.

The Benetton's front suspension was badly deranged, and Pirro at first suffered considerable shock. 'I don't know what they were doing there anyway,' said Prost of the blocks after the race. Happily, McLaren's former test driver didn't suffer any lasting harm, but when he was clumsily and limply extracted from the car one feared the worst.

Lotus hadn't been having a happy two weeks with one director facing court hearings, and Peter Warr having left. The genial Tony Rudd had taken up the reins with Rupert Mainwaring as team manager, and although the Tickford engine seemed more suitable with its top-end power, it was the four-valve Judd which powered Piquet to eighth on the grid.

In spite of using the spare car, Piquet said that it got better and better

on its way to fifth place; and Nakajima might have been sixth but for losing a brake contest with the clutchless Derek Warwick with nine laps to go. Derek's sixth place, from 17th on the grid, was a dogged performance.

RACE DEBRIEF

McLaren, Ferrari, Williams, Benetton seemed to be the order for most of the weekend. Thanks to the circuit configuration, it seemed to be one of the more predictable races, and only that fine duel between the McLarens saved it from being tedious.

Not that there wasn't plenty going on further back. Pre-qualifying, livened up by Aguri Suzuki with an accident and a spin, was immediately

Alesi straightlines the Tyrrell.

action-packed. Gone with the mid-term re-shuffle were the Brabhams, Caffi and Weidler, replaced by the Lola-Lamborghinis, the point-winning Tarquini and Moreno.

Apart from Suzuki's dramas, Alliot stopped out on the circuit, but Lola had a squadron of scooters at strategic points for just such an eventuality, and he was rushed back to pre-qualify third while new teammate Alboreto pipped the man he had replaced, Yannick Dalmas, by just one thousandth of a second. Heading the pre-qualifiers were the Onyxes, Gachot however damaging his undertray and suffering a transmission problem.

From there on, everything went wrong for the Belgian, and in the end he failed to qualify for the race, after a succession of electrical problems and a spectacular collision with the polystyrene blocks, later upstaged by Pirro. Alboreto continued to live precariously, making the grid by 16/1000ths of a second.

Apart from that the grid was pretty much according to the established hierarchy, although Alesi shone where Palmer suffered traffic, the Marches were suffering from handling and traction and the Arrows were slow in a straight line. The grid was made up of times set on both Friday and Saturday, the three-degree warmer weather of Saturday being blamed for lack of improvements, although both Lotuses and Johansson's Onyx were at least a second quicker on the second day.

The main drama during the warm-up was Mansell's spin when chopped by Johansson at the Sachs Curve, the stationary Ferrari nearly being T-boned by teammate Berger. Senna and Prost were out front, then came Mansell, then the Benettons (Pirro ahead) followed by Williamses and Berger. Alesi was best of the rest.

In spite of the non-pre-qualification of the Zakspeeds, and the non-qualifications of the Rials, the vast 58,000-seat stadium was remarkably full for the race. There were a couple of pre-race dramas. Piquet took the spare when his own race car suffered a misfire, and Palmer felt a warm glow down his back, and realised that he had a petrol leak.

And what a start Gerhard Berger made from fourth on the grid when the lights turned green! The Ferrari jinxed from the right of the grid across to the left and then gave Senna a shock by coming round the outside at the first corner and into the lead. It must have been depressing for him the way Senna then came past on the way down to the first chicane, and Prost did likewise before the second.

At the back, Alliot was nudged into a harmless spin off the grid which showered Capelli's March with dirt and caused a throttle failure, while the other Lola-Lamborghini was soon out with engine trouble. Alliot would go the same way with a fiery spin later in the race.

At the front, though, the confusion had been resolved, as Senna and Prost gradually eased away. The Ferraris of Berger and Mansell were left with their own battle, joined by lap eight by Mansell, eager to get past. Indeed, he gestured his intention at the start of lap 14, and his wish came

true, although not in a conventional way.

Going into the first chicane, Berger's Ferrari became unstable. There was no air in the right rear tyre, which unbalanced the car, lifting the front left into the air. With no brakes on one side, Berger was just a passenger as the car hit the chicane kerb, bucking into the air and coming down on its nose (which broke off), and then careering across the track and on to the grass. No result for Berger again, but there was no sign of a puncture; marks on the wheel suggested persistent kerbing was to blame.

Mansell was now in a safe third behind the McLarens, while further back there had been a sort-out between the Benettons and Williamses. Nannini had got ahead of Boutsen on lap three but when Pirro tried to do the same thing a lap later, the pair collided, sending Boutsen backwards into the barrier at the third chicane, which put him out and damaged the Benetton's front suspension.

Nannini retired to the pits with a misfire on the next lap; so when Berger also went out, the McLarens were out front, Mansell was third,

Pirro fourth, Patrese a lonely fifth, Piquet was up to sixth and Alesi was seventh, while Gugelmin was already up to eighth from 14th on the grid.

At lap 17, the tyre stops were coming thick but not always fast. There was Prost's delay, and a lap later Mansell had a slow stop to have the left front wheel tightened. Patrese's stop was clean. And on lap 19 came Senna, delayed, and Pirro. Last to stop was Piquet on lap 21. Alesi disappeared from his fine sixth place with a spin at the Sachs Curve from which he had to be rescued by Range Rover, later doing the same again. Teammate Palmer's warm feeling had been petrol burns for which he had needed a shower after a couple of laps, and then the throttle cable mercifully broke.

The McLarens had changed positions due to their differing-length delays, so now Senna spent the rest of the race catching his teammate. Mansell, third, was being gained on just a little by Pirro when the Italian, having trouble with stability under braking and downshifting, got up on the kerb at the entrance to the stadium. His car crashed into three of the polystyrene blocks and out of the race.

Clockwise from right: Ciao Gerhard! Brundle checks his mirrors before turning. Prost leads Alesi and Caffi into the forest.

This promoted Patrese to fourth, his gearbox stiffening, and Gugelmin up to a remarkable fifth ahead of Piquet and Warwick, neither the March nor clutchless Arrows driver having stopped for tyres. Gugelmin, however, had been suffering from locking rear brakes, but no sooner had he taken fifth than his car stuck in fifth gear and was out.

In the closing laps, the McLarens gradually closed on one another, while Warwick's sixth place was under threat from Nakajima. However the Japanese lost out in a late braking contest and Warwick was home and dry with one point. Behind the Arrows and de Cesaris's Dallara, Brundle, Modena, Martini and Cheever had been scrapping over eighth, but then Modena dropped out with engine problems and Cheever's car failed to pick up the last of its fuel, leaving Brundle in eighth and Martini ninth.

All eyes were on the front as Senna closed on Prost, then suddenly swept past when Prost couldn't find sixth gear with only three laps left. It was Senna's fourth win in 1989, and he had closed the points gap on Prost, but there was still a long way to go.

MILESTONES

- Tony Rudd takes over chairmanship of Team Lotus from Fred Bushell; Peter Warr leaves the team
- Michele Alboreto replaces Eric Bernard in the Larrousse Lola-Lamborghini team
- Alboreto, teammate Alliot, Tarquini and Moreno are the new pre-qualifiers, replacing Brabham drivers Brundle and Modena plus Weidler and Caffi

FORMULA 1 WORLD CHAMPIONSHIP

GROSSER MOBIL 1 PREIS VON DEUTSCHLAND

ENTRIES · PRACTICE · RESULTS

Pos	Driver/Nationality		No.	Car/Engine	P.Q. (sunny)	Practice 1 (cloudy, warm)	Practice 2 (sunny, warm)	Warm-up (pos) (hazy, warm)	Laps (warm, cloudy)	Time/Retirement
1	A. Senna	BR	1	McLaren M4/5 Honda V10	–	**42.300**	1:42.790	1:46.433 (1)	45	1hr21m43.302
2	A. Prost	F	2	McLaren M4/5 Honda V10	–	1:43.306	**1:43.295**	1:46.826 (2)	45	1hr22m01.453
3	N. Mansell	GB	27	Ferrari 641 Ferrari V12	–	**1:44.020**	1:44.076	1:47.784 (3)	45	1hr23m06.556
4	R. Patrese	I	6	Williams FW12C Renault V10	–	1:45.062	**1:44.511**	1:48.908 (7)	46	1hr22m09.156
5	N. Piquet	BR	11	Lotus 101 Judd V10	–	1:47.316	**1:45.475**	1:49.921 (11)	44	1hr22m24.769
6	D. Warwick	GB	9	Arrows A11 Ford DFR V8	–	1:47.756	**1:47.533**	1:49.698 (10)	44	1hr22m46.298
7	A. de Cesaris	I	22	Dallara BMS 189 Ford DFR V8	–	**1:47.879**	1:48.005	1:51.138 (18)	44	1hr22m59.924
8	M. Brundle	GB	7	Brabham BT58 Judd V8	–	**1:47.216**	1:47.796	1:51.569 (20)	44	1hr23m10.230
9	P. Martini	I	23	Minardi M189 Ford DFR V8	–	1:48.222	**1:47.380**	1:51.744 (21)	44	1hr23m15.278
10	J. Alesi	F	4	Tyrrell 018 Ford DFR V8	–	1:47.551	**1:46.888**	1:49.647 (9)	43	1hr22m57.379
11	R. Arnoux	F	25	Ligier JS33 Ford DFR V8	–	**1:48.266**	1:48.598	1:52.881 (24)	42	1hr23m16.418
12	E. Cheever	USA	10	Arrows A11 Ford DFR V8	–	**1:48.396**	1:48.553	1:50.796 (17)	41	out of fuel
13	S. Modena	I	8	Brabham BT58 Judd V8	–	**1:47.511**	1:47.552	1:50.029 (12)	37	engine
14	S. Nakajima	J	12	Lotus 101 Judd V8	–	1:48.782	**47.663**	1:50.753 (16)	36	spin
15	I. Capelli	I	16	Leyton House CG891 Judd V8	–	1:48.239	**1:48.078**	2:16.896 (26)	32	throttle sensor
16	M. Gugelmin	BR	15	Leyton House CG891 Judd V8	–	**1:47.387**	1:47.578	1:50.157 (13)	28	gearbox
17	E. Pirro	I	20	Benetton 189 Ford HB V8	–	**1:46.521**	1:45.845	1:47.787 (4)	26	accident
18	P. Alliot	F	30	Lola LC89 Lamborghini V12I	1:47.746	**1:47.486**	1:47.566	1:50.309 (14)	20	oil leak-engine
19	J. Palmer	GB	3	Tyrrell 018 Ford DFR V8	–	1:47.836	**1:47.676**	1:53.523 (25)	16	fuel injector
20	G. Berger	A	28	Ferrari 641 Ferrari	–	**1:44.467**	1:44.509	1:49.043 (8)	13	tyre exploded
21	S. Johansson	S	36	Onyx ORE1 Ford DFR V8	1:47.700	1:49.935	**1:48.348**	1:52.051 (23)	8	rear wheel bearing seal
22	A. Nannini	I	19	Benetton B188 Ford DFR V8	–	**1:45.033**	1:45.040	1:48.268 (5)	6	ignition
23	T. Boutsen	B	5	Williams FW12C Renault V10	–	1:45.520	**1:44.702**	1:48.826 (6)	4	collision/Pirro
24	A. Caffi	I	21	Dallara BMS 189 Ford DFR V8	–	1:48.671	**1:47.679**	1:51.934 (22)	2	electrics
25	M. Alboreto	I	29	Lola LC89 Lamborghini V12I	1:47.919	**48.670**	1:48.726	1:51.403 (19)	1	clutch
26	O. Grouillard	F	26	Ligier JS33 Ford DFR V8	–	47.408	**1:46.893**	1:50.367 (15)	–	clutch
27	L. Sala	E	24	Minardi M189 Ford DFR V8	–	1:49.587	**1:48.686**	DNQ		
28	B. Gachot	B	37	Onyx ORE1 Ford DFR V8	1:47.283	1:49.252	**1:49.004**	DNQ		
29	C. Danner	D	38	Rial ARC02 Ford DFR V8	–	1:50.678	**1:49.767**	DNQ		
30	V. Weidler	D	39	Rial ARC02 Ford DFR V8	–	1:50.673	**1:49.770**	DNQ		
–	Y. Dalmas	F	41	GS JH23 Ford DFR V8	1:47.920	DNPQ	DNPQ			
–	N. Larini	I	17	Osella FA1M Ford DFR V8	1:48.301	DNPQ	DNPQ			
–	G. Tarquini	I	40	AGS JG 23 Ford DFR V8	1:48.558	DNPQ	DNPQ			
–	P. Ghinzani	I	18	Osella FA1M Ford DFR V8	1:48.564	DNPQ	DNPQ			
–	R. Moreno	BR	31	Coloni C3 Ford DFR V8	1:48.567	DNPQ	DNPQ			
–	P. Raphanel	F	32	Coloni C3 Ford DFR V8	1:48.780	DNPQ	DNPQ			
–	G. Foitek	S	33	EuroBrun189 Judd V8	1:49.458	DNPQ	DNPQ			
–	A. Suzuki	J	35	Zakspeed ZK189 Yamaha V8	1:49.527	DNPQ	DNPQ			
–	B. Schneider	D	34	Zakspeed ZK189 Yamaha V8	1:50.455	DNPQ	DNPQ			

Circuit Data: Hockenheimring, length 4.223 miles/6.223 km, race distance 45 laps = 190 miles/305.9 km, race weather cloudy and warm.
Notes: Alboreto (I) in Lola No. 29, replacing Bernard. Pirro, No. 20, now has Benetton B189 and Ford HB V8 engine also EuroBrun is now ER189 rather than ER188B, but still with Judd V8 engine. Newcomers to pre-qualifying are Larrousse, Moreno and Tarquini; no longer do Brabham, Weidler and Caffi have to pre-qualify.

1. A SENNA	
	2. A PROST
27. N MANSELL	
	28. G BERGER
6. R PATRESE	
	5. T BOUTSEN
19. A NANNINI	
	11. N PIQUET
20. E PIRRO	
	4. J ALESI
26. O GROUILLARD	
	7. M BRUNDLE
23. P MARTINI	
	15. M GUGELMIN
30. P ALLIOT	
	8. S MODENA
9. D WARWICK	
	12. S NAKAJIMA
3. J PALMER	
	21. A CAFFI
22. A DE CESARIS	
	16. I CAPELLI
25. R ARNOUX	
	36. S JOHANSSON
10. E CHEEVER	
	29. M ALBORETO

LAP CHART

Grid Order	Driver	Laps 1–45 (car numbers)
1	A. Senna	1 1 1 1 1 1 1 1 1 1 1 1 1 1 1 1 1 1 1 1 1 2 2 2 2 2 2 2 2 2 2 2 2 2 2 2 2 2 2 2 2 2 1 1 1
2	A. Prost	2 2 2 2 2 2 2 2 2 2 2 2 2 2 2 2 2 2 2 27 2 1 1 1 1 1 1 1 1 1 1 1 1 1 1 1 1 1 1 1 1 1 1 2 2 2
27	N. Mansell	28 28 28 28 28 28 28 28 28 28 28 28 28 27 27 27 27 20 20 20 27 27 27 27 27 27 27 27 27 27 27 27 27 27 27 27 27 27 27 27 27 27 27 27 27
28	G. Berger	27 27 27 27 27 27 27 27 27 27 27 27 27 20 20 20 20 2 27 20 20 20 20 20 20 20 6 6 6 6 6 6 6 6 6 6 6 6 6 6 6 6 6 6 6
6	R. Patrese	5 5 19 19 19 20 20 20 20 20 20 20 20 6 6 6 6 6 11 11 11 6 6 6 6 6 15 11 11 11 11 11 11 11 11 11 11 11 11 11 11 11 11 11 11
5	T. Boutsen	19 19 5 5 20 6 6 6 6 6 6 6 6 11 11 11 11 11 4 4 15 15 15 15 15 15 11 9 9 9 9 9 9 9 9 9 9 9 9 9 9 9 9 9 9
19	A. Nannini	20 20 20 20 6 11 11 11 11 11 11 11 11 4 4 4 4 4 15 15 6 11 11 11 11 11 9 15 12 12 12 12 12 12 12 22 22 22 22 22 22 22 22 22 22
11	N. Piquet	6 6 6 6 11 4 4 4 4 4 4 4 15 15 15 15 15 6 6 9 9 9 9 9 9 22 22 22 22 22 22 22 22 22 7 7 7 7 7 7 7 7 7
20	E. Pirro	11 11 11 11 4 7 7 7 8 8 8 15 15 12 12 12 12 12 9 9 8 8 8 8 8 22 12 16 16 16 8 8 8 8 7 23 23 10 10 23 23 23 23
4	J. Alesi	4 4 4 4 7 8 8 8 7 15 15 8 12 8 8 8 9 9 8 8 23 23 23 22 8 8 8 8 8 8 8 7 7 7 7 8 10 10 23 23 4 4 4
26	O. Grouillard	7 7 7 7 8 15 15 15 7 12 12 8 9 9 9 8 8 23 23 22 22 22 23 12 16 16 7 7 7 23 23 23 23 23 8 4 4 4 25 25
7	M. Brundle	8 8 8 8 15 9 9 9 9 12 9 9 9 7 7 7 7 23 23 22 22 10 10 10 12 12 16 7 7 23 23 23 10 10 10 10 10 4 25 25 25
23	P. Martini	15 15 15 15 9 12 12 12 12 9 7 7 7 23 23 23 22 22 10 10 16 16 16 10 10 23 23 23 10 10 10 16 25 4 4 4 25
15	M. Gugelmin	9 9 9 9 12 19 23 23 23 23 23 23 22 22 7 10 16 16 12 12 16 16 10 10 23 23 10 10 16 25 4 4 4 25
30	P. Alliot	21 21 12 12 23 23 22 22 22 22 22 22 20 10 10 10 16 12 12 7 7 7 7 7 25 25 4 4 4
8	S. Modena	12 12 23 23 22 22 25 10 10 10 10 10 16 16 16 16 7 7 7 25 25 25 25 25 4 4
9	D. Warwick	23 23 22 22 25 25 10 10 10 10 16 16 16 16 7 7 7 25 25 25 25 25 4 4
12	S. Nakajima	22 22 25 25 10 10 36 16 16 25 25 25 25 25 25 25 25 25
3	J. Palmer	25 25 10 10 36 36 16 30 30 30 30 30 30 3 3 3
21	A. Caffi	10 10 36 36 16 16 30 30 36 3 3 3 3 3
22	A. de Cesaris	36 36 3 16 30 30 30 3 3
16	I. Capelli	3 3 16 30 3 3
25	R. Arnoux	29 16 30 3
36	S. Johansson	16 30
10	E. Cheever	30
29	M. Alboreto	

FASTEST LAPS

Pos.	Car No./Driver/Team		Time
1	1	A. Senna/McLaren	1:45.884
2	2	A. Prost/McLaren	1:45.977
3	27	N. Mansell/Ferrari	1:48.722
4	28	G. Berger/Ferrari	1:48.931
5	20	E. Pirro/Benetton	1:49.005
6	12	S. Nakajima/Lotus	1:49.311
7	19	A. Nannini/Benetton	1:49.665
8	6	R. Patrese/Williams	1:49.910
9	11	N. Piquet/Lotus	1:49.917
10	10	E. Cheever/Arrows	1:50.216
11	15	M. Gugelmin/Leyton House	1:50.493
12	23	P. Martini/Minardi	1:50.676
13	4	J. Alesi/Tyrrell	1:50.817
14	9	D. Warwick/Arrows	1:50.899
15	7	M. Brundle/Brabham	1:51.012
16	5	T. Boutsen/Williams	1:51.168
17	16	I. Capelli/Leyton House	1:51.362
18	22	A. de Cesaris/BMS Dallara	1:51.495
19	8	S. Modena/Brbaham	1:52.562
20	30	P. Alliot/Larrousse	1:52.638
21	3	J. Palmer/Tyrrell	1:52.888
22	21	A. Caffi/BMS Dallara	1:52.417
23	36	S. Johansson/Onyx	1:53.686
24	25	R. Arnoux/Ligier	1:53.907
25	29	M. Alboreto/Tyrrell	2:10.370

CHAMPIONSHIP POINTS

Drivers

1	A. Prost	53 pts
2	A. Senna	36 pts
3	N. Mansell	25 pts
4	R. Patrese	25 pts
5	T. Boutsen	13 pts
6	A. Nannini	12 pts
7	N. Piquet	8 pts
8	M. Alboreto	6 pts
9	J. Herbert	5 pts
10	D. Warwick	5 pts
11	A. de Cesaris	4 pts
	M. Gugelmin	4 pts
	E. Cheever	4 pts
	S. Modena	4 pts
15	A. Caffi	4 pts
16	C. Danner	3 pts
	J. Alesi	3 pts
18	S. Johansson	2 pts
	R. Arnoux	2 pts
	P. Martini	2 pts
21	G. Tarquini	1 pt
21	O. Grouillard	1 pt
	L. Sala	1 pt
	M. Brundle	1 pt
	J. Palmer	1 pt

Drivers/Constructors

1	McLaren	89 pts
2	Williams	38 pts
3	Ferrari	25 pts
4	Benetton	17 pts
5	Tyrrell	10 pts
6	Arrows	9 pts
7	Dallara	8 pts
	Lotus	8 pts
9	Brabham	5 pts
10	Leyton House	4 pts
11	Rial	3 pts
	Ligier	3 pts
	Minardi	3 pts
14	Onyx	2 pts
15	AGS	1 pt

Existing qualifying lap record: Keke Rosberg, McLaren-TAG MP4/2C, 1m 42.013s at 239.864 kph/149.045 mph in 1986

Existing race lap record: Nigel Mansell, Williams-Honda FW11B, 1m 45.716s, 231.462 kph/143.824 mph in 1987

Existing distance record: Nelson Piquet, Williams-Honda FW11B, 44 laps in 1hr 21m 25.091s at 220.394 kph/136.946 mph in 1987

PAST WINNERS

Year	Driver	Nat.	Car	Circuit
1979	Alan Jones	AUS	3.0 Williams FW07 Ford	Hockenheim
1980	Jacques Laffite	F	3.0 Ligier JS 11/15 Ford	Hockenheim
1981	Nelson Piquet	BR	3.0 Brabham BT49C Ford	Hockenheim
1982	Patrick Tambay	F	1.5 Ferrari 126C2 t/c	Hockenheim
1983	René Arnoux	F	1.5 Ferrari 126C3 t/c	Hockenheim
1984	Alain Prost	F	1.5 McLaren MP4/2 TAG t/c	Hockenheim
1985	Michele Alboreto	I	1.5 Ferrari 156/85 t/c	New Nürburgring
1986	Nelson Piquet	BR	1.5 Williams FW11 Honda t/c	Hockenheim
1987	Nelson Piquet	BR	1.5 Williams FW11B Honda t/c	Hockenheim
1988	Ayrton Senna	BR	1.5McLaren MP4/4 Honda t/c	Hockenheim

Budapest

POP 84 MAGYAR NAGYDÍJ · 13 AUGUSZTUS

'The best race of the season' and 'the best race of my career' were just two views of the 1989 Pop 84 Hungarian Grand Prix at the Hungaroring. The latter comment, of course, came from the winner, Nigel Mansell. The former comment was in no small way due to his gritty performance.

Foitek's new Eurobrun failed to pre-qualify, leaving him plenty of time to appreciate Budapest's stunning architecture.

After all, you simply don't win Grand Prix races in 1989 from 12th on the grid. It isn't – or allegedly can't be – done. Usually you don't even overtake people to win Grand Prix races. But happily for nearly everyone, Mansell confounded all that. And by doing so, he not only put the racing back into Grand Prix racing, but his performance restored many outsiders' faith in the sport.

Yet the stage for his most challenging of performances was also tight. This twisty but billiard-table smooth circuit was also responsible for the weekend of changing fortunes. It brought the field closer together, produced surprises and frustrations and to some extent equalised the field. The Hungaroring, ironically, was a great leveller.

In these days of unlimited budgets, where McLaren had been testing future Honda engines for five days only the previous week, many were looking for a factor which tightened up the field, one which made all men equal, would bring back some racing at the head of a Grand Prix pack.

And where better than (increasingly less) Communist Hungary, where all men should be equal? A combination of that smooth surface, the twisty circuit, few straights and traffic put Ricardo Patrese on pole position, Caffi third on the grid, six V8s ahead of a Ferrari V12 – and that in qualifying alone.

Admittedly the so-called multi-cylinders came into their own in the race itself but at least it was on an equal basis. Patrese's Williams-Renault, the two McLarens, first Berger, then Mansell rejoined by Berger, all fought it out in the front-running bunch. 'What was also good,' as Mansell pointed out, 'was that I raced against all the top teams, and had to overtake them, and I beat them. It was a very good race for me.'

Racing, of course, is all about overtaking people, the challenge of the man and machine in front and behind. Some people had forgotten this, perhaps. The competition in recent months had clouded some memories.

In spite of the lack of straights, this was a race where the winner had to overtake, to race for his points. In Mansell's case, he overtook nine people, and was justly rewarded with the same number of points for his win. For once, Senna didn't overtake anyone for his second place, while

A kaleidoscope of colour, Ford power,
but only eighth place for Pirro.

Brundle spins,
Piquet and Gachot dive through.

incident with Jean Alesi when the frustrated Frenchman 'brake-tested' his peer, Mansell was still relaxed.

Twelfth the next afternoon would seem to be a disaster, and in some ways it was. Yet Nigel had a card up his sleeve. The qualifiers wouldn't work, sure, so he'd spent time on soft race tyres. And on those same soft race tyres, the next morning in the race day warm-up, he set fastest time overall, ahead of Jonathan Palmer, Senna and Berger. 'We understood what the problem was last night. I knew I'd be competitive for the race.'

While front-row men Patrese and Senna plus Prost and Cheever went for the harder B compound Goodyear, Mansell went for the softer C. And as he would explain, he was able to preserve them. 'I made a bansai [*sic*] start and overtook four cars. Then I had to wait. I had a quiet, Sunday afternoon drive for 20 laps.

'It was probably a good thing that I was caught up in a five-car battle at the start because it meant that I didn't over-use my tyres. They were good almost all the way to the end. But then I got angry.'

Japanese computer games.

championship leader Prost was overtaken by Mansell and overtook Caffi and Cheever on his way to fourth place.

Hungary was the stage for a great race. The host country and its capital, Budapest, become more attractive and popular every year. And although the tighter, twistier circuits may be less popular with drivers, they have their place in the championship, and for spectactors they sometimes artificially create the closest racing.

BRIGHT SPARKS

Nigel Mansell had said in Germany that he really expected to be at the front at the Hungaroring. There was no doubt about it. So it came as a nasty shock when the qualifiers didn't work. He was second in Friday's free session, but only ninth that afternoon. He was tenth the next morning, and had slipped to 12th on the grid by the end of qualifying.

'We went completely the wrong way on settings and we're going to change everything for tomorrow,' he explained on Friday. 'We're trying to get grip while not upsetting the handling.' In spite of an

*A pit stop to replace a punctured tyre
dropped Alesi out of contention.*

The overtaking began. Nannini's pit stop for tyres put the Ferrari in seventh place, just behind Boutsen and Caffi. Mansell disposed of the Belgian on lap 20, the Italian a lap later. Now he had to make up the gap between himself and the quartet of Patrese, Senna, Prost and Berger ahead of him. He replaced Berger, who stopped for tyres at lap 37, half distance.

Prost was swiftly disposed of. 'Alain was very fair,' said Mansell. 'I got alongside him, and then he let me go. But not one overtaking manoeuvre was comfortable.'

For eleven laps, Patrese, Senna, Mansell and Prost formed a high speed quartet. Then Patrese dropped back, and the duel was on: Senna from Mansell. Yet it lasted just five laps. On lap 58 they came up on Johansson. He'd been having trouble with his gear selection, and as they came up on him out of the third corner, his Onyx slipped out of fourth gear. Senna was right behind him. 'I nearly hit the back of Senna's car,' said Mansell, who 'threw the car to the right and slingshot past'.

It was an incredible manoeuvre, the decision taken in a split second, but it gave him the lead. 'Then I pushed hard to pull away from Senna,' and pull away he did: fastest lap on lap 66 of the race, and he was home and dry.

The hero of the day was Mansell, without doubt. He dedicated his win

Clockwise from left: Alboreto enjoys Lamborghini power, but no results. Only fourth for Prost. Iron curtain mania: they couldn't afford one, but loved the win.

to Enzo Ferrari, the day before the first anniversary of the death of the man who would have been so proud of the Englishman's victory.

But others should not be forgotten. Patrese's pole position ending McLaren's run of poles in the Italian's 185th Grand Prix was a popular demonstration of the Italian's impressive motivation and talent. He controlled the race superbly for 52 laps under the utmost pressure, and was cruelly robbed of the lead by a punctured radiator.

Caffi's third on the grid was immensely popular and perhaps the young Italian deserved more than seventh place at the end. Eddie Cheever certainly deserved more than fifth from what he called 'the race of which I've been most proud in Formula One'. He held off Nannini and Boutsen, and nearly Prost during the closing stages, doing the whole race on one set of Goodyear's Bs.

RACE DEBRIEF

The smooth and slightly quicker revised Hungaroring circuit provided shocks and surprises from the first day of practice. Johansson was quickest in pre-qualifying, but Ghinzani was a surprising second fastest, getting through the Friday morning barrier for the first time in 1989. Alboreto straightlined chicanes – and consequently cracked a rib – to pre-qualify third, with Bertrand Gachot having to take his qualifiers early after a puncture on a circuit that he didn't know.

Prost, Mansell, Patrese and Caffi were quickest that morning, but in the afternoon, as Patrese set a time 1.3s quicker than anyone, it all came home to the quick boys: traffic and this non-abrasive surface would play a great part. Caffi was second, McLarens and Ferraris searched for grip.

There were many problems here and there. Palmer had a brake cable wear through and crashed. Fortunately, for the first time since Imola, Tyrrell had a spare car. Ligier were in deep trouble: Arnoux didn't do a lap on Saturday morning, and didn't qualify that afternoon. The Williamses suffered some handling problems like their multi-cylindered partners; McLaren, Ferrari and March were having trouble with their qualifiers.

Although the track was faster on Saturday afternoon, not everyone improved. Senna made a demon effort but it resulted in mistakes, Nannini and Pirro both spun, and Boutsen's gearbox jammed. Patrese, then, was on pole, Senna pipped Caffi who lost an engine, Boutsen came

up to fourth from Prost and Berger. Mansell, on both B and C race tyres, slipped to 12th.

The warm-up was just as surprising. Mansell was happy with both race and spare chassis, Palmer adopted Alesi's settings and was second quickest. Senna was third, Prost had pick-up problems, and Boutsen needed a new engine. When that was found to misfire, he would start in Patrese's spare which was set up, inside and out, for the Italian.

Caffi was only 14th and first of the Pirelli runners. Pirro had a fuel fire and would start in the spare, and Capelli would do likewise after crashing.

The crowd, slightly larger than the previous year, saw Senna challenging Patrese down into the first corner, but it was the Italian who emerged ahead from Senna with Caffi being strongly challenged by a fast-starting Berger in fourth. Caffi, however, simply didn't have the speed of the Goodyear-shod multi-cylinders, and while Patrese and Senna rushed off into the distance, Caffi found Berger, Prost, Boutsen and Nannini, soon joined by Mansell, bottled up behind him.

Berger got by on lap four and by lap eight was challenging Senna which actually allowed Patrese to pull away a little. The gap of 2.8s between first and second would not be matched for another 59 laps.

It was on this lap also that Prost took Caffi and began to gnaw away at the 7.3s gap between himself and the three in front. Eight laps later, that had all but disappeared.

Prost left Boutsen and Mansell (making up four places at the start) behind Caffi. Nannini had been there as well, but stopped early for tyres, saying that 'the car was going better and better, and I wanted it to be in good shape at the end'. He wouldn't be there, however, the car's gear linkage falling apart after 46 laps.

Instead, the battle for fifth place was joined by Derek Warwick who was being shadowed by the Marches of Capelli and Gugelmin. But at the 20-lap mark, Mansell began to move. He overtook Boutsen and then Caffi, while Boutsen headed for the pits and new tyres. 'I couldn't overtake Caffi, so I decided to stop early, and then had a faster, clearer race.' The Marches also disappeared: Capelli first when his wheel pegs sheared, and then Gugelmin when the electric pump for his drinks bottle shorted out, which left Warwick and teammate Cheever challenging Caffi for his sixth place.

At the front, Senna had been waiting for Patrese to run into backmarkers, surely a problem on this tight circuit, but when he did, it was Senna who nearly lost out when Alboreto took his racing line and briefly delayed the McLaren. Behind the leading quartet, covered by mere seconds, Mansell was steadily making up time, and when teammate Berger, the only one of the leading quartet on the softer Cs like Mansell, pitted for Bs, his English teammate took over fourth place.

Berger rejoined behind Caffi but quickly overtook him, while the Italian's second biggest challenger, Warwick, left him in peace when the

Brabhams over Hungary: both finished, albeit out of the points.

Ch. Danner
V. Weidler

Briton felt that he had a problem with the rear end. A lengthy pit stop revealed nothing but the problem was cured with a change of tyres, suggesting a loose wheel nut might have been the culprit. On rejoining, Warwick was 'tripped over' by Nakajima, determined to take his usual racing line in spite of the presence of the slower car trying to keep out of the way. Soon after Caffi pitted for tyres, promoting Cheever to sixth, being closed on by Nannini and Boutsen.

As they came up to half distance, Mansell was threatening Prost, and his excellent speed on softer C tyres down the hill through the third corner was enough to bring him alongside the Frenchman, who wisely let the Briton through to third place.

By now, Berger had joined the four ahead of him, although Warwick was running between him and Prost. Warwick would complain (quietly) that the leaders were holding him up. Berger complained rather more loudly that Warwick was holding him up. But on lap 53, that wasn't important. A haze behind Patrese's Williams revealed that he was in trouble. Senna was through in a flash, and Mansell followed two corners later. Patrese managed to keep Prost and Berger behind him, but already he was four seconds behind Mansell. That became nine seconds when Patrese pulled off. A piece of metal had punctured his radiator. Unlike Silverstone, where he crashed on his own water, this time the engine had lost power and then the Italian had disconsolately pulled off, his race over.

Prost, however, had received a haze of oil and water on his visor, and in trying to avoid it, had run wide on to the marbles and his tyres had

picked up debris. He and Berger were suddenly 16 seconds down on the leading duo – but more importantly, only three seconds ahead of Cheever and Boutsen who had closed in behind.

There was bad news for Ferrari on lap 57: Berger pulled off. He'd had gearbox trouble in the warm-up but it hadn't been fixed correctly and had broken again. Then there was good news for Ferrari. Senna had been boxed in behind Johansson and Mansell had ducked round them both to take the lead.

Mansell put the hammer down, and ten laps later, with another nine to go, he was 4.6s ahead of the McLaren. Both had tyre vibration and Senna had brake trouble too.

Behind them, Cheever and Boutsen were closing rapidly on Prost. He had no alternative but to pit for new tyres. Cheever lost out to Boutsen while Prost came charging up. And although Prost had trouble with a cutting engine, he managed to overtake Cheever at the start of the very last lap to take fourth place, the disappointed Cheever back in fifth. It was that sort of a race.

MILESTONES

- Patrese's third pole position brings to an end McLaren's run of 17 consecutive poles
- Ghinzani's first race of the year

FORMULA 1 WORLD CHAMPIONSHIP

POP 84 MAGYAR NAGYDÍJ

ENTRIES · PRACTICE · RESULTS

Pos	Driver/Nationality		No.	Car/Engine	P.Q. (cool, hazy)	Practice 1 (warm, hazy)	Practice 2 (warm, cloudy)	Warm-up (pos) (warm, cloudy)	Laps	Time/Retirement (warm, cloudy)
1	N. Mansell	GB	27	Ferrari 649 Ferrari V12	–	1:22.544	1:21.951	1:23.965 (1)	77	1hr49m38.650
2	A. Senna	BR	1	McLaren MP4/5 Honda V10	–	1:21.576	1:20.039	1:24.176 (3)	77	1hr50m04.617
3	T. Boutsen	B	5	Williams FW12C Renault V10	–	1:23.492	1:21.001	1:24.604 (9)	77	1hr50m17.004
4	A. Prost	F	2	McLaren MP4/5 Honda V10	–	1:21.076	1:22.267	1:24.590 (7)	77	1hr50m22.827
5	E. Cheever	USA	10	Arrows A11 Ford DFR V8	–	1:23.251	1:22.374	1:25.322 (13)	77	1hr50m23.756
6	N. Piquet	BR	11	Lotus 101 Judd V8	–	1:22.837	1:22.406	1:24.454 (5)	77	1hr50m50.629
7	A. Caffi	I	21	Dallara BMS 189 Ford DFR V8	–	1:21.040	1:20.704	1:25.635 (14)	77	1hr51m02.875
8	E. Pirro	I	20	Benetton B189 Ford DFR V8	–	1:23.772	1:23.399	1:25.674 (15)	76	1hr49m40.374
9	J. Alesi	F	4	Tyrrell 018 Judd V8	–	1:23.853	1:21.799	1:24.591 (8)	76	1hr50m14.589
10	D. Warwick	GB	9	Arrows A11 Ford DFR V8	–	1:23.111	1:21.617	1:26.092 (17)	76	1hr50m29.917
11	S. Modena	I	8	Brabham BT58 Judd V8	–	1:23.090	1:21.472	1:26.491 (21)	76	1hr50m45.815
12	M. Brundle	GB	7	Brabham BT58 Judd V8	–	1:22.970	1:22.296	1:26.746 (22)	75	1hr50m36.986
13	J. Palmer	GB	3	Tyrrell 018 Judd V8	–	1:24.670	1:22.578	1:24.097	73	1hr50m05.093
14	L. Sala	S	24	Minardi M189 Ford DFR V8	–	1:23.017	1:24.188	1:27.751 (26)	57	collision/Modena
15	G. Berger	A	28	Ferrari 640 Ferrari V12	–	1:21.304	1:21.270	1:24.212 (4)	56	clutch
16	R. Patrese	I	6	Williams FW12C Renault V10	–	1:19.726	1:20.644	1:24.534 (6)	54	holed radiator/engine
17	S. Johansson	S	36	Onyx ORE1 Ford DFR V8	1:22.836	1:23.372	1:23.148	1:24.937 (36)	48	gearbox mounting
18	A. Nannini	I	19	Benetton B189 Ford HB V8	–	1:21.448	1:21.301	1:25.078 (11)	46	gear linkage
19	B. Gachot	B	37	Onyx ORE1 Ford DFR V8	1:24.412	1:22.634	1:23.720	1:25.945 (16)	38	gearbox
20	S. Nakajima	J	12	Lotus 101 Judd V8	–	1:23.996	1:22.630	1:26.198 (19)	33	collision/Warwick
21	M. Gugelmin	BR	15	Leyton House CG891 Judd V8	–	1:22.949	1:22.083	1:25.150 (12)	27	loom short
22	I. Capelli	I	16	Leyton House CG 891 Judd V8	–	1:22.445	1:22.088	1:26.182 (18)	26	wheel pegs
23	M. Alboreto	I	29	Lola LC89 Lamborghini V12	1:24.323	1:23.733	1:25.660	1:26.996 (24)	26	engine
24	P. Ghinzani	I	18	Osella FA1M Ford DFR V8	1:24.086	1:23.091	1:22.763	1:27.463 (25)	20	electrics
25	P. Martini	I	23	Minardi M189 Ford DFR V8	–	1:21.746	1:32.546	1:26.935 (23)	19	wheel bearing
26	A. de Cesaris	I	22	Dallara BMS 189 Ford DFR V8	–	1:23.463	1:22.410	1:26.379 (20)	–	clutch
27	R. Arnoux	F	25	Ligier JS33 Ford DFR V8	–	1:25.862	1:24.003	DNQ		
28	O. Grouillard	F	26	Ligier JS33 Ford DFR V8	–	1:24.702	1:25.169	DNQ		
29	C. Danner	D	38	Rial ARC02 Ford DFR V8	–	1:26.485	1:25.017	DNQ		
30	V. Weidler	D	39	Rial ARC02 Ford DFR V8	–	Time d/a	1:26.320	DNQ		
–	N. Larini	I	17	Osella FA1M Ford DFR V8	1:24.601	DNPQ	DNPQ			
–	P. Alliot	F	30	Lola LC89 Lamborghini V12	1:24.928	DNPQ	DNPQ			
–	Y. Dalmas	F	41	AGS JH23 Ford DFR V8	1:25.571	DNPQ	DNPQ			
–	B. Schneider	D	34	Zakspeed ZK189 Yamaha DFR V8	1:25.613	DNPQ	DNPQ			
–	G. Tarquini	I	40	AGS JH24 Ford DFR V8	1:25.685	DNPQ	DNPQ			
–	R. Moreno	BR	31	Coloni C3 Ford DFR V8	1:26.903	DNPQ	DNPQ			
–	G. Foitek	S	33	EuroBrun ER189 Judd V8	1:27.478	DNPQ	DNPQ			
–	A. Suzuki	J	35	Zakspeed ZK189 Ford DFR V8	1:28.113	DNPQ	DNPQ			

Circuit Data: Hungaroring, circuit changes mean existing records no longer apply, circuit length is now: 2.463 miles/3.964 kms, race distance 77 laps = 189.6 miles/305.5 km, race weather cloudy and warm.

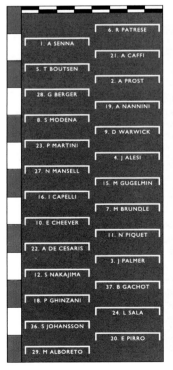

1. A SENNA
6. R PATRESE
5. T BOUTSEN
21. A CAFFI
28. G BERGER
2. A PROST
8. S MODENA
19. A NANNINI
23. P MARTINI
9. D WARWICK
27. N MANSELL
4. J ALESI
16. I CAPELLI
15. M GUGELMIN
10. E CHEEVER
7. M BRUNDLE
22. A DE CESARIS
11. N PIQUET
12. S NAKAJIMA
3. J PALMER
18. P GHINZANI
37. B GACHOT
36. S JOHANSSON
24. L SALA
29. M ALBORETO
20. E PIRRO

LAP CHART

Grid Order	Lap-by-lap positions (laps 1–77)
6 R. Patrese	6 6 6 6 6 6 6 6 6 6 6 6 6 6 6 6 6 6 6 6 6 6 6 6 6 6 6 6 6 6 6 6 6 6 6 6 6 6 6 6 6 6 6 6 6 6 6 6 6 6 6 6 6 6 6 6 6 6 6 6 6 6 6 6 6 6 6 6 1 1 1 1 27 27 27 27 27 27 27 27 27 27 27 27 27 27 27 27 27 27
1 A. Senna	1 1 1 1 1 1 1 1 1 1 1 1 1 1 1 1 1 1 1 1 1 1 1 1 1 1 1 1 1 1 1 1 1 1 1 1 1 1 1 1 1 1 1 1 1 1 1 1 1 1 1 1 1 1 1 1 1 1 1 1 1 1 1 1 1 1 1 1 27 27 27 27 27 1 1 1 1 1 1 1 1 1 1 1 1 1 1 1 1 1 1 1 1
21 A. Caffi	21 21 21 28 28 28 28 28 28 28 28 28 28 28 28 28 28 28 28 28 28 28 28 28 28 28 2 2 2 2 2 2 2 2 2 27 27 27 27 27 27 27 27 27 27 27 6 2 2 2 2 2 2 2 2 2 2 2 10 10 10 5 5 5 5 5 5 5 5 5 5 5 5 5 5 5 5
5 T. Boutsen	28 28 28 21 21 21 21 2 2 2 2 2 2 2 2 2 2 2 2 2 2 2 2 2 2 2 2 28 27 27 27 27 27 27 27 27 27 27 2 2 2 2 2 2 2 2 2 2 2 28 28 28 10 10 10 10 10 5 5 5 10 10 10 10 10 10 10 10 10 10 10 10 2
2 A. Prost	2 2 2 2 2 2 21 21 21 21 21 21 21 21 21 21 21 21 27 27 27 27 27 27 27 27 27 21 28 28 28 28 28 28 28 28 28 28 28 28 28 28 28 28 28 6 10 10 5 5 5 5 5 2 2 2 2 2 2 2 2 2 2 2 2 2 2 2 2 10
28 G. Berger	5 5 5 5 5 5 5 5 5 5 5 5 5 5 5 5 27 27 21 21 21 21 21 21 21 21 28 28 21 21 21 10 10 10 10 10 10 10 10 10 10 10 10 10 10 10 5 5 1 1 1 1 1 1 1 1 1 1 1 1 1 1 1 1 1 1 1 1 1 1 1 1 1 1 1 1
19 A. Nannini	19 19 19 19 19 19 19 19 19 19 27 27 27 27 27 27 5 5 9 9 9 9 9 9 9 9 9 9 9 10 10 10 19 19 19 19 19 19 19 19 19 19 19 5 5 5 5 5 5 5 5 5 11 11 21 21 21 21 21 21 21 21 21 21 21 21 21 21 21 21 21 21 21
8 S. Modena	27 27 27 27 27 27 27 27 27 27 9 9 9 9 9 9 9 9 16 16 16 16 15 10 10 10 10 10 11 19 19 5 5 5 5 5 5 5 5 5 11 11 11 11 11 11 11 11 11 11 11 11 21 20 20 20 20 20 20 20 20 20 20 20 20 20 20 20 20 20 20 20 20
9 D. Warwick	9 9 9 9 9 9 9 9 9 9 16 16 16 16 16 16 16 15 15 15 10 10 11 11 11 11 11 11 11 19 11 5 21 11 11 11 11 11 11 11 21 21 21 21 21 21 21 21 20 20 8 8 8 4 4 4 4 4 4 4 4 4 4 4 4 4 4 4 4
23 A. de Cesaris	16 16 16 16 16 16 16 16 16 19 23 15 15 15 15 15 15 10 10 10 10 11 19 19 19 19 9 5 11 11 21 21 21 21 21 21 21 19 3 3 3 20 20 20 20 8 8 4 4 4 8 8 8 8 8 8 8 8 9 9 9 9 9 9 9 9 9 9
4 J. Alesi	23 23 23 23 23 23 23 23 23 23 15 23 10 10 10 10 10 5 11 11 11 11 19 12 12 12 5 5 3 3 3 3 3 3 3 3 3 3 8 20 20 20 8 8 8 4 4 9 9 9 9 9 9 9 9 9 9 8 8 8 8 8 8 8 8
27 N. Mansell	4 8 8 8 8 8 8 8 8 15 8 10 23 23 11 11 11 11 12 12 19 12 12 36 5 5 12 3 8 8 8 8 8 8 8 8 8 20 8 8 8 4 4 4 9 24 7 7 7 7 7 7 7 7 7 7 7 7 7 7 7 7 7
15 M. Gugelmin	8 15 15 15 15 15 15 15 15 8 10 8 11 11 11 23 3 12 12 12 19 19 36 36 5 36 3 3 8 20 20 20 20 20 20 20 20 4 4 4 9 9 9 24 24 7 3 3 3 3 3 3 3 3 3 3 3 3 3 3 3 3 3
16 I. Capelli	15 12 10 10 10 10 10 10 10 10 10 11 11 8 3 3 3 12 19 19 36 36 5 5 3 3 3 8 8 20 7 7 7 4 4 4 4 4 9 9 9 9 3 24 24 24 7 7 7 3
7 M. Brundle	10 10 11 11 11 11 11 11 11 11 11 3 3 3 8 12 19 36 36 5 5 5 16 3 8 8 8 37 20 7 4 4 36 36 36 36 36 9 9 9 24 24 24 24 24 7 7 7 3
10 E. Cheever	11 11 3 3 3 3 3 3 3 3 37 12 12 12 8 8 8 3 3 3 3 3 8 37 37 37 20 7 4 36 36 36 9 9 9 9 36 24 24 24 7 7 7 7 3 3 3
11 N. Piquet	37 37 37 37 37 37 37 37 37 37 12 36 36 36 36 19 36 8 8 8 8 8 37 20 20 20 7 4 12 9 9 24 24 24 24 24 24 7 7 7 36 36
22 P. Martini	3 3 12 12 12 12 12 12 12 12 12 19 19 19 19 36 19 37 37 37 37 37 37 20 7 7 7 4 36 36 24 24 24 7 7 7 7 7 36 36 36
3 J. Palmer	12 4 24 24 24 24 24 36 36 36 36 19 37 37 37 37 37 20 20 20 20 20 7 4 4 4 36 24 24 37 37 37 37
12 S. Nakajima	24 24 36 36 36 36 24 24 20 20 20 20 20 20 20 7 7 7 7 7 4 24 24 24 37 37
37 B. Gachot	18 36 18 18 20 20 20 20 20 7 7 7 7 7 7 7 4 24
18 P. Ghinzani	36 18 20 20 18 7 7 7 4 4 4 4 4 4 4 24 24 24 24 24 24
24 L. Sala	20 20 7 7 18 18 18 4 24 24 24 24 24 24 24 24 29 29 29 29 29 29
36 S. Johansson	29 7 29 29 29 29 29 29 29 29 29 29 29 29 29 29 29 18
20 E. Pirro	7 29 4 4 4 4 4 18 18 18 18 18 18 18 18 18 18
29 M. Alboreto	

FASTEST LAPS

Pos.	Car No./Driver/Team	Time
1	27 N. Mansell/Ferrari	1:22.637
2	2 A. Prost/McLaren	1:22.654
3	28 G. Berger/Ferrari	1:23.214
4	1 A. Senna/McLaren	1:23.313
5	5 T. Boutsen/Williams	1:23.396
6	7 M. Brundle/Brabham	1:23.442
7	11 N. Piquet/Lotus	1:23.620
8	19 A. Nannini/Benetton	1:23.702
9	10 E. Cheever/Arrows	1:23.894
10	21 A. Caffi/BMS Dallara	1:24.075
11	3 J. Palmer/Tyrrell	1:24.166
12	9 D. Warwick/Arrows	1:24.197
13	20 E. Pirro/Benetton	1:24.305
14	36 S. Johansson/Onyx	1:24.464
15	6 R. Patrese/Williams	1:24.559
16	15 M. Gugelmin/Leyton House	1:24.664
17	4 J. Alesi/Tyrrell	1:24.741
18	12 S. Nakajima/Lotus	1:24.903
19	8 S. Modena/Brabham	1:25.149
20	37 B. Gachot/Onyx	1:25.207
21	16 I. Capelli/Leyton House	1:25.710
22	24 L. Sala/Minardi	1:26.185
23	23 P. Martini/Minardi	1:26.691
24	18 P. Ghinzani/Osella	1:27.012
25	29 M. Alboreto/Larrousse	1:27.840

CHAMPIONSHIP POINTS

	Drivers			Drivers/Constructors	
1	A. Prost	56 pts		O. Grouillard	1 pt
2	A. Senna	42 pts		L. Sala	1 pt
3	N. Mansell	34 pts		M. Brundle	1 pt
	R. Patrese	25 pts		J. Palmer	1 pt
5	T. Boutsen	17 pts			
6	A. Nannini	12 pts	1	McLaren	98 pts
7	N. Piquet	9 pts	2	Williams	42 pts
8	M. Alboreto	6 pts	3	Ferrari	34 pts
	E. Cheever	6 pts	4	Benetton	17 pts
10	J. Herbert	5 pts	5	Arrows	11 pts
	D. Warwick	5 pts	6	Tyrrell	10 pts
12	A. de Cesaris	4 pts	7	Lotus	9 pts
	M. Gugelmin	4 pts	8	Dallara	8 pts
	S. Modena	4 pts	9	Brabham	5 pts
	A. Caffi	4 pts	10	Leyton House	4 pts
16	C. Danner	3 pts	11	Rial	3 pts
	J. Alesi	3 pts		Ligier	3 pts
18	S. Johansson	2 pts		Minardi	3 pts
	R. Arnoux	2 pts	14	Onyx	2 pts
	P. Martini	2 pts	15	AGS	1 pt
21	G. Tarquini	1 pt			

PAST WINNERS

Year	Driver	Nat.	Car	Circuit
1986	Nelson Piquet	BR	1.5 Williams FW11 Honda t/c	Hungaroring
1987	Nelson Piquet	BR	1.5 Williams FW11B Honda t/c	Hungaroring
1988	Ayrton Senna	BR	1.5 McLaren MP4/4 Honda t/c	Hungaroring

Left: an early start for the
Zakspeed team, but still no joy.

Spa

CHAMPION BELGIAN GRAND PRIX · 27 AOUT

The sight of 26 cars accelerating down the hill, out of the La Source hairpin, into one of the most daunting and spectacular combinations of corners, Eau Rouge

Spa is famous for torrential rain – start delayed by 30 minutes as the water sweepers descend into Eau Rouge.

and Le Raidillon, is always an impressive one. When it takes place in conditions that only 30 minutes previously had caused a delayed start, then one has to be in awe of the commitment of those involved.

It is a paradox of the sport that one of Formula One's most favourite circuits is also affected, all too often, by its least favourite track conditions. The ups and downs of the pine-clad Ardennes, with every variety of corner, test the drivers and their commitment, particularly in qualifying, as Senna underlined.

He'd shattered the previous pole-winning record, set by Nigel Mansell, by 1.2s, but explained that it was all down to commitment. With only one dry qualifying session – Friday's was a wash-out – there were just two chances on qualifiers, and it was all about knowing – imagining? – how much grip the qualifiers would give and then exploiting that grip.

Senna, then, revealed the commitment needed to set such a sparkling lap, and although he did admit that this was one of his best poles, he wouldn't say that it was the best.

Sunday's race weather called for more soul-searching from the drivers. The warm-up was already wet. The weather closed in more than ever as race time approached. The organisers, with FISA starter Roland Bruynserade making use of local knowledge, wisely delayed the start.

When it did happen, it was to everyone's surprise and the drivers' credit that they gave one another space and kept out of trouble. Forward and rearward visibility was virtually nil. Yet around half of the field felt capable of racing hard. They kept out of trouble early on, allowing their tyres to clear water from the track and minimise spray and then went racing.

Their progress was held up by backmarkers, of course. In the spray, marshals were unable to see the leaders behind slower cars and couldn't show the blue flag, and in a bunch of cars, it was unlikely that the backmarker could see either the blue flag or the car behind. Consequently, the use of the black and white flag to warn one driver that he was holding up others showed a lack of imagination on the part of those who demanded it, and was not entirely appropriate.

If there was one other impression from the Belgian Grand Prix, it was the absence of one of racing's establishment teams on the grid. A Grand Prix without Lotus is as unthinkable as a Grand Prix without Ferrari. But circumstances and a degree of bad luck for both dictated that there was no healthy car for Piquet to drive at the end of the one dry session. It was only the fourth time in Lotus's long history that they failed to start a Grand Prix.

Clockwise from top right corner: Birthday boy Warwick shelters under a makeshift marquee during the delayed start. Martini was impressive on Pirelli's hand-grooved slicks. Cheever received the black-and-white flag (unsportsmanlike behaviour) for holding up the leaders.

BRIGHT SPARKS

There were a number of people who held high hopes of this Grand Prix. At the start of the weekend, Zakspeed had hoped that testing and Yamaha engine progress might elevate them to become one of the chosen four to go into qualifying, but a spin from Bernd Schneider and uncompetitive Pirellis put paid to that. Roberto Moreno was also hopeful after an encouraging Coloni test, but again, it was not to be.

The rest of the day was wet but whereas at Monza, for instance, you might find a few drivers going out, expecting it to dry, everyone went out in the wet, knowing that Spa's traditional weather could well be in for the weekend. Behind Senna, Mansell and Berger, Arnoux, Johansson and Piquet followed in Friday morning's session, and that afternoon, Prost put his McLaren fifth with scarcely any complaint about his least favourite weather. 'He'll be racing hard, whatever the conditions,' pointed out a McLaren team member, 'the championship depends on it.'

The next day was dry and Prost went quickest in the morning session, and was second quickest to Senna's remarkable time that afternoon. It was multi-cylinders all the way, with McLarens on the front row, followed by Ferraris and Renaults.

The gap between Mansell's Ferrari (1m 52.898s) and Nannini's following Benetton (1m 55.075s) told the power story. Modena, in eighth place, was the first of the Pirelli runners which made things look encouraging for them. Gugelmin was much happier in ninth than he had been the previous day which he described as his worst day in Grand Prix racing. Warwick, sixth in the wet on Friday, had slipped to tenth but was still optimistic after a good test at Monza. Herbert, replacing F3000 driver Jean Alesi at Tyrrell, was encouraged to be quicker than teammate Palmer, in spite of a couple of excursions into the gravel traps.

The multi-cylinders were again dominant in the wet warm-up — but behind Pierluigi Martini for whom Pirelli hand-grooved some slicks. Their reaction to their wet weather problem slightly back fired when first Martin Brundle and then Stefano Modena crashed on the grooved slicks during the pre-race laps, but bold Martini and de Cesaris would set superb times on these tyres when the track began to dry and they changed on to them, later in the race.

Warwick's sixth place in the warm-up, ahead of Prost, Nannini and Boutsen, proved that he was willing to tackle the conditions, even on his birthday, and so it would prove in the race with the first of the DFR-powered runners coming home sixth, perhaps deserving more.

Fellow Anglo-Saxon Nigel Mansell was not one to let the weather get the better of him either, worrying Alain Prost during a superb final eight laps when the Briton used all the road and more in an effort to loom as large in Alain's mirrors as possible/find the best grip/cool the tyres/be in an overtaking position should anything happen. It didn't, but it was one of the best battles of the race.

You couldn't fault Ivan Capelli for his constant worrying of Pierluigi Martini, while Gugelmin did a good job to attempt to tame his bouncing March.

But the real winners were more general. Spa had done a great job to make the track safer. The drivers themselves had relatively few incidents in unfavourable conditions and the Belgians still turned out in full force, 65,000, in spite of them.

Clockwise from above: Nakajima contemplates — P6 in the wet — disaster in the dry and no Lotuses in the race. Boutsen's century at home.
Running blind in the mid-field. Successful pre-qualifiers Johansson's Onyx and Alliot (top) in the Lola at La Source.

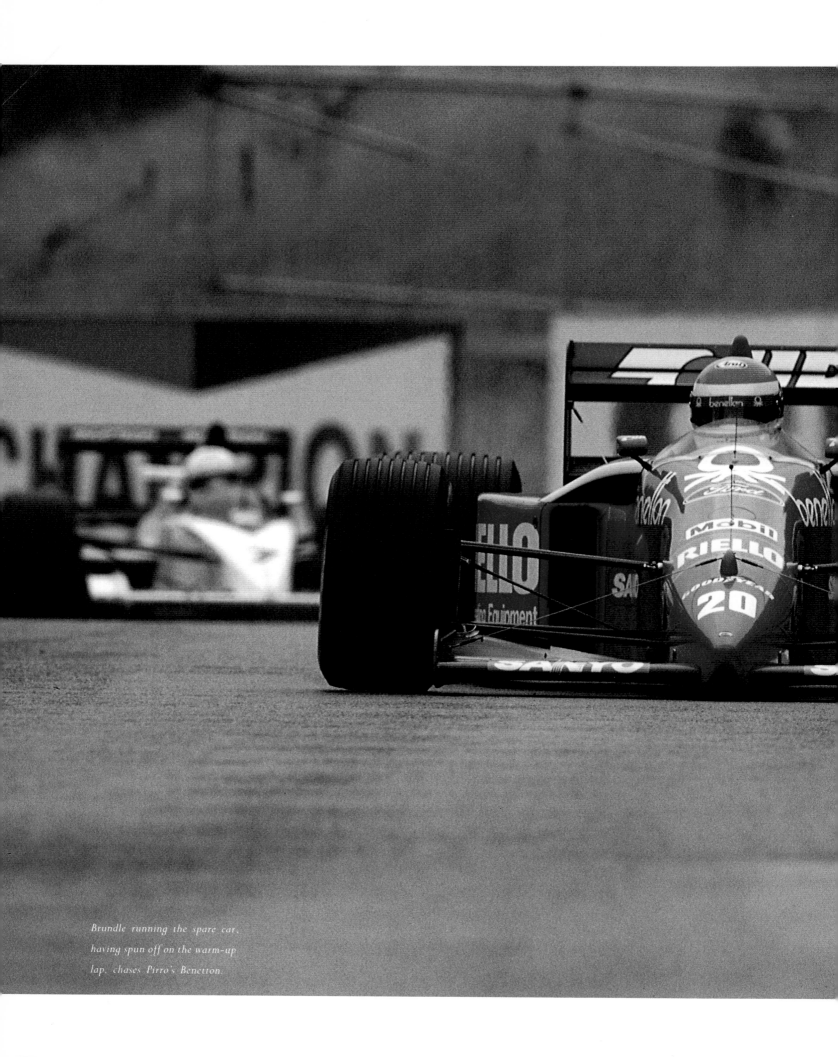

*Brundle running the spare car,
having spun off on the warm-up
lap, chases Pirro's Benetton.*

RACE DEBRIEF

It was, for everyone, a weekend of ebb and flow. One moment things were going great with records set and progress made. The next moment it was hold station, hang back, let things settle.

It was that way right from the start. Johansson's quickest lap in dry pre-qualifying would have put him fifth on the grid for the previous year's race. He bettered it only by a tenth of a second in Saturday's dry qualifying. The Onyx team, along with Lola-Lamborghini, eclipsed the rest in pre-qualifying, but whatever the slippery conditions, it was soon obvious that the multi-cylinders still had the advantage, and the rest should really have Goodyear tyres if the weather was very wet.

The ebb, then, was on Friday when it was wet, everyone hoping for a dry flow on Saturday, which duly occurred. Here the multi-cylinders came into their own, with prodigious power. The V8s were left miles behind but the qualifiers didn't include the Lotuses. Piquet had a misfiring engine in one car, and then spun off in his spare when put off line by Grouillard.

Nigel Mansell felt that the McLarens would have the edge in qualifying, but that Ferrari might be able to give them a good race. And that, in terms of the lead, was pretty much the way it worked out. They all got through La Source unharmed first time round but then it was ebb time again as everyone held station for several laps, trying to clear the water and waiting for visibility to improve.

Mansell's lively start round the outside of the Williamses had elevated him to fourth place, so that it was Senna from Prost for McLaren, Berger and Mansell for Ferrari, and then Boutsen from Patrese for Williams. Nannini, Warwick and Gugelmin led the V8 field behind, but Arnoux and Alliot tangled on lap one and had a replay two laps later when Alliot spun and Arnoux ran into him which put out the Ligier.

If anyone was looking threatening amongst the first six it was Berger who, 30 that day, was putting a certain amount of pressure on Prost. But on lap ten, all that came to an end when the Austrian slid wide into the barrier, and although there wasn't much damage done, he was out of the race for the tenth time in as many races.

Mansell now closed on Prost, leaving the Williams pair to fight their own battle behind. But on lap 14, Prost got caught behind Cheever. The gap between himself and Senna ahead rose from 6.2s to nearly 15s in three laps behind backmarkers, while Mansell was also held up and from being two seconds behind Prost, he dropped to over 15s.

He virtually fell back into the clutches of the Williams, but then left them to get past Alboreto. The Italian pulled over to let Boutsen through, but then pulled back again just as Patrese was about to follow through. Patrese and Alboreto tangled and went off into the sand trap, the Lola driver apologising to the Williams man but it was all over for the two of them.

It began to dry out at about half distance, but then down came the rain again, albeit briefly, at the 26-lap mark. The lead gap had dropped to less than six seconds when Senna was behind Martini, but rose back up to eight. Mansell, however, was setting one fastest lap after another – including a quick trip to the grass – and steadily he pulled himself away from Boutsen in fourth and up to Prost in second. By lap 36, Mansell was ready to pounce.

But there was never an opportunity. He and Prost were never much more than a couple of lengths apart, and while Mansell took some remarkable lines, including a wide kerb hop at La Source to try and slingshot past Prost on the run down to Eau Rouge and up to Les Combes, he was never quite close enough. He showed Prost every angle he could of the Ferrari, but never really poked his nose in front.

There was no doubt that the Frenchman was driving defensively, 'and I don't know how much longer I could have driven like that', admitted Prost. Mansell pointed out that 'Alain was very fair. It was a good race with him.'

The pair caught Senna during the final laps, but the Brazilian was well aware of what was going, saying that he had no particular problem, although both he and particularly Prost complained that their engines lacked driveability in the conditions, a complaint that Mansell said he could live with.

Boutsen, in his 100th Grand Prix and on his sixth anniversary in Grand Prix racing, finished a popular fourth, sometimes being caught by Nannini who in turn was occasionally caught by the following Warwick.

Boutsen said that he was able to control Nannini behind, although the Italian said that he was able to close up in the wet but that Boutsen pulled away in the dry. With Warwick behind, Nannini didn't have a moment's relaxation, but the English driver, consistently competitive all weekend, admitted that the more it dried, the more understeer he had. Gugelmin and Johansson were just out of the points, Martini was next after a pit stop for grooved slicks, Pirro had a spin but was lucky to reach the grass and rejoin while de Cesaris also stopped for tyres. There were 16 classified finishers which, for the conditions and speed of the Spa circuit, was testimony to the drivers on a very difficult day.

Clockwise from left: view through the pine trees. Ken's new boy, Herbert, was quick – when he was on the track. Ken never fails to recognise talent. A new helmet in the Rial, Raphanel was out of pre-qualifying, but still failed to get on the grid.

MILESTONES

- Johnny Herbert replaces Tyrrell's Jean Alesi who is racing F3000
- Thierry Boutsen's 100th Grand Prix
- Honda's 50th Grand Prix win
- McLaren's 50th pole position in Grand Prix racing
- Pierre-Henri Raphanel moves to Rial in place of Volker Weidler
- Enrico Bertaggia replaces Raphanel at Coloni
- Gordon Message now team manager for Benetton in place of Peter Collins

CHAMPION BELGIAN GRAND PRIX

ENTRIES · PRACTICE · RESULTS

Pos	Driver/Nationality		No.	Car/Engine	P.Q. (wet later)	Practice 1 (damp)	Practice 2 (overcast)	Warm-up (pos) (wet)	Laps (raining)	Time/Retirement
1	A. Senna	BR	1	McLaren MP4/4 Honda V10	–	2:11.171	**1:50.867**	2:16.252 (5)	44	1hr40m54.196
2	A. Prost	F	2	McLaren MP4/4 Honda V10	–	2:12.721	**1:51.463**	2:17.188 (7)	44	1hr40m55.500
3	N. Mansell	GB	27	Ferrari 640 Ferrari V12	–	2:12.042	**1:52.989**	2:14.150 (2)	44	1hr40m56.020
4	T. Boutsen	B	5	Williams FW12C Honda V10	–	2:13.030	**1:52.786**	2:17.619 (9)	44	1hr41m48.614
5	A. Nannini	I	19	Benetton B189 Ford HB V8	–	2:14.117	**1:55.075**	2:14.150 (8)	44	1hr42m03.001
6	D. Warwick	GB	9	Arrows A11 Ford DFR V8	–	2:13.005	**1:55.864**	2:17.168 (6)	44	1hr42m12.512
7	M. Gugelmin	BR	15	Leyton House CG891 Judd V8	–	2:16.401	**1:55.729**	2:21.379 (22)	43	1hr41m29.221
8	S. Johansson	S	36	Onyx ORE1 Ford DFR V8	1:56.279	2:17.329	**1:56.129**	2:20.326 (17)	43	1hr41m56.884
9	P. Martini	I	23	Minardi M189 Ford DFR V8	–	2:15.515	**1:56.115**	2:13.822 (1)	43	1hr41m58.324
10	E. Pirro	I	20	Benetton B189 HBV8	–	2:15.068	**1:55.902**	2:19.323 (12)	43	1hr42m01.895
11	A. de Cesaris	I	22	Dallara BMS 189 Ford DFR V8	–	2:17.512	**1:56.257**	2:19.863 (14)	43	1hr42m10.091
12	I. Capelli	I	16	Leyton House CG891 Judd V8	–	2:15.863	**1:56.291**	2:21.674 (24)	43	1hr42m25.545
13	O. Grouillard	F	26	Ligier JS33 Ford DFR V8	–	2:18.175	**1:57.027**	2:20.204 (16)	43	1hr43m09.007
14	J. Palmer	GB	3	Tyrrell 018 Ford DFR V8	–	2:18.405	**1:56.600**	2:19.545 (13)	42	1hr41m53.847
15	L. Sala	S	24	Minardi M189 Ford DFR V8	–	2:18.907	**1:56.957**	2:24.017 (25)	41	1hr41m56.548
16	P. Alliot	F	30	Lola LC89 Lamborghini V12	1:57.748	2:14.357	**1:55.890**	2:21.079 (20)	39	engine
17	E. Cheever	USA	10	Arrows A11 Ford DFR V8	–	2:14.641	**1:56.748**	2:28.382 (11)	38	loose wheel nut
18	B. Gachot	B	37	Onyx ORE1 Ford DFR V8	1:57.720	2:18.151	**1:56.716**	2:20.029 (15)	21	wheel bearing seal
19	R. Patrese	I	6	Williams FW12C Renault V10	–	2:12.581	**1:52.875**	2:15.123 (3)	20	collision/Alboreto
20	M. Alboreto	I	29	Lola LC89 Lamborghini V12	1:57.509	2:17.240	**1:56.616**	2:21.095 (21)	19	collision/Patrese
21	A. Caffi	I	21	Dallara BMS 189 Ford DFR V8	–	2:17.604	**1:55.892**	2:20.355 (18)	13	spin
22	M. Brundle	GB	7	Brabham BT58 Judd V8	–	2:18.663	**1:56.327**	2:21.562 (23)	12	brakes
23	G. Berger	A	28	Ferrari 640 Ferrari V12	–	2:11.102	**1:52.391**	2:15.273 (4)	9	accident
24	S. Modena	I	8	Brabham BT58 Judd V8	–	2:19.161	**1:55.642**	2:24.594 (26)	9	handling
25	R. Arnoux	F	25	Ligier JS33 Ford DFR V8	–	2:14.344	**1:56.251**	2:18.217 (10)	4	collision/Alliot
26	J. Herbert	GB	4	Tyrrell 018 Ford DFR V8	–	2:17.714	**1:56.248**	2:20.998 (19)	3	accident
27	S. Nakajima	J	12	Lotus 101 Judd V8	–	2:13.677	**1:57.251**	DNQ		
28	N. Piquet	BR	11	Lotus 101 Judd V8	–	2:14.358	**1:57.771**	DNQ		
29	C. Danner	D	38	Rial ARC02 Ford DFR V8	–	2:29.503	**2:00.247**	DNQ		
30	P. Raphanel	F	39	Rial ARC02 Ford DFR V8	–	2:21.180	**2:02.937**	DNQ		
–	N. Larini	I	17	Osella FA1M Ford DFR V8	1:58.065	DNPQ	DNPQ			
–	P. Ghinzani	I	18	Osella FA1M Ford DFR V8	1:58.209	DNPQ	DNPQ			
–	R. Moreno	BR	31	Coloni C3 Ford DFR V8	1:58.650	DNPQ	DNPQ			
–	G. Tarquini	I	40	AGS JH24 Ford DFR V8	1:59.432	DNPQ	DNPQ			
–	B. Schneider	F	34	Zakspeed ZK189 Yamaha V8	2:00.713	DNPQ	DNPQ			
–	A. Suzuki	J	35	Zakspeed ZK189 Yamaha V8	2:00.757	DNPQ	DNPQ			

Circuit Data: Circuit de Spa-Francorchamps, length 4.312 miles/6.940 km, race distance 44 laps = 189.7 miles/305.4 km, race weather heavy rain.
Notes: Enrico Bertaggia (I) replaces Pierre-Henri Raphanel in Coloni No. 32. Pierre-Henri Raphanel (F) replaces Volker Weidler in Rial No. 39. Johnny Herbert (GB) replaces Jean Alesi in Tyrrell No. 4.

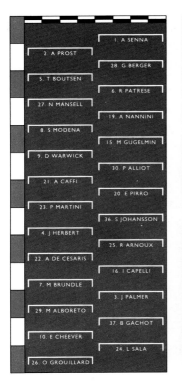

1. A SENNA
2. A PROST
28. G BERGER
5. T BOUTSEN
6. R PATRESE
27. N MANSELL
19. A NANNINI
8. S MODENA
15. M GUGELMIN
9. D WARWICK
30. P ALLIOT
21. A CAFFI
20. E PIRRO
23. P MARTINI
36. S JOHANSSON
4. J HERBERT
25. R ARNOUX
22. A DE CESARIS
16. I CAPELLI
7. M BRUNDLE
3. J PALMER
29. M ALBORETO
37. B GACHOT
10. E CHEEVER
24. L SALA
26. O GROUILLARD

LAP CHART

Grid Order	1	2	3	4	5	6	7	8	9	10	11	12	13	14	15	16	17	18	19	20	21	22	23	24	25	26	27	28	29	30	31	32	33	34	35	36	37	38	39	40	41	42	43	44
1 A. Senna	1	1	1	1	1	1	1	1	1	1	1	1	1	1	1	1	1	1	1	1	1	1	1	1	1	1	1	1	1	1	1	1	1	1	1	1	1	1	1	1	1	1	1	1
2 A. Prost	2	2	2	2	2	2	2	2	2	2	2	2	2	2	2	2	2	2	2	2	2	2	2	2	2	2	2	2	2	2	2	2	2	2	2	2	2	2	2	2	2	2	2	2
28 G. Berger	28	28	28	28	28	28	28	28	28	27	27	27	27	27	27	27	27	27	27	27	27	27	27	27	27	27	27	27	27	27	27	27	27	27	27	27	27	27	27	27	27	27	27	27
5 T. Boutsen	27	27	27	27	27	27	27	27	27	5	5	5	5	5	5	5	5	5	5	5	5	5	5	5	5	5	5	5	5	5	5	5	5	5	5	5	5	5	5	5	5	5	5	5
6 R. Patrese	5	5	5	5	5	5	5	5	5	6	6	6	6	6	6	6	6	6	6	6	6	19	19	19	19	19	19	19	19	19	19	19	19	19	19	19	19	19	19	19	19	19	19	19
27 N. Mansell	6	6	6	6	6	6	6	6	6	19	19	19	19	19	19	19	19	19	19	19	19	9	9	9	9	9	9	9	9	9	9	9	9	9	9	9	9	9	9	9	9	9	9	9
19 A. Nannini	19	19	19	19	19	19	19	19	19	9	9	9	9	9	9	9	9	9	9	9	9	15	15	15	15	15	15	15	15	15	15	15	15	15	15	15	15	15	15	15	15	15	15	15
8 S. Modena	9	9	9	9	9	9	9	9	9	15	15	15	15	15	15	15	15	15	15	15	15	36	36	36	36	36	36	36	36	36	36	36	36	36	36	36	36	36	36	36	36	36	36	36
15 M. Gugelmin	15	15	15	15	15	15	15	15	15	21	21	21	21	36	36	36	36	36	36	36	36	20	20	20	20	20	20	20	20	20	20	20	20	20	20	20	20	20	20	20	20	20	23	23
9 D. Warwick	21	21	21	21	21	21	21	21	21	20	20	36	36	22	22	22	22	22	20	20	22	22	22	22	22	22	22	22	22	22	16	16	16	16	16	22	22	22	22	22	23	20	20	
30 P. Alliot	20	20	20	20	20	20	20	20	20	36	36	22	22	20	20	20	20	20	22	22	23	23	23	23	23	23	23	16	16	22	22	22	22	22	22	16	16	23	23	23	22	22	22	
21 A. Caffi	36	36	36	36	36	36	36	36	36	22	22	20	20	23	23	23	23	23	23	23	16	16	16	16	16	16	16	23	10	10	23	23	23	23	23	23	23	16	16	16	16	16	16	
20 E. Pirro	4	4	4	22	22	22	22	22	22	23	23	23	23	16	16	16	16	16	16	16	26	26	10	10	10	10	10	10	23	23	10	10	10	10	10	10	10	10	10	26	26	26	26	26
23 P. Martini	23	22	22	23	23	23	23	23	23	16	16	16	16	26	26	26	26	26	26	26	10	10	26	26	26	26	26	26	26	26	26	26	26	26	26	26	26	26	30	3	3	3		
36 S. Johansson	22	23	23	16	16	16	16	16	16	7	7	26	26	29	29	29	29	29	29	29	10	3	3	3	3	3	3	3	30	30	30	30	30	30	30	30	30	3	24	24				
4 J. Herbert	10	10	10	7	7	7	7	7	7	7	26	26	29	29	10	10	10	10	10	10	3	37	30	30	30	30	30	30	3	3	3	3	3	3	3	3	3	3	3	24				
25 R. Arnoux	16	16	16	26	26	26	26	26	26	29	29	10	10	3	3	3	3	3	3	37	30	24	24	24	24	24	24	24	24	24	24	24	24	24	24	24	24	24	24					
22 A. de Cesaris	7	7	7	10	29	29	29	29	29	3	3	3	3	37	37	37	37	37	37	37	30	24																						
16 I. Capelli	26	26	26	29	3	3	3	3	3	10	10	24	24	30	30	30	30	30	30	30	24																							
7 M. Brundle	30	30	30	3	24	24	24	10	10	24	24	30	37	24	24	24	24	24	24																									
3 J. Palmer	29	29	25	25	8	10	10	24	24	30	30	37	30																															
29 M. Alboreto	37	25	37	24	10	8	30	30	30	37	37	7																																
37 B. Gachot	3	37	29	8	30	30	8	8	37																																			
10 E. Cheever	24	3	3	30	37	37	37	37	8																																			
24 L. Sala	25	24	24	37																																								
26 O. Grouillard	8	8	8																																									

FASTEST LAPS

Pos.	Car No./Driver/Team	Time
1	2 A. Prost/McLaren	2:11.571
2	27 N. Mansell/Ferrari	2:11.736
3	23 P. Martini/Minardi	2:12.101
4	1 A. Senna/McLaren	2:12.890
5	22 A. de Cesaris/BMS Dallara	2:13.176
6	5 T. Boutsen/Williams	2:13.842
7	9 D. Warwick/Arrows	2:14.106
8	19 A. Nannini/Benetton	2:14.399
9	30 P. Alliot/Larrousse	2:14.675
10	16 I. Capelli/Leyton House	2:15.701
11	20 E. Pirro/Benetton	2:15.868
12	10 E. Cheever/Arrows	2:16.727
13	26 O. Grouillard/Ligier	2:17.253
14	36 S. Johansson/Onyx	2:17.294
15	15 M. Gugelmin/Leyton House	2:17.411
16	6 R. Patrese/Williams	2:18.273
17	28 G. Berger/Ferrari	2:18.865
18	37 B. Gachot/Onyx	2:19.405
19	3 J. Palmer/Tyrrell	2:19.772
20	29 M. Alboreto/Larrousse	2:21.323
21	24 L. Sala/Minardi	2:22.222
22	21 A. Caffi/BMS Dallara	2:22.790
23	4 J. Herbert/Tyrrell	2:26.020
24	25 R. Arnoux/Ligier	2:26.022
25	7 M. Brundle/Brabham	2:27.325
26	8 S. Modena/Brabham	2:31.976

CHAMPIONSHIP POINTS

	Drivers			Drivers/Constructors	
1	A. Prost	62 pts		O. Grouillard	1 pt
2	A. Senna	51 pts		L. Sala	1 pt
3	N. Mansell	15 pts		M. Brundle	1 pt
4	R. Patrese	25 pts		J. Palmer	1 pt
5	T. Boutsen	20 pts			
6	A. Nannini	14 pts	1	McLaren	113 pts
7	N. Piquet	9 pts	2	Williams	45 pts
8	M. Alboreto	6 pts	3	Ferrari	38 pts
9	E. Cheever	6 pts	4	Benetton	19 pts
10	D. Warwick	6 pts	5	Arrows	12 pts
11	J. Herbert	5 pts	6	Tyrrell	10 pts
12	A. de Cesaris	4 pts	7	Lotus	9 pts
	M. Gugelmin	4 pts	8	Dallara	8 pts
	S. Modena	4 pts	9	Brabham	5 pts
15	A. Caffi	4 pts	10	Leyton House	4 pts
16	J. Alesi	3 pts	11	Rial	3 pts
	C. Danner	3 pts		Ligier	3 pts
18	S. Johansson	2 pts		Minardi	3 pts
	R. Arnoux	2 pts	14	Onyx	2 pts
	P. Martini	2 pts	15	AGS	1 pt
21	G. Tarquini	1 pt			

Existing qualifying lap record: Nigel Mansell, Williams-Honda FW11B, 1m 52.026s at 223.020 kph/138.578 mph in 1987

Existing race lap record: Alain Prost, McLaren-TAG MP4/3, 1m 57.153s at 213.260 kph/132.514 mph in 1987

Existing distance record: Alain Prost, McLaren-TAG MP4/3, 43 laps in 1hr 27m 03.217s at 205.680 kph/127.804 mph in 1987

PAST WINNERS

Year	Driver	Nat.	Car	Circuit
1979	Jody Scheckter	ZA	3.0 Ferrari 312T 4	Zolder
1980	Didier Pironi	F	3.0 Ligier JS11/15 Ford	Zolder
1981	Carlos Reutemann	RA	3.0 Williams FW07C Ford	Zolder
1982	John Watson	GB	3.0 McLaren MP4B Ford	Zolder
1983	Alain Prost	F	1.5 Renault RE40 t/c	Francorchamps
1984	Michele Alboreto	I	1.5 Ferrari 126C4 t/c	Zolder
1985	Ayrton Senna	BR	1.5 Lotus 97T Renault t/c	Francorchamps
1986	Nigel Mansell	GB	1.5 Williams FW11 Honda t/c	Francorchamps
1987	Alain Prost	F	1.5 McLaren MP4/3 TAG t/c	Francorchamps
1988	Ayrton Senna	BR	1.5 McLaren MP4/4 Honda t/c	Francorchamps

Monza

COCA COLA GRAN PREMIO D'ITALIA · 10 SETTEMBRE

Off-track politics occasionally over-shadow on-track performances in motor racing. While McLaren-Honda's second successive Con-structors' Championship, Ayrton Senna's 38th pole position and Alain Prost's 39th Grand Prix victory provided their own talking points, it was Prost's post-race comments that made the head-lines.

*That very week, the French-*man had signed to drive for Ferrari in 1990. There had been some who thought that when he announced in France that he

More success for Martini's Minardi has not dulled the team's idea of good taste — espresso and pasta.

would leave McLaren at the end of the year, he would be taking a year's sabbatical. He didn't give any indication of that, saying at the time that he would probably be in Grand Prix racing in 1990. So his signing for Ferrari shouldn't have come as much of a surprise.

However, the World Championship leader considered that he had put himself in a precarious position. Should he win the World Championship (which seemed fairly likely, particularly after the race), he would be taking the number one to Ferrari. This, he thought, was more than some people could take. Not so McLaren's Ron Dennis who declared before the race that 'more important than winning the World Championship is the fundamental integrity of the company and the team'.

But Prost clearly thought that his engine was inferior to Senna's throughout the weekend and made his thoughts known to Honda personnel. When he felt that nothing had been done, that his engine was still poor at low revs and in acceleration during the race, he decided to give his views a wider audience.

He did not point out that he had set fastest race lap, although that was set on the same lap on which Senna was easing up with low oil pressure and coincidentally setting his own fastest race lap, only hundredths of a second slower than Prost's. This simply made the situation more complex.

Prost was no doubt reacting to previous claims by both Keke Rosberg and Nigel Mansell that outgoing Honda drivers are less in favour than those remaining with the team, and are therefore not given the same machinery.

Honda, however, claimed that both drivers had identical machinery, including the engine management chip. They were obviously disappointed in their championship leader, and that impression was also given by McLaren team personnel too, specifically people who had long been loyal to the Frenchman.

Prost pointed out that he had been two seconds slower than Senna in qualifying, so his engine obviously wasn't the same. Honda gave the impression that they were disappointed with Prost's performance, that he simply couldn't match Senna.

It was a sad end to a race that should have been more joyful, but then there were many who were disappointed, including Mansell and Senna who both might have hoped for more. Berger, finishing for the first time this year, was the happiest man around.

BRIGHT SPARKS

Ferrari versus McLaren; even if you weren't Italian, this was the way the Italian Grand Prix looked. Providing the hype were the tifosi, giving it a Roman Games atmosphere. Thumbs down for McLaren (or Senna more specifically), thumbs up for anything Ferrari red, including incoming Prost, not forgetting outgoing Berger.

No one else really mattered as far as the tifosi were concerned. Riccardo Patrese had his fans and their polite round of applause, and so did Michele Alboreto, but that was about it.

So Ferrari's bounce back, with engine modifications to even out the power curve, received a rapturous welcome. Berger's fastest time on Friday morning – one of the coolest Italian Grand Prix meetings for some years, incidentally – was followed by a great Ferrari battle that afternoon, with Berger coming in late with a lap that pipped teammate Mansell by just five hundredths of a second.

The tifosi watched their every move the next afternoon: could they go even quicker, and keep the dreaded McLaren from pole? Neither Ferrari driver did so. Flashes of opposite lock revealed minute mistakes, with the drivers taking bigger bites of the kerbs than ever.

No improvement for Ferrari, then. Overnight rain had perhaps slowed the track. Not for Senna, however. Ferrari bigwigs watched his lap on the giant screen overlooking the start/finish line. There it was, for all to see. Ron Dennis watched it too. Senna admitted a little mistake on the second run at the first chicane, he brought the qualifiers in differently, but the time was there – and how. He was a second quicker than the Ferraris had been the previous evening, and they had been

0.3s quicker than Senna. 'There was a little satisfaction at seeing the Christian eat the lion for a change,' said Dennis.

Of course Senna's performance in the race seemed dominant. He even remarked that he didn't have to use maximum revs. Berger, meanwhile, gave valiant chase, although he admitted that he was more interested in finishing than challenging for the lead. Prost first, Berger second was like a Ferrari one-two as far as the locals were concerned.

Those with broader minds noted Alliot seventh in qualifying, but an early race retirement. Pirro was right up with Nannini, the first of the V8-powered runners, but Emanuele retired even earlier than Alliot. Alesi followed up tenth on the grid with a tigering fifth, two weeks after his Birmingham F3000 victory. Minardi and Dallara battled hard, victory going to Minardi after two late race blow-ups for Scuderia Italia. Behind Martini came Sala who had unofficially crash tested a Minardi in

within 0.3s of the Swede.

Friday, then, was Ferrari day; Ron Dennis's men had their revenge the next day. Berger was quickest in both sessions on Friday, the 1988 grid times rapidly fading into insignificance. It was damp on Saturday morning, however, and Berger was soon spinning off into a gravel trap. That afternoon neither he nor Mansell improved, both drivers getting out of shape on quick laps while Mansell also ran out of fuel.

Senna's lap in the 1m 23s bracket seemed brilliant, but what looked like a perfectly executed parallel ski turn into the first chicane wasn't ideal and the Brazilian admitted the loss of a tenth of a second or so. Behind the Ferraris, Prost was already mystified by the 1.8s difference between himself and Senna.

At Williams, the atmosphere was mixed, the good-natured Patrese pleased with row three, although Prost was a tantalising 35/1000ths

Toeing the line: Pirro, Patrese and Piquet.

qualifying. But these promising performances were of no consequence to most of Italy – sadly.

RACE DEBRIEF

The impartial doesn't exist in Italy, but there were other happenings during the weekend apart from the red versus red-and-white duel. Pre-qualifying saw V12 power come to the fore in the shape of the Lamborghinis in the back of the Lolas, with Alliot heading Alboreto, the Frenchman with a time good enough for third on the previous year's grid. Larini took advantage of his Pirelli tyres to go further. Bertrand Gachot made it into number four spot, pipping Onyx teammate Johansson who found he had more time than he would have liked to celebrate his birthday after his race car's clutch slipped and the spare car wasn't set up for him. Tarquini, Moreno and Ghinzani were all

ahead. The normally placid Boutsen, however, was furious after an unfortunate mechanic wrongly fitted two gears. At least they had the new FW13 to look forward to, this being FW12C's last race.

Alliot's pace continued all the way through qualifying to seventh on the grid from Nannini, who of course should have been best of the V8s but had teammate Pirro just behind. Things now began to get very tight: the next eight places were covered by a second, another one covering the next ten. Out of a race was Modena, unfortunately disqualified for not stopping at a weigh-in which let in Luis Sala who had crashed a Minardi, fortunately without injury.

The warm-up gave the many Italians flooding through the gates a glimmer of hope. After all, it was their three drivers (Mansell, Prost and Berger in that order) against one: Senna. Unfortunately it was he who was quickest – but by just 0.3s from Mansell. However, Prost was 1.2s further back from Alesi, Nannini, Alliot and Palmer. Berger was 19th after his gearbox's hydraulic valve had unscrewed itself once again.

The tifosi might have hoped that one of their beloved V12s might out-accelerate Honda's V10 on the drag down to the first chicane, but there was no such luck as Senna led Mansell, Berger and Prost. Gugelmin went auto-crossing with Grouillard while Pirro instantly lost his clutch.

Another of the top ten qualifiers disappeared on the next lap when Alliot spun out of tenth. By this stage, however, Senna had extended his lead to 1.2s and by lap ten it was up to 4.2s. Berger, with the idea of a finish firmly fixed in his mind, was quite content to settle into second and see what might happen. Behind Mansell, however, Prost came under considerable pressure from Boutsen being pushed by Nannini and momentarily Patrese who then faded. Alesi was next.

Mansell found his engine down on power from the start, and once Prost had shaken off those behind, he was able to think about challenging the Ferrari ahead. But it took many laps before he actually caught the Ferrari, contact finally being made (figuratively speaking) on lap 16. Five laps later, Prost was past and rapidly pulling away. Mansell was in trouble.

Looming large behind the Ferrari now was Boutsen. The Belgian had been rid of the Benetton threat on lap 16 when Nannini pitted early for new tyres which left the two Williamses, a few seconds apart, safely in fifth and sixth places. Then came a big gap to Capelli who had fought through the field overtaking Brundle, Piquet and Alesi to head the rest.

However, just as he was caught by Nannini's re-shod Benetton, so Boutsen was worrying Mansell's Ferrari. But there was little that the Belgian could do. 'He was quicker on the straights than I was, and you can only overtake on the straights, so I was never really in a position to get past.'

Behind Patrese, Nannini had got ahead of Capelli, only for the March to disappear when its engine blew. 'The oil pressure was low,' said the Italian, 'and I hoped that the computer had made a mistake – but it

Above: Berger on his way to his first finish of '89. The fans were also happy.

Below left: Grouillard suggests a new line through the Rettifilo. Below: Capelli's Judd V8 will go no further.

hadn't.' However, Nannini was not to last either, suffering brake trouble which saw him pit and hand seventh place to ever-attendant Alesi on lap 34. Brundle was the only other unlapped runner.

At this stage, two battles were brewing: Berger, with the chequered flag in his mind, was being caught by Prost while Mansell, now in gearbox trouble, had both Williamses breathing down his neck. First, however, Prost caught and passed Berger, although it took him most of Monza's long straight to do it. And a lap later, the end was nigh for Mansell. Coming into the second chicane, Boutsen pulled alongside and even

caused Mansell to lock up as he hugged the line into fourth place. The Ferrari driver fought back viciously until he again lost gears – and the following Patrese nearly hit him as he slowed. It was all over for Mansell, however.

Senna led by 21s from Prost pulling away from Berger while Boutsen was less than ten seconds behind the Ferrari, Patrese now dropping behind his teammate. The rest, led by Alesi and Brundle, were lapped. Indeed, all that seemed left were the Minardis and Dallaras having their own private battle.

But on lap 45, with eight to go, Senna's engine suddenly blew at the start of the back straight. 'Maybe that's because it had so much power,' suggested his bitter teammate after the race, but it was Prost who now inherited a win to give McLaren the Constructors' Championship. Berger was happy in second place, with Boutsen and Patrese pleased to give FW12C a good send-off in third and fourth places. Behind final points scorers Alesi and Brundle, Minardi won the Italian second

division after the Dallaras suffered coincidental self-destruction of the engine department.

The fireworks, however, were still to come: Prost's trophy went to the crowd to Ron Dennis's disgust. The Constructors' trophy ended up at Prost's feet, and then the Frenchman made his feelings known about the team and engine supplier and everyone had a sour taste in their mouths.

Clockwise from above: Brundle on his way to a sixth place. Prost commits a cardinal sin, but is praised by his new fans. Rial blues – DNQ.

MILESTONES

- McLaren clinch Constructors' Championship
- Honda's 50th Grand Prix win
- Oscar Larrauri replaces Foitek at EuroBrun
- Ferrari announces Prost will join Mansell in 1990
- Lotus announces Lamborghini, Camel, Warwick and Donnelly for 1990
- Ghinzani announces retirement at the end of the year

COCA-COLA GRAN PREMIO D'ITALIA

ENTRIES · PRACTICE · RESULTS

Pos	Driver/Nationality		No.	Car/Engine	P.Q. (cool, overcast)	Practice 1 (hazy)	Practice 2 (damp)	Warm-up (pos) (hazy, sun)	Laps (sunny)	Time/Retirement
1	A. Prost	F	2	McLaren MP4/5 Honda V10	–	1:25.872	**1:25.510**	1:29.149 (3)	53	1hr19m27.550
2	G. Berger	A	28	Ferrari 640 Ferrari V12	–	**1:24.734**	1:24.998	1:31.261 (19)	53	1hr19m34.876
3	T. Boutsen	B	5	Williams FW12C Renault V10	–	**1:26.155**	1:26.392	1:30.127 (10)	53	1hr19m42.525
4	R. Patrese	I	6	Williams FW12C Renault V10	–	1:26.195	**1:25.545**	1:30.161 (12)	53	1hr20m06.272
5	J. Alesi	F	4	Tyrrell 018 Ford DFR V8	–	time d/a	**1:27.399**	1:29.773 (4)	52	1hr19m41.097
6	M. Brundle	GB	7	Brabham BT58 Judd V8	–	**1:27.627**	1:27.637	1:30.764 (15)	52	1hr19m56.173
7	P. Martini	I	23	Minardi M189 Ford DFR V8	–	1:28.397	**1:27.923**	1:30.001 (8)	52	1hr20m44.089
8	L. Sala	S	24	Minardi M189 Ford DFR V8	–	1:29.592	**1:29.293**	1:32.774 (26)	51	1hr19m36.571
9	R. Arnoux	F	25	Ligier JS33 Ford DFR V8	–	**1:28.685**	1:28.843	1:31.526 (23)	51	1hr20m09.652
10	S. Nakajima	J	11	Lotus 101 Judd V8	–	1:28.769	**1:28.441**	1:30.971 (16)	51	rear suspension
11	A. Caffi	I	21	Dallara BMS 189 Ford DFR V8	–	**1:28.596**	1:28.708	1:31.035 (18)	47	exhaust valve
12	A. de Cesaris	I	22	Dallara BMS 189 Ford DFR V8	–	**1:28.129**	1:28.180	1:31.417 (21)	45	exhaust valve
13	A. Senna	BR	1	McLaren MP4/5 Honda V10	–	1:25.021	**1:23.720**	1:27.637 (1)	44	engine
14	N. Mansell	GB	27	Ferrari 640 Ferrari V12	–	**1:24.739**	1:24.979	1:27.934 (2)	44	gearbox
15	B. Gachot	B	37	Onyx ORE1 Ford DFR V8	1:28.344	**1:28.684**	1:29.058	1:30.736 (14)	38	engine/accident
16	A. Nannini	I	19	Benetton Ford HBV8	–	1:27.162	**1:27.052**	1:29.867 (5)	33	brakes
17	I. Capelli	I	16	Leyton House CG891 Judd V8	–	1:31.969	**1:28.430**	1:31.931 (24)	30	engine
18	O. Grouillard	F	26	Ligier JS33 Ford DFR V8	–	**1:28.669**	1:29.537	1:30.994 (17)	30	exhaust and gearbox
19	N. Piquet	BR	11	Lotus 101 Judd V8	–	1:28.135	**1:27.508**	1:30.465 (13)	23	accident
20	J. Palmer	GB	3	Tyrrell 018 Ford DFR V8	–	1:29.187	**1:27.822**	1:29.981 (76)	18	oil leak
21	D. Warwick	GB	9	Brabham BT58 Judd V8	–	**1:28.092**	1:29.031	1:31.399 (20)	18	electrics
22	N. Larini	I	17	Osella FA1M Ford DFR V8	1:27.980	1:29.265	**1:28.773**	1:31.465 (22)	18	gearbox
23	M. Alboreto	I	29	Lola LC89 Lamborghini V12	1:27.829	**1:28.586**	1:27.803	1:30.140 (11)	14	camshaft pick-up
24	M. Gugelmin	BR	15	Leyton House CG891 Judd V8	–	1:29.192	**1:28.923**	1:32.553 (25)	14	throttle
25	P. Alliot	F	30	Lola LC89 Lamborghini V12	1:26.623	1:27.118	**1:26.985**	1:29.921 (6)	1	jammed throttle/spin
26	E. Pirro	I	20	Benetton B189 Ford HBV8	–	1:28.367	**1:27.397**	1:30.110 (9)	–	clutch
27	E. Cheever	USA	10	Arrows A11 Ford DFR V8	–	1:29.884	**1:29.554**	DNQ		
28	C. Danner	D	38	Rial ARC02 Ford DFR V8	–	1:32.074	**1:31.830**	DNQ		
29	P. Raphanel	F	39	Rial ARC02 Ford DFR V8	–	time d/a	**1:36.295**	DNQ		
30	S. Modena	I	8	Brabham BT58 Judd V8	–	**1:28.017**	disqualified from event			
–	B. Gachot	B	37	Onyx ORE1 Ford DFR V8	1:28.344	DNPQ	DNPQ			
–	S. Johansson	S	36	Onyx ORE1 Ford DFR V8	1:28.588	DNPQ	DNPQ			
–	G. Tarquini	I	40	AGS JH24 Ford DFR V8	1:28.813	DNPQ	DNPQ			
–	R. Moreno	BR	31	Coloni C3 Ford DFR V8	1:28.864	DNPQ	DNPQ			
–	P. Ghinzani	I	18	Osella FA1M Ford DFR V8	1:28.884	DNPQ	DNPQ			
–	B. Schneider	D	34	Zakspeed ZK189 Yamaha V8	1:29.472	DNPQ	DNPQ			
–	A. Suzuki	J	35	Zakspeed ZK189 Yamaha V8	1:30.085	DNPQ	DNPQ			
–	O. Larrauri	Arg	33	EuroBrun ER189 Judd V8	1:30.089	DNPQ	DNPQ			
–	Y. Dalmas	F	41	AGS JH24 Ford DFR V8	1:30.382	DNPQ	DNPQ			
–	E. Bertaggia	I	32	Coloni C3 Ford DFR V8	1:31.606	DNPQ	DNPQ			

Circuit Data: Autodromo Nazionale di Monza, length 3.604 miles/5.800 km, race distance 53 laps = 191 miles/307.4 km, race weather sunny and warm.
Notes: Jean Alesi (F) drives Tyrrell No. 4 again. Oscar Larrauri (RA) replaces Gregor Foitek in EuroBrun No. 33.

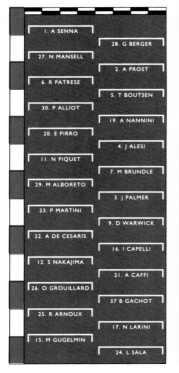

1. A SENNA	
	28. G BERGER
27. N MANSELL	
	2. A PROST
6. R PATRESE	
	5. T BOUTSEN
30. P ALLIOT	
	19. A NANNINI
20. E PIRRO	
	4. J ALESI
11. N PIQUET	
	7. M BRUNDLE
29. M ALBORETO	
	3. J PALMER
23. P MARTINI	
	9. D WARWICK
22. A DE CESARIS	
	16. I CAPELLI
12. S NAKAJIMA	
	21. A CAFFI
26. O GROUILLARD	
	37 B GACHOT
25. R ARNOUX	
	17. N LARINI
15. M GUGELMIN	
	24. L SALA

Ferrari's new addition.

LAP CHART

Lap columns: 1 2 3 4 5 6 7 8 9 10 11 12 13 14 15 16 17 18 19 20 21 22 23 24 25 26 27 28 29 30 31 32 33 34 35 36 37 38 39 40 41 42 43 44 45 46 47 48 49 50 51 51 53

Grid Order	Lap positions
1 A.Senna	1 1 1 1 1 1 1 1 1 1 1 1 1 1 1 1 1 1 1 1 1 1 1 1 1 1 1 1 1 1 1 1 1 1 1 1 1 1 1 1 1 1 1 1 2 2 2 2 2 2 2 2 2
28 G.Berger	28 28 28 28 28 28 28 28 28 28 28 28 28 28 28 28 28 28 28 28 28 28 28 28 28 28 28 28 28 28 28 28 28 28 28 28 28 28 28 28 28 28 28 2 2 2 2 28 28 28 28 28 28
27 N.Mansell	27 27 27 27 27 27 27 27 27 27 27 27 27 27 27 27 27 27 2 2 2 2 2 2 2 2 2 2 2 2 2 2 2 2 2 2 2 2 2 2 2 2 2 2 28 28 28 28 5 5 5 5 5 5 5 5 5 5
2 A.Prost	2 2 2 2 2 2 2 2 2 2 2 2 2 2 2 2 2 2 2 2 2 2 27 27 27 27 27 27 27 27 27 27 27 27 27 27 27 27 27 27 27 27 27 27 27 5 5 5 6 6 6 6 6 6 6 6
6 R.Patrese	5 5 5 5 5 5 5 5 5 5 5 5 5 5 5 5 5 5 5 5 5 5 5 5 5 5 5 5 5 5 5 5 5 5 5 5 5 5 5 5 5 5 5 5 6 6 6 4 4 4 4 4 4 4
5 T.Boutsen	19 19 19 19 19 19 19 19 19 19 19 19 19 19 19 6 6 6 6 6 6 6 6 6 6 6 6 6 6 6 6 6 6 6 6 6 6 6 6 6 6 6 6 4 4 4 7 7 7 7 7 7 7
30 P.Alliot	6 6 6 6 6 6 6 6 6 6 6 6 6 6 6 4 16 16 16 16 16 16 16 16 16 16 19 19 19 19 19 19 19 4 4 4 4 4 4 4 4 7 7 7 21 21 21 23 23 23 23
19 A.Nannini	4 4 4 4 4 4 4 4 4 4 4 4 4 4 16 4 4 4 4 19 19 19 19 16 16 16 16 4 4 4 7 7 7 7 7 7 7 7 23 23 23 23 23 23 24 24 24 24
20 E.Pirro	7 7 7 7 11 11 11 11 11 11 16 16 16 16 16 19 11 11 11 19 19 4 4 4 4 4 4 4 4 7 7 23 23 23 23 23 23 23 23 21 21 21 21 24 24 12 12 25 25
4 J.Alesi	30 11 11 11 7 7 16 16 16 16 11 11 11 11 11 11 11 19 19 11 11 11 11 11 11 7 7 7 7 7 7 7 23 23 23 21 21 21 21 21 21 21 21 22 22 22 24 12 12 25 25 12 12
11 N.Piquet	11 16 16 16 16 16 7 7 7 7 7 7 7 7 7 7 7 7 7 7 7 7 7 7 23 23 23 23 23 21 21 21 22 22 22 22 22 22 22 22 22 24 24 24 12 25 25
7 M.Brundle	16 29 29 29 29 29 23 23 23 23 23 23 23 23 23 23 23 23 23 23 23 21 21 21 21 21 21 21 21 22 22 22 24 24 24 24 24 24 24 24 25 12 12 25
29 M.Alboreto	29 23 23 23 23 29 29 29 29 29 29 29 29 29 9 21 21 21 21 21 21 21 22 22 22 22 22 22 24 24 24 25 25 25 25 25 25 25 25 12 12 25 25
3 J.Palmer	23 9 9 9 9 9 9 9 9 9 9 9 9 9 9 9 21 9 22 22 22 22 22 22 22 12 12 12 12 12 12 12 25 25 12 12 12 12 12 12 12 12 12 12
23 P.Martini	9 26 26 26 26 26 26 26 26 26 21 21 21 22 22 12 12 12 12 12 12 24 24 24 24 24 24 24 12 12 12 37 37 37 37 37 37
9 D.Warwick	26 21 21 21 21 21 21 21 21 21 17 17 17 22 12 12 3 3 24 24 24 24 25 25 25 25 25 25 25 25 37 37 37
22 A.de Cesaris	21 17 17 17 17 17 17 17 17 21 21 22 22 17 17 3 25 25 25 25 25 25 37 37 37 37 37 37 37 37
16 I.Capelli	17 12 22 22 22 22 22 22 22 22 22 12 12 12 3 25 24 24 37 37 37 37 26 26 26 26 26 26
12 S.Nakajima	22 22 12 12 25 25 12 12 12 12 3 3 3 25 24 37 37 26 26 26 26 26
21 A.Caffi	12 25 25 12 12 12 25 25 25 25 25 25 24 24 37 26 26
26 O.Grouillard	25 37 3 3 3 3 3 3 3 3 24 24 24 37 17 9 9
37 B.Gachot	37 3 37 37 37 37 24 24 24 24 24 37 37 37 26 26
25 R.Arnoux	3 24 24 24 24 24 37 37 37 37 37 15 15 15
17 N.Larini	24 15 15 15 15 15 15 15 15 15 26 26 26
15 M.Gugelmin	15
24 L.Sala	

FASTEST LAPS

Pos.	Car No./Driver/Team	Time
1	2 A.Prost/McLaren	1:28.107
2	1 A.Senna/McLaren	1:28.179
3	5 T.Boutsen/Williams	1:28.245
4	28 G.Berger/Ferrari	1:28.712
5	27 N.Mansell/Ferrari	1:28.820
6	6 R.Patrese/Williams	1:28.857
7	19 A.Nannini/Benetton	1:29.726
8	16 I.Capelli/Leyton House	1:30.236
9	7 M.Brundle/Brabham	1:30.437
10	4 J.Alesi/Tyrrell	1:30.588
11	11 N.Piquet/Lotus	1:30.976
12	21 A.Caffi/BMS Dallara	1:31.112
13	22 A.de Cesaris/BMS Dallara	1:31.138
14	23 P.Martini/Minardi	1:31.468
15	24 L.Sala/Minardi	1:31.535
16	26 O.Grouillard/Ligier	1:31.639
17	12 S.Nakajima/Lotus	1:31.931
18	9 D.Warwick/Arrows	1:32.302
19	17 N.Larini/Osella	1:32.416
20	3 J.Palmer/Tyrrell	1:32.474
21	29 M.Alboreto/Larrousse	1:32.548
22	25 R.Arnoux/Ligier	1:32.577
23	37 B.Gachot/Onyx	1:32.691
24	15 M.Gugelmin/Leyton House	1:33.571
25	30 P.Alliot/Larrousse	1:44.035
26	20 E.Pirro/Benetton	0 laps

Existing qualifying lap record: Nelson Piquet, Williams-Honda FW11B, 1m 23.460s at 250.180 kph/155.455 mph in 1987

Existing race lap record: Ayrton Senna, Lotus-Honda 99T, 1m 26.796s at 240.564 kph/149.480 mph in 1987

Existing distance record: Nelson Piquet, Williams-Honda FW11B, 50 laps in 1 hr 14m 47.707s at 232.636 kph/144.553 mph in 1987

CHAMPIONSHIP POINTS

Drivers			Drivers/Constructors	
1	A.Prost	71 pts	22 M.Brundle	2 pts
2	A.Senna	51 pts	23 G.Tarquini	1 pt
3	N.Mansell	38 pts	O.Grouillard	1 pt
4	R.Patrese	28 pts	L.Sala	1 pt
5	T.Boutsen	24 pts	J.Palmer	1 pt
6	A.Nannini	14 pts		
7	N.Piquet	9 pts	1 McLaren	122 pts
8	G.Berger	6 pts	2 Williams	52 pts
	M.Alboreto	6 pts	3 Ferrari	44 pts
	E.Cheever	6 pts	4 Benetton	19 pts
	D.Warwick	6 pts	5 Arrows	12 pts
12	J.Herbert	5 pts	Tyrrell	12 pts
	J.Alesi	5 pts	7 Lotus	9 pts
14	A.de Cesaris	4 pts	8 Dallara	8 pts
	M.Gugelmin	4 pts	9 Brabham	6 pts
	S.Modena	4 pts	10 Leyton House	4 pts
	A.Caffi	4 pts	11 Rial	3 pts
18	C.Danner	3 pts	Ligier	3 pts
19	S.Johansson	2 pts	Minardi	3 pts
	R.Arnoux	2 pts	14 Onyx	2 pts
	P.Martini	2 pts	15 AGS	1 pt

PAST WINNERS

Year	Driver	Nat.	Car	Circuit
1979	Jody Scheckter	ZA	3.0 Ferrari 312T-4	Monza
1980	Nelson Piquet	BR	3.0 Brabham BT49 Ford	Imola
1981	Alain Prost	F	1.5 Renault RE30 t/c	Monza
1982	René Arnoux	F	1.5 Renault RE30B t/c	Monza
1983	Nelson Piquet	BR	1.5 Brabham BT52B BMW t/c	Monza
1984	Niki Lauda	A	1.5 McLaren MP4/2 TAG t/c	Monza
1985	Alain Prost	F	1.5 McLaren MP4/2B TAG t/c	Monza
1986	Nelson Piquet	BR	1.5 Williams FW11 Honda t/c	Monza
1987	Nelson Piquet	BR	1.5 Williams FW11B Honda t/c	Monza
1988	Gerhard Berger	A	1.5 Ferrari F1/87/88C t/c	Monza

Carbon fibre in all directions on Capelli's CG189 monocoque.

Estoril

GRANDE PRÉMIO DE PORTUGAL · 24 SETEMBRO

It was a very innocent mistake which grew into a soap opera. Nigel Mansell even threatened to quit motor racing as a consequence — although if the truth be known, *few insiders thought that he would. In the end — three weeks later — Ferrari did the best*

A lobster entrée and champagne aperitif for Berger — Mansell wasn't so fortunate.

thing. They took the emphasis off politics by dropping the appeal and going back to racing. But in the meantime we endured a Grand

Prix which could only have been enlivened by the one man who was in fact banned from it.

It all started with a pit stop. Mansell pitted for tyres from the lead on lap 39 of the 71-lap Portuguese Grand Prix. He might have come in too fast. Certainly when he saw his pit he locked up a brake, but by then it was too late. He overshot, and when no one pulled him back, he naturally and easily pressed the reverse button in the Ferrari cockpit and back he went under power.

And that isn't allowed. In a crowded pit lane, vehicles under power coming in the opposite direction to usual traffic can well be dangerous. There's a rule against it and, like it or not, it exists for the wellbeing of those working in the pit lane. Mansell, quite innocently, had broken that law, and the penalty was the black flag. First, however, his team manager, Cesare Fiorio, was informed that his driver would be given the black flag, with the suggestion that Fiorio might like to bring him in rather than suffer the more public display from the start/finish line. Fiorio had two available options: the pit-to-car radio (which Mansell underlined had disadvantages due to the screaming V12 behind his head) and the pit board which, although relatively low down, was still against bright sunlight.

Mansell did not react to either of these, and after three or four laps the black flag was hung out. Again, there was no reaction. Only three flags are shown at the start/finish line, the black flag, the chequered flag and the red flag. Each suggests that at least one driver should slow, two of them suggest that all drivers should slow.

Mansell was now battling with Senna. No driver fights quite like Mansell, and both his concentration and Senna's were 100 per cent on the battle. Senna admits that he did know that something – but what? – was going on at the start/finish line. Mansell saw nothing.

Senna was informed on the pit-to-car radio, after three laps of the black flag, that Mansell was being given a black flag. It was a lap too late, Ron Dennis admits, and Senna didn't hear what his team manager was saying.

Just as he was saying 'repeat', so Mansell was coming down the inside of the McLaren into the first corner, as he had 41 laps before. Mansell

was committed to overtaking. But Senna took his rightful racing line and found himself ahead. The two came together, Mansell's front wheel hooking Senna's rear.

A classic racing accident, you may say. But Mansell shouldn't have been there at all, and Senna had too much to lose to be fighting. The stewards fined Mansell $50,000 and recommended to FISA that he should be banned for one race. Two days later, after members of the World Motorsports Council had been canvassed, he was indeed excluded from the Spanish event.

Mansell appealed, via the RAC, to the FIA International Court of Appeal. Only five of the court's fifteen delegates are needed to form a quorum, but they could not be assembled before the Spanish race, which Mansell duly missed.

On 5 October the court eventually met in Paris to hear appeals from Mansell and Ferrari. A decision was deferred, but four days later FISA decreed that the Spanish Grand Prix results would stand, and Ferrari decided to drop their appeal.

The circumstances were too varied and complex for anyone to know what the verdict should have been. Sides were taken, but generally in ignorance. Mud was thrown, and Ferrari putting an end to the saga was the best thing that could have happened.

BRIGHT SPARKS

It was unfortunate that so many of the less savoury aspects of motor racing dominated the Portuguese Grand Prix, because there were excellent performances from many drivers.

The Ferraris and McLarens, of course, were at the forefront, with Senna fighting Mansell and Berger, while Prost admitted to feeling unmotivated and maintaining a low profile further back.

Mansell, the only man to have caught and overtaken Senna in straight racing circumstances in 1989, proceeded to do the same thing twice at Estoril, even if the second manoeuvre did end in disaster.

Berger meanwhile, took the lead at the start from second on the grid

and pulled away from Senna, opening up a lead of over nine seconds during the first eight laps. The pace had taken much out of Berger's tyres, however, and when Mansell came up to challenge in amongst the backmarkers, Berger had little reply. But the two red cars were at least holding the red-and-whites at bay. This was a day for Ferrari.

Berger stopped for tyres on lap 34. He'd been calling for tyres on his radio but received no reply, so went in anyway and the result was a superb 6.84s stop. He was back in the lead and pulling away from Senna within six laps. Perhaps the most difficult moments were after Senna

Anti-clockwise from left:
leader of the pack – Brundle.
Before and after. Senna assures
Ron Dennis that he can win.

and Mansell had tangled and Berger simply had to maintain his lead for the last 23 laps. But this he did for an excellent victory after a season that had brought little success so far.

Behind Prost in second place might have been the Williams-Renault of Riccardo Patrese once he had won the Williams battle with Thierry Boutsen, who wasn't entirely happy with that situation. The new Williams-Renault FW13 had proved very efficient in testing and practice, almost too much so, for the older rear suspension, remaining in service until the new spec Renault engine is ready, was not up to the new front suspension, resulting in oversteer. Patrese caught and passed Stefan Johansson, the Williams on new tyres, and a place on the rostrum was a certainty, until an old Williams chestnut reared its head. The radiators became blocked and both cars overheated simultaneously.

Johansson then claimed a great third place for Onyx, having picked up places during the opening stint, then staying out on one set of tyres throughout the race. The problems with the sacked Bertrand Gachot were briefly forgotten in the euphoria. Onyx's driver became the tenth team of the year to mount the rostrum.

And mention should be made of both Roberto Moreno and Pierluigi Martini. The former made great use of new aerodynamics on the Coloni to make his way through pre-qualifying and qualifying to start 15th on the grid, but by this stage the aerodynamics were destroyed in a spectacular qualifying accident with Eddie Cheever. Recurring misfiring problems stopped the Brazilian in the race.

Martini, however, was one of the heroes of the weekend, with a great fifth on the grid on an intriguing mix of Pirelli qualifiers, and so good was the balance of his Martini, he was able to hold off the Williamses when other Pirelli runners were going backwards. He even led a lap before pitting for new tyres which dropped him to an unworthy ninth but retirements saw him finish fifth and a points scorer.

RACE DEBRIEF

Nothing seemed to go according to plan in the Portuguese Grand Prix. There were surprises even in pre-qualifying. While Johansson was quickest and Alliot followed, two other marques should have filled the next two places: AGS and Coloni. But while the Coloni was going superbly thanks to new aerodynamics, Dalmas's AGS was thrown out as the Frenchman used unmarked tyres, which let in Alboreto's Lola. Lehto would have been next, but had to abandon the Onyx he inherited from Gachot after a suspension failure, and few Grand Prix drivers could have qualified a car that they hadn't driven before on qualifiers of which they had no experience. Meanwhile Larini was also excluded for not stopping at a weigh check.

Practice was twice stopped that afternoon, once due to a power failure and the second time when Herbert spun. Mansell was involved in a collision with Danner's Rial on which something had broken.

Johansson was the main benefactor of the Senna/Mansell incident, netting four points for Onyx.

Senna slotted in one quick one to go quickest in the warm-up but had a spin. Mansell, who lost first and second gears, Prost and Warwick, on relatively low tanks, Berger and Johansson were close behind.

But the real question mark was over tyres, and when the cars took up their grid positions, it was clear that the field, on Goodyears at least, was divided. Arrows, Benetton, Berger, Patrese and Alboreto all went for the harder Bs. McLaren, Lotus, March plus Arnoux, Mansell, Boutsen, Johansson and Alliot were all on Cs, while Palmer chose a mixture of Bs and Cs.

Berger made a demon start and had pulled out a lead of 2.1s by the end of the first lap. Senna, Mansell, Prost, Martini, Patrese, Caffi, Boutsen and the Brabhams followed. And while Senna coped with Mansell, Berger was able to extend his lead out to more than six seconds by lap five.

At the same time, Martini, being left behind by Prost ahead, was having to cope with the two Williamses behind, once Boutsen had left Caffi in the capable hands of Brundle and then Johansson. But of those, it was the Onyx driver who was moving up having overtaken Sala, Modena and then Brundle on lap eight. Caffi went the same way on lap ten. Johansson was now eighth.

While that had been going on, Mansell had overtaken Senna in a clean manoeuvre on lap eight, and promptly pulled away, cutting the gap between himself and Ferrari teammate Berger. The McLarens seemed powerless to do anything about the Ferraris, and although the gaps

With a strong following wind, Senna was quickest, already under his outright qualifying record from Berger, while Martini was a tremendous third.

Next morning, Boutsen had lost his nose section within minutes of the start of the session and both new Williamses, suffering badly from oversteer, spent long minutes in the pits having their teething troubles sorted out.

The previous afternoon, some drivers had been just as happy on race tyres as qualifiers, and with just one lap available on what was now a clear, calm day, there was some doubt as to which rubber would be best.

Yet on his second run, Senna went even quicker than the previous day in second qualifying, while both Berger and Mansell also improved ahead of Prost who had minor problems on both runs. Martini was bumped down to fifth from Patrese, Caffi reinforcing the Pirelli programme with seventh ahead of Boutsen while Sala and Brundle did more for Pirelli completing the top ten. Johansson was the best of the V8s on Goodyears, the Benettons were in trouble on the bumps, and Johansson, Nakajima, Cheever and Gugelmin were among those who went slower than they had that morning.

There was a better crowd than for previous Portuguese Grands Prix.

Clockwise from right: Berger never looked back. Both Williams FW13s were overcome by the heat. Moreno's bravado in qualifying was spectacular but it didn't impress Cheever.

weren't enormous, there was no way that Prost was challenging Senna, or that Senna was able to maintain any sort of challenge to Mansell ahead. But behind them, Martini was still holding up or holding off the Williamses, while Johansson had broken free of the rest where Nannini was closing on Caffi and Brundle, both in tyre trouble.

Berger later admitted that he'd gone too hard, too early, and that his tyres had consequently suffered. He was therefore powerless as Mansell came charging up, but what was going to influence things was a huge and, for the participants, marvellous battle going on at the back of the field.

On lap 18, the gap from first to second was 4.7s. A lap later it was 2.5s but when they hit the backmarkers the gap plummeted to 0.8s. Mansell tailed Berger for three laps but on lap 23 Mansell overtook Berger as the pair came up on Warwick and Modena. Senna closed up too, and the trio was covered by four seconds.

Prost was the first to pit for tyres from fourth place on lap 27. Mansell was still easing away from Berger as the Austrian appealed to his pit to give him more tyres. When there was no reply, he came in anyway and was sent away again in 6.84s in a fine stop. Senna came in a lap later; it was not a perfect stop and lost him six seconds in comparison to Berger,

while Boutsen was next to stop. Mansell and Patrese stopped on lap 39, all of which left Martini leading – for a lap.

Mansell's stop, however, was a mess. He came in, couldn't see where to turn, overshot the pit and then waited for someone to pull him back. 'All I could see was a wall of people and then at the last moment I saw the yellow shirts,' he would say later. 'When no one pulled me back, I automatically took reverse . . .'

The stop took many seconds, and while FISA's men checked their rule books concerning the use of reverse gear in the pit lane, Mansell came out just in front of Prost.

It all left Martini leading but he was soon overtaken by Berger, Senna and then Mansell before the Minardi headed for the pits. Berger was almost comfortably in the lead, some 4.8s ahead as Mansell caught Senna. Mansell's team was soon told that he would be black-flagged and they not only told him over the radio but he was also shown a pit board telling him to come in.

Mansell was battling hard and when the Ferrari team's efforts came to naught, the black flag was duly shown at the start/finish line. Still there was no reaction.

On lap 49, Mansell made his move to pass Senna, ducking out of the slipstream and heading down the inside of the McLaren-Honda down into the first corner. The two cars were level into the braking area with Mansell dropping back slightly under braking. Senna came across to take the racing line, fine as long as there was no one on the inside, but his rear wheel hit Mansell's front, the McLaren going off quickly into the sand while Mansell's Ferrari spun. Both were out of the race.

At the front, Berger was left with a lead over Prost that he would simply extend. Prost, in chassis trouble with tyre vibration, was happy to inherit second place. Johansson had plugged away in third, not stopping for tyres and heading for the rostrum, denied him when his Onyx ran out of fuel on the slowing-down lap.

He had been overtaken by Patrese whose shadow, teammate Boutsen, was unhappy at the end because Patrese wouldn't move over. But then they both suffered blocked radiators, due to rubber and debris on the track, and up went the temperatures, both Williamses pulling out on lap 61. Nannini salvaged a poor weekend for Benetton with fourth, having a spin, oversteer early on, and then poor handling when the fuel load lightened. Martini finished a fine fifth with a stiff neck while Palmer reckoned that he might have gone all the way through on Cs, another with a stiff neck.

However, the results sheet was not the last that one would hear of this Portuguese Grand Prix . . .

MILESTONES

- Prost's 150th Grand Prix
- Ferrari fined $50,000 as Mansell ignored black flag
- J. J. Lehto replaces Gachot in Onyx team
- Dalmas and Larini excluded from pre-qualifying

Clockwise from left: more points for Martini. Alboreto in shadow. Benetton plays follow-my-leader, Nannini salvaging three points.

FORMULA 1 WORLD CHAMPIONSHIP

GRANDE PRÉMIO DE PORTUGAL

ENTRIES · PRACTICE · RESULTS

Pos	Driver/Nationality		No.	Car/Engine	P.Q. (sunny, cool)	Practice 1 (sun, windy)	Practice 2 (warm, sun)	Warm-up (pos) (warm, sun)	Laps (warm, sun)	Time/Retirement
1	G. Berger	A	28	Ferrari 640 Ferrari V12	–	1:16.799	**1:16.059**	1:20.730 (5)	71	1hr36m48.546
2	A. Prost	F	2	McLaren MP4/5 Honda V10	–	1:17.336	**1:16.204**	1:20.219 (3)	71	1hr37m21.183
3	S. Johansson	S	36	Onyx ORE1 Ford DFR V8	1:18.623	1:19.281	**1:18.105**	1:20.932 (6)	71	1hr37m43.871
4	A. Nannini	I	19	Benetton B189 HBV8	–	**1:18.115**	1:18.359	1:22.074 (17)	71	1hr38m10.915
5	P. Martini	I	23	Minardi M189 Ford DFR V8	–	**1:16.938**	1:17.161	1:21.533 (9)	70	1hr36m54.373
6	J. Palmer	GB	3	Tyrrell 018 Ford DFR V8	–	1:19.172	**1:18.404**	1:21.733 (14)	70	1hr37m15.830
7	S. Nakajima	J	12	Lotus 101 Judd V8	–	1:19.278	**1:19.165**	1:22.073 (16)	70	1hr37m48.693
8	M. Brundle	GB	7	Brabham BT58 Judd V8	–	**1:17.874**	1:17.995	1:23.043 (23)	70	1hr37m58.667
9	P. Alliot	F	30	Lola LC89 Lamborghini V12	1:19.164	1:19.306	**1:18.386**	1:21.641 (12)	70	1hr37m58.920
10	M. Gugelmin	BR	15	Leyton House CG891 Judd V8	–	**1:18.124**	1:18.277	1:21.545 (10)	69	1hr37m00.756
11	M. Alboreto	I	29	Lola LC89 Lamborghini V12	1:19.869	**1:18.563**	1:18.846	1:22.448 (20)	69	1hr37m33.401
12	L. Sala	S	42	Minardi M189 Dore DFR V8	–	**1:17.844**	1:18.305	1:23.217 (24)	69	1hr37m54.600
13	R. Arnoux	F	25	Ligier JS33 Ford DFR V8	–	**1:18.767**	1:19.979	1:22.175 (18)	69	1hr37m58.6454
14	S. Modena	I	8	Brabham BT58 Judd V8	–	1:18.589	**1:18.093**	1:24.561 (26)	69	1hr37m59.633
15	R. Patrese	I	6	Williams FW13 (p) FW12C (r) Renault V10	–	**1:17.281**	1:17.852	1:21.566 (11)	60	overheating
16	T. Boutsen	B	5	Williams FW13 Renault V10	–	**1:17.801**	1:17.888	1:21.059 (7)	60	overheating
17	A. Senna	BR	1	McLaren MP4/5 Honda V10	–	1:15.496	**1:15.468**	1:19.795 (1)	48	accident/Mansell
18	N. Mansell	GB	27	Ferrari 640 Ferrari V12	–	1:17.387	**1:16.193**	1:20.063 (2)	48	accident/Senna
19	D. Warwick	GB	9	Arrows A11 Ford DFR V8	–	**1:18.711**	1:18.892	1:20.693 (4)	37	accident damage
20	N. Piquet	BR	11	Lotus 101 Judd V8	–	**1:18.482**	1:18.682	1:22.991 (22)	33	accident/Caffi
21	A. Caffi	I	21	Dallara BMS 189 Ford DFR V8	–	1:18.623	**1:17.661**	1:22.311 (19)	33	accident/Piquet
22	E. Pirro	I	20	Benetton B189 HB V8	–	**1:18.340**	1:18.328	1:21.662 (13)	29	shock absorber
23	I. Capelli	I	16	Leyton House CG891 Judd V8	–	1:19.076	**1:18.785**	1:22.472 (21)	25	engine
24	E. Cheever	USA	10	Arrows A11 Ford DFR V8	–	**1:19.247**	1:20.006	1:21.244 (8)	24	accident
25	A. de Cesaris	I	22	Dallara BMS 189 Ford DFR V8	–	**1:18.442**	1:18.511	1:22.010 (15)	17	wiring loose
26	R. Moreno	BR	31	Coloni C3 Ford DFR V8	1:19.780	**1:18.196**	1:20.512	1:23.306 (25)	11	electrics
27	J. Herbert	GB	4	Tyrrell 018 Ford DFR V8	–	1:19.515	**1:19.264**	DNQ		
28	O. Grouillard	F	26	Ligier JS33 Ford DFR V8	–	1:19.605	**1:19.436**	DNQ		
29	P. Raphanel	F	39	Rial ARC02 Ford DFR V8	–	no time	**1:21.435**	DNQ		
30	C. Danner	D	38	Rial ARC02 Ford DFR V8	–	**1:21.678**	1:22.423			
–	J. J. Lehto	F	37	Onyx ORE1 Ford DFR V8	1:20.880	DNPQ	DNPQ			
–	P. Ghinzani	I	18	Osella FA1M Ford DFR V8	1:21.021	DNPQ	DNPQ			
–	O. Larrauri	ARG	33	EuroBrun ER189 Judd V8	1:21.326	DNPQ	DNPQ			
–	G. Tarquini	I	40	AGS JH24 Ford DFR V8	1:21.881	DNPQ	DNPQ			
–	A. Suzuki	J	35	Zakspeed ZK189 Yamaha V12	1:24.116	DNPQ	DNPQ			
–	B. Schneider	F	34	Zakspeed ZK189 Yamaha V12	1:24.732	DNPQ	DNPQ			
–	E. Bertaggia	I	32	Coloni C3 Ford DFR V8	1:28.526	DNPQ	DNPQ			
–	N. Larini	I	17	Osella FA1M Ford DFR V8	excluded	DNPQ	DNPQ			
–	Y. Dalmas	F	41	AGS JH24 Ford DFR V8	excluded	DNPQ	DNPQ			

Circuit Data: Autodromo do Estoril, length 2.703 miles/4.350 km, race distance 71 laps = 191.9 miles/308.8 km, race weather sunny and warm.
Notes: J. J. Lehto (SF) replaces Bertrand Gachot in Onyx No. 37. No times for either Dalmas or Larini, excluded from pre-qualifying for various reasons. Both Patrese and Boutsen driving Williams FW13s. Alesi replaced by Johnny Herbert (GB) in Tyrrell No. 4 again.

Grid Order	1 2 3 4 5 6 7 8 9 10 11 12 13 14 15 16 17 18 19 20 21 22 23 24 25 26 27 28 29 30 31 32 33 34 35 36 37 38 39 40 41 42 43 44 45 46 47 48 49 50 51 52 53 54 55 56 57 58 59 60 61 62 63 64 65 66 67 68 69 70 71
1 A. Senna	28 28 28 28 28 28 28 28 28 28 28 28 28 28 28 28 28 28 28 28 28 28 28 27 27 27 27 27 27 27 27 27 27 27 27 27 27 27 27 27 27 27 23 28 28 28 28 28 28 28 28 28 28 28 28 28 28 28 28 28 28 28 28 28 28 28 28 28 28 28 28
28 G. Berger	1 1 1 1 1 1 1 27 27 27 27 27 27 27 27 27 27 27 27 27 27 27 27 27 27 28 28 28 28 28 28 28 1 1 23 23 23 23 28 1 1 1 1 1 1 1 1 1 2 2 2 2 2 2 2 2 2 2 2 2 2 2 2 2 2 2 2 2
27 N. Mansell	27 27 27 27 27 27 27 1 1 1 1 1 1 1 1 1 1 1 1 1 1 1 1 1 1 1 1 1 1 28 23 6 6 6 28 1 23 27 27 27 27 27 27 27 36 36 36 36 36 36 36 6 6 6 36 36 36 36 36 36 36 36 36 36
2 A. Prost	2 2 2 2 2 2 2 2 2 2 2 2 2 2 2 2 2 2 2 2 2 2 2 23 23 23 23 23 23 23 6 28 28 28 1 27 27 23 2 2 2 2 6 6 6 6 6 6 36 36 36 19 19 19 19 19 19 19 19 19 19 19 19 19
23 P. Martini	23 23 23 23 23 23 23 23 23 23 23 23 23 23 23 23 23 23 23 23 23 23 2 6 6 6 6 6 28 1 1 1 2 2 2 2 36 36 36 36 36 5 5 5 5 5 5 5 5 5 19 23 23 23 23 23 23 23 23 23 23 23
6 R. Patrese	6 6 6 6 6 6 6 6 6 6 6 6 6 6 6 6 6 6 6 6 6 6 6 5 5 5 5 5 36 36 2 2 6 36 36 23 19 6 6 6 19 19 19 19 19 19 19 19 19 19 23 3 3 3 3 3 3 3 3 3 3
21 A. Caffi	21 21 5 5 5 5 5 5 5 5 5 5 5 5 5 5 5 5 5 5 5 5 5 5 36 36 36 36 36 36 2 2 36 36 19 19 19 6 5 5 5 23 23 23 23 23 23 23 23 23 5 12 12 12 12 12 12 12 12 12 12
5 T. Boutsen	5 5 21 21 21 21 21 21 36 36 36 36 36 36 36 36 36 36 36 36 36 36 36 2 2 2 2 2 2 5 19 19 19 6 6 6 6 5 19 19 19 19 3 3 3 3 3 3 3 3 3 3 3 7 7 7 7 7 7 7 7 7
24 L. Sala	7 7 7 7 7 7 36 36 21 21 21 21 21 21 21 21 21 21 19 19 19 19 19 19 19 19 19 19 19 5 5 5 5 5 5 5 23 23 23 23 23 12 12 12 12 12 12 12 12 12 12 30 30 30 30 30 30 30 30
7 M. Brundle	8 8 8 8 36 36 36 7 7 7 7 7 7 7 7 7 19 19 19 21 21 21 21 21 21 21 15 15 11 3 3 3 3 3 3 3 3 3 3 3 3 7 7 7 7 7 7 7 7 7 15 15 15 15 15 15 15 15 15
8 S. Modena	24 24 24 36 8 19 19 19 19 19 19 19 19 19 19 19 7 7 7 7 7 7 15 15 15 15 11 11 3 11 7 7 7 7 7 7 7 7 7 7 12 30 30 30 30 30 30 30 30 30 29 29 29 29 29 29 29 29 29
36 S. Johansson	36 36 36 24 19 8 15 15 15 15 15 15 15 15 15 15 15 15 15 15 15 15 11 11 11 11 3 15 12 12 12 12 12 12 12 12 12 30 7 15 15 15 15 15 15 15 15 15 24 24 24 24 24 24 24
19 A. Nannini	19 19 19 19 24 15 8 8 8 11 11 11 11 11 11 11 11 11 11 11 11 11 7 3 3 21 21 7 30 30 30 30 30 30 30 30 30 7 30 29 29 29 29 29 29 29 29 25 25 25 25 25 25 25 25
15 M. Gugelmin	15 15 15 15 24 20 24 11 8 8 8 3 3 3 3 3 3 3 3 3 3 30 30 30 30 7 7 12 24 24 24 24 24 24 15 15 15 15 15 15 24 24 24 24 24 24 24 8 8 8 8 8 8 8 8
31 R. Moreno	20 20 20 20 20 20 24 11 24 3 3 30 30 30 30 30 30 30 30 30 30 7 7 7 12 30 9 9 9 15 15 15 24 24 24 24 24 24 25 25 25 25 25 25 25 25 25 25
20 E. Pirro	11 11 11 11 11 11 11 3 3 24 30 30 8 8 16 16 16 16 16 16 16 16 12 12 12 12 12 30 30 24 15 15 15 25 25 25 29 29 29 29 29 29 8 8 8 8 8 8 8 8 8
30 P. Alliot	31 3 3 3 3 3 3 30 30 30 24 16 16 8 8 8 8 8 8 24 12 12 24 24 24 24 24 24 9 29 29 29 29 29 29 29 25 25 25 25 25 25 25 25
3 J. Palmer	3 30 30 30 30 30 20 20 20 16 16 24 24 24 24 24 24 24 12 24 24 9 9 9 9 9 9 15 8 25 25 25 8 8 8 8 8 8 8 8 8 8
22 A. de Cesaris	22 31 22 22 22 22 22 22 16 20 20 20 20 20 20 12 12 12 8 9 29 29 29 29 29 29 29 25 8 8 8
11 N. Piquet	30 22 31 9 9 9 9 16 22 22 9 9 9 9 22 9 12 9 9 9 9 8 16 8 8 8 8 8 8 8
29 M. Alboreto	9 9 9 31 29 29 16 16 9 9 9 22 22 22 22 9 22 9 20 29 29 29 29 9 8 25 25 25 25 25 25 25
9 D. Warwick	29 29 29 29 16 16 29 29 29 29 29 29 29 12 12 29 29 10 10 10 10 10 25 20 20 20 20
25 R. Arnoux	25 25 16 16 10 10 10 10 12 12 10 10 10 10 12 29 29 10 10 20 20 20 20 20 20
16 I. Capelli	16 16 25 10 12 12 12 12 10 10 12 12 12 10 10 10 25 25 25 25 25 25
12 S. Nakajima	10 10 10 12 31 31 25 25 25 25 25 25 25 25 25 25
10 E. Cheever	12 12 12 25 25 25 31 31 31 31 31

FASTEST LAPS

Pos.	Car No./Driver/Team	Time
1	28 G. Berger/Ferrari	1:18.986
2	27 N. Mansell/Ferrari	1:19.047
3	2 A. Prost/McLaren	1:19.385
4	1 A. Senna/McLaren	1:19.490
5	5 T. Boutsen/Williams	1:19.575
6	6 R. Patrese/Williams	1:19.796
7	15 M. Gugelmin/Leyton House	1:20.571
8	30 P. Alliot/Larrousse	1:20.697
9	19 A. Nannini/Benetton	1:20.722
10	7 M. Brundle/Brabham	1:21.167
11	23 P. Martini/Minardi	1:21.170
12	36 S. Johansson/Onyx	1:21.224
13	21 A. Caffi/BMS Dallara	1:21.300
14	8 S. Modena/Brabham	1:21.451
15	3 J. Palmer/Tyrrell	1:21.562
16	25 R. Arnoux/Ligier	1:21.603
17	29 M. Alboreto/Lola	1:21.756
18	12 S. Nakajima/Lotus	1:21.794
19	24 L. Sala/Minardi	1:22.114
20	11 N. Piquet/Lotus	1:22.356
21	16 I. Capelli/Leyton House	1:22.873
22	9 D. Warwick/Arrows	1:22.926
23	22 A. de Cesaris/BMS Dallara	1:23.592
24	10 E. Cheever/Arrows	1:23.732
25	20 E. Pirro/Benetton	1:24.080
26	31 R. Moreno/Coloni	1:25.411

CHAMPIONSHIP POINTS

Drivers			Drivers/Constructors		
1	A. Prost	75 pts	22	M. Brundle	2 pts
2	A. Senna	51 pts		J. Palmer	2 pts
3	N. Mansell	38 pts	24	G. Tarquini	1 pt
4	R. Patrese	28 pts		O. Grouillard	1 pt
5	T. Boutsen	24 pts		L. Sala	1 pt
6	A. Nannini	17 pts			
7	G. Berger	15 pts	1	McLaren	128 pts
8	N. Piquet	9 pts	2	Ferrari	53 pts
9	S. Johansson	6 pts	3	Williams	52 pts
	M. Alboreto	6 pts	4	Benetton	22 pts
	E. Cheever	6 pts	5	Tyrrell	13 pts
12	D. Warwick	6 pts	6	Arrows	12 pts
13	J. Alesi	5 pts	7	Lotus	9 pts
	J. Herbert	5 pts	8	Dallara	8 pts
15	A. de Cesaris	4 pts	9	Onyx	6 pts
	M. Gugelmin	4 pts		Brabham	6 pts
	S. Modena	4 pts	11	Minardi	5 pts
18	A. Caffi	4 pts	12	Leyton House	4 pts
19	P. Martini	4 pts	13	Rial	3 pts
20	C. Danner	3 pts		Ligier	3 pts
21	R. Arnoux	2 pts	15	AGS	1 pt

Existing qualifying lap record: Ayrton Senna, Lotus-Renault 98T, 1m 16.673s at 204.244 kph/126.911 mph in 1986

Existing race lap record: Gerhard Berger, Ferrari F1/87, 1m 19.282s at 197.523 kph/122.735 in 1987

Exisiting distance record: Alain Prost, McLaren-TAG MP4/3, 70 laps in 1 hr 37m 03.906s at 188.224 kph/116.957 mph in 1987

PAST WINNERS

Year	Driver	Nat.	Car	Circuit
1958	Stirling Moss	GB	2.5 Vanwall	Oporto
1959	Stirling Moss	GB	2.5 Cooper T51 Climax	Monsanto
1960	Jack Brabham	AUS	2.5 Cooper T53 Climax	Oporto
1984	Alain Prost	F	1.5 McLaren MP4/2 TAG t/c	Estoril
1985	Ayrton Senna	BR	1.5 Lotus 97T Renault t/c	Estoril
1986	Nigel Mansell	GB	1.5 Williams FW11 Honda t/c	Estoril
1987	Alain Prost	F	1.5 McLaren MP4/3 TAG t/c	Estoril
1988	Alain Prost	F	1.5 McLaren MP4/4 Honda t/c	Estoril

Patrese in the FW13 — but he wouldn't race it.

Jerez

GRAN PREMIO TIO PEPE DE ESPAÑA · 1 OCTUBRE

Tio Pepe's sherry man is a familiar sight in Andalucia.

Spanish Grand Prix of most of its interest – at least as far as the leaders were concerned. Senna won, and kept his championship hopes alive, and after the Portuguese fiasco there were many who were quite glad about that. But on a track that has habitually hosted thrillers, this was an impotent affair. Was Nigel Mansell the missing vital ingredient?

Fatigue, off-track politics, heat and mechanical problems sadly contrived to rob the 73-lap

It would be a sad reflection on Grand Prix racing to say that just one driver makes a race, but not even Mansell's detractors would deny that he puts his heart, soul and everything else into his racing, and often that produces the real excitement of a weekend.

This weekend, however, he put in just a token appearance to explain his view of (sub judice) events days previously, and once it became plain that there would be no Court of Appeal prior to the Spanish Grand Prix, he was gone.

One Ferrari versus two McLarens, then; but where would the supporting cast come from? Williams's new FW13 was obviously having teething troubles with the imbalance between old rear and new front suspension, causing Patrese to revert to a FW12C in which he might be expected to run with, but perhaps not challenge, the aforementioned dominators.

Pirelli runners Martini and Brundle looked good in practice, but we'd seen what can happen in a race the week before. However, they could be joined by the V8-powered cars from Piquet, Alesi and Pirro which might make a race. Alliot's fifth-placed Lola-Lamborghini had shown

reliability the previous weekend, but even he didn't consider himself capable of challenging the fellow 'multi-cylinders' ahead.

In the event Senna grabbed the lead and Berger tentatively challenged for 20 laps until the fuel stops. Prost was happy with third place, with Patrese not far behind. Everyone's pit stops went perfectly.

Berger began to drop back when his engine started smoking soon after the stops, leaving Senna to win. Berger was second and Prost lost Patrese after the tyre stops. None of them appeared to draw much pleasure from the race, even though they had accomplished what they set out to do. A tired Senna had kept his championship hopes alive, an equally exhausted Berger had finished again, and Prost was happy with third place on a circuit where, he said, you can't overtake.

Spectators, happily, were able to look further back to see more interesting battles, watching new F3000 champion Alesi just holding off the twice pitting Patrese for fourth place, and Luis Perez Sala assaulting Gugelmin's March. The front runners promised better in Japan.

BRIGHT SPARKS

Senna's dogged winning performance was preceded by his 40th pole position, a somewhat controversial affair after his first quickest time on Friday afternoon was discounted when he failed to slow for black flags being shown around the circuit after Gregor Foitek had crashed his Rial. A $20,000 fine was included in the penalty.

But next afternoon he put his McLaren-Honda on pole position with a lap that was 3.8s quicker than last year's pole-winning time, and 1.4s quicker than the outright qualifying lap record. Cooler conditions had a little to do with it, but it was still an excellent performance.

Clockwise from right: Onyx's new boy J. J. Lehto leads a Minardi and Boutsen's FW13. Larrousse keeping the tyres warm. A hive of activity for pre-qualifying.

Pierluigi Martini had explained in Portugal the reasons for his Minardi and Pirelli being so competitive, and the same rule applied in Spain where the team had done so much of its testing. Fourth on the grid was the team's best-ever performance, but he was comfortably ahead of Brundle, the next Pirelli runner in eighth spot with Modena next into twelfth place.

Although both he and fifth-placed Philippe Alliot were overtaken by Patrese at the start, they were soon running solidly in fifth and sixth places. Martini's tyre stop – 'I asked a lot of my tyres in the first twenty laps' – dropped him back into the battle behind de Cesaris's Dallara from which he spun out rather ignominiously after 27 laps.

Alliot, however, did all that was asked of him. Fifth was both his and the team's best-ever placing and he shadowed Martini during the early laps. But in order not to overheat the tyres, they'd taken off front wing. Afterwards, Alliot felt that a little more front wing might have brought them fourth place, but he scored the Lola-Lamborghini team's first-ever World Championship with sixth place.

While one championship point was not about to save the team from the problems of pre-qualifying in 1990, it did point towards reliability

and competitiveness. It also went some way to demonstrating that Alliot can race reliably and without incident, Friday morning apart, for spins are the rule rather than the exception in Philippe's case.

Ahead of him, however, were Patrese and Alesi. The Frenchman had missed the previous weekend's Portuguese Grand Prix as he was busy clinching the F3000 championship. Back in Formula One again, he admitted making the fundamental mistake of going out too early on his qualifiers in the first session but with a new engine, better grip and a circuit that he likes, he set ninth fastest time.

The warm-up was good in parts: Alesi was second to Prost but went off and damaged the underside of the car avoiding Berger, which put him in the spare for the race. He had a fraught battle with Brundle for most of the first 20 laps, then, after overtaking him, quickly took Alliot and found himself fourth until a relatively late stop for tyres on lap 36. Later he caught Patrese (who promptly stopped for tyres), taking over fourth place and even unlapping himself from the leader. In the closing laps, however, Patrese was catching him, and Alesi didn't want to overtake Senna again. He just hung on to fourth place by a tenth of a second, his third points score in his six-race Grand Prix career.

RACE DEBRIEF

Once again, the Pirelli factor weighed quite heavily during pre-qualifying and qualifying itself. Both Osellas got through pre-qualifying, with Larini quickest in spite of having to take the spare car when his own car's gearbox failed. Lehto came in with a late second quickest time, while Alliot completed the top four.

There was disappointment for AGS who thought that they would be competitive, but didn't take the Pirelli factor into account. Johansson was also out of a race after his engine failed and the spare car lacked grip, while fellow former Ferrari driver Michele Alboreto parked his Lola with an electrical problem, and then couldn't find a balance with the spare.

In practice and qualifying, there was much talk of traffic, lack of grip, and front qualifiers going off before the lap was completed. Once again, Martini was the number-one interloper, setting fastest time on Friday morning, second-fastest time that afternoon, second again the next morning and then slipping to fourth in the final qualifying session, feeling the effect of ribs bruised in a spin at Estoril.

The Brabhams also shone in the unofficial sessions, ending up eighth (Brundle) and twelfth (Modena) thanks to traffic. Piquet was also looking competitive, in spite of a slight moment at the esses and failing front tyres at the end of the lap. And looking particularly good was Pirro in spite of similar front-tyre problems, making his point by out-qualifying teammate Nannini who was also suffering from the same complaint.

Larini did well with his Osella, putting it in 11th place, his best of the year by several places, while Lehto would make his Grand Prix debut from 17th on the grid, in spite of a landing helicopter drowning him in dust; surely one of the most original excuses for a ruined lap!

It was quasi-disaster for March: mechanical problems on two cars and a crashed third on Saturday morning meant that neither driver had a real chance to improve, particularly when more problems arose.

The Spanish Grand Prix is rarely blessed with an enormous crowd, in spite of the closeness of previous races. But the absence of Mansell meant that expatriate Brits from the nearby Costa del Sol were less inclined to make the short trip. It's still one of the best and easiest Grand Prix to visit from a spectator's point of view.

The stands, then, were less full than they might have been elsewhere as a stiff breeze blew dust back on to the track which the organisers had spent five hours sweeping the night before. Prost was again troubled

by gearchange problems in the warm-up but set quickest time from Alesi, who damaged his car, and Senna, who found understeer on full tanks. Berger was only 20th, with gearbox failure in both race and spare Ferraris.

There was much speculation as to what might happen should Berger manage to dispute the first corner with future teammate Senna. However, in the event, it was Senna who made the cleaner start to lead Berger into the first corner from Prost and then Patrese getting ahead of Martini and Alliot. Nakajima and Capelli tangled at turn two, the Japanese going no further, while the Italian pitted for suspension replacements.

The story of the first three is swiftly told. Senna, out in front and leading, was harrassed by Berger for the first 20 laps or so before a gap began to open up as they came up to their first tyre stops. Prost had gradually fallen back, particularly in the laps prior to the tyre stops which he initiated on lap 26. Patrese was close behind the Frenchman.

Prost stopped on lap 26 (7.9s), Berger made a good one (6.2s) on lap 28, Senna's was a lap later (7.5s). All of which left Senna still ahead of Berger, the pair of them leaving Prost.

Clockwise from right: Nannini dug in. A lonesome Ferrari, Berger scores again. A space left for Nigel? Prost motors.

But each had his own story. 'It was a very stressful race', admitted Senna, 'and Berger's pressure made it that much more stressful. Physically it was very tiring too, and I had gearbox problems for the last twenty-five laps, and brake problems for the last twenty.'

But Berger was not in a position to challenge. 'I tried hard during the first part of the race, but it was impossible to overtake, so I just waited to see what happened at the pit stops. Then the engine started smoking and the oil pressure was going down, so I settled for second place.'

Prost was also in trouble. 'I missed so many gear changes that I'm really happy to have finished. It was impossible to overtake here, and my visor was covered in oil from Gerhard's car, so I drove my "taxi" to third, which is what I wanted from this race.'

No change in the first three then, but Patrese's fourth place disappeared at the pit stops when an on-form Emanuele Pirro overtook him. The Benetton driver had overtaken Brundle, then Alliot and finally Martini before the pit stops. Patrese's pit stop was a little slow, and Pirro found himself in a fine fourth place for the middle section of the race. Indeed, it was quite a safe fourth place – from the outside. Inside the car, however, was a different matter as poor Pirro struggled with cramp which ultimately got the better of him on lap 60 when his solid braking leg just failed to react and he spun out as teammate Nannini had done earlier.

That elevated Patrese to fourth place, but he was being caught hand

Left: the close confines of Jonathan Palmer's Tyrrell. Above: Tyrrell hotshot Alesi duels with Brundle. Right: Spanish eyes!

over fist by Alesi thanks to understeer with his second set of tyres. The only solution was to change them, and that's just what he did with ten laps to go.

It gave Alesi fourth place, running with Senna, and the Frenchman even unlapped himself. In those final ten laps, Patrese cut the gap between himself and the Tyrrell driver from 19.4s to a tenth of a second at the flag, Alesi being in a real quandary as to whether and how he should overtake Senna as Patrese closed, but fortunately Patrese was not quite close enough.

Alliot, Alesi and Martini were all together as they approached the first tyre stops, but Martini spun soon after he stopped. Alliot's stop took a little longer than it should have done, after trouble with the left rear, but the Frenchman spent a while battling with Palmer (who would slow drastically with an awful misfire) and Brundle, whose exhaust broke, leading to over-heating, mechanical seizure and a spin. Sixth place, then, went to a delighted Alliot.

Behind him at 46 laps were Gugelmin battling with Sala and Warwick with Piquet. Both groups tangled within two laps, the former pair being sidelined, while for Warwick it was the second incident in the race, having earlier been hit up the back by his own teammate when both were caught out by de Cesaris going into the pits. The Dallara driver then went on to finish seventh in what was one of the year's less exciting races from a front runner's point of view.

MILESTONES

- J. J. Lehto makes Grand Prix debut in Onyx
- Senna's 40th pole position
- Mansell excluded from race
- Foitek replaces Danner at Rial
- Alliot becomes points scorer number 27, equalling the record set in 1960
- Lola-Lamborghini become 16th team to score points
- Best-ever grid positions for Minardi (4th) and Larrousse Lola (5th)

FORMULA 1 WORLD CHAMPIONSHIP

GRAN PREMIO TIO PEPE DE ESPAÑA

ENTRIES · PRACTICE · RESULTS

Pos	Driver/Nationality		No.	Car/Engine	P.Q. (sunny)	Practice I (hot, sunny)	Practice 2 (warm, sunny)	Warm-up (pos) (wind, sunny)	Laps	Time/Retirement (breezy, sunny)
I	A. Senna	BR	I	McLaren MP4/5 Honda V10	–	1:21.855	1:20.291	1:25.552 (3)	73	1hr47m48.264
2	G. Berger	A	28	Ferrari 640 Ferrari V12	–	1:22.276	1:20.565	1:28.223 (20)	73	1hr48m15.315
3	A. Prost	F	12	McLaren MP4/5 Honda V10	–	1:23.113	1:21.368	1:25.157 (1)	73	1hr48m42.052
4	J. Alesi	F	4	Tyrrell 018 Ford DFR V8	–	1:24.615	1:22.363	1:25.551 (2)	72	1hr47m48.759
5	R. Patrese	I	6	Williams FW13 Renault V10	–	1:24.033	1:21.777	1:25.726 (4)	72	1hr47m48.759
6	P. Alliot	F	30	Lola LC89 Lamborghini V12	–	1:23.597	1:21.708	1:27.074 (11)	72	1hr48m41.496
7	A. de Cesaris	I	22	Dallara BMS 189 Ford DFR V8	–	1:24.900	1:23.186	1:28.949 (23)	72	1hr48m43.316
8	N. Piquet	BR	II	Lotus 101 Judd V8	–	1:23.235	1:21.922	1:27.703 (16)	71	1hr47m52.737
9	D. Warwick	GB	9	Arrows A11 Ford DFR V8	–	1:24.161	1:23.222	1:27.408 (13)	71	1hr48m03.056
10	J. Palmer	GB	3	Tyrrell 018 Ford DFR V8	–	1:23.494	1:23.052	1:28.275 (21)	71	1hr49m00.319
11	E. Cheever	USA	10	Arrows A11 Ford DFR V8	–	1:24.222	1:23.729	1:27.944 (19)	61	engine
12	E. Pirro	I	20	Benetton B189 HB V8	–	1:24.647	1:22.567	1:26.407 (6)	59	cramp/spin
13	A. Caffi	I	21	Dallara BMS 189 Ford DFR V8	–	1:24.658	1:23.763	1:28.951 (24)	55	valve spring
14	M. Brundle	GB	7	Brabham BT58 Judd V8	–	1:23.761	1:22.133	1:27.473 (14)	51	spin
15	M. Gugelmin	BR	15	Leyton House CG891 Judd V8	–	1:24.707	no time	1:26.410 (7)	47	collision/Sala
16	L. Sala	E	24	Minardi M189 Ford DFR V8	–	1:23.908	1:23.443	1:28.368 (22)	47	collision/Gugelmin
17	T. Boutsen	B	5	Williams FW13 Renault V10	–	1:24.838	1:23.657	1:26.874 (8)	40	fuel pump
18	O. Grouillard	F	26	Ligier JS33 Ford DFR V8	–	1:24.991	1:23.931	1:27.930 (18)	34	injection trumpet
19	P. Martini	I	23	Minardi M189 Ford DFR V8	–	1:22.243	1:21.479	1:27.639 (15)	47	spin
20	I. Capelli	I	16	Leyton House CG891 Judd V8	–	1:23.401	no time	1:27.033 (10)	23	transmission
21	J. J. Lehto	F	37	Onyx ORE1 Ford DFR V8	1:23.958	1:24.322	1:23.243	1:27.235 (12)	20	transmission
22	P. Ghinzani	I	18	Osella FA1M Ford DFR V8	1:24.586	1:26.147	1:24.003	1:30.331 (26)	17	gearbox
23	A. Nannini	I	19	Benetton B189 HBV8	–	1:24.233	1:23.105	1:26.402 (5)	14	spin
24	S. Modena	I	8	Brabham BT58 Judd V8	–	1:23.679	1:22.826	1:29.337 (25)	11	engine cut
25	N. Larini	I	17	Osella FA1M Ford DFR V8	1:23.566	1:23.538	1:22.620	1:27.777 (17)	6	accident
26	S. Nakajima	J	12	Lotus 101 Judd V8	–	time d/a	1:23.309	1:27.004 (9)	–	collision/Capelli
27	R. Arnoux	F	25	Ligier JS33 Ford DFR V8	–	1:26.767	1:25.190	DBQ		
28	P. Raphanel	F	39	Rial ARC02 Ford DFR V8	–	1:28.311	1:25.443	DBQ		
28	G. Foitek	S	38	Rial ARC02 Ford DFR V8	–	1:29.226	no time	DBQ		
–	G. Tarquini	I	40	AGS JH24 Ford DFR V8	1:24.847	DNPQ	DNPQ			
–	S. Johansson	S	36	Onyx ORE1 Ford DFR V8	1:24.944	DNPQ	DNPQ			
–	R. Moreno	BR	31	Coloni C3 Ford DFR V8	1:25.074	DNPQ	DNPQ			
–	M. Alboreto	I	29	Lola LC89 Lamborghini V12	1:25.646	DNPQ	DNPQ			
–	B. Schneider	D	34	Zakspeed ZK189 Yamaha V8	1:25.673	DNPQ	DNPQ			
–	Y. Dalmas	F	41	AGS JH24 Ford DFR V8	1:26.131	DNPQ	DNPQ			
–	A. Suzuki	J	35	Zakspeed ZK189 Yamaha V8	1:26.609	DNPQ	DNPQ			
–	O. Larrauri	ARG	33	Eurobrun ER189 Judd V8	1:26.803	DNPQ	DNPQ			
–	E. Bertaggia	I	32	Coloni C3 Ford DFR V8	1:27.236	DNPQ	DNPQ			

Circuit Data: Circuito de Jerez, length 2.6209 miles/4.218 km, race distance 61 laps = 191.3 miles/307.9 km, race weather sunny and breezy.
Notes: Jean Alesi (F) back in Tyrrell No. 4. Gregor Foitek (CH) replaces Christian Danner in Rial No. 38. Riccardo Patrese drives Williams FW12C rather than FW13, but Boutsen continues to drive newer car. Nakajima's first qualifying times were discounted.

Grid Order	1 2 3 4 5 6 7 8 9 10 11 12 13 14 15 16 17 18 19 20 21 22 23 24 25 26 27 28 29 30 31 32 33 34 35 36 37 38 39 40 41 42 43 44 45 46 47 48 49 50 51 52 53 54 55 56 57 58 59 60 61 62 63 64 65 66 67 68 69 70 71 72 73
1 A. Senna	1 1 1 1 1 1 1 1 1 1 1 1 1 1 1 1 1 1 1 1 1 1 1 1 1 1 1 1 1 1 1 1 1 1 1 1 1 1 1 1 1 1 1 1 1 1 1 1 1 1 1 1 1 1 1 1 1 1 1 1 1 1 1 1 1 1 1 1 1 1 1 1 1
28 G. Berger	28 28 28 28 28 28 28 28 28 28 28 28 28 28 28 28 28 28 28 28 28 28 28 28 28 28 28 28 28 28 28 28 28 28 28 28 28 28 28 28 28 28 28 28 28 28 28 28 28 28 28 28 28 28 28 28 28 28 28 28 28 28 28 28 28 28 28 28 28 28 28 28 28
2 A. Prost	2 2 2 2 2 2 2 2 2 2 2 2 2 2 2 2 2 2 2 2 2 2 2 2 2 2 2 6 2 2 2 2 2 2 2 2 2 2 2 2 2 2 2 2 2 2 2 2 2 2 2 2 2 2 2 2 2 2 2 2 2 2 2 2 2 2 2 2 2 2 2 2 2
23 P. Martini	6 6 6 6 6 6 6 6 6 6 6 6 6 6 6 6 6 6 6 6 6 6 20 20 4 4 4 4 4 4 4 20 20 20 20 20 20 20 20 20 20 20 20 20 20 20 20 20 20 20 20 20 20 20 20 20 20 20 20 20 20 6 6 6 4 4 4 4 4 4 4 4 4
30 P. Alliot	23 23 23 23 23 23 23 23 23 23 23 23 23 23 23 23 23 23 20 20 20 20 4 4 20 20 20 20 20 20 6 6 6 6 6 6 6 6 6 6 6 6 6 6 6 6 6 6 6 6 6 6 6 6 4 4 4 6 6 6 6 6 6 6 6 6 6
6 R. Patrese	30 30 30 30 30 30 30 30 30 30 30 20 20 20 20 20 20 23 23 23 4 4 6 6 6 6 6 6 6 6 4 4 4 4 4 4 4 4 4 4 4 4 4 4 4 4 4 4 4 4 4 30 30 30 30 30 30 30 30 30 30 30 30
11 N. Piquet	7 7 7 7 7 7 7 7 20 20 20 20 20 30 30 30 30 30 30 30 30 4 30 30 30 3 3 3 3 7 7 7 7 7 7 7 7 7 7 7 7 7 7 7 7 7 7 30 30 30 30 30 22 22 22 22 22 22 22 22 22 22 22
7 M. Brundle	20 20 20 20 20 20 20 20 7 7 7 7 7 7 7 7 7 7 4 30 3 3 3 3 7 7 7 7 3 3 30 30 30 30 30 30 30 30 30 30 30 30 30 30 22 22 22 22 22 22 22 22 3 3 3 3 3 3 3 1 1 1 1 1 1 1 1 1
4 J. Alesi	4 4 4 4 4 4 4 4 4 4 4 4 4 4 4 4 4 4 4 7 3 22 22 7 7 22 22 15 30 30 30 3 3 3 15 15 15 15 15 15 15 15 15 15 15 22 22 22 22 3 3 3 3 3 3 3 1 1 1 1 1 1 1 1 1 1 1 9 9 9 9
20 J. Herbert	1 1 1 1 1 1 1 1 1 1 1 1 19 19 19 19 19 1 1 1 1 1 1 3 3 3 3 3 3 3 7 9 7 22 22 9 9 30 15 15 15 15 15 24 24 24 24 24 24 24 24 24 3 3 3 1 1 1 1 1 1 1 1 1 1 1 9 9 9 9 9 9 9 3 3 3 3
17 N. Larini	8 8 8 19 19 19 1 1 1 1 1 1 1 1 3 3 3 22 22 22 22 22 22 22 7 9 9 9 10 10 10 11 11 11 11 11 11 24 3 3 3 1 1 1 1 1 1 1 1 22 22 21 1 1 1 21 21 21 21 9 9 9 10 10
8 S. Modena	19 19 19 8 8 8 8 8 8 8 8 22 22 22 22 9 9 9 9 9 9 9 24 24 10 23 15 15 11 24 24 24 24 11 11 11 11 11 9 9 9 9 9 9 3 1 11 11 21 21 9 9 9 10 10 10 10
3 J. Palmer	3 3 3 3 3 3 3 3 3 3 9 9 9 37 37 37 37 24 24 24 10 10 23 10 30 30 24 22 22 22 22 22 22 22 22 9 22 22 22 22 22 22 11 9 9 9 10 10 10 10
19 A. Nannini	17 17 17 17 17 17 22 22 22 22 22 37 37 37 24 24 24 24 10 10 10 23 23 15 15 5 11 22 26 9 9 9 9 9 9 22 3 3 3 3 3 3 32 1 10 10 10 10
22 A. de Cesaris	22 22 22 22 22 22 9 9 9 9 24 24 24 24 5 5 5 5 10 5 5 5 5 5 5 11 24 9 9 5 5 5 5 5 5 5 5 5 21 21 21 21 21 21 9
9 D. Warwick	9 9 9 9 9 37 37 37 37 5 5 5 10 10 10 10 5 15 15 15 15 15 11 11 24 26 26 5 26 26 26 21 21 21 21 21 10 10 10 10 10 10 10 10
37 J. J. Lehto	37 37 37 37 37 37 24 24 24 24 10 10 10 10 11 15 15 15 15 11 11 11 11 11 26 24 26 5 5 21 21 21 10 10 10 10 10 10
12 S. Nakajima	24 24 24 24 24 24 5 5 5 5 19 21 19 21 15 11 11 11 11 11 26 26 26 26 26 24 26 21 21 21 10 10 10 10
16 I. Capelli	5 5 5 5 5 5 10 10 10 10 10 21 19 21 15 21 21 21 26 26 21 21 21 21 21 21
24 L. Sala	10 10 10 10 10 10 10 21 21 21 21 21 15 15 15 26 26 26 26 21 21 16 16 16
5 T. Boutsen	21 21 21 21 21 21 15 15 15 15 15 26 26 26 18 18 18 18 16 16 16
10 E. Cheever	15 15 15 15 15 15 18 18 18 26 26 18 18 18 18 16 16 16
21 A. Caffi	18 26 26 26 26 26 26 26 26 18 18 6 1 16 16 16
26 O. Grouillard	26 18 18 18 18 18 18 16 16 16 16 16
18 P. Ghinzani	16 16 16 16 16 16 16
15 M. Gugelmin	

Pos.	Car No./Driver/Team		Time
1	1	A. Senna/McLaren	1:25.799
2	6	R. Patrese/Williams	1:26.211
3	28	G. Berger	1:26.213
4	30	P. Alliot/Larrousse	1:26.272
5	11	N. Piquet/Lotus	1:26.476
6	10	E. Cheever/Arrows	1:26.650
7	2	A. Prost/McLaren	1:26.758
8	4	J. Alesi/Tyrrell	1:26.807
9	9	D. Warwick/Arrows	1:27.186
10	20	E. Pirro/Benetton	1:27.272
11	19	A. Nannini/Benetton	1:27.301
12	3	J. Palmer/Tyrrell	1:27.540
13	7	M. Brundle/Brabham	1:27.870
14	22	A. de Cesaris/BMS Dallara	1:28.016
15	15	M. Gugelmin/Leyton House	1:28.285
16	24	L. Sala/Minardi	1:28.322
17	16	I. Capelli/Leyton House	1:28.582
18	23	P. Martini/Minardi	1:29.000
19	21	A. Caffi/BMS Dallara	1:29.338
20	5	T. Boutsen/Williams	1:29.457
21	26	O. Grouillard	1:29.611
22	8	S. Modena/Brabham	1:30.142
23	37	J. J. Lehto/Onyx	1:30.206
24	17	N. Larini/Osella	1:30.578
25	18	P. Ghinzani/Osella	1:31.570

	Drivers			Drivers/Constructors	
1	A. Prost	76 pts	24	G. Tarquini	1 pts
2	A. Senna	60 pts		P. Alliot	1 pt
3	N. Mansell	38 pts		O. Grouillard	1 pt
4	R. Patrese	30 pts		L. Sala	1 pt
5	T. Boutsen	24 pts			
6	B. Berger	21 pts	1	McLaren	141 pts
7	A. Nannini	27 pts	2	Ferrari	59 pts
8	N. Piquet	9 pts	3	Williams	54 pts
9	J. Alesi	8 pts	4	Benetton	22 pts
10	S. Johansson	6 pts	5	Tyrrell	16 pts
	M. Alboreto	6 pts	6	Arrows	12 pts
	E. Cheever	6 pts	7	Lotus	9 pts
13	D. Warwick	6 pts	8	Dallara	8 pts
14	J. Herbert	5 pts	9	Onyx	6 pts
15	A. de Cesaris	4 pts		Brabham	6 pts
	M. Gugelmin	4 pts	11	Minardi	5 pts
	S. Modena	4 pts	12	Leyton House	4 pts
18	A. Caffi	4 pts	13	Rial	3 pts
19	P. Martini	4 pts		Ligier	3 pts
20	C. Danner	3 pts	15	AGS	1 pt
21	R. Arnoux	6 pts		Larrousse	1 pt
	J. Palmer	2 pts			

Existing qualifying lap record: Ayrton Senna, Lotus-Renault 98T, 1m 21.605s, 186.077 kph/115.623 mph in 1986

Existing race lap record: Gerhard Berger, Ferrari F1/87, 1m 26.986s, 174.566 kph/108.470 mph in 1987

Existing distance record: Alain Prost, McLaren-Honda MP4/4, 72 laps in 1hr 48m 43.851s at 167.586 kph/104.133 mph in 1988

Year	Driver	Nat.	Car	Circuit
1975	Jochen Mass	D	3.0 McLaren M23 Ford	Montjuich
1976	James Hunt	GB	3.0 McLaren M23 Ford	Járama
1977	Mario Andretti	USA	3.0 JPS/Lotus 78 Ford	Járama
1978	Mario Andretti	USA	3.0 JPS/Lotus 79 Ford	Járama
1979	Patrick Depailler	F	3.0 Ligier JS11 Ford	Járama
1980	Alan Jones	AUS	3.0 Williams FW07B Ford	Járama
1981	Gilles Villeneuve	CDN	1.5 Ferrari 126CK t/c	Járama
1986	Ayrton Senna	BR	1.5 Lotus 96T Renault t/c	Jerez
1987	Nigel Mansell	GB	1.5 Williams FW11B Honda t/c	Jerez
1988	Alain Prost	F	1.5 McLaren MP4/4 Honda t/c	Jerez

Schneider's Zakspeed in the race

at last!

Suzuka

FUJI TELEVISION JAPANESE GRAND PRIX · 22 OCTOBER

It would be a saga that would drag on long after the race itself, but the immediate feeling was that this was a messy way to end a championship.

It had been a fabulous race, with the sport's top two protagonists — forgetting their personal feelings towards one another — battling it out lap after lap, whittling away the race record, and watching one another's every move.

But Prost was totally prepared for what came his way on lap 47 of this most professionally organised race. There were many reasons why he knew, he would explain, and you had to agree with some of them. Ayrton Senna is a fairly uncompromising racing driver, but then you don't get much beyond Formula Ford if you don't push sometimes.

No one could have predicted how much hot air the Japanese controversy would cause.

On that vital lap, Senna, who admitted he wasn't as quick as Prost on the straight, ducked out of the slipstream and came down the inside of Prost into the very slow and unpopularly tight chicane. Prost, however, turned in on him, and, judging by the groans at the subsequent McLaren showing of a video taken from overhead, turned in unnecessarily early. He would deny this, but the general opinion was that he'd turned in sooner than he should have.

Of course, most of those condemning him had never driven a race car, just as those who subsequently disqualified Senna had not done so either. Senna's car was pushed away down an escape road, one that is not governed by supplementary regulations requiring those leaving the track to rejoin at the same point. Such regulations cover escape roads at a number of other circuits.

Senna was now being pushed by the marshals who eventually push-started him, so that he was able to take the chequered flag and win. Within a few minutes, the rostrum ceremony, usually vital, was held up, and Senna was subsequently disqualified. Nannini, naturally delighted, was acclaimed as the winner, although he preferred to win by the usual method.

Prost was hailed World Champion, but Dennis, adhering to his view of part of his job being one of 'keeping happy the driver who is not winning rather than the one who is', now lodged his appeal against Senna's disqualification.

Four days later, he and Senna were in Paris for the hearing where they felt that they were dealt a bad deal, and said so. The appeal went against them, and arriving in Adelaide, they said that they would 'fight for the fundamental values of fairplay and honesty' to have procedures changed which they considered 'grossly unfair'.

To Dennis's credit, he was not seeking to change the identity of the World Champion, or the World Championship itself. This was now decided in Prost's favour, yet there was that feeling that it didn't bring him quite the same satisfaction as it might have done had the series been decided by the chequered flag in Japan or Adelaide.

Arriving in Australia, the reigning World Champion and his successor both agreed on one thing, to go racing and put the immediate past behind them. But the taste was still somewhat sour, with the feeling that somehow we'd been denied the final shoot-out.

BRIGHT SPARKS

The battle of the giants dominated the Japanese Grand Prix, of course, but there were other performances worthy of note. From the start of the weekend, Nicolo Larini was looking good with quickest time in pre-qualifying for the second race running, followed by tenth on the grid for the race, surely the best-ever Grand Prix grid position for an Osella. The race, however, doesn't always go so well for Larini, and after a moment on the first lap, he retired with brake

problems.

It was good to see Bernd Schneider make it into the race after one of those years that are best forgotten. Unlike Brazil where he made it through pre-qualifying based on fifth and an ill-judged technicality, he was third in Japan and proceeded to qualify 21st. Again, it was a race that ended prematurely with gearbox-related retirement.

The same could certainly be said of Paolo Barilla's race. The Italian had taken over the Minardi from his good friend Pierluigi Martini who was still suffering rib injuries from an off-track excursion in Estoril. Barilla is a talented driver, but not one of the greatest single-seater drivers. He has tested a variety of Formula One cars, and has always maintained contact with Minardi as reserve driver. Given a Formula One chance, he acquitted himself extremely well, qualifying ahead of Gugelmin, both Arrows and Palmer, but again it was a race that ended earlier than it might have done with transmission failure.

Benetton bounced back here too. With a development Ford engine that gave improvements all through the power band, Nannini put himself well in amongst the 'multi-cylinders' on Friday, but a potential weakness saw him shift back to the standard engine on Saturday, qualifying sixth.

But Pirro used a development engine for the race, and flew through

Above: Ford's development engine and McLaren team tactics served to give Nannini his first GP win.
Below: Larrousse leads Coloni in pre-qualifying; only the Larrousse will go through.

the field. From a lowly 22nd on the grid (caused by a misfire), he had picked up eight places in five laps, but then came up on an equally determined driver, Jean Alesi, who was also making good progress.

The two tangled at the hairpin, more to Alesi's disadvantage as he lost two places, while Pirro soon overtook Nakajima and spent a long time tailing Piquet. After the pit stops he found himself ninth behind the Williamses only to 'have a misunderstanding with de Cesaris' as he generously put it, and that was that.

Alesi had been picking off one car after another but then lost fifth gear which eventually caused his retirement, progress ceasing soon after the Pirro incident. After a poor practice due to handling problems on qualifiers, Warwick raced hard to overtake the Osellas, Larini, Cheever, Nakajima and Gugelmin at the end, which gave him a well-deserved sixth place until Senna's disqualification.

It wasn't hard to find deserving drivers in the latter half of the grid – but behind the stars, there wasn't a lot of action.

RACE DEBRIEF

The Japanese Grand Prix was a two-horse race as far as many people were concerned, and for much of the time, there wasn't a lot of real place changing and wheel-to-wheel battling amongst the top six.

That, some may say, is nothing new, but there was much more going on than just the World Championship contest. In pre-qualifying, for instance, Larini, the Lolas and Schneider made it where Onyx, Ghinzani and Moreno didn't. The second Coloni didn't even complete a lap before part of its front suspension broke.

Senna was the star of qualifying itself. Berger laughed openly in disbelief when the 1m 38.041s came up on the TV screen; no one else got within 1.7s of the time and it was a full two seconds quicker than Berger's previous qualifying lap record! Senna even went on to say that his 41st pole position wasn't as smooth as it might have been, and he'd fumbled a couple of gearchanges.

He'd started on one set of race tyres, set the really quick time on qualifiers (although his race tyre lap was also quick enough for pole) and then gone back on to the race tyres to continue sorting the car. 'There are two priorities here, a well-balanced car and the start,' said the Brazilian, who had to win here to stay in contention.

On Friday, he and Prost tried different specification engines in the two cars that were available to each of them. Prost had specificaton four engines (with greater top-end power) and didn't think they were so good, but it was that specification which they both chose ultimately for the race.

After suffering traffic on his first set of tyres on Saturday afternoon, Prost was ultra-careful on the second set, extremely mindful that he must start from the front row of the grid, but he need not have worried unduly: Berger was unable to get his front right tyre to last a qualifying lap, and Prost was 0.4s quicker than the Austrian.

McLarens on row one, then, Ferraris on row two. Berger's front right tyre usually had a dark ring of blisters around it before the lap of the challenging Suzuka was out, and Mansell usually had a slightly less obtrusive ring. But the English driver might well have been less supportive of his new home than he usually is after qualifying. He was late out because of a differential change, had to abort the first lap because a piece of bodywork was loose, and then set a time 0.3s slower than the troubled Berger. We were all looking forward to see what he could do on the second set, but he cruised past the start/finish line – out of petrol! Ferraris on the second row then,

The Williams drivers both found their FW13s difficult to drive, Patrese pointing out that they are very sensitive in the fast corners. Boutsen was sure that he would get closer to Patrese on his second lap, but the tyres blistered within two corners, which suggested a rogue set.

So they were split by Nannini's Benetton which was powered by Ford's new V8 development engine in first qualifying: fifth quickest, 0.4s behind the slower of the Ferraris. Like teammate Pirro, Nannini was slowed by a misfire on Saturday but had a clear lap to set his time.

Alliot was once again on form with eighth quickest and close behind Boutsen and Nannini, as were Modena and Larini in the first of the

Pirelli-shod runners. Piquet had Nakajima beside him on row six, the Japanese driver in determined mood here, while Brundle was accompanied by Sala taking over the role of team leader following Martini's withdrawal. Names unexpectedly far back are best explained by their set-up not allowing Goodyears qualifier to last a full lap . . .

This was a phenomenal Grand Prix in many ways. With Japanese sponsorship more and more apparent, and two more companies (ESPO and Footwork) taking a financial interest in teams (Lola and Arrows), Formula One racing is clearly another area in which the Japanese are happy to sink their money.

The Japanese people showed their interest in Grand Prix racing with their feet. By seven on Saturday evening there was a kilometre-long queue of people, five deep, sitting it out waiting to get into the circuit. With 130,000 in the circuit on raceday, it was one of the biggest Grands Prix of the year.

The race itself, it must be said, was a little boring if pregnant with possibility. Prost made a great start to head Senna into the first corner, followed by Berger, Nannini, Patrese (soon overtaken by Mansell) and then Boutsen and Modena.

Once Mansell had overtaken Patrese on lap three, and Alliot had got by Modena on lap seven, these leading positions altered little apart from during the pit stops. Prost was never more than 4.9s ahead of Senna, who slowly but surely pulled away from Berger in third place. He in turn was four to five seconds ahead of Nannini in fourth place, who had Mansell looking threatening in fifth. The Williams pair tussled over

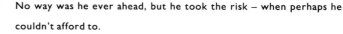

sixth place, Patrese constantly ahead of Boutsen.

Mansell was the first to stop for tyres on lap 18, followed by Nannini two laps later; Prost on lap 21, Boutsen on lap 22, Senna and Berger on lap 23, and Patrese on lap 24. Sole interloper was Piquet who was yet to stop, but generally the pit stops went well, Senna being the biggest loser with a 9.8s stop after a problem with one front wheel.

Battle rejoined after the stops, with Senna taking up position just a couple of seconds behind Prost, the pair forming an immensely talented and competitive high-speed duo, whittling down the fastest lap some 30 times between them.

As their battle came to its almost inevitable head, so the Ferraris ran into trouble. Berger pitted from third with a failed gearbox on lap 34, Mansell's challenge to Nannini faded with gearbox trouble, and then the engine began to smoke on lap 36, finally succumbing eight laps later.

By this time, however, Senna had closed up once on Prost so that the difference between them was negligible. Prost, not feeling threatened, but in charge of the race, pulled away again after three laps, but his one second lead dipped back to half that by lap 46.

'The chicane was the one place that I could overtake,' said Senna later. 'I overtook a lot of people there last year. I was quicker in most places, but he was quicker on the straight.' On lap 47, Senna ducked out of Prost's slipstream and came down the inside of Prost into the chicane.

No way was he ever ahead, but he took the risk – when perhaps he couldn't afford to.

Prost turned in – and the two McLarens interlocked wheels and slid off to the outside of the circuit. Prost was ahead but he proceeded to get out of his car. Senna stayed in his, however, getting marshals to push his stalled car backwards and then, once free of Prost's car, steering down the escape road towards a safe place to park. He was unbuckling his belts but the marshals continued to push, so he selected a gear, the engine fired up, and with a damaged nosecone he was back out on the track and away again.

By the time he'd done one lap and made a 21s stop for a new nosecone, the lead had gone to Nannini, who crossed the line 4.7s ahead on lap 49 with three to go. Next time round, there was no gap and at the end of lap 51, Senna dived down the inside of Nannini, as he had done with Prost, surprised Nannini, who locked up a brake, and took the lead and the chequered flag.

Then came disqualification, disappointment, confusion and appeal.

For others, such as Nannini, Patrese, an ill-handling Boutsen, a surprised and almost engineless Piquet, Brundle in the spare and Warwick from the back row of the grid, this was a more action-packed race, for the right reasons. Sadly they were little more than supporting cast for all eyes were on those up front.

Clockwise from left: development ensures results as Patrese takes the FW13 to a rostrum finish. Paolo Barilla deputises for his good friend, the injured Martini. 'You've won!' – Patrese to Nannini.

MILESTONES

- Senna's disqualification seals World Championship for Prost
- Barilla replaces injured Martini in the Minardi
- Arrows and Larrousse announce Japanese tie-ups
- Ford debuts development V8
- Gachot joins Rial in place of Foitek

FUJI TELEVISION JAPANESE GRAND PRIX

ENTRIES · PRACTICE · RESULTS

Pos	Driver/Nationality		No.	Car/Engine	P.Q. (sunny, bright)	Practice 1 (warm, sunny)	Practice 2 (overcast)	Warm-up (pos) (overcast)	Laps (overcast)	Time/Retirement
1	A. Nannini	I	19	Benetton B189 Ford HB V8	–	1:41.601	1:41.103	1:46.390 (10)	53	1hr35m06.277
2	R. Patrese	I	6	Williams FW13 Renault V10	–	1:42.397	1:40.936	1:45.646 (6)	53	1hr35m18.181
3	T. Boutsen	B	5	Williams FW13 Renault V10	–	1:42.943	1:41.324	1:46.583 (11)	53	1hr35m19.723
4	N. Piquet	BR	11	Lotus 101 Judd V8	–	1:43.386	1:41.802	1:46.998 (14)	53	1hr36m50.502
5	M. Brundle	GB	7	Brabham BT58 Judd V8	–	1:44.236	1:42.182	1:47.620 (16)	52	1hr35m09.012
6	D. Warwick	GB	9	Arrows A11 Ford DFR V8	–	1:44.288	1:43.599	1:44.897 (4)	52	1hr35m19.112
7	M. Gugelmin	BR	15	Leyton House CG891 Judd V8	–	1:44.805	1:42.880	1:46.838 (13)	52	1hr35m37.237
8	E. Cheever	USA	10	Arrows A11 Ford DFR V8	–	1:44.501	1:43.511	1:48.054 (18)	52	1hr36m12.091
9	A. Caffi	I	21	Dallara BMS 189 Ford DFR V8	–	1:43.171	1:42.488	1:48.571 (23)	52	1hr36m56.031
10	A. de Cesaris	I	22	Dallara BMS 189 Ford DFR V8	–	1:43.904	1:42.581	1:47.849 (17)	51	1hr35m08.582
11	A. Prost	F	2	McLaren MP4/5 Honda V10	–	1:40.875	1:39.771	1:44.079 (1)	46	collision/Senna
12	S. Modena	I	8	Brabham BT58 Judd V8	–	1:42.909	1:41.458	1:48.108 (19)	46	alternator
13	N. Mansell	GB	27	Ferrari 640 Ferrari V12	–	1:40.608	1:40.406	1:44.469 (2)	43	engine
14	S. Nakajima	J	12	Lotus 101 Judd V8	–	1:43.370	1:41.988	1:45.787 (7)	41	overheating
15	J. Alesi	F	4	Tyrrell 108 Ford DFR V8	–	1:43.306	1:42.709	1:46.087 (9)	37	gearbox
16	P. Alliot	F	30	Lola LC89 Lamborghini V12	1:43.089	1:42.534	1:41.336	1:48.323 (22)	36	engine
17	G. Berger	A	28	Ferrari 640 Ferrari V12	–	1:41.253	1:40.187	1:45.611 (5)	34	gearbox
18	E. Pirro	I	20	Benetton B189 Ford HB V8	–	1:43.217	1:43.063	1:46.029 (8)	33	collision/de Cesaris
19	O. Grouillard	F	26	Ligier JS33 Ford DFR V8	–	1:45.801	1:43.379	1:46.702 (12)	31	engine
20	I. Capelli	I	16	Leyton House CG891 Judd V8	–	1:43.851	1:42.672	1:48.161 (20)	27	front upright
21	N. Larini	I	17	Osella FA1M Ford DFR V8	1:43.035	1:42.483	1:41.519	1:48.300 (21)	21	brakes
22	J. Palmer	GB	3	Tyrrell 018 Ford DFR V8	–	1:43.955	1:43.757	1:47.162 (15)	20	fuel tank
23	B. Schneider	F	34	Zakspeed ZK189 Yamaha V8	1:44.053	1:44.323	1:42.892	1:51.599 (26)	1	gearbox
24	P. Barilla	I	23	Minardi M189 Ford DFR V8	–	1:46.096	1:42.780	1:49.279 (25)	–	clutch
25	L. Sala	E	24	Minardi M189 Ford DFR V8	–	1:43.107	1:42.283	1:49.190 (24)	–	collision/Nakajima
26	A. Senna	BR	1	McLaren MP4/5 Honda V10	–	1:39.493	1:38.041	1:44.801 (3)	–	excluded from results
27	R. Arnoux	F	25	Ligier JS33 Ford DFR V8	–	1:44.221	1:44.030	DNQ		
28	M. Alboreto	I	29	Lola LC89 Lamborghini V12	1:44.075	1:44.063	1:44.101	DNQ		
29	P. Raphanel	F	38	Rial ARC02 Ford DFR V8	–	2:11.328	1:47.160	DNQ		
30	B. Gachot	B	39	Rial ARC02 Ford DFR V8	–	1:50.883	1:47.295	DNQ		
–	P. Ghinzani	I	18	Osella FA1M Ford DFR V8	1:44.313	DNPQ	DNPQ			
–	R. Moreno	BR	31	Coloni C3 Ford DFR V8	1:44.498	DNPQ	DNPQ			
–	S. Johansson	S	36	Onyx ORE1 Ford DFR V8	1:44.582	DNPQ	DNPQ			
–	A. Suzuki	J	35	Zakspeed ZK189 Yamaha V8	1:44.780	DNPQ	DNPQ			
–	O. Larrauri	ARG	33	EuroBrun ER189 Judd V8	1:45.446	DNPQ	DNPQ			
–	J. J. Lehto	F	37	Onyx ORE1 Ford DFR V8	1:45.787	DNPQ	DNPQ			
–	G. Tarquini	I	40	AGS JH24 Ford DFR V8	1:46.705	DNPQ	DNPQ			
–	Y. Dalmas	F	41	AGS JH24 Ford DFR V8	1:48.306	DNPQ	DNPQ			
–	E. Bertaggia	I	32	Coloni C3 Ford DFR V8	no time	DNPQ	DNPQ			

Circuit Data: International Racing Course, Suzuka, length 3.641 miles/5.859 km, race distance 53 laps = 192.9 miles/310.5 km, race weather grey and overcast.
Notes: Bertaggia didn't do a lap in pre-qualifying, suspension broke. Gachot now in Rial No. 39. Paolo Barilla (I) replaces Pierluigi Martini in Minardi No. 23. Both Boutsen and Patrese driving Williams FW13.

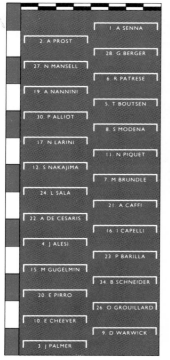

	1. A SENNA
2. A PROST	
	28. G BERGER
27. N MANSELL	
	6. R PATRESE
19. A NANNINI	
	5. T BOUTSEN
30. P ALLIOT	
	8. S MODENA
17. N LARINI	
	11. N PIQUET
12. S NAKAJIMA	
	7. M BRUNDLE
24. L SALA	
	21. A CAFFI
22. A DE CESARIS	
	16. I CAPELLI
4. J ALESI	
	23. P BARILLA
15. M GUGELMIN	
	34. B SCHNEIDER
20. E PIRRO	
	26. O GROUILLARD
10. E CHEEVER	
	9. D WARWICK
3. J PALMER	

LAP CHART

Grid Order		1	2	3	4	5	6	7	8	9	10	11	12	13	14	15	16	17	18	19	20	21	22	23	24	25	26	27	28	29	30	31	32	33	34	35	36	37	38	39	40	41	42	43	44	45	46	47	48	49	50	51	52	53
1	A. Senna	2	2	2	2	2	2	2	2	2	2	2	2	2	2	2	2	2	2	2	2	2	1	1	1	2	2	2	2	2	2	2	2	2	2	2	2	2	2	2	2	2	2	2	2	2	2	1	1	19	19	1	1	1
2	A. Prost	1	1	1	1	1	1	1	1	1	1	1	1	1	1	1	1	1	1	1	1	1	2	2	2	1	1	1	1	1	1	1	1	1	1	1	1	1	1	1	1	1	1	1	1	1	1	1	1	1	1	19	19	19
28	G. Berger	28	28	28	28	28	28	28	28	28	28	28	28	28	28	28	28	28	28	28	28	28	28	28	28	28	28	28	28	19	19	19	19	19	19	19	19	19	19	19	19	19	19	19	19	6	6	6	6	6	6	6		
27	N. Mansell	19	19	19	19	19	19	19	19	19	19	19	19	19	19	19	19	19	19	19	6	6	6	19	19	19	19	19	19	19	19	19	28	27	27	27	27	27	27	27	27	6	6	6	5	5	5	5	5	5	5			
6	R. Patrese	6	6	27	27	27	27	27	27	27	27	27	27	27	27	27	27	6	6	5	19	19	27	27	27	27	27	27	27	27	6	6	6	6	6	6	6	6	6	5	5	5	11	11	11	11	11	11	11	11				
19	A. Nannini	27	27	6	6	6	6	6	6	6	6	6	6	6	6	6	6	5	5	19	5	27	6	11	11	11	11	6	6	6	6	6	6	5	5	5	5	5	5	11	11	11	7	7	7	7	7	7						
5	T. Boutsen	5	5	5	5	5	5	5	5	5	5	5	5	5	5	5	5	27	27	27	27	11	11	6	6	6	6	11	11	5	5	5	30	30	11	11	11	11	11	8	8	8	9	9	9	9	9	9						
30	P. Alliot	8	8	8	8	8	8	30	30	30	30	30	30	30	30	30	30	30	30	30	20	5	5	5	5	5	5	20	20	20	30	11	11	8	8	8	8	8	8	15	7	7	15	15	15	15	15	15						
8	S. Modena	30	30	30	30	30	30	8	8	11	11	11	11	11	11	11	11	11	11	11	11	5	20	20	20	20	20	11	30	30	11	8	8	15	15	15	15	15	15	7	15	10	10	10	10	10	10	10						
17	N. Larini	7	7	7	7	11	11	11	8	8	20	20	20	20	20	20	20	20	20	30	30	30	30	30	30	30	11	11	8	15	15	12	7	7	7	7	7	7	9	9	9	21	21	21	21	21	21							
11	N. Piquet	17	11	11	11	11	7	4	4	12	12	8	8	8	8	8	8	8	8	8	8	8	4	4	4	4	4	4	4	8	15	12	12	7	12	12	12	12	9	9	10	10	10	22	22	22	22							
12	N. Nakajima	11	12	12	12	4	20	20	20	20	12	12	12	4	4	4	4	4	4	4	16	16	16	16	16	8	8	8	8	15	12	4	4	9	9	9	9	9	10	10	21	21	21											
7	M. Brundle	12	21	4	4	12	7	12	4	4	4	4	12	12	12	16	16	16	16	8	8	8	8	7	7	15	15	15	12	4	7	7	4	10	10	10	10	21	22	22	22													
24	L. Sala	21	17	21	21	20	20	12	7	7	7	16	16	16	16	16	12	12	7	7	7	7	7	7	15	12	12	12	4	7	9	10	21	21	21	21	22	22																
21	A. Caffi	22	4	17	20	21	21	21	16	7	7	7	7	7	7	7	15	15	15	15	15	15	15	9	12	7	7	7	7	9	10	10	21	22	22	22																		
22	A. de Cesaris	4	22	22	17	17	22	16	16	16	16	21	21	15	15	15	15	15	9	9	9	9	9	12	9	9	9	9	9	10	21	21	22																					
16	I. Capelli	16	16	20	22	16	22	22	22	22	15	15	15	21	21	21	21	9	21	21	21	22	12	21	21	26	26	21	10	21	22																								
4	J. Alesi	15	20	16	16	16	15	15	15	15	22	22	22	22	22	22	22	21	22	22	22	12	21	26	26	21	10	21	22																										
23	P. Barilla	20	15	15	15	15	26	26	26	26	9	9	9	9	9	9	9	22	12	12	12	21	10	10	10	10	22	22																											
15	M. Gugelmin	26	26	26	26	26	9	9	9	9	26	26	26	26	26	26	26	12	10	10	10	10	26	10	22	22	22	22																											
34	B. Schneider	10	10	10	9	9	17	17	17	17	10	10	10	10	10	10	10	26	26	26	26	10	22	22																														
20	E. Pirro	9	9	9	10	10	10	10	10	10	17	3	3	3	3	3	3	3	3	3	3	3	17																															
26	O. Grouillard	3	3	3	3	3	3	3	3	3	3	17	17	17	17	17	17	17	17	17																																		
10	E. Cheever	34																																																				
9	D. Warwick																																																				
3	J. Palmer																																																				

FASTEST LAPS			
Pos.	**Car No./Driver/Team**		**Time**
1	2	A. Prost/McLaren	1:43.506
2	28	G. Berger/Ferrari	1:44.189
3	19	A. Nannini/Benetton	1:44.919
4	20	E. Pirro/Benetton	1:45.069
5	27	N. Mansell/Ferrari	1:45.077
6	5	T. Boutsen/Williams	1:45.115
7	6	R. Patrese/Williams	1:45.335
8	30	P. Alliot/Larrousse	1:45.353
9	7	M. Brundle/Brabham	1:46.194
10	22	A. de Cesaris/BMS Dallara	1:46.225
11	11	N. Piquet/Lotus	1:46.420
12	4	J. Alesi/Tyrrell	1:46.674
13	9	D. Warwick/Arrows	1:47.069
14	12	S. Nakajima/Lotus	1:47.338
15	16	I. Capelli/Leyton House	1:47.465
16	10	E. Cheever/Arrows	1:47.920
17	15	M. Gugelmin/Leyton House	1:47.976
18	26	O. Grouillard/Ligier	1:48.145
19	8	S. Modena/Brabham	1:48.609
20	21	A. Caffi/BMS Dallara	1:49.322
21	17	N. Larini/Osella	1:49.479
22	3	J. Palmer/Tyrrell	1:49.910
23	34	B. Schneider/Zakspeed	2:11.970

CHAMPIONSHIP POINTS

Drivers			Drivers/Constructors		
1	A. Prost	76 pts		J. Palmer	2 pts
2	A. Senna	60 pts	24	G. Tarquini	1 pt
3	N. Mansell	38 pts		P. Alliot	1 pt
4	R. Patrese	36 pts		O. Grouillard	1 pt
5	T. Boutsen	28 pts		L. Sala	1 pt
6	A. Nannini	26 pts			
7	G. Berger	21 pts	1	McLaren	141 pts
8	N. Piquet	12 pts	2	Williams	64 pts
9	J. Alesi	8 pts	3	Ferrari	59 pts
10	D. Warwick	7 pts	4	Benetton	31 pts
11	S. Johansson	6 pts	5	Tyrrell	16 pts
	M. Alboreto	6 pts	6	Arrows	13 pts
	E. Cheever	6 pts	7	Lotus	12 pts
14	J. Herbert	5 pts	8	Dallara	8 pts
15	A. de Cesaris	4 pts		Brabham	8 pts
	M. Gugelmin	4 pts	10	Onyx	6 pts
	S. Modena	4 pts	11	Minardi	5 pts
	A. Caffi	4 pts	12	Leyton House	4 pts
	P. Martini	4 pts	13	Rial	3 pts
	M. Brundle	4 pts		Ligier	3 pts
21	C. Danner	3 pts	15	AGS	1 pt
22	R. Arnoux	2 pts		Larrousse	1 pt

Left: Ferrari count the cost of two DNFs.

Existing qualifying lap record: *Gerhard Berger, Ferrari F1/87, 1m 40.042s, 210.835 kph/131.007 mph in 1987*

Existing race lap record: *Alain Prost, McLaren MP4/3, 1m 43.844s, 203.116 kph/126.210 mph in 1987*

Existing distance record: *Gerhard Berger, Ferrari F1/87, 51 laps in 1hr 32m 58.072s at 192.847 kph/119.830 mph in 1987*

PAST WINNERS

Year	Driver	Nat.	Car	Circuit
1976	Mario Andretti	USA	3.0 Lotus 77 Ford	Fuji
1977	James Hunt	GB	3.0 McLaren M23 Ford	Fuji
1987	Gerhard Berger	A	1.5 Ferrari F1/87 t/c	Suzuka
1988	Ayrton Senna	BR	1.5 McLaren MP4/4 Honda t/c	Suzuka

F is for Ferrari

Adelaide

FOSTER'S AUSTRALIAN GRAND PRIX · 5 NOVEMBER

'The race they couldn't stop' and 'Grand Prix turns into near farce' were just two of the local headlines which screamed out at visitors departing from the Australian Grand Prix on Monday morning as Adelaide and more particularly Grand Prix racing tried to recover from a damp raceday Down Under.

Standing water on a street circuit built for public use rather than racing had provoked drivers to plead for a delay in raceday proceedings, but although conditions did improve, the drivers wanted a further delay, while officials wanted the race to be run. There was simply no provision for common ground. The race had to go ahead, was one view; it was too dangerous to do so, came the view from the other side.

Down under it wasn't only the Koalas that needed eucalyptus.

rost, the most vociferous critic of Grand Prix racing in the wet, pulled together colleagues Mansell (who had already crashed on the straight in the second raceday warm-up), Berger, Boutsen and others to plead with clerks of the course Roland Bruynseraede and Tim Schenken for a further postponement.

But there is no provision for such matters in Grand Prix racing. Any postponement might well have led to the end of the Australian Grand Prix – at least in Adelaide. And that, as any visitor to one of Grand Prix racing's best events know, would have been a tragedy.

Certainly the drivers and officials were at loggerheads and it's all very well to say that Thierry Boutsen then went out and didn't put a foot wrong in winning the race, but 13 of his colleagues, including World Champions past and present, crashed out of the event. Luck, said Boutsen's rivals, played a considerable part in whether you stayed on the track or aquaplaned off it.

Boutsen did not suggest that this was one of the hardest races in his career. However, 'the organisers should have delayed the start longer,' he said. 'By the time of the second start the conditions were better, but they were still worse than in Canada and Belgium this year. The trouble is that on a street circuit there's no provision for any error if things go wrong. The barrier is too close.'

Prost nearly succeeded in banding his colleagues into what could only be called a near-strike. The World Champion elect stuck to his guns by doing one lap and retiring, simply unwilling to take any further risks. Teammate Senna, who had nothing to do with the pre-race politics, stayed out to take risks, led the race incredibly comfortably, and then whacked into the back of Brundle's Brabham which put them both out of the race.

But the strongest memory is that of a quasi-prepared grid being green-flagged away when there were cars, equipment, mechanics and drivers still patently out of place and not ready. Although there was no obvious danger, it did not present Grand Prix racing in its best possible light. Indeed, the loser in all this was the sport.

The Australian Grand Prix was faced with possible extinction through no fault of its own, and escaped by the skin of its teeth. But there was no get-out clause for when weather conditions dictate such measures. Some will say it's up to the drivers to race whenever they are told to do so; others will say that it's just another battle in the continuing power struggle.

BRIGHT SPARKS

You could say that Satoru Nakajima is used to the kind of spray and standing water experienced in the Australian Grand Prix. After all, Japanese race conditions are frequently much worse. But the Japanese driver was without doubt one of the stars of Adelaide.

After the disappointment of his home Grand Prix, he went to Australia hoping that he would finally score points after a lean year. Friday's qualifying saw him struggling with a broken exhaust and undertray problems and in spite of an improvement in handling, he slipped a place on the grid to 23rd, having failed to go quicker, although he had beaten teammate Piquet in the second session.

In the first start he was hit by another car and needed a new front wing. There was more trouble at the next start when he tangled with a Ligier and spun. But he overtook Gugelmin on lap two, Ghinzani on lap three and Modena plus Alliot on lap four. Piquet slipped behind on lap six, Grouillard went the same way on lap eight, Pirro on lap nine and then Brundle and Lehto on lap 11. His front wing was damaged again when he ultimately managed to get by Martini on lap 17 and he was now sixth. Mansell's retirement brought him up to fifth, he overtook Cheever on lap 24 and was now fourth, nearly 40 seconds behind Patrese with a projected 50 laps to go.

dubious honour of causing the race to be stopped when 'my car had a misfire and as I got going it cleared and with the extra power I just got sideways'.

Taking a spare car, J. J. Lehto drove impeccably to find himself fifth after 27 laps with seventh-fastest lap of the race. But then the engine suddenly cut out and his very promising race was over.

Pierluigi Martini was the star of practice and qualifying with the best-ever performance for himself and Minardi, but Pirelli's race tyres were not up to Goodyear's best and he struggled home to finish sixth, certainly deserving his single point although it might have been much more on dry tyres.

RACE DEBRIEF

That the Australian Grand Prix should be so affected by the weather was particularly sad and inappropriate. The weather during practice and qualifying had been literally brilliant, with a superb

Clockwise from left: Berger's last race for Ferrari was a troubled one. Blue skies on Saturday gave no warning for race day. Pre-qualifying — no problem for J.J.

His intentions became clear on lap 29 when he set fastest lap of the race. The gap was under 30 seconds on lap 35. Another fastest lap 12 laps later brought it down to 20 seconds and this was followed by two more fastest laps in three laps. After another fastest lap on lap 56, the gap was down to nine seconds with a projected 24 laps to go. On lap 64 he set fastest lap of the race. By lap 67 he was just 1.7s behind Patrese.

But he got no closer. 'I would have got past him,' said Nakajima, 'but as I got up behind him the spray from his car was causing mine to misfire, so I decided to ease off and make sure of fourth place. It's a nice way to end my three years with Camel Team Lotus.'

Pirro was two laps down but also a newcomer to the World Championship table after starting a more encouraging 13th on the grid. 'Just after the first start, I drove over a piece of driveshaft from another car,' explained Emanuele. 'I heard a strange noise for most of the race and it changed the aerodynamics and I had too much oversteer. But it was nice to score points.'

Out of luck was J. J. Lehto, the Finn who bumped teammate Johansson out of the pre-qualifying. After getting a little lost on Friday, he and his teammate got the set-up together on Saturday morning when the Finn was seventh fastest with a time which would eventually have put him eighth on the grid. Instead, he had to settle for 17th and then had the

light and clear blue skies over Adelaide.

Pre-qualifying was held for the first time on Thursday in spite of earlier dissension. Although there had been other practice sessions, the track was still dusty and slippery and not surprisingly there were a number of spins as there usually are in Adelaide, although none were car-damaging.

Throughout the next three days there would be difficulties with

qualifying tyres. Goodyear suggested their own method of warming up the tyres, but it was only on Saturday that they really began to work. Two sets of race tyres for pre-qualifying might have been more advisable, but none of the pre-qualifiers had much experience of Adelaide.

But both Osellas made it through, plus Alliot, while Lehto just bumped out teammate Johansson on his final lap, the Swede having been held up by Larini for three corners on his quick one. Alboreto didn't make it either, his car's transmission failing, and Moreno was very disappointed to be handicapped with no clutch and engine trouble.

The fabulous weather saw the field split roughly 50-50 between those who did improve on the Saturday and those who didn't.

On the Friday, in fact, it was very difficult to set a quick time because there were so many others pounding round and round on race tyres. Senna was second to Prost, having been held up, he said, by a Ferrari — and a McLaren.

But the next day he went out to claim his 42nd pole position with a lap that was smoother, he said, than his first effort. Behind Prost, who didn't improve, came Martini in the Minardi, admitting that there was still work to do on the race set up, while Nannini, once again using Ford's development engine for qualifying, was fourth quickest. The Williams-Renaults might have hoped for better on this circuit where traction is important, but Ferrari were having substantial problems. Berger had a

succession of failures while Mansell was in trouble with handling and using the development engine in the spare car which Berger was not allowed to drive. Mansell would at least start seventh, but Berger was only 14th.

All the pre-qualifiers made it into the race, and so too did the departing Ghinzani, Arnoux and Cheever, who crashed heavily at the end of the final qualifying session. This spoiled Palmer's qualifying lap, which saw him join Sala and the Rials as non-qualifiers.

Clockwise from above: not a fan of street circuits, 'Naka' excelled himself, clocking fastest lap. Pirro — last race for Benetton — best finish to date. Nelson to Ricardo — 'I'll race if you will!' Martini makes his car very difficult to pass.

The weather turned sour on Sunday, even more sour than forecast. The warm-up took place under cloudy skies with Senna ahead of Berger from Patrese and then three Pirelli-shod cars, suggesting race-tyre performance may be much improved. Prost, with oversteer, was seventh.

But that was academic when it began to rain and rain. When there seemed no let-up, the second warm-up/acclimatisation session was organised in the wet, and it was soon obvious that the conditions were treacherous, mainly due to standing water and consequent spray. Senna had a wild spin, Alliot damaged the front of his car, and then Nannini spun off and into the barrier on the straight, and the session was stopped. When it resumed, both Mansell and Prost spun, the former at the same spot as Nannini, and now the session was abandoned.

The paddock was full of discussion about conditions for the next couple of hours. The Ferrari drivers didn't want to race. Prost was doubtful. Boutsen went to see compatriot and clerk of the course Roland Bruynseraede. As drivers picked their way through the puddles there was no doubt that they felt the conditions were too dangerous to race in.

But race they did. Admittedly there was much discussion beforehand, a lot of lobbying and the extraordinary sight of half the grid moving off on the final parade lap while the rest were still being prepared for the off. It made for a huge traffic jam in Adelaide's Foster's hairpin for the start...

Prost made a great start, but Senna was through and into the lead by the first chicane, leading across the finishing line at the end of the first lap by 7.9s but not from Prost. The Frenchman ducked into the pits and out of the race, saying that conditions were too dangerous. And then out came the black flag, stopping the race. Lehto had hit the wall and damaged his car, and it was parked in a dangerous position.

The more orderly restart lacked Prost and finally Larini whose car

stalled twice and was pushed off. Again Senna had a huge lead at the end of lap one, some 8.7s ahead and that became 17.2s and then 21.5s on subsequent laps, rising to nearly half a minute by lap seven.

The main cause of this was that Boutsen, Patrese and Nannini were bottled up behind Martini for a couple of laps, the Minardi driver not at home on Pirelli's wets. But he was relegated to fifth by lap four and the Williamses were pulling away from Nannini, his Benetton now fitted with a standard engine.

Martini dropped back behind an advancing Mansell to battle with de Cesaris and Warwick, both of whom would spin out of the race within a few laps. But ahead, the Williamses were having their own private tussle as they gradually reduced Senna's lead. Patrese managed to get ahead of Boutsen but promptly spun back again.

Senna had been in amongst the backmarkers since lap seven and on lap 14 – after not even 30 minutes of racing – he came up on Brundle whose car suddenly aquaplaned. The Briton lifted off and Senna came hurtling up the back of him, ripping a front wheel off the McLaren and putting both cars out of the race.

Which left Boutsen leading from Patrese – but only for one lap, until the Italian had another spin and dropped to fourth place, putting Mansell third. But that only lasted another three laps before the Englishman spun and damaged his Ferrari. He clearly thought that this was a race he might have won.

The first three were established for the rest of the race, Boutsen taking his second Grand Prix victory, saying that his car was perfect and seeming not unhappy with the conditions. Nannini finished second, unable to catch the Williams-Renault, while Patrese held third, mindful that it would be good enough to take third in the championship off Mansell.

Fourth was held by Cheever who overtook Martini, but then Nakajima came charging up, and Lehto came past the Arrows too. But like teammate Warwick, Cheever spun out when his car misfired. Then Lehto's engine cut out and Nakajima nearly caught Patrese, only for his engine too to start misfiring. Pirro caught Martini and finished fifth, while Gugelmin and Modena were the only other finishers.

It certainly wasn't the perfect end to the championship, and though there *were* bright moments in this Grand Prix there are probably some people who would be hard-pushed to find them.

Above: young gun Modena must hope for better results in 1990. Left: a second win for Boutsen, now a wet weather specialist.

MILESTONES

- Senna's 42nd pole position
- Martini back in his Minardi again
- First-ever World Championship points for Pirro
- Points for Nakajima and Pirro mean record number of 29 points-scorers in 1989, beating previous record of 27 in 1960
- Last Grand Prix for Ghinzani and Arnoux

FOSTER'S AUSTRALIAN GRAND PRIX

ENTRIES · PRACTICE · RESULTS

Pos	Driver/Nationality		No.	Car/Engine	P.Q. (overcast)	Practice 1 (hot, sunny)	Practice 2 (hot, sunny)	Warm-up (pos) (wet)	Laps (wet, rain)	Time/Retirement
1	T. Boutsen	B	5	Williams FW13 Renault V10	–	1:17.791	1:18.586	1:23.162 (19)	70	2h00m17.421
2	A. Nannini	I	19	Benetton B189 Ford HB V8	–	1:18.271	1:17.762	1:22.599 (9)	70	2h00m46.079
3	R. Patrese	I	6	Williams FW13 Renault V10	–	1:18.636	1:17.827	1:21.689 (3)	70	2h00m55.104
4	S. Nakajima	J	12	Lotus 101 Judd V8	–	1:20.066	1:20.333	1:23.326 (20)	70	2h00m59.752
5	E. Pirro	I	20	Benetton B189 Ford HB V8	–	1:19.710	1:19.217	1:23.913 (21)	68	2h02m03.998
6	P. Martini	I	23	Minardi M189 Ford DFR V8	–	1:18.043	1:17.623	1:21.995 (5)	67	2h01m18.164
7	M. Gugelmin	BR	15	Leyton House CG891 Judd V8	–	1:20.191	1:20.200	1:24.302 (23)	66	2h00m24.757
8	S. Modena	I	8	Brabham BT58 Judd V8	–	1:18.750	1:20.076	1:23.022 (15)	64	2h01m51.005
9	E. Cheever	USA	10	Arrows A11 Ford DFR V8	–	1:19.922	1:21.206	1:26.646 (25)	42	spin
10	J. J. Lehto	F	37	Onyx ORE1 Ford DFR V8	1:19.442	1:20.767	1:19.309	1:22.758 (11)	27	engine cut
11	O. Grouillard	F	26	Ligier JS33 Ford DFR V8	–	1:21.882	1:20.073	1:24.834 (24)	22	accident
12	N. Piquet	BR	11	Lotus 101 Judd V8	–	1:19.392	1:20.622	1:22.670 (10)	19	collision/Ghinzani
13	P. Ghinzani	I	18	Osella FA1M Ford DFR V8	1:19.153	1:19.691	1:20.718	1:23.057 (16)	18	collision/Piquet
14	N. Mansell	GB	27	Ferrari 640 Ferrari V12	–	1:19.525	1:18.313	1:22.938 (14)	17	accident
15	A. Senna	BR	1	McLaren MP4/5 Honda V10	–	1:17.712	1:16.665	1:21.306 (1)	13	collision/Brundle
16	A. Caffi	I	21	Dallara BMS 189 Ford DFR V8	–	1:18.857	1:18.899	1:22.340 (8)	13	accident
17	I. Capelli	I	16	Leyton House CG891 Ford DFR V8	–	1:19.269	1:19.294	1:26.682 (26)	13	holed radiator
18	A. de Cesaris	I	22	Dallara BMS 189 Ford DFR V8	–	1:18.828	1:19.487	1:21.798 (4)	12	spin
19	M. Brundle	GB	7	Brabham BTR58 Judd V8	–	1:19.136	1:19.428	1:22.876 (13)	12	collision/Senna
20	D. Warwick	GB	9	Arrows A11 Ford DFR V8	–	1:19.599	1:19.622	1:23.086 (18)	7	accident
21	P. Alliot	F	30	Lola LC89 Lamborghini V12	1:18.523	1:19.568	1:19.579	1:22.795 (12)	6	collision/Berger
22	G. Berger	A	28	Ferrari 640 Ferrari V12	–	1:19.238	1:20.615	1:21.656 (2)	6	collision/Alliot
23	L. Alesi	F	4	Tyrrell 108 Ford DFR V8	–	1:19.363	1:19.259	1:23.928 (22)	5	electrics
24	R. Arnoux	F	25	Ligier JS33 Ford DFR V8	–	1:20.872	1:20.391	1:23.075 (17)	4	accident
25	N. Larini	I	17	Osella FA1M Ford DFR V8	1:18.379	1:19.305	1:19.110	1:22.062 (6)	–	stalled on line
26	A. Prost	F	2	McLaren MP4/5 Honda V10	–	1:17.403	1:17.624	1:22.179 (7)	–	did not start
27	J. Palmer	GB	3	Tyrrell 108 Ford FR V8	–	1:20.428	1:20.451	DNQ		
28	L. Sala	E	24	Minardi M189 Ford DFR V8	–	1:20.633	1:20.866	DNQ		
29	B. Gachot	B	39	Rial ARC02 Ford DFR V8	–	1:22.267	1:24.913	DNQ		
30	P. Raphanel	F	38	Rial ARC02 Ford DFR V8	–	1:22.305	1:22.391	DNQ		
–	S. Johansson	S	36	Onyx ORE1 Ford DFR V8	1:19.539	DNPQ	DNPQ			
–	M. Alboreto	I	29	Lola LC89 Lamborghini V12	1:20.129	DNPQ	DNPQ			
–	B. Schneider	F	34	Zakspeed ZK189 Yamaha V8	1:20.179	DNPQ	DNPQ			
–	R. Moreno	BR	31	Coloni C3 Ford DFR V8	1:20.183	DNPQ	DNPQ			
–	O. Larrauri	ARG	33	EuroBrun ER189 Judd V8	1:20.750	DNPQ	DNPQ			
–	A. Suzuki	J	35	Zakspeed ZK189 Yamaha V8	1:21.012	DNPQ	DNPQ			
–	Y. Dalmas	F	41	AGS JH24 Ford DFR V8	1:21.022	DNPQ	DNPQ			
–	G. Tarquini	I	40	AGS JH24 Ford DFR V8	1:21.600	DNPQ	DNPQ			
–	E. Bertaggia	I	32	Coloni C3 Ford DFR V8	1:24.081	DNPQ	DNPQ			

Circuit Data: Adelaide Grand Prix Circuit, length 2.347 miles/3.777 km, race distance 70 laps = 164.3 miles/264.4 km, race weather very wet and raining.

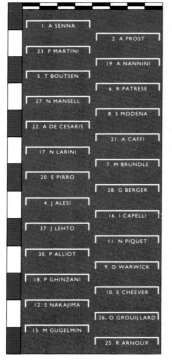

1. A SENNA	
23. P MARTINI	2. A PROST
	19. A NANNINI
5. T BOUTSEN	
	6. R PATRESE
27. N MANSELL	
	8. S MODENA
22. A DE CESARIS	
	21. A CAFFI
17. N LARINI	
	7. M BRUNDLE
20. E PIRRO	
	28. G BERGER
4. J ALESI	
	16. I CAPELLI
37. J LEHTO	
	11. N PIQUET
30. P ALLIOT	
	9. D WARWICK
18. P GHINZANI	
	10. E CHEEVER
12. S NAKAJIMA	
	26. O GROUILLARD
15. M GUGELMIN	
	25. R ARNOUX

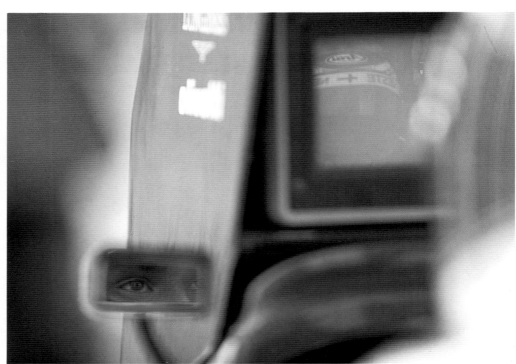

LAP CHART

Grid Order	Driver	Laps (1–70)
1	A. Senna	1 1 1 1 1 1 1 1 1 1 1 1 1 1 1 5 5 5 5 5 5 5 5 5 5 5 5 5 5 5 5 5 5 5 5 5 5 5 5 5 5 5 5 5 5 5 5 5 5 5 5 5 5 5 5 5 5 5 5 5 5 5 5 5 5 5 5 5 5 5
2	A. Prost	23 23 5 5 5 5 5 5 5 5 5 5 6 19 19 19 19 19 19 19 19 19 19 19 19 19 19 19 19 19 19 19 19 19 19 19 19 19 19 19 19 19 19 19 19 19 19 19 19 19 19 19 19 19 19 19 19 19 19 19 19 19 19 19 19 19 19 19 19 19
23	P. Martini	5 5 6 6 6 6 6 6 6 6 6 6 6 19 27 27 27 6 6 6 6 6 6 6 6 6 6 6 6 6 6 6 6 6 6 6 6 6 6 6 6 6 6 6 6 6 6 6 6 6 6 6 6 6 6 6 6 6 6 6 6 6 6 6 6 6 6 6 6 6
19	A. Nannini	6 6 23 19 19 19 19 19 19 19 19 19 27 6 6 6 10 10 10 10 10 10 12 12 12 12 12 12 12 12 12 12 12 12 12 12 12 12 12 12 12 12 12 12 12 12 12 12 12 12 12 12 12 12 12 12 12 12 12 12 12 12 12 12 12 12 12 12 12 12
5	T. Boutsen	19 19 19 23 23 27 27 27 27 27 27 27 23 10 10 12 12 12 12 12 10 37 37 10 10 10 10 10 10 10 10 10 10 10 10 10 10 10 20 20 20 20 20 20 20 20 20 20 20 20 20 20 20 20 20 20 20 20 20 20 20 20 20 20 20 20 20 20 20 20
6	R. Patrese	22 22 22 22 27 23 23 23 23 22 23 10 10 23 12 37 37 37 37 37 37 10 10 23 23 23 23 23 23 23 23 23 23 23 23 23 23 23 23 23 23 23 23 23 23 23 23 23 23 23 23 23 23 23 23 23 23 23 23 23 23 23 23 23 23 23 23 23 23 23
27	N. Mansell	27 21 21 27 22 22 9 22 22 22 23 21 21 12 12 12 37 23 23 23 23 23 23 20 20 20 20 20 20 20 20 20 15 15 15 15 15 15 15 15 15 15 15 15 15 15 15 15 15 15 15 15 15 15 15 15 15 15 15 15 15 15 15 15 15 15 15 15 15 15
8	S. Modena	21 27 27 21 9 9 22 21 21 21 10 10 37 37 37 23 11 11 20 20 20 20 20 20 15 15 15 15 15 15 15 15 15 15 8 8 8 8 8 8 8 8 8 8 8 8 8 8 8 8 8 8 8 8 8 8 8 8 8 8 8 8 8 8 8 8 8 8 8 8
22	A. de Cesaris	8 9 9 9 21 21 21 10 10 10 10 22 12 11 11 11 11 11 20 20 26 26 26 15 15 15 15 15 8 8 8 8 8 8 8 8 8 8 8 8
21	A. Caffi	7 11 11 11 11 11 7 10 7 7 7 12 12 37 20 20 20 20 20 26 26 15 15 15 8 8 8 8 8
17	N. Larini	9 7 7 7 7 10 7 20 37 37 37 37 11 26 26 26 26 15 15 8 8 8
7	M. Brundle	11 28 10 10 10 20 20 37 12 12 7 7 20 15 15 15 15 15 18 8
20	A. Nannini	28 8 25 20 20 37 37 12 20 20 11 11 26 18 18 18 18 8
28	G. Berger	20 10 20 37 37 26 26 26 11 11 20 20 15 8 8 8 8
4	J. Alesi	10 25 37 26 26 12 12 11 26 26 26 16
16	I. Capelli	37 20 26 12 12 11 11 11 15 15 15 15 15 18
37	J.J. Lehto	25 37 8 8 30 30 15 16 16 16 16 16 8
11	N. Piquet	26 26 30 30 8 28 16 18 18 18 18 18
30	P. Alliot	30 30 12 18 28 15 18 8 8 8 8 8
9	D. Warwick	18 18 18 15 15 16 8
18	P. Ghinzani	15 12 15 28 18 8
10	E. Cheever	12 15 16 16 16 18
12	S. Nakajima	16 16 28 25 4
26	O. Grouillard	4 4 4 4
15	M. Gugelmin	
25	R. Arnoux	

FASTEST LAPS

Pos.	Car No./Driver/Team	Time
1	12 S. Nakajima/Lotus	1:38.480
2	6 R. Patrese/Williams	1:38.685
3	19 A. Nannini/Benetton	1:40.336
4	5 T. Boutsen/Benetton	1:40.380
5	1 A. Senna/McLaren	1:41.159
6	27 N. Mansell/Ferrari	1:42.406
7	37 J.J. Lehto/Onyx	1:42.509
8	20 E. Pirro/Benetton	1:43.144
9	1 N. Piquet/Lotus	1:44.277
10	10 E. Cheever/Arrows	1:44.305
11	15 M. Gugelmin/Leyton House	1:44.734
12	4 J. Alesi/Tyrrell	1:44.900
13	9 D. Warwick/Arrows	1:45.700
14	23 P. Martini/Minardi	1:46.189
15	28 G. Berger/Ferrari	1:46.911
16	26 O. Grouillard/Ligier	1:46.973
17	21 A. Caffi/BMS Dallara	1:47.255
18	22 A. de Cesaris/BMS Dallara	1:47.525
19	8 S. Modena/Brabham	1:48.171
20	7 M. Brundle/Brabham	1:48.366
21	16 I. Capelli/Leyton House	1:48.521
22	30 P. Alliot/Larrousse	1:49.251
23	25 R. Arnoux/Ligier	1:50.375
24	18 P. Ghinzani/Osella	1:51.975

CHAMPIONSHIP POINTS

	Drivers			Drivers/Constructors	
1	A. Prost	76 pts		E. Pirro	2 pts
2	A. Senna	60 pts		J. Palmer	2 pts
3	R. Patrese	40 pts	26	G. Tarquini	1 pt
4	N. Mansell	38 pts		P. Alliot	1 pt
5	T. Boutsen	37 pts		O. Grouillard	1 pt
6	A. Nannini	32 pts		L. Sala	1 pt
7	G. Berger	21 pts			
8	N. Piquet	12 pts	1	McLaren	141 pts
9	J. Alesi	8 pts	2	Williams	77 pts
10	D. Warwick	7 pts	3	Ferrari	59 pts
11	S. Johansson	6 pts	4	Benetton	39 pts
	M. Alboreto	6 pts	5	Tyrrell	16 pts
	E. Cheever	6 pts	6	Lotus	15 pts
14	J. Herbert	5 pts	7	Arrows	13 pts
15	P. Martini	5 pts	8	Dallara	8 pts
16	A. de Cesaris	4 pts		Brabham	8 pts
	M. Gugelmin	4 pts	10	Onyx	6 pts
	S. Modena	4 pts		Minardi	6 pts
	A. Caffi	4 pts	12	Leyton House	4 pts
	M. Brundle	4 pts	13	Rial	3 pts
21	C. Danner	3 pts		Ligier	3 pts
	S. Nakajima	3 pts	15	AGS	1 pt
23	R. Arnoux	2 pts		Larrousse	1 pt

Existing qualifying lap record: Gerhard Berger, Ferrari F1/87, 1m 17.267s, 176.117 kph/109.434 mph in 1987

Existing race lap record: Gerhard Berger, Ferrari F1/87, 1m 20.416s, 169.220 kph/105.148 mph in 1987

Existing distance record: Gerhard Berger, Ferrari F1/87, 82 laps in 1hr 52m 56.144s at 164.674 kph/102.324 mph in 1987

Left: veteran of three races, Lehto has his eyes firmly fixed on 1990.

PAST WINNERS

Year	Driver	Nat.	Car	Circuit
1985	Keke Rosberg	SF	1.5 Williams FW10 Honda t/c	Adelaide
1986	Alain Prost	F	1.5 McLaren MP4/2C TAG t/c	Adelaide
1987	Gerhard Berger	A	1.5 Ferrari F1/87 t/c	Adelaide
1988	Alain Prost	F	1.5 McLaren MP4/4 Honda t/c	Adelaide

Smudgers

The excellent photography appearing in the FIA Formula One World Championship Yearbook has been contributed by the photographers named below. W.H. Allen & Co., publisher Nick Hervey, editor Bob Constanduros, and design consultants Carter Wong would like to thank each and every one of them for their superb support and contribution to this publication.

Zooom Photographic,
John Dunbar, Lee Farrant,
David Winter, Darren Heath, Patrick
Gosling, LAT, Steven Tee, Allsport, Keith
Sutton, John Blakemore, Peter Nygaard,
Lukas Gorys, Colorsport, David Phipps,
Ferdi Kraling, Sporting Pictures, Hiroshi
Kaneko, Pamela Lausen, Bernard Asset,
Stephen Davis, Jon Eisberg, Jeff Bloxham,
Ercole Colombo, Agence Vandystadt,
Nigel Snowdon, Diana Burnet, Herke de
Vries, Dominique Leroy, Dave Kennard,
Pascal Rondeau, Alois Rottensteiner,
Jean-Francois Galeron of Autopresse,
Steve Domenjoz, Kaz Winiemko, Jens
Hoffmeister, Jori Potiker, Wolfgang
Scholvien, Justin de Villeneuve,
Alain Patrice, Jean-Marc Loubat